Adolescence in Context

Rainer K. Silbereisen   Eberhard Todt
Editors

Adolescence in Context

The Interplay of Family, School,
Peers, and Work in Adjustment

With 50 Illustrations

Springer-Verlag
New York Berlin Heidelberg London Paris
Tokyo Hong Kong Barcelona Budapest

Rainer K. Silbereisen, Ph.D.
Department of Human
 Development and Family Studies
College of Health and Human
 Development
The Pennsylvania State University
University Park, PA 16802-6504
 USA

Eberhard Todt, Ph.D.
Department of Psychology
University of Giessen
D-35394 Giessen
Germany

Library of Congress Cataloging-in-Publication Data
Adolescence in context : the interplay of family, school, peers, and
 work in adjustment / Rainer K. Silbereisen, Eberhard Todt, editors.
   p. cm.
 Includes bibliographical references and index.
 ISBN 0-387-94060-X
 1. Adolescence. 2. Teenagers—Employment. 3. Education,
Secondary. 4. Adolescent psychology. I. Silbereisen, R. K.
(Rainer K.). 1944– . II. Todt. Eberhard.
HQ796.A3325   1993
305.23′5—dc20   93-3850

Printed on acid-free paper.

Production coordinated by Chernow Editorial Services, Inc., and managed by
 Christin R. Ciresi; manufacturing supervised by Jacqui Ashri.
Typeset by Best-set Typesetter Ltd., Hong Kong.
Printed and bound by Edwards Brothers, Inc., Ann Arbor, MI.
Printed in the United States of America.

9 8 7 6 5 4 3 2 1

ISBN 0-387-94060-X Springer-Verlag New York Berlin Heidelberg
ISBN 3-540-94060-X Springer-Verlag Berlin Heidelberg New York

Preface

Development takes place in contexts. The processes and outcomes of change depend on the interplay between developmentally instigative personal attributes and contextual features conducive to development. This general notion is illuminated for development in adolescence.

Although person and context vary on a multitude of dimensions, recent research has demonstrated the relevance of a smaller number of important aspects. Concerning developmentally instigative attributes of the person, agency beliefs and other motivational resources represent a major source of differential use of contextual opportunities. For instance, adolescents high in external control beliefs are likely to lack the social skills required in order to integrate themselves into age-adequate peer groups.

Concerning contexts, various approaches have characterized the developmental impact of social situations within contexts. Such settings may provide role models and exhibit behavioral routines conducive to the resolving of age-typic developmental tasks. For example, commercial leisure settings such as discotheques offer opportunities to socialize with peers and to learn by observation how to make contacts with prospective romantic friends.

In addition to single contexts, such as one's peer group or work party, the interaction among contexts provides opportunities for development in its own right. The mutual influence of family and peers on the development of social competence is a case in point. Assume a youngster living in a hazardous environment, characterized by violence and criminality. Against this background, the risk of affiliating with problematic peers may be substantially reduced by strict parental discipline, whereas under normal circumstances such parenting would be negative for healthy development.

Research on the impact of contexts on development was particularly promoted by Bronfenbrenner's (Bronfenbrenner & Crouter, 1983) plea for person-process-context paradigms. Although a growing body of knowledge emerged over the last decade, not until recently has systematic research begun on commonalities and differences in developmental processes across contexts.

This volume brings together recent research on the impact of contexts on adolescent development. Studies were located that investigate processes and outcomes across contexts, such as cultural belief systems or groups characterized by different family structures, and within interacting contexts, such as the link between school and adolescents' part-time work or family and parents' jobs. The contributions concentrate on the continuum of positive adjustment to maladaptive outcomes during the adolescent transitions, tapping not only setting-specific behaviors, but also attitudes, beliefs, and values that give one's actions direction.

As Heron and Kroeger (1981) claimed, research on human action ought to be developmental in depth and cross-cultural in breadth. Accordingly, comparative perspectives within national contexts and across cultures are well represented. Moreover, the better part of the studies reported relies on longitudinal data sets. The investigators come from the the United States, Australia, and Europe.

Research on adolescence is an interdisciplinary subject. Consequently, the approaches represented in this volume were initiated by investigators from various disciplines, namely, psychology, sociology, education, and epidemiology. The book is aimed at informing students and the research community of these disciplines about recent approaches and empirical results.

The chapters are based on papers discussed at an international conference, held in May 1991 at Schloss Rauschholzhausen, Germany. We would like to thank the German Research Council and our universities for the funds and support we received. Special thanks go to Ute Schönwetter whose help in organizing the conference was invaluable, and to Kathie Vondracek for her assistance in preparing the indices.

It was a great pleasure to bring such a distinct group together. Our discussions were lively and highly stimulating. We all enjoyed Roberta Simmons's thoughtful and provoking contributions. Shortly before this book went to print, we learned that she had passed away. We will miss her.

References

Bronfenbrenner, U. & Crouter, A.C. (1983). The evolution of environmental models in developmental research. In W. Kessen (Ed.), *Handbook of child psychology: History, theories, and methods* (Vol. 1, pp. 357–414). New York: Wiley.

Heron, A. & Kroeger, E. (1981). Introduction to developmental psychology. In H.C. Triandis & A. Heron (Eds.), *Handbook of cross-cultural psychology* (Vol. 4, pp. 1–15). Boston: Allyn & Bacon.

Contents

Part I   Introduction

Part II   Social Contexts and the Development of Orientations for Life

Part III   The Impact of Cultural and Ethnic Contexts

Part IV   The Family-Work Nexus

Part V   The Interplay between School and Work

Part VI   The Sample Case of Aggressive Behavior

Contributors

David M. Almeida, Ph.D. Department of Psychology, University of Victoria, Victoria, British Columbia V8W 3P5, Canada

Phame M. Camarena, Ph.D. Department of Child Development and Family Studies, Purdue University, West Lafayette, IN 47907, USA

Rand D. Conger, Ph.D. Department of Sociology, Iowa State University, Ames, IA 50011, USA

Nancy Darling, Ph.D. Department of Psychology, Temple University, Philadelphia, PA 19122, USA

Ralf Drewes, Ph.D. Department of Psychology, University of Giessen, D-35394 Giessen, Germany

Glen H. Elder Jr., Ph.D. Department of Sociology, University of North Carolina at Chapel Hill, Hamilton, Chapel Hill, NC 27599-3210, USA

Uwe Engel, Ph.D. Department of Sociology, University of Duisburg, D-47048 Duisburg, Germany

David P. Farrington, Ph.D. Institute of Criminology, Cambridge University, Cambridge CB3 9DT, England

S. Shirley Feldman, Ph.D. Center for Study of Families, Children and Youth, Stanford University, Stanford, CA 94305-2135, USA

Nancy L. Galambos, Ph.D. Department of Psychology, University of Victoria, Victoria, British Columbia V8W 3P5, Canada

Anthony Glendinning, B.Sc. (Hons.) Department of Education, King's College, University of Aberdeen, Aberdeen AB9 2UB, Scotland

Ann Hagell, Ph.D. Department of Sociology, University of North Carolina at Chapel Hill, Hamilton Hall, Chapel Hill, NC 27514, USA. Present address: Policy Studies Institute, London NW1 3SR, England

Stephen F. Hamilton, Ed.D. Department of Human Development and Family Studies, Cornell University, Ithaca, NY 14853-4401, USA

Sigrid Heils, Dipl.-Psych. Department of Psychology, University of Giessen, D-35394 Giessen, Germany

Leo B. Hendry, Ph.D. Department of Education, King's College, University of Aberdeen, Aberdeen AB9 2UB, Scotland

Klaus Hurrelmann, Ph.D. University of Bielefeld, Research Center Prevention and Intervention in Childhood and Adolescence, D-33501 Bielefeld, Germany

Sheppard G. Kellam, Ph.D. Prevention Research Center, Department of Mental Hygiene, School of Hygiene and Public Health, The Johns Hopkins University, Baltimore, MD 21205, USA

Reed Larson, Ph.D. Division of Human Development and Family Studies, University of Illinois at Urbana-Champaign, Urbana, IL 61801, USA

John Love, Ph.D. Department of Education, King's College, University of Aberdeen, Aberdeen AB9 2UB, Scotland

Lawrence S. Mayer, Ph.D. Prevention Research Center, Department of Mental Hygiene, School of Hygiene and Public Health, The Johns Hopkins University, Baltimore, MD 21205, USA

Jeylan T. Mortimer, Ph.D. Sociology Life Course Center, University of Minnesota, Minneapolis, MN 55455, USA

Peter Noack, Ph.D. Department of Education, University of Mannheim, D-68131 Mannheim, Germany

Hans Oswald, Ph.D. Institute of Sociology of Education, Free University of Berlin, D-14195 Berlin 33, Germany

Anne C. Petersen, Ph.D. University of Minnesota, Graduate School, Minneapolis, MN 55455, USA

George W. Rebok, Ph.D. Prevention Research Center, Department of Mental Hygiene, School of Hygiene and Public Health, The Johns Hopkins University, Baltimore, MD 21205, USA

Doreen A. Rosenthal, Ph.D. Department of Psychology, University of Melbourne, Victoria, Australia

Laura Rudkin, Ph.D. Carolina Population Center, University of North Carolina at Chapel Hill, Chapel Hill, NC 27516-3997, USA

Seongryeol Ryu, Ph.D. Sociology Life Course Center, University of Minnesota, Minneapolis, MN 55455, USA

Ute Schönpflug, Ph.D. Department of Education, Free University of Berlin, D-14195 Berlin 33, Germany

Jeanette Scott, M.A. (Hons.) Department of Education, King's College, University of Aberdeen, Aberdeen AB9 2UB, Scotland

Michael Shanahan, Ph.D. Sociology Life Course Center, University of Minnesota, Minneapolis, MN 55455, USA

Janet Shucksmith, M.A. (Cantab.) Department of Education, King's College, University of Aberdeen, Aberdeen AB9 2UB, Scotland

Rainer K. Silbereisen, Ph.D. Department of Human Development and Family Studies, College of Health and Human Development, The Pennsylvania State University, University Park, PA 16802-6504, USA

Roberta G. Simmons, Ph.D. Department of Psychiatry, University of Pittsburgh, Pittsburgh, PA 15213-2593, USA

Laurence Steinberg, Ph.D. Department of Psychology, Temple University, Philadelphia, PA 19122, USA

Mark Stemmler, Ph.D. Psychiatric Clinic, University of Erlangen-Nuremberg, D-91054 Erlangen, Germany

Klaus-Uwe Süss, Ph.D. Institute of Education, Free University of Berlin, D-14195 Berlin, Germany

Eberhard Todt, Ph.D. Department of Psychology, University of Giessen, D-35394 Giessen, Germany

Fred W. Vondracek. Ph.D. Department of Human Development and Family Studies, The Pennsylvania State University, University Park, PA 16802, USA

Sabine Walper, Ph.D. Department of Psychology, University of Munich, D-80802 Munich, Germany

Renate Wilson, Ph.D. Prevention Research Center, Department of Mental Hygiene, School of Hygiene and Public Health, The Johns Hopkins University, Baltimore, MD 21205, USA

Yingzhi Zhou, Ph.D. Department of Psychiatry, University of Pittsburgh, Pittsburgh, PA 15213-2593, USA

Part I
Introduction

1
Adolescence—A Matter of Context

RAINER K. SILBEREISEN AND EBERHARD TODT

In a recent presentation, Steinberg (1990) characterized the 1980s as the decade when the study of adolescence finally came of age, and the decade when researchers finally began to put the ecological perspective into practice. This volume is concerned with both.

Various new journals, handbooks, and scientific societies devoted to the study of the second decade of life reveal the growing interest in adolescent development. According to Petersen's definitive review (1988; see Petersen, Silbereisen, & Soerensen, 1993, for an update including recent international research), in recent studies particularly, three domains can be distinguished. First, research on adolescent adjustment challenged previous beliefs that turmoil during adolescence is a normative state of affairs. Rather, most adolescents resolve the new challenges without any serious difficulties. Nevertheless, questions remain concerning some aspects of mental health such as depression. It may be higher in subgroups typically underrepresented in past research on large, nonclinical samples.

Second, puberty and its effects on psychosocial adjustment became a main focus of research. For instance, girls' timing of puberty (early vs. late) turned out to be relevant for some aspects of their adjustment during adolescence. The response of others to the physical changes seems to lead to differential association with peers who encourage precocious social behaviors. However, as societal norms regarding weight and body shape also play a role, comparative and cross-cultural research is needed.

Third, research cumulated in the area of adolescent-family interactions. Despite the apparent generation gap, parents and children share their basic beliefs. As conflicts typically concerning mundane issues increase during early adolescence, this points to problems in adjusting the adolescent-parent relationship to increasing maturity and the young's growing expectations for greater autonomy. Presumably the family context plays a role: In families involving single parents, for instance, less conflict is observed and some studies point to more rapid maturation among adolescent daughters (Surbey, 1990).

Seen against this background, the topics covered in this volume mainly represent and discuss research on the broad issue of psychosocial adjustment in various groups of adolescents. This is accomplished, however, in a specific perspective characterized by Petersen (1988) as the common thread underlying the new research efforts—contexts of development.

The relevance of contextual features for adolescent development is illuminated by the fact that even biological processes such as puberty cannot be fully understood without considering the effects of nutrition, exercise, and societal norms. These variables differ greatly depending on the living circumstances and the cultural background. As shown by the sad example of anorexia nervosa, through manipulating eating behaviors, adolescents can even gain control over the pace of their maturation.

In the remainder of this chapter, we first highlight the quality of adolescents' interactions with leisure contexts. Our particular point of view is that of active individuals who "produce" their pathways through adolescence by utilizing contextual potentials conducive for development. Next, despite our strong belief in the genuine role of contexts in development, we need to discuss a recently suggested radical shift in the understanding of contexts as merely reflecting individual differences in stable personal characteristics. Following, three main foci of research on adolescence in context are illuminated by the studies collected in this volume: approaches toward the processes that make contexts developmental, research on differences and commonalities in developmental mechanisms across contexts, and investigations of context-context interactions. The latter refers to synergies and conflicts between the challenges of contexts such as families and school or school and work. Finally, we comment shortly on the organization of this volume.

Leisure Contexts and Adolescent Development

The more researchers became aware of the role that processes of interaction with contexts play, the more various contexts other than family and school came into focus. As a matter of fact, research on adolescence began to include proximal contexts such as peer groups, as well as more distal contexts such as the community. In a parallel manner, the qualities of particular contexts received attention. Instead of counting the number of friends, investigators became interested in the what and how of interactions within various peer cliques (Brown, 1990).

The new deal regarding ecological research on adolescent development focused attention on contexts that were widely overlooked in the past. In particular, researchers learned about the structure and impact of the "fourth environment" (Van Vliet, 1983), that is, settings that allow adolescents to exert more self-induced control than is characteristic of school and other normative, adult-supervised contexts: youth clubs, shopping malls, sports centers, gambling arcades, and discotheques, to mention a few.

More specifically, activities in such settings provide links between the free play of childhood and the challenge of adult obligatory activities (Larson, this volume). In the eyes of the actors, the activities are characterized by intrinsic motivation, feelings of being challenged, and opportunities to learn control over such motivational resources. Additionally, they give a unique chance to plan and manage "personal projects" (Little, 1983), that is, cumulative series of tasks undertaken towards a common, self-determined end. Differences in the content of these tasks are likely to reflect more general developmental orientations. Zank (1988), for instance, found young solvent experimenters to report fewer tasks related to education than is common among normative age-mates.

Furthermore, in times where a growing number of young people are lacking normative social roles due to unemployment and many other reasons, leisure contexts and other instances of the fourth environment fulfill important compensatory functions. The company and activities youths are able to enjoy there allow aspects of the transition to proceed despite the problems culminating in the spheres of vocational training and work. Examples are the establishment of more mature social relations and the development of commitments that give one's life direction and purpose (Hendry, Glendinning, Shucksmith, Long, & Scott, this volume).

The negative relation some researchers see between school achievement and part-time work (Greenberger & Steinberg, 1986) may actually indicate a selection effect—those who are not satisfied with school look for alternative domains of fulfillment, and part-time work gives at least some of the status attributes adolescents want (Mortimer, Shanahan, & Ryu, this volume).

By far, not all environments outside school fulfill the qualification as being productive concerning the development of mature identity. Some fail because they are actually adult-dominated and likely to imply achievement orientations similar to school, others because the projects adolescents enjoy imply risks for maladjustment (Larson, this volume).

Reflecting general trends in life-span developmental psychology (Baltes, 1987), but also instructed by the results of field research on the behavior of adolescents in everyday contexts, various researchers began to focus on the "efficacy" the young develop concerning their own development: Adolescents not only shape direction and content of their development by evoking reactions from parents, teachers, peers, mentors, and many other categories of people, but also play an active part as "producers of their development" (Lerner & Busch-Rossnagel, 1982).

Inspired by such approaches, some years ago we (Silbereisen, Eyferth, & Rudinger, 1986) edited a book with the title *Development as Action in*

Context. The idea put forward in some of the chapters was to show how adolescents utilize the latent potential that leisure settings and other contexts provide for their development—latent, because quite often it is the young's goal-directed, intentional behavior vis-à-vis the environment that brings to bear the developmental impact of such contexts. Parts of our own research attempted to give substance to this notion. As the results directly relate to the topic of the present endeavor, a short example may be helpful.

One of the premium challenges adolescents face is the formation of romantic friendships. While future-time perspectives concerning intimate relationships evolve, the young compare the actual state of fulfillment with their hopes and wishes for the future. The basic hypothesis tested in the study of Silbereisen, Noack, and von Eye (1992) was that a mismatch between actual and aspired state (e.g., no romance despite strong wishes to establish such a relation) would motivate adolescents to undertake steps to overcome the unpleasent situation. More specifically, we assumed they would change their preferred leisure contexts in order to increase the likelihood of opportunities and activities that are known to mediate the right kind of interpersonal contacts. Thus, instead of spending one's spare time at the parental home or at other places characterized by close supervision, the adolescents were predicted to change to discotheques and comparable locales.

Utilizing a prospective data set, the role of "going places" in adolescent development was confirmed. As expected, youths who wished to establish romantic friendships attended leisure locales that provide this possibility. Understandably enough, once they had established a close relationship, they were more likely to seek out settings where the possibility of privacy is greatest (with homes again receiving quite a reputation). According to a recent study on a similar data set, stricter parents risk even more pronounced attempts of their offspring to utilize the pleasure in development-prone settings (Müller, 1992).

Certainly, such results can only be understood on the basis of our knowledge about the kind of experiences young people are likely to make within such contexts. Thanks to several studies, mainly conducted during the 1980s, we know a lot more about the specific nature of the actions and interactions that translate contextual potentials into developmental outcomes (Silbereisen & Noack, 1988).

A case in point is the "alternative scripts" (Spencer, Blades, & Morsley, 1989) in use by adolescents who inhabit adult spaces but for reasons different from those of adult users. Interestingly enough, a telling example was already observed and described almost 60 years ago. In their landmark study, Muchow and Muchow (1935) showed how adolescents utilized props like escalators in a department store not for the actual purpose but rather as a way to show off to their imagined or real audience. To attract girls' attention, for instance, boys walked the escalator against the intended direction—a little step that makes a big difference.

In thinking about the impact of contexts on adolescents, the growing sociocognitive capabilities and their consequences for the self are important to consider. Other than during childhood, adolescents experiment with possible selves, supported by their growing awareness of the role of contexts in person perception. As adolescents try to utilize and even shape contextual features, what they see is in part a reflection of what they did or were allowed to do. Thus, constraints in the environment tell about constraints concerning one's self, which are likely to have negative consequences (Fuhrer & Kaiser, 1993). For instance, a higher risk of affiliating with deviant peers was observed among adolescents who perceived a mismatch between their self-related expectations and the actual quality of their living quarters (Boehnke, Silbereisen, & Noack, 1992).

Taken together, adolescents not only visit, occupy, and even defend territories they were not able to access during childhood, they also have their own understanding of proper use. Conflicts with adult users (shop owners, guards, etc.) are part of the game. Judged from such examples, the genuine role contexts play in adolescent development seems to be beyond any doubt.

Yet, referring to the results of behavioral genetic studies, which showed rather high heritability estimates for a variety of traits, Scarr (1992) suggested that differences in individuals' environments should not be seen as origins of the individual differences in developmental outcomes; rather, they are "merely a reflection of the (genetic) characteristics of both parents and child" (p. 9). This radical shift in the conception of how contexts impact human development would explain why a wide range of family environments appears to be "functionally equivalent" concerning growth.

Contexts Matter—Do They?

Scarr (1992) confines her model to environments that fall within the range of "average expectable environments" for the species. Outside this range, and thus detrimental and causally related to development, are environments somewhat vaguely characterized as deprived, abusive, and neglectful.

As originally described by Scarr and McCartney (1983), individuals are conceived as influencing their environments in three different ways. The early, passive form of genotype-environment relation is represented by the fact that parents offer environmental opportunities not accidentally but correlated with their genetic endowment. For instance, many books in the family home, at least in part, are a product of parents' reading abilities and preferences. Evocative genotype-environment effects com-

prise circumstances where genetically driven individual differences provoke different reactions from other people. Thus, a difficult temperament
may result in rejection from caretakers. Finally, particularly adolescents
begin to show what the authors call active genotype-environment effects,
that is, the young influence the course of their development by selecting,
shaping, and producing environments according to their interests, talents,
and personality. It is this latter way of influencing the environment that
reminds Scarr (1992) of certain branches of research on adolescence,
including our view on development as action in context.

Scarr's provocative argument is that the differences in environments
thus provided are not essential for the development of personality above
and beyond the differences produced by genetic factors, provided individuals have the choice to sort themselves into environments according
to their genetic dispositions. However, depending on the living circumstances and the developmental domain studied, not too many people may
be lucky enough to fall within the limits—for instance, what about the
choices of the long-term unemployed or single mothers in poverty? One
should add, however, that several kinds of contexts adolescents attend
are especially characterized by the choices they allow to make, independent from adult control.

Is this approach a danger to the ecological perspective, which attributes
to contexts a genuine role in development? Certainly not, and hopefully
this book contributes a little to our growing understanding, although, we
should hasten to add, studies utilizing behavioral genetic methods are
not included. The following reasons speak for the fruitfulness of the
ecological perspective (see Bronfenbrenner, Lenzenweger, & Ceci, 1992).

First, the family is no longer the main context for development. Although the present formulation leaves it open whether other developmental contexts are deemed similarly weak in their impact on personality,
it is quite unlikely that the influences stemming from peer groups, work
environments, mass media, and many other contexts are mainly due to
choices based on genetic endowment.

Second, although not all research on developmental effects of genetics
and environments can be characterized in this way, Scarr's (1992) model
is based on a research strategy that essentially treats the environment
as residual: Its impact is what is left after calculating coefficients of
heritability. As the latter are bound to the particular population under
study, little environmental variation (e.g., due to neglect of ethnic minor-
ities) will result in higher heritability estimates. More specifically, neither
is the environment assessed in terms of the concrete people, activities,
and physical properties, nor is the way characterized in which people
interact with their environment.

Third, the approach is focused on behaviors that show considerable
stability across many contexts and periods of the life span, that is, traits.
Thus, even within this approach environmental impact does play a role in

temporally less stable but consistent responses to concurrent contexts, and/or in situation-specific behaviors.

In contrast, most studies claiming a genuine impact of contexts on adolescent development include contexts other than family, assess concrete attributes of contexts and specify person-context interactions, and they have less stable and thus more context-affected behaviors as their target.

Nevertheless, contexts cannot be conceived of without the developing person herself. Individual differences on some personality attributes are known to influence the way individuals interact with contexts. Control beliefs exemplify such developmentally instigative personal characteristics. Depending on whether adolescents trust in their capability to exert control over behavioral outcomes, they are likely to handle contextual opportunities in a different way (Skinner, 1990). Interests as studied by Todt, Drewes, and Heils (this volume) represent another example of relatively stable motivational structures that shape development by influencing the choice of contexts. Adolescents who share interests in topics such as physics and technology are likely to sort themselves in appropriate settings.

How Contexts Get Developmental

In the following, we discuss some issues concerning the interaction processes that "yield" the developmental potential of contexts. Before we go on, however, some comments on the use of the terms *process* and *context* are required.

According to Bronfenbrenner (1989), contexts can be seen as organized somewhat similar to onion skins: Highly abstract and impersonal contexts like the basic technologies or belief systems of the culture we live in encompass other, less distal but still remote contexts as exemplified by the political institutions or, even closer to the people and their everyday life, the community in which they live. This system of layers within layers ends at the premium microsystem, the family. Thus, the term *context* covers a wide range, from the immediate setting where the developing individual acts, to distal structures.

By *process* we refer to the interaction between the person and the immediate setting, that is, the nature and quality of personally induced exchanges with the people and objects around (Bronfenbrenner et al., 1992). For instance, although the availability of drugs on school yards may increase the risk of getting involved, having close friends who take drugs and with whom one frequently interacts presents the actual process (Kandel, 1986).

As the developmentally instigative potential of contexts is reflected in more than just the most obvious features, such as physical props or the crowds present, careful description is a must. At a closer look, discotheques, for instance, reveal quite different "affordances" such as dancing and its opportunities for making friends, the gambling machines, the various opportunities and requisites to observe people, etc. (Silbereisen & Noack, 1988). In order to compare the potential that contexts offer, they could be conceived and assessed with respect to the major developmental tasks the young have to face. Examples are the prevalence and quality of behavioral models for particular achievements, the accessibility of relevant information, the adaptability to individual differences in personality, and many other aspects.

It is important that the analyses encompass more than whether individuals attended particular contexts, but rather which of the many distinct features they were actually able to utilize. In this respect, researchers on the "new territories" in adolescent development are still too easily satisfied with simple labels or "social addresses" (Bronfenbrenner, 1989).

How contexts are perceived and how they impact outcomes is age-graded or, put more generally, a function of the developmental status of the person. For instance, adolescents seem to value the kinds of work that are known to have negative psychological consequences for adults as quite satisfying and challenging. Working part-time in a fast-food restaurant is viewed differently if done the first time, despite the lack of authority and prestige resulting from it (Mortimer et al., this volume).

It is obvious that many features of contexts, whether physical attributes of buildings or social structures within a community, cannot directly be related to development. Rather, it needs a translation into the "biopsychosocial" system of the individual. Hamilton (this volume) provides an excellent example of how features of even distal contexts can be assessed in terms of their potential psychological impact. Bearing on the concept of self-efficacy (Bandura, 1986), the transparency and permeability of the school-work linkage is used to compare and explain national differences in school performance. Presumably due to the low transparency of future career trajectories, many noncollege youths in the United States have no chance to experience psychological control and thus lose track.

Thus far, we illustrated the assessment of contexts in a way appropriate for psychological study. Once this is accomplished, the question arises as to which processes or interactions between the individual and the proximal context the effects of the latter are brought about. Obviously, insights concerning the latter depend in part on how the context at stake was described.

In most cases it is more than a single process that links distal features of contexts to the developing person. The research initiated by Elder (Elder, Van Nguyen, & Caspi, 1985) on the impact of economic hardship on the family and adolescent adjustment is a major example of how complex the chaining of such processes may look like. Whether adolescent problem behaviors indeed turn up largely depends on mediating experiences such as the worsening of the marital relationship, itself a consequence of nagging disputes over scarce financial resources, which subsequently undermines the quality of parenting and hampers supervision of the adolescent children.

How families cope with such strains depends not only on the current situation but may be deeply rooted in past experiences, such as their familiarity with similar hardships (Walper & Silbereisen, this volume), or in stable personal characteristics like irritability. Strains may accentuate problems that existed long before but did not yet express themselves, rather than produce new outcomes. Divorce, for instance, accentuated depressive mood in girls that developed during prior periods of apparent parental harmony (Doherty & Needle, 1991).

The quality of the parent-adolescent relationship seems to be a major mediating link between experiences in various extra-familial domains and adolescents' psychosocial development. In their study of dual-earner families, Galambos & Almeida (this volume) showed that work strains increased the likelihood of adolescent problem behavior. Whereas in the case of mothers, lower acceptance of the child played a role, work strains led to increased conflicts between fathers and adolescents. Thus, depending on the family role and presumably affected by the kind of the problem, different processes in parent-child interaction are affected.

In sum, contexts cannot be fully understood without investigating the person-context interaction. Of course, there is no a priori limit as to the number or quality of such processes. Rather, their specific content depends on the particular domain of development, characteristics of the person, and features of the context. Nevertheless, some more general notions have been developed on how adolescents face age-typic challenges and interact with usual contextual opportunities. Coping and identity processes illustrate such attempts.

Oerter (1986), for instance, describes the ways adolescents master everyday manifestations of developmental tasks within the general framework of coping research. A number of stimulating studies were initiated by Seiffge-Krenke (1990). Whereas most adolescents use functional strategies such as seeking information or taking advice vis-à-vis normative demands, according to her results only about one in five of the responses qualify as denial or withdrawal, and this ratio also applied in a cross-cultural framework. A collection of recent approaches was edited by Bosma and Jackson (1990).

Another example is the model of identity formation put forward by Marcia (1980). As this concept plays a role in some of the research reported in this volume (Vondracek, this volume), a few remarks may be in place. The way adolescents deal with the foremost task of developing a sense of identity is described in terms of two processes, namely, exploration and commitment. Whereas the first characterizes the quantity and quality of "outreach" into as yet uncharted opportunities for future selves, the second refers to the adolescents' felt obligation to live up to identity decisions they made. For instance, exhibiting firm commitments on the basis of little exploration seems to be characteristic of political beliefs among German students who attended the lowest track of secondary schooling. Such a foreclosure status may be a particular risk for extremist political positions (Fend, 1991).

Much more can be done in order to characterize youthful person-context interactions. It may be worthwhile to look at recent research on resilience or studies on risk and protective factors in general (Loesel & Bliesener, in press). Whereas risk factors are quite often contextual conditions, many known protective factors can be seen as indicating particular qualities of the person-context interaction. We take an example from our own research. Silbereisen, Nowak, and Schwarz (1992) compared developmental timetables of adolescents from families high (upper 10%) and low in cumulated adversities such as divorce, economic hardship, and illness of parents. The expectation was that such adverse living circumstances would cause the young to develop autonomy a little faster (see Simmons & Zhou, this volume). The effect was pronounced only in cases where parents were reported to show little monitoring of their offspring. In other words, the negative potential of an highly adverse context could be balanced by higher levels of monitoring.

Comparison across Contexts

Once the role of contexts is on the agenda, a widely applied strategy in analyzing developmental data no longer holds. As Steinberg and Darling (this volume) put it: "if we believe that context matters, we certainly do not want to control it away." Thus, rather than statistically control differences in antecedents and/or outcomes as a function of contextual variation, systematic comparisons across contexts are at stake. A main question is whether the same or different developmental mechanisms are operative depending on the context.

Although comparing contexts in their impact on development has an established tradition in cross-cultural psychology, the body of studies on adolescence is not too impressive (Kagitcibasi & Berry, 1989). In many cases, researchers are satisfied with nominal classifications of contexts (nationality, ethnicity, etc.), and quite often the aim simply is to study the generalizability of an antecedent-outcome relation. Based on discrepant results, new hypotheses may emerge.

The study by Walper and Silbereisen (this volume) is characteristic of this approach. Drawing on their research with a German sample, it was predicted that economic hardship among Polish families would impact adolescents' adjustment indirectly, mediated mainly by a worsening of family cohesion due to the financial strains. As the German results fit well to earlier research by others (see McLoyd, 1989 for an overview), the resulting lack of generalizability came as a surprise at the first place. However, in thinking about the results, the potential role of a much higher adaptation to hardships among the Polish families emerged. Living under adverse conditions may help to establish mechanisms that protect family cohesion against getting disturbed by financial constraints.

Likewise, Simmons and Zhou (this volume) replicated their earlier research on the transition from junior to senior high school among European-American students with African-American samples. In general, the changes showed similar patterns, with problem behaviors most consistently affected. Judged by such indicators as deviant activities or precocious sexual relations, however, African-American males changed more in the direction of the cultural stereotype of adolescence. In addition to institutional racism, this effect could originate in a number of conditions, including minority status and differences in ethnically-based timetabling, particularly concerning males. Silbereisen, Noack, and Schönpflug (this volume) raise similar arguments when comparing differences between German and Polish adolescents' substance use and their likely antecedents.

Generalizability studies are a worthwhile endeavor in and of itself. Replication helps to get sensitized for context-specific limits of one's approach. Nevertheless, one would like to come closer to a more elaborated goal: Exactly why do contexts exert differential impact on development? A step toward this aim is to compare developmental processes across a number of contexts that differ in theoretically meaningful respects. The research reported by Steinberg and Darling (this volume) is an exemplary case. In order to investigate whether the benefits of authoritative parenting (Baumrind, 1991) transcend the demographic lines present in normal United States populations, the researchers compared samples covering a large number of "ecological niches." (Super & Harkness, 1986), defined by cross-classifications according to ethnicity, socioeconomic status, and family structure. Despite remarkable differences in the prevalence of authoritative parenting in favor of European-American, economically prosperous contexts, the positive role of authoritative parenting in psychosocial adjustment was rather uniform across all niches studied.

Obviously there are pragmatic limits as to the number of contexts one can distinguish and analyze comparatively—sample size and statistical power. Depending on the actual effect sizes, which may be quite small, huge samples are required in order to guarantee replicability of the results (Cohen, 1992). Studies emphasizing an ecological approach may be particularly affected by such problems because a breakdown of samples into subgroups is part of the strategy most often used.

In the study just described, for many niches the covariation of parenting and adjustment within groups corresponded to the differences in mean levels of both variables across groups. Assuming that predictors of individual differences would also explain group differences is the essence of the so-called individual-level approach in cross-cultural research (Leung & Bond, 1989).

Starting from this approach, Feldman and Rosenthal (this volume) explicitly asked whether differences in value orientations and family environments they found across ethnic groups would also help to explain level differences in outcome, namely, adolescent misconduct. However, despite parental demandingness showing level differences, there was no relation with misconduct within the contexts studied. Conversely, monitoring revealed no differences across cultural groups, but was substantively related to misconduct within each group.

Although there is no statistical reason to expect a specific relation between the two kinds of differences between contexts (Feldman & Rosenthal, this volume), the question remains whether certain processes follow similar patterns across a heterogeneous array of contexts. In this respect, authoritative parenting and parental monitoring seem to exemplify such a robust pattern: They share similar relations with indices of adjustment irrespective of the level or prevalence within groups. In his cross-cultural work on aggression in childhood, Rohner (1986) identifies parental warmth as such a universal.

Interacting Contexts

During the last years, investigators attempted to distinguish multiple contexts and to study their concurrent or consecutive interplay: "Adolescents do not come of age in society as a whole, but rather in a particular community, school, and family," as Elder put it, one of the intellectual forerunners in this field of investigation (Elder, Hagell, Rudkin, & Conger, this volume).

The following example from our research (Silbereisen, Boehnke, & Crockett, 1991) demonstrates how the impact of school tracking on adolescents' problem behavior depends on the socioeconomic ecology of the neighborhood. A sample of middle track secondary school students (in Germany, a school type for better achievers among noncollege youth) was split into halves according to a composite index, reflecting individual family income and economic prosperity of the neighborhood according to census tract information. In contrast to the general trend among students in secondary schools, those students of the middle track who lived in the more prosperous context drank alcohol more frequently than their agemates who attended middle track schools located in the less prosperous contexts.

Thus, what matters is not the single context but its interaction with other contexts. If one takes drinking among adolescents aged 14 on average as indicating actual psychosocial problems and/or as foreshadowing later maladaptations (McCord, 1990), the fact that students who live under seemingly better conditions drink more appears quite surprising. However, for them, attending the "atypical" school may actually indicate a mismatch to their expectations, implying the risk of downward mobility, whereas their age-mates living in the less prosperous contexts deem attending the middle track as success. Engel and Hurrelmann (this volume) discuss a similar problem when comparing students' mental health across school systems.

Bronfenbrenner (1979) coined the term "mesosystem" to denote a particular feature of contexts that several chapters of this volume address: Ecological systems of the same and/or of hierarchically distinct levels interact, and it is this very aspect that we need to study. Due to such mutual influences, apparently identical contexts may be different in their impact on development. As it requires one to look beyond the boundaries of the particular context under study, multisystem studies and respective research strategies are sorely needed.

Seen in a life-span perspective, the mesosystems an individual experiences do not represent a constant. Rather, the ins and outs of ecological systems are governed by the passage of normative developmental tasks and nonnormative life events. Thus, leaving school and starting vocational training builds up a new mesosystem, as does reentering the labor force as a consequence of the death of one's spouse.

Studying context-context interactions still is a rather new endeavor. As Farrington (this volume) points out, his present analyses represent the first systematic attempt in empirical research on offending. Rather than analyzing main effects of prior risks on future offending, all possible two-way interactions were investigated. Despite this purely inductive strategy, some interesting results turned up concerning changes in number and kind of interactions across adolescence and adulthood. Whereas offending earlier in life seems to depend on some synergies between contexts, later on less plasticity in the target behavior is revealed by an absolute preponderance of main effects. It would be interesting to discuss such results against the arguments Scarr (1992) raised concerning the impact of genetic factors.

The abstract category mesosystem can be differentiated in various ways. Not unimportantly, one may ask whether the young themselves see contexts as interacting or not. Concerning part-time work and school, the adolescents Mortimer et al. (this volume) studied deemed contexts not as isolated but functioning in a positive, synergistic way.

The interaction between school and work is a case of a mesosystem characterized by institutional links. As discussed by Hamilton (this volume), countries differ in how they are used to establish this connection.

In contrast to the United States, where work during secondary education is given an ambiguous role, Germany and Sweden offer apprenticeships and other linkages that strengthen the relation and controllability between school performance and career entry.

The specific way mesosystems work is a function of personal attributes as well, gender being not the least among them. For instance, due to gender-typic role expectations, male and female adolescents have different experiences concerning the interplay between family and work; moreover, negotiating a personally acceptable balance between demands originating in these contexts is of much higher significance for females. As shown by Camarena, Stemmler, & Petersen (this volume), males manage to arrange the two domains as parallel, whereas females see it as conflictual, and the balance they ultimately achieve is much more dependent on specific experiences with such role conflicts in their family during adolescence.

With regard to a particular developmental outcome the interaction among contexts can result in either synergistic or conflictual effects. The research reported by Steinberg and Darling (this volume) is a case in point. While confirming the unique role attributed to authoritative parenting, at closer look the strength of the association between this form of parenting and the outcomes studied was higher in intact, middle-class families of European-American origin. Based on this observation, the differential role of other, interacting contexts comes into play, namely, peer groups. In contrast to other groups, the peers of African-American students seem not to encourage academic achievement and thus counterbalance parental interest and investment in school success.

Plan of the Book

In thinking about how to organize a volume on the role of contexts and interaction among contexts in adolescent development, various ways come to mind. One is to focus on mesosystems and thus have chapters representing systematic combinations of contexts, such as family and school or family and work. Following this principle mechanically, however, would overlook the actual foci of research efforts. For instance, there is considerable research on the family-school link but almost nothing relevant for a better understanding of the relation between adolescents' work experiences and leisure contexts.

Moreover, in addition to the horizontal interplay among microsystems, the hierarchical dimension of contexts is of no less import. Contexts on the microsystem level interact with broader and more distal contexts such as the community or contexts characterized by cultural belief systems. In essence, understanding one context requires considering its relation with and embedding in other contexts. Research on the explanation of cross-cultural differences in parent-adolescent relations is a good example.

Additionally, we have to bear in mind that the developmental potential of some contexts is widely unexplored. Concerning the impact of extra-curricular activities, for instance, even the features impacting develop-ment still need to be distinguished and investigated.

Finally, we were interested in presenting research from different parts of the world. After all, adolescence is a cultural phenomenon, and con-texts provided to and used by adolescents differ as a function of national and ethnic standards. In particular, research from the United States and Europe was collected in order to give a broader view on adolescence in context.

In sum, there are three main topics we wanted to address. As it was clear from the onset that a comprehensive overview on relevant research activities would exceed space limits, we had to restrict ourselves. The following characterizes the final selection of papers.

In the first section (Social Contexts and the Development of Orien-tations for Life), the chapter by Steinberg and Darling reports about an approach that is almost prototypical for the new deal in ecological research on adolescent development. It shows the necessity of looking beyond the limits of single contexts, studies a major antecedent of ado-lescent adaptation, and in general provides the ground for many chapters in this volume. The other chapters in this section demonstrate the import of careful studies of the developmental potential of youthful contexts for the development of orientations and life-styles.

In the second section (The Impact of Cultural and Ethnic Contexts), chapters deal with comparisons across ethnical and national contexts. Group differences in the development of various aspects of adaptive (school achievement, positive resolving of developmental tasks) and maladaptive (age-inappropriate conduct such as early sexual activity or drinking) behaviors are studied, comparing Chinese and American samples, European-American with African-American, and Polish with German samples. The studies vary in the degree to which their designs allow one to explain the differences and commonalities found in terms of proximal processes.

The following sections are focused on different domains of context-context interactions.

In the third section (The Family-Work Nexus), one of the chapters compares genders and shows the much more complex interaction between these domains in the prediction of young adult females' expectations concerning the import of work and family in their life. Another chapter analyzes the impact of work-related strains on problem behaviors in adolescence. In particular, hypotheses are tested concerning moderating processes and their dependence on contextual features. The final chapter demonstrates differences in the antecedents of future-time orientations, depending on the quality of the rural context.

The main focus of the fourth section (The Interplay between School and Work) is on aspects of the spillover between school and work. In one chapter, some peculiarities of the construction of this mesosystem in the United States are characterized by comparing it with other countries, including Germany and Japan. Following that, chapters on the role of work in identity development, and on the relation between part-time work and adolescents' school activities exemplify some of the problems identified on the macro level. Finally, school-type differences in students' mental health are discussed as a joint function of parental expectations and achievement.

The fifth section (The Sample Case of Aggressive Behavior) presents research on the interplay among various contexts in the development of aggressive behavior. Contributions cover aggression in schools and offending across adolescence and young adulthood. Although the concluding chapter by Kellam, Rebok, Mayer, and Wilson refers mainly to children, the approach has implications for adolescence. Last but not least this line of research belongs among the forerunners of the ecological perspective.

References

Baltes, P.B. (1987). Theoretical propositions of life-span developmental psychology: On the dynamic between growth and decline. *Developmental Psychology, 23*, 611–626.

Bandura, A. (1986). *Social foundations of thought and action: A social cognitive theory*. Englewood Cliffs, NJ: Prentice Hall.

Baumrind, D. (1991). The influence of parenting style on adolescent competence and substance use. *Journal of Early Adolescence, 11*, 56–95.

Boehnke, K., Silbereisen, R.K., & Noack, P. (1992). Experiencing urban environment in adolescence: A study on the perception and evaluation of environmental characteristics and their impact on substance use. In H. Dettenborn (Ed.), *Berichte aus der Arbeit des Instituts für Pädagogische Psychologie am Fachbereich Erziehungswissenschaften der Humboldt-Universität zu Berlin*. Berlin: Humboldt Universität.

Bosma, H. & Jackson, S. (Eds.). (1990). *Coping and self-concept in adolescence*. Berlin: Springer.

Bronfenbrenner, U. (1979). *The ecology of human development: Experiments by nature and by design*. Cambridge: Harvard University Press.

Bronfenbrenner, U. (1989). Ecological systems theory. In R. Vasta (Ed.), *Six theories of child development: Revised formulations and current issues* (Annals of Child Development, Vol. 6, pp. 187–249). Greenwich, CT: JAI Press.

Bronfenbrenner, U., Lenzenweger, M.F., & Ceci, S.J. (1992). Heredity, environment, and the question "How?" In R. Plomin & J. McClearn, *Nature, nurture, and psychology*. Washington, DC: ATA Books.

Brown, B.B. (1990). Peer groups and peer cultures. In S.S. Feldman & G.R. Elliott (Eds.), *At the threshold: The developing adolescent* (pp. 171–196). Cambridge: Harvard University Press.

Cohen, J. (1992). A power primer. *American Psychologist, 112*, 155–159.

Doherty, W.J. & Needle, R.H. (1991). Psychological adjustment and substance use among adolescents before and after a parental divorce. *Child Development*, *62*, 328–337.

Elder, G.H., Jr., Van Nguyen, T., & Caspi, A. (1985). Linking family hardship to children's lives. *Child Development*, *56*, 361–375.

Fend, H. (1991). *Identitätsentwicklung in der Adoleszenz* [Identity development during adolescence]. Bern: Huber.

Fuhrer, U. & Kaiser, F.G. (1993). Ortsbindung: Ursachen und deren Konsequenzen für die Wohn-und Siedlungsgestaltung [Place bonding: Causes and consequences for architectural and urban design]. In H.J. Harloff (Ed.), *Psychologie des Wohnungs- und Siedlungsbaus. Psychologie im Dienste von Architektur und Stadtplanung* (pp. 57–73). Göttingen: Hogrefe.

Greenberger, E. & Steinberg, L.D. (1986). *When teenagers work: The psychological and social costs of adolescent employment*. New York: Basic Books.

Kagitcibasi, C. & Berry, J.W. (1989). Cross-cultural psychology: Current research and trends. *Annual Review of Psychology*, *40*, 493–531.

Kandel, D.B. (1986). Processes of peer influences in adolescence. In R.K. Silbereisen, K. Eyferth, & G. Rudinger (Eds.), *Development as action in context: Problem behavior and normal youth development* (pp. 203–227). New York: Springer.

Lerner, R.M. & Busch-Rossnagel, N.A. (Eds.). (1981). *Individuals as producers of their development: A life-span perspective*. New York: Academic Press.

Leung, K. & Bond, M.H. (1989). On the empirical identification of dimensions for cross-cultural comparisons. *Journal of Cross-Cultural Psychology*, *20*, 133–151.

Little, B.R. (1983). Personal projects: A rationale and method for investigation. *Environment and Behavior*, *15*, 273–309.

Loesel, F. & Bliesener, T. (in press). Why do high-risk adolescents not develop conduct disorders? A study on protective factors. *International Journal of Behavioural Development*.

Marcia, J.E. (1980). Identity in adolescence. In J. Adelson (Ed.), *Handbook of adolescent psychology* (pp. 158–187). New York: Wiley.

McCord, J. (1990). Problem behaviors. In S.S. Feldman & G.R. Elliott (Eds.), *At the threshold: The developing adolescent* (pp. 414–430). Cambridge: Harvard University Press.

McLoyd, V.C. (1989). Socialization and development in a changing economy. The effects of paternal job and income loss on children. *American Psychologist*, *44*, 293–302.

Muchow, M. & Muchow, H. (1935). *Der Lebensraum des Großstadtkindes* [The lifespace of the urban child]. Hamburg: Martin Riegel Verlag.

Müller, M. (1992). *Der Einfluß des elterlichen Erziehungsstils und des Partnerschaftswunsches von Jugendlichen auf ihr Freizeitverhalten* [The impact of parental attitudes and the state in the development of romantic friendship on adolescents' leisure time activities]. Unpublished thesis, University of Giessen.

Oerter, R. (1986). Developmental task through the life span: A new approach to an old concept. In P.B. Baltes, L. Featherman, & R. Lerner (Eds.), *Life-span development and behavior*, Vol. 7. Hillsdale, NJ: Lawrence Erlbaum.

Petersen, A.C. (1988). Adolescent development. *Annual Review of Psychology*, *39*, 583–607.

Petersen, A.C., Silbereisen, R.K., & Soerensen, S. (1993). Adolescent develop-
ment: A global perspective. In W. Meeus, M. de Goede, W. Kox, & K.
Hurrelmann (Eds.), *Adolescence, careers and cultures* (pp. 1–34). Berlin/New
York: De Gruyter.

Rohner, R.P. (1986). *The warmth dimension.* Beverly Hills: Sage.

Scarr, S. (1992). Developmental theories for the 1990s: Development and individual differences. *Child Development, 63,* 1–19.

Scarr, S. & McCartney, K. (1983). How people make their own environments:
A theory of genotype → environment effects. *Child Development, 54,* 424–
435.

Seiffge-Krenke, I. (1990). Developmental processes in self-concept and coping
behaviour. In H. Bosma & S. Jackson (Eds.), *Coping and self-concept in
adolescence* (pp. 51–68). New York: Springer.

Silbereisen, R.K., Boehnke, K., & Crockett, L. (1991). Zum Einfluß von
Schulmilieu und elterlicher Erziehungshaltung auf Rauchen und Trinken im
mittleren Jugendalter [On the impact of school milieu and parental attitudes on
smoking and drinking in mid-adolescence]. In R. Pekrun & H. Fend (Eds.),
Schule und Persönlichkeitsentwicklung: Ein Resumée der Längsschnittforschung
(pp. 272–293). Stuttgart: Enke.

Silbereisen, R.K., Eyferth, K., & Rudinger, G. (Eds.). (1986). *Development as
action in context: Problem behavior and normal youth development.* New York:
Springer.

Silbereisen, R.K. & Noack, P. (1988). On the constructive role of problem
behavior in adolescence. In N. Bolger, A. Caspi, G. Downey, & M.
Moorehouse (Eds.), *Person and context: Developmental processes* (pp. 152–
180). Cambridge: Cambridge University Press.

Silbereisen, R.K., Noack, P., & von Eye, A. (1992). Adolescents' development
of romantic friendship and change in favorite leisure contexts. *Journal of
Adolescent Research, 7,* 80–93.

Silbereisen, R.K., Nowak, M., & Schwarz, B. (1992). *Belastung der Eltern-Kind-
Beziehung und Tempo der psychosozialen Entwicklung im Jugendalter* [Strains
in parent-child relationships and variation in the timing of adolescents' psychosocial development]. Unpublished manuscript, University of Giessen.

Skinner, E.A. (1990). What causes success and failure in school and friendship?
Developmental differentiation of children's beliefs across middle childhood.
International Journal of Behavioral Development, 13, 157–176.

Spencer, C., Blades, M., & Morsley, K. (1989). *The child in the physical environment. The development of spatial knowledge and cognition.* Chichester:
Wiley.

Super, C. & Harkness, S. (1986). The developmental niche: A conceptualization
at the interface of society and the individual. *International Journal of Behavioral
Development, 9,* 545–570.

Surbey, M.K. (1990). Family composition, stress, and human menarche. In T.E.
Ziegler & F.B. Bercovitch (Eds.), *Socioendocrinology of primate reproduction*
(pp. 11–32). New York: Wiley.

Steinberg, L. (1990). Adolescent development in ecological perspective. Invited
address presented at the 98th Annual Convention of the American Psychological Association, Boston.

Van Vliet, W. (1983). Exploring the fourth environment. *Environment and Behavior, 15*, 567–588.

Zank, S. (1988). *Zur Entwicklung des Lösungsmittelschnüffelns bei Jugendlichen und jungen Erwachsenen* [On the development of solvent use among adolescents and young adults]. Berlin: Arno Spitz.

Part II

Social Contexts and the Development of Orientations for Life

2
The Broader Context of Social Influence in Adolescence

LAURENCE STEINBERG AND NANCY DARLING

The research reported in this chapter derives from a larger, short-term longitudinal study of adolescent adjustment and behavior in a multiethnic, multiclass, multiregional sample of over 20,000 United States high school students between the ages of 14 and 18. Specifically, we focus on four aspects of adolescent adjustment: (a) academic competence, as assessed in terms of school performance, school engagement, and educational ambitions; (b) psychosocial adjustment, as assessed in terms of psychosocial maturity, social competence, self-esteem, and susceptibility to peer pressure; (c) behavior problems, including drug and alcohol use, delinquency, and school misconduct; and (d) internalized distress, including both psychological and somatic symptoms. Our interest is in understanding how functioning in each of these areas is affected by the context in which the adolescent lives, including the separate and combined influences of family, peers, schools, and community.

Although the overall program of work has permitted us to collect extensive information on several domains of contextual influence, our primary interest—and the focus of this paper—is on one particular context of development during adolescence: the family. More specifically, we are interested in examining whether, and through what mechanisms, parents of high-school-aged adolescents continue to influence their children to develop in healthy ways. Although the prevailing 'wisdom'' has been that the significance of parents decreases markedly during the high school years, we believe that this view inheres in an antiquated view of adolescence and of adolescent-parent relationships.

Most research on the influence of the family on adolescent development focuses on early adolescence, rather than on development during the high school years (see Collins, 1990; Steinberg, 1990). A small, but growing body of research, however, suggests that high school students who grow up in families characterized by different child-rearing practices show differential patterns of school performance (Dornbusch, Ritter, Leiderman, Roberts, & Fraleigh, 1987) and drug use (Baumrind, 1991a).

These studies support the general contention that family relations continue to matter well into the high school years.

Parental influence does not occur in a social vacuum, however. During middle and late adolescence, in particular, the influence of parents is likely to be moderated by forces outside the family, including the adolescent's peer group and the broader community in which the family lives. No complete discussion of the family's role in adolescent development, therefore, can ignore the fact that the norms, expectations, and influences of the family are experienced by the adolescent alongside the norms, expectations, and influences of his or her friends. In some cases, these two agents of influence (the family and the peer group) are likely to have synergistic effects, with support for healthy behavior from peers enhancing the potency of parental support. In other instances, however, the combined effects of family and peer influences may be antagonistic, with one group undermining the best intentions of the other. Without taking peer influences into account, one may end up with an incomplete—or even distorted—picture of the family's significance.

A similar argument can be made in favor of studying parental influences within the context of the broader community. As we shall demonstrate, the degree to which family factors influence student achievement (one of our indicators of academic competence) varies across ethnic and socioeconomic groups. In particular, parental behaviors "known" to positively affect student achievement are more likely to be associated with adolescent academic success in some subgroups than others. Indeed, in some ethnic groups, the adolescent's immediate family does not appear to be an important influence on achievement at all (Steinberg, Lamborn, Dornbusch, & Darling, 1992; Steinberg, Mounts, Lamborn, & Dornbusch, 1991). Obviously, findings of this sort have important implications for researchers and practitioners, since they may indicate that school programs for parents developed from research within one population may not be applicable to other groups.

The data we draw upon in this chapter—all derived from self-report questionnaires completed by the adolescents—present several unique opportunities to study the influence of parents within a broader context. First, because we have extensive data on each adolescent's ethnic background and living arrangements (including each parent's ethnicity, each parent's level of education and employment status, the family's immigration history, patterns of language usage, the parents' marital history, the number of adults living in the home, and so on), we are able to examine parenting practices and adolescent outcomes across environments defined by family structure, ethnicity, and socioeconomic status. Here our work bridges approaches typically found in sociology (in which researchers have asked about differences between demographic groups either in adolescent outcomes or in their family relationships) with those typically found in the field of child development (in which questions have concerned the relation between parenting practices and child outcomes). Instead of treating these demographic variables as controls, however, our approach has been to examine how patterns of relations between parenting and child development vary across demographic groups.

Second, out data base allows us to examine the processes through which peers moderate the impact of parents on adolescents at three distinct levels of potential peer influence. First, we have data on each participating adolescent's peer crowd affiliation. (By "crowd," we refer to the reputation-based groups that structure the social system of the high school, e.g., "jocks," "druggies," etc.). These peer crowds play an important role in determining norms and values during high school (Brown, 1990; Eckert, 1989). Second, because each adolescent has provided us with the names of his or her five closest friends, we are able to examine the influence of each adolescent's immediate social network, or clique. Finally, within each clique, we are able to identify each adolescent's closest friend.

Third, we have information about the neighborhood and communities in which the families function. (In our program of research, "community" is defined both in the sense of residential community—i.e., the neighborhood—and more broadly, in terms of the extent to which families know one another and share norms and values.) Far less is known about community influences on adolescent adjustment than is known about familial or peer influences (Steinberg, 1989). Although several researchers have purported to examine community, or neighborhood, effects on academic performance (see Jencks & Mayer, 1988 for a review and critique), this literature is composed almost exclusively of studies of between-school differences in educational attainment or cognitive performance, rather than community differences in these outcomes (the contrast is typically between or among schools that vary with respect to the mean family socioeconomic status of the student body). Indeed, Jencks and Mayer (1988) could locate only two studies—one published (Datcher, 1982), one unpublished (Corcoran, Gordon, Laren, & Solon, 1987)—of the relation between neighborhood of residence and educational attainment. Interestingly, each of these studies suggests that growing up in a more affluent neighborhood is associated with increases in educational attainment above and beyond the contribution of family socioeconomic status. Disadvantaged students who grow up in a more affluent neighborhood achieve more than do comparably disadvantaged students who grow up in a poor neighborhood.

In this chapter, we present findings that address four specific questions relevant to the broader issue of the family's influence on adolescent adjustment. First, to what extent, and through what mechanisms, do family factors continue to exert an influence on adjustment during the high school years? Second, to what extent are these processes of parental influence consistent across different subpopulations of families? Third, how do the influences of families on adolescent adjustment differ depending upon the behavior and expectations of the adolescent's peers? Finally, how do familial influences on middle adolescent adjustment differ depending upon the context in which the family lives, in terms of the type and functioning of the neighborhood and community?

The Power of Authoritative Parenting

Our battery concerning family relations is aimed primarily at understanding authoritative parenting and its impact on youngsters' development. Authoritative parenting is a term coined by Diana Baumrind (1967) to describe a constellation of parenting practices, values, and beliefs that combines warmth, acceptance, and involvement with structure, maturity demands, and firm behavioral control. In most studies of authoritative parenting, scores on two dimensions—one tapping warmth, the other tapping control—are used to classify parents, typically into one of three groups: authoritative (high warmth and high control), authoritarian (low warmth and high control), and permissive (high warmth and low control).

The inventory we use includes measures of both warmth and behavioral control, but also includes a third dimension of authoritativeness that may be particularly important during adolescence: psychological autonomy-granting. This dimension parallels a similar dimension identified by Earl Schaefer nearly 30 years ago in his landmark studies of parent behavior (1965). It is also quite similar to the converse of a construct recently described by Baumrind, which she calls "directive/conventional control" (1991b). Parents who score high on our measure of psychological autonomy-granting encourage the child to have and express her own opinions, tolerate individual differences in the family, legitimate their authority, and rarely use coercive disciplinary techniques. In contrast, parents who score low on this dimension believe that children should be seen and not heard, expect their children to accept their authority unquestioningly, and frequently use guilt-induction, power assertion, and other coercive disciplinary techniques.

In our model, authoritative parents are defined as those who score high in acceptance, high in behavioral control, and high in psychological autonomy-granting. Although it may seem contradictory to describe a group of parents as being both high in behavioral control and high in psychological autonomy-granting, our behavioral control and psychological autonomy-granting scales tap quite different aspects of the parent-child relationship. Authoritative parents encourage their children to have their own opinions, and use induction when disciplining their children; this is what we mean by psychological autonomy-granting. But they also have firm and clearly articulated standards, expect their children to behave in mature ways, and have made it clear what the consequences of violating these expectations are; this is what we mean by behavioral control. In other words, authoritative parents exert control over the child's behavior, but not over the child's sense of self.

In general, we find that scores on the three dimensions—warmth, behavioral control, and psychological autonomy-granting—are independently related to various measures of adolescent competence and adjustment. Overall, it appears that warmth primarily facilitates the development of positive self-conceptions and social skills, psychological autonomy-granting mainly facilitates the development of responsibility and competence, and behavioral control chiefly contributes to the development of impulse control and deterrence of deviance (Steinberg, 1990). Not surprisingly, however, these parenting dimensions are moderately intercorrelated with each other, and with other aspects of the parent-child relationship as well. By assessing these dimensions simultaneously and drawing on them together, it is possible to capture a parenting style that is characterized by a specific constellation of behavioral and attitudinal manifestations (see also Darling & Steinberg, 1993).

The overall pattern of intercorrelations among parental behaviors and attitudes is quite sensible. Authoritative parents are not only warmer, firmer, and more democratic. They are also more involved in their child's schooling, are more likely to engage in joint decision making, and are more likely to maintain an organized household with predictable routines. Authoritarian parents, in addition to being relatively high in control and in coerciveness, and relatively low on warmth, are less involved in their child's schooling and more likely to make decisions unilaterally. Indulgent parents, in addition to being high on warmth and low on both types of control, score low in involvement and family organization and are likely to defer decision making to the adolescent. In view of these patterns, we have been employing a categorical approach to the study of parenting, in which we use scores on each of these dimensions to assign families to one of several categories.

In a first test of this model (Lamborn, Mounts, Steinberg, & Dornbusch, 1991), using the four-fold typology of parenting style outlined by Maccoby and Martin (1983), we categorized families into one of four groups— authoritative, authoritarian, indulgent, or neglectful—on the basis of scores on our parenting dimensions. We then contrasted the four groups of youngsters on our four sets of outcome measures: psychosocial adjustment, schooling, behavior problems, and internalized distress. The findings indicated that there are theoretically predictable differences among adolescents raised in authoritative, authoritarian, indulgent, and neglectful homes.

For the authoritative and neglectful groups, the findings were consistent across the four sets of outcomes. Adolescents raised in authoritative homes are better adjusted and more competent; they are confident about their abilities, competent in areas of achievement, and less likely than their peers to get into trouble. In sharp contrast, adolescents raised in neglectful homes are consistently compromised, whether the index examined taps competence, self-perceptions, misbehavior, or psychological distress.

Adolescents in the other two groups showed a mixture of positive and negative traits; the specific pattern is quite interesting, however. As one might expect, adolescents raised in authoritarian homes score reasonably well on measures of obedience and conformity to the standards of adults; they do well in school and they are less likely than their peers to be involved in deviant activities. At the same time, however, these youngsters appear to have paid a price where self-confidence is concerned—both in terms of self-reliance and in terms of their perceptions of their own social and academic abilities. The overall pattern suggests a group of young people who have been overpowered into obedience.

The adolescents from indulgent homes presented an especially intriguing picture. Like their counterparts from neglectful homes, these adolescents are relatively disengaged from school and show a higher frequency of involvement in certain deviant behaviors, including drug and alcohol use and school misconduct. These are two aspects of deviance that are both peer-oriented and, in some circles of adolescents in contemporary America, "normative." However, the fact that adolescents from indulgent homes do not score higher than the authoritative or authoritarian groups on the measure of more serious delinquency and the fact that they do score relatively high on measures of social competence and self-confidence suggests a picture of psychologically adjusted youngsters who are especially oriented toward their peers, and toward the social activities valued by adolescents—including some activities not especially valued by adults.

Because these analyses are cross-sectional, it is impossible to say with any certainty that the parenting practices examined in fact caused or even preceded the outcomes assessed. It could well be the case, for example, that competent adolescents elicit authoritativeness from their parents, or that less well-adjusted youth provoke parental neglect (see Lewis, 1981). We therefore undertook a series of longitudinal analyses designed to get at this issue more directly, with our initial focus on adolescent academic performance (Steinberg, Lamborn et al., 1992). In these analyses, we used multiple regression to predict adolescents' school achievement from their parents' practices assessed one year earlier while controlling for adolescents' initial achievement scores. This design permitted us to ask whether authoritative parenting (again, defined as parenting that is high in warmth, behavioral control, and psychological autonomy-granting) actually *leads to* improvements in adolescents' school performance.

The results of the 1-year longitudinal analyses suggest quite clearly that authoritative parenting leads to (and does not simply accompany) higher school performance. That is, all other factors being equal—including initial levels of achievement—adolescents whose parents were warm, firm, and democratic showed greater improvements in school performance and greater increases in school engagement over the one-year period than did their peers. Given the fact that our sample is already well into adolescence, the fact that parenting practices make *any* contribution to school performance over and above prior levels of achievement is noteworthy. We are now investigating whether this pattern of longitudinal effects holds true in other outcome domains. Thus far, it appears to be the case for externalizing problems as well as achievement (that is, authoritative parenting leads to a decline in externalizing) but not so clearly for other outcomes.

Authoritative Parenting: Transcontextual Validation

Our findings on the power of authoritative parenting parallel those reported by a number of different investigators, including Baumrind herself. Most of these other studies, however, have focused on middle-class, European-American youngsters growing up in two-parent households, and it is not clear from this work whether the benefits of authoritative parenting transcend demographic lines.

There are a number of ways to approach this question. For developmental psychologists, the conventional approach is to treat factors like socioeconomic status, ethnicity, or family structure as nuisance variables, and to take these variables into account through selective sampling or statistical control. In a regression model or an analysis of covariance, one would control for these factors and look to see if the relation between authoritative parenting and adolescent adjustment holds after the effects of these demographic factors are taken into account.

Although this is a widely used technique, it does not answer the question that should be of primary interest to the contextually minded researcher—namely, whether the relation between authoritative parenting and adolescent adjustment is the same for adolescents growing up under one set of circumstances as it is for adolescents growing up under another. We want to know whether the effects of authoritative parenting on minority youth are the same as on majority youth, the same for poor youth as for affluent ones, the same for youngsters from nonintact homes as for those whose biological parents are married. The covariance approach may make sense mathematically, but it makes no sense within the ecological perspective. If we believe that context matters, we certainly do not want to control it away.

The size and heterogeneity of our sample permitted us to look at this issue directly. We examined the association between authoritativeness and adolescent outcomes in 16 ecological niches (Steinberg et al., 1991). Each niche was defined by three variables: ethnicity (four categories—

African-American, Asian-American, Hispanic-American, and European-American), socioeconomic status (two categories—working-class and below versus middle-class and above), and family structure (two categories—biological two-parent and nonintact). Crossing these dimensions resulted in ecological niches such as intact, working-class, European-Americans; intact working-class Asian-Americans; intact, middle-class African-Americans, and so on. As in previous analyses, families who had scored above the entire sample median on warmth, behavioral control, and psychological autonomy-granting were categorized as authoritative. Families who had scored below the entire sample median on any of the three dimensions were categorized as nonauthoritative. (The reliability of each of the three parenting scales was examined and found to be adequate within every ecological niche.)

Adolescents from authoritative and nonauthoritative homes within each niche were then contrasted on four outcome variables, one from each of our outcome sets: grade point average, self-reliance, depression, and delinquency. Although the *prevalence* of authoritativeness varies across different ecological niches—it is most prevalent among European-Americans, middle-class families, and intact families—the *effect* of authoritativeness varies much less so. Indeed, the results of the contrasts between authoritatively and nonauthoritatively-reared adolescents were remarkably consistent. Across the 16 ecological groups, and across the four outcome variables, youngsters from authoritative homes fared better than their counterparts from nonauthoritative homes. Authoritatively-reared adolescents perform better in school, are more self-reliant, are less likely to report feeling depressed, and are less likely to be involved in delinquent activity. Out of the 64 contrasts (4 outcomes by 16 niches), 40 were statistically significant, each favoring youngsters from authoritative homes. Out of the remaining 24 contrasts, all but 3 were in the expected direction. In no case were youngsters from nonauthoritative homes significantly better off than youngsters from authoritative homes. This consistency is all the more noteworthy because the "nonauthoritative" group included many adolescents whose parents scored above the sample median on two of the three parenting dimensions.

Our working hypothesis was that authoritativeness would be more strongly related to child adjustment in middle-class, intact, European-American homes. In order to examine whether the strength of the relation between authoritative parenting and adolescent adjustment varied across the ecological niches, effect sizes were calculated for each contrast. Our hypothesis was only partially borne out, however. When we considered youngsters' psychosocial development, depression, and the likelihood of delinquency, we found that growing up in an authoritative home has comparable benefits, regardless of the family's ethnicity, class, or composition. When we looked at youngsters' school performance, however, we found that European- and Hispanic-American youngsters are more likely to benefit from authoritative parenting than are African- or Asian-American youngsters. That is, within the African- and Asian-American groups, youngsters whose parents are authoritative do not perform better in school than youngsters whose parents are not.

As will be detailed later, we do not find strong evidence of parental influence on academic achievement for either Asian- or African-American adolescents, regardless of how our measure of parental influence is operationalized. Virtually regardless of their parents' practices, the Asian-American students in our sample receive higher grades in school than other youngsters. And, unfortunately, virtually regardless of their parents' practices, the African-American students in our sample receive relatively lower grades than other students.

Family Influences on School Performance: The Moderating Role of Peers

Studies of adolescent school achievement generally point to the family as the single most important influence in the domain of socialization. Yet, our findings suggested that ethnic differences in school performance cannot be explained as a result of factors within the family, and that in some ethnic groups, parents are relatively unimportant influences on youngsters' school performance. In order to better understand this unexpected set of results, we decided to look at the influence of yet another context—the peer group—and how it interacts with that of the family. As we shall detail, our findings suggest that only by looking at these two contexts simultaneously can we understand ethnic differences in school performance.

Many of the items on our questionnaire asked students directly about the extent to which their friends and parents encouraged them to perform well in school. For parents, the questions concerned their involvement in school activities, their performance standards, and their expectations for their child's achievement. For peers, the questions concerned the degree of importance they placed on academic success and the extent to which they supported achievement among their friends. We used these items to calculate the degree to which a student felt he or she received support for academic accomplishment from parents and, independently, from peers, and then used these composite indices of parental and peer support to predict various aspects of students' attitudes and behaviors toward school. We found, as have others, that although parents are the most salient influence on youngsters' long-term educational plans, peers are the most potent influence on their day-to-day behaviors in school: how much time they spend on homework, whether they enjoy coming to school each day, and how they behave in the classroom (Steinberg & Brown, 1989).

There are interesting ethnic differences in the relative influence of parents and peers on student achievement and engagement, however (Brown, Steinberg, Mounts, & Philipp, 1990). These differences help to shed light on some of the difficulties we encountered in predicting the school performance of minority youngsters from information on their parents' practices. Our analyses suggested that peers are relatively more potent sources of influence, and parents relatively less potent sources of influence, on Asian-, African- or Hispanic-American youngsters' schooling than they are on European-American youngsters. This is not to say that the mean levels of parental encouragement are necessarily lower in minority homes than in majority homes. Rather, it is that the size of the correlations between parental encouragement and academic success and between peer encouragement and academic success are different for minority than for majority youth. In comparison to European-American youngsters, minority youngsters' peers are relatively more influential, and their parents relatively less influential. This pattern of results suggested that in order to better understand influences on the school achievement of minority youth, we needed to look less at the family (the traditional focus of research on influences on school achievement) and more closely at the peer group.

To fully appreciate the nature of peer influence on the academic achievement of minority youth, one must recognize the tremendous level of ethnic segregation that characterizes the social structure of most ethnically mixed high schools in the United States. In the course of conducting our interviews designed to reveal the social structure of each school, we spoke with students from each ethnic group in each school. We found that for the most part, students from one ethnic group did not know their classmates from other ethnic groups very well. When presented with the name of a European-American classmate, for instance, a European-American student could usually assign that classmate to one of several differentiated peer crowds—"jocks," "populars," "brains," "nerds," and so forth. When presented with the name of a African-American classmate, however, a European-American student would typically not know the group that this student ran with, or might simply say that the student was a part of the "black" crowd. The same was true for Hispanic- and Asian-American students. In other words, within ethnic groups, youngsters have a very differentiated view of their classmates; across ethnic groups, however, youngsters see their classmates as members of an ethnic group first, and members of a more differentiated crowd second, if at all.

The location of an adolescent within the school's social structure is very important, because peer crowd membership exerts an impact on school achievement above and beyond that of the family. Across all ethnic groups, youngsters who are members of academically oriented crowds and whose friends support achievement perform better than their peers, and these effects are over and above the contribution of the family (Steinberg & Brown, 1989). Indeed, an important predictor of academic success for an adolescent is the level of congruence between parent and peer support for academics: Students who receive academic support from both parents and peers perform better in school than those who receive support from only one source. But the likelihood of experiencing such congruence is greater for European-American youngsters, than for their African- and Hispanic-American peers.

For European-American students, especially those in the middle-class, the forces of parents and peers typically converge around an ethic that supports success in school (see also Ianni, 1983). For example, we find that, among European-American youth, youngsters from authoritative homes are more likely to belong to peer crowds that encourage academic achievement and school engagement—the "jocks" and the "populars" (Durbin, Steinberg, Darling, & Brown, 1993). As a result, middle-class European-American youngsters (who are more likely than their peers to reside in authoritative homes) receive encouragement for school success from virtually everyone important in their lives. For these youngsters, authoritative parenting is related to academic achievement not only because of the direct effect it has on the individual adolescent's work habits, but because of the impact it has on the adolescent's crowd affiliation. Simply put, authoritatively raised adolescents are more likely to run with other youngsters who value school and behave in ways that earn them good grades.

The situation is more complicated for youngsters from minority backgrounds, because the ethnic segregation characteristic of most high schools limits their choices for peer crowd membership. We replicated our analyses on the relation between parenting practices and peer crowd affiliation among European-American youth separately within our other ethnic subsamples (Steinberg, Dornbusch, & Brown, 1992). Among African- and Asian-American students, there is no relation between parenting practices and peer crowd membership. In other words, authoritatively raised minority youngsters are no more likely to belong to peer groups that encourage academic success than are youngsters from less academically oriented homes. Authoritatively reared minority youngsters who are in academically-oriented peer groups—whose peers and parents push them in the same positive direction—perform quite well in school. But for authoritatively reared minority youth who are not part of a peer crowd that emphasizes achievement, the influence of peers offsets the influence of parents.

Our working hypothesis is that in ethnically mixed high schools, Asian-, African-American and, to a lesser extent, Hispanic-American students find their choices of peer groups more restricted than do European-American students. But the nature of the restriction varies across ethnic groups, which helps to account for the generally higher school performance of Asian-American youngsters and the generally poorer performance of their African- and Hispanic-American peers (Steinberg, Dornbusch, & Brown, 1992). More often than not, Asian-American students belong to a peer group that encourages and rewards academic excellence. Asian-American youngsters report the highest level of peer support for academic achievement. We have found, through our student interviews, that social supports among Asian-American students for help with academics—studying together, explaining difficult assignments, and so on—is pervasive. Interestingly, and in contrast to popular belief, Asian-American students' parents are the least involved in their youngsters' schooling, in terms of attendance at school programs, parent-teacher conferences, and school-sponsored extracurricular activities, and they are among the least authoritative in our sample (see also Dornbusch et al., 1987; Sue & Okazaki, 1990).

African-American students face quite a different dilemma. Although their parents are, as a rule, supportive of academic success (they score among the highest on our measure of parental involvement in schooling), these youngsters, we have learned from our interviews, find it much more difficult to join a peer group that encourages the same goal. Our interviews with high-achieving African-American students indicate that peer support for academic success is so limited that many successful African-American students eschew contact with other African-American students and affiliate primarily with students from other ethnic groups. As has been reported by Fordham, in her ethnographic studies of African-American teenagers (Fordham & Ogbu, 1986), we find that African-American students are more likely than others to be caught in a bind between performing well in school and being popular among their peers.

Understanding African- and Asian-American students' experiences in their peer groups helps to account for the finding that authoritative parenting practices, while predictive of psychological adjustment, appear almost unrelated to school performance among these youngsters. For Asian-American students in nonauthoritative homes, the potential negative effects of these parenting practices on schooling are offset by the homogeneity of influence these youngsters encounter, in favor of academic success, in the peer group. For African-American youngsters in authoritative homes, the benefits of this type of parenting to schooling are offset by the lack of support for academic excellence that these youngsters enjoy among their peers.

Social Networks and Functional Communities

In addition to our interest in examining familial influences alongside the moderating influence of the peer group, we have also begun to examine the role of the broader community in which the family lives. Our notion of the way in which community factors moderate familial influences on children's adjustment draws heavily on the work of Coleman and Hoffer (1987), who have advanced the concept of the "functional community." According to them, functional communities are communities "in which social norms and sanctions, including those that cross generations, arise out of the social structure itself, and both reinforce and perpetuate that structure" (p. 7). Coleman and Hoffer suggest that functional communities promote adolescent competence through their impact on parenting practices. We hypothesize that membership in a functional community has certain "protective" effects—that community membership modulates the potentially deleterious effects of growing up in a "high-risk" family environment. In other words, we believe (as do Coleman and Hoffer), that the benefits of living in a strong community are greatest for those families who are the most vulnerable.

As a hypothetical illustration, consider the question of parental monitoring of youngsters' after-school activities. Nonvigilant monitoring, as well as parental permissiveness in general, is associated with a host of behavior problems in childhood and adolescence, and it is likely to be associated, directly or indirectly, with school-related difficulties (Dornbusch et al., 1985; Patterson & Stouthamer-Loeber, 1984). It has been shown as well that monitoring is less vigilant, and discipline more permissive, in single-parent than in two-parent households (see Dornbusch et al., 1985). Because membership in a functional community increases parents' contact with their children's friends and with the families of their children's friends, one by-product of living in such a community should be increased vigilance and monitoring by parents and other adults, regardless of the individual adolescent's household composition. As adolescents move through high school and spend less and less time without direct supervision, such indirect monitoring may become increasingly important. Membership in a functional community should therefore enhance parental monitoring and, more importantly, benefit families with more limited economic and personal resources most—in the case at hand, single-parent families.

Consensus among parents within a functional community about the ways in which they socialize their children may also enhance parental effectiveness both directly and indirectly. First, support and agreement among parents may increase consistency within each family. Second, because adolescents within the community are exposed to similar norms and values from adults other than their own parents, these contacts serve to reinforce those they are exposed to at home. Third, to the extent that adolescents come to internalize the norms and values of their parents, the peer group within a functional community will tend to bolster, rather than undermine, the influence of the family.

Our findings concerning adolescents' crowds suggest that the norms and values of the peer crowd may strengthen or weaken the impact of parenting practices on the individual adolescent's behavior. But members of the adolescent's crowd themselves have been socialized by their own parents. Another way to think of this, then, especially in connection with Coleman's work on communities, is that peers provide the bridge between nonfamilial adults' values and adolescents' behaviors. We examined this hypothesis through an analysis of adolescents' social networks and the extended communities they comprise.

One seldom-studied function of peers during adolescence is to introduce adolescents to adults outside of their immediate family—in this case, to the peers' parents. Within the Coleman and Hoffer "functional community" framework, these social contacts provide opportunities for "intergenerational closure"—overlap between the norms and values of adolescents and adults. Do parents in the community influence other families' adolescents, either directly or through their influence they have on their own children (who transmit this influence to their friends within the peer group)?

As part of our questionnaire, students were asked to name their five closest friends from school. Because our approach was to administer questionnaires schoolwide, we were able to match each respondent's file with that of his or her closest friend. (Here we define the closest friend as that named first.) Because each friend provided information about his or her behavior and family relationships, we were able to ask whether having a best friend from an authoritative home is beneficial to the adolescent above and beyond the effect of his or her own parents. We need to look at community influence "over and above" the family because we find, as one would expect, that characteristics of adolescents' social networks are highly correlated with characteristics of their home environment (i.e., authoritatively reared adolescents are more likely than their peers to have authoritatively reared friends).

Our analyses proceeded as follows. First, we attempted to predict each individual adolescent's score on three measures of adjustment (grade point average [GPA], work orientation, and substance use) from his or her parents' scores on the three dimensions defining authoritativeness: involvement, behavioral control, and psychological autonomy-granting. As we have amply demonstrated, adolescents whose parents are characterized by aspects of authoritativeness score higher than their peers on each indicator of adjustment (see columns A and D in Table 2.1).

Next, in order to understand the influence of the adolescents' peers' parents, the peer's parents' scores on our indices of authoritativeness were entered into the regression equation after taking into account the influence of the adolescent's own parents (see columns B and E in Table 2.1). Although the specific results vary depending upon the outcome examined and the adolescent's gender, in each case, the analyses indicate that more authoritativeness on the part of the peer's parents is significantly

TABLE 2.1. Impact on grade point average, work orientation, and substance use of parental authoritativeness, friend's parents' authoritativeness, and friend's behavior.

| | Grade point average | | | | | |
| | Boys | | | Girls | | |
Predictor	A	B	C	D	E	F
Year	−.02	−.03	−.02	.04	.03	.03
Respondent's Parents						
Responsiveness	.71**	.62*	.59*	.75**	.66**	.61**
Behavioral control	.83**	.81**	.68**	.32	.28	.11
Autonomy-granting	1.55**	1.47**	1.30**	1.20**	1.19**	.97**
Peer's Parents						
Responsiveness	—	.20	−.03	—	−.11	−.44*
Control	—	.37	.21	—	.75**	.47**
Autonomy-granting	—	.63**	.28	—	.56**	.25
Peer GPA	—	—	.33**	—	—	.30**
Model *R*	.33	.36	.47	.28	.32	.43
Year	−0.1	−0.1	−0.1	−0.1	−0.1	−0.1
Respondent's Parents						
Responsiveness	.74**	.72**	.69**	.60**	.54**	.54**
Behavioral control	.62**	.58**	.57**	.53**	.53**	.52**
Autonomy-granting	.83**	.83**	.81**	.64**	.62**	.61**
Peer's Parents						
Responsiveness	—	.01	−.05	—	.06	.04
Control	—	.29*	.24	—	.26*	.24
Autonomy-granting	—	.04	−.05	—	.40**	.35**
Peer Work Orientation	—	—	.11**	—	—	.05
Model *R*	.34	.35	.37	.29	.32	.32
Year	−.27**	−.24**	−.16**	−.17**	−.14**	−.09**
Respondent's Parents						
Responsiveness	.30	.41	.33	−.14	.02	.06
Behavioral control	−2.43**	−2.31**	−1.78**	−3.18**	−3.06**	−2.61**
Autonomy-granting	−1.36**	−1.29**	−1.00**	−1.09**	−1.12**	−.82**
Peer's Parents						
Responsiveness	—	.11	.14	—	.00	.09
Control	—	−1.22**	−.37	—	−1.57**	.01
Autonomy-granting	—	−.90**	−.58	—	−.62*	−.16
Peer Substance Use	—	—	.38**	—	—	.43**
Model *R*	.39	.42	.54	.40	.44	.59

Note: Respondent's year in school was entered into the regression equation first, followed by variables assessing parental authoritativeness (column A), variables assessing friend's parents' authoritativeness (column B), and the friend's behavior (column C).
* $p < .05$; ** $p < .01$

associated with higher scores for the target adolescent on our measures of adjustment.

Although these results suggest that adolescents whose best friend comes from an authoritative family fare better than those whose friend does not, these analyses do not indicate whether this influence is *directly* from the peer's parents to the target adolescent or, alternatively, whether the peer's parents influence their own child, who in turn influences the target adolescent (an *indirect* effect). This question is addressed in the third step of the analyses (reported in columns C and F of Table 2.1). Here, we once again examined the relation between the parenting practices of the peer's parents and the target adolescent's outcomes, this time, however, controlling both for the influence of the target adolescent's own family and for the adolescent's friend's score on the target measure (i.e., peer substance use, GPA, or work orientation, respectively).

The results of these analyses indicate that among boys, the benefits of having friends whose parents are authoritative come indirectly, through the influence of the friends' parents on their own children. The process is seen most clearly when one examines the results of analyses concerning substance use, which indicate that the significant effect of nonfamilial adults' authoritativeness on the respondent's substance use (see column B) disappears once the mediating effect of the respondent's friend's drug use is taken into account (see column C). In other words, adolescents whose parents are high in behavioral control and psychological autonomy-granting are less likely to be involved in substance use than their peers, and being friends with such peers lowers the likelihood that one will be involved with substance use himself. Importantly, the positive effect of associating with authoritatively raised peers is over and above the effect of having authoritative parents.

The results of parallel analyses among girls suggest, however, that friends' parents have a direct influence on girls' adjustment, at least with respect to school performance and work orientation (as well as an additional indirect effect on school performance). Specifically, girls whose friends' parents are high in involvement and behavioral control perform better in school than those with equally high-achieving peers whose parents are not. Similarly, girls with friends whose parents are high in psychological autonomy-granting have more positive work orientations than those whose friends do not, even controlling for the friends' own work orientation. In the case of substance use, however, the findings are identical to those among boys: The positive influence of knowing authoritative nonfamilial adults is mediated through the impact that these adults have on their children.

Together, these results suggest that growing up in a context in which the nonfamilial adults one knows are authoritative may be beneficial in two ways. First, it makes it more likely that one will associate with competent friends. Second, at least for girls, living in a community that includes authoritative adults other than one's parents may help encourage competence in adolescents directly, above and beyond the effect of one's own parents and friends.

Neighborhood Effects

These last findings suggest that living in a community characterized by a high number of authoritative parents is likely to foster the development of adolescent above and beyond the influence of one's own family. The final set of analyses we present examines the moderating role of neighborhoods on parental influence. As we shall see, these findings replicate, on a different level of analysis, the results just reported.

We were able to collect information on the specific addresses of virtually all of our California subsample, and by using these addresses, we were able to map onto each respondent's file information about the characteristics of his or her neighborhood, which we obtained from the U.S. Census Bureau. A census tract is actually a good deal larger than a neighborhood—in our sample, the average tract contained about 4,500 individuals. Nevertheless, our analyses (see Dornbusch, Ritter, & Steinberg, 1991) point to the importance of looking at community effects—even when "community" is as grossly defined as it is here—in understanding the impact of parenting on adolescents' behavior. In these analyses, for reasons that will become apparent, we focused on European- and African-American adolescents only.

We noted earlier that we are much better able to predict European-American students' school performance from their parents' practices than we are in predicting African-American students' performance from the same parenting variables. This general finding is also true in the prediction of adolescent school performance from family status variables, such as family structure or parental education. That is, whereas European-American students' academic performance varies as a function of their parents' education and their family background, the same is not true for African-American students. Given the presumed importance of the family as an influence on achievement, why should family variables not be predictive of academic achievement among African-American students? We discussed earlier the likely role that peers play in undermining positive parental influences among African-American youngsters. Here, we look at another explanation: differences between the neighborhoods of European-American and African-American students.

Using census data, we categorized each respondent as living in a predominantly European-American tract (more than 75% European-American) or a substantially African-American tract (more than 30% African-American). We then reran the analyses linking family process and family status variables to school outcomes separately for African-

and European-American youngsters living in the two different types of neighborhoods.

The results are quite provocative. Among African-American youngsters living in predominantly European-American neighborhoods, we are just as able to predict school performance from family variables as we are among majority youngsters from majority neighborhoods. But among families living in neighborhoods with a high concentration of African-American families, the prediction of adolescent school performance from family variables is not significant. Interestingly enough, this is true whether the family is European- or African-American. In other words, in minority neighborhoods, the positive impact of individual family factors on adolescent school performance appears to be overwhelmed by forces in the broader the community. Another way of looking at this is that some communities allow families to take advantage of their advantages, whereas other communities do not.

How does this fit in with the finding that authoritative parenting may have more of a payoff for some adolescents than others? Because European-American adolescents are more likely to live in communities that permit families to take advantage of their advantages, they are more likely to reap the benefits of good parenting when their parents provide it. Conversely, because African-American adolescents are less likely to live in these sorts of communities, even those with authoritative parents may not enjoy the outcomes generally associated with this style of child-rearing.

We do not yet know which community factors make a difference. One hypothesis, based on the findings we discussed previously, is that communities that are predominantly European-American have a higher concentration of authoritative families. It may be the case that a "critical mass" of parental authoritativeness is necessary in the community in order for authoritative parenting to have an impact within individual households.

Some Concluding Comments

These findings reported in this chapter should serve to illustrate the complex mechanisms through which the contexts in which adolescents live influence their lives and their behavior. We began by looking at one process occurring within the microsystem of the family: the relation between authoritative parenting and adolescent adjustment. We find, in general, that adolescents whose parents are warm, firm, and democratic are better adjusted and more competent than their peers. Adolescents whose parents are more authoritarian tend to behave obediently but evince diminished self-confidence and self-reliance. Adolescents whose parents are more indulgent have healthy self-conceptions, but are more likely to behave in ways that adults find troublesome. Adolescents whose parents are uninvolved or neglectful show problems in competence and adjustment across numerous indicators. Our longitudinal analyses suggest that authoritative parenting leads to improvements in adolescent adjustment (rather than simply accompanying it), even during the high school years. Moreover, our findings suggest that the benefits of parental authoritativeness may not be limited, as has been argued, to European-American youngsters from middle-class homes.

At the same time, however, our findings suggest that the effects of authoritative parenting must be examined within the broader context in which the family lives and in which youngsters develop. The family is not the only source of influence on adolescents' development and behavior. This appears to be especially true where school performance is concerned. Our findings suggest that the impact of parenting practices on youngsters' academic performance and behavior is moderated to large extent by the social milieu they encounter in their peer crowd, among their close friends, within their social network, and in their neighborhood. Although authoritative parenting "works," generally speaking, it works better in some contexts than others. Indeed, in certain contexts overarching forces may actually overwhelm the beneficial effects of authoritative parenting in the home. Ironically, then, the key to understanding the influence of the family during adolescence may inhere in looking beyond the boundaries of this particular context and at the broader context in which the adolescent lives.

Acknowledgments. Preparation of this chapter was supported by a grant to the first author from the Lilly Endowment and by a grant to both authors from the William T. Grant Foundation. The research on which the paper draws was supported by a grant to Laurence Steinberg and B. Bradford Brown from the U.S. Department of Education, through the National Center on Effective Secondary Schools at the University of Wisconsin-Madison, and from the Spencer Foundation, to Sanford Dornbusch and P. Herbert Leiderman of the Stanford University Center for Families, Children, and Youth. Address correspondence to the authors, Department of Psychology, Temple University, Philadelphia, PA 19122.

References

Baumrind, D. (1967). Child care practices anteceding three patterns of preschool behavior. *Genetic Psychology Monographs, 75*, 43–88.

Baumrind, D. (1991a). The influence of parenting style on adolescent competence and substance use. *Journal of Early Adolescence, 11*, 56–95.

Baumrind, D. (1991b). Parenting styles and adolescent development. In J. Brooks-Gunn, R. Lerner, & A.C. Petersen (Eds.), *The encyclopedia of adolescence.* New York: Garland.

Brown, B.B. (1990). Peer groups and peer cultures. In S.S. Feldman & G.R. Elliott (Eds.), *At the threshold: The developing adolescent.* pp. 171–196. Cambridge: Harvard University Press.

Brown, B., Steinberg, L., Mounts, N., & Philipp, M. (1990, March). *The comparative influence of peers and parents on high school achievement: Ethnic differences.* Paper presented as part of a symposium entitled "Ethnic Variations in Adolescent Experience" at the biennial meetings of the Society for Research on Adolescence, Atlanta.

Coleman, J.S. & Hoffer, T. (1987). *Public and private high schools: The impact of communities.* New York: Basic Books.

Collins, W.A. (1990). Parent-child relationships in the transition to adolescence: Continuity and change in interaction, affect, and cognition. In R. Montemayor, G. Adams, & T. Gullotta (Eds.), *Advances in adolescent development: Volume 2. The transition from childhood to adolescence.* Beverly Hills: Sage.

Corcoran, M., Gordon, R., Laren, D., & Solon, G. (1987). *Intergenerational transmission of education, income, and earnings.* Unpublished paper. Ann Arbor: Institute for Public Policy Studies, University of Michigan.

Darling, N. & Steinberg, L. (1993). Parenting style as context: An integrative model. *Psychological Bulletin.*

Datcher, L. (1982). Effects of community and family background on achievement. *The Review of Economics and Statistics, 64,* 32–41.

Dornbusch, S.M., Carlsmith, J.M., Bushwall, S.J., Ritter, P.L., Leiderman, P.H., Hastorf, A.H., & Gross, R.T. (1985). Single parents, extended households, and the control of adolescents. *Child Development, 56,* 326–341.

Dornbusch, S.M., Ritter, P.L., Leiderman, P.H., Roberts, D.F., & Fraleigh, M.J. (1987). The relation of parenting style to adolescent school performance. *Child Development, 58,* 1244–1257.

Dornbusch, S., Ritter, P., & Steinberg, L. (1991). Community influences on the relation of family statuses to adolescent school performance: An attempt to understand a difference between African-Americans and non-Hispanic Whites. *American Journal of Education, August,* 543–567.

Durbin, D.L., Steinberg, L., Darling, N., & Brown, B.B. (1993). Parenting style and peer group membership in European-American adolescents. *Journal of Research on Adolescence, 3,* 87–100.

Eckert, P. (1989). *Jocks and burnouts: Social categories and identity in the high school.* New York: Teachers College Press.

Fordham, S. & Ogbu, J.U. (1986). Black students' school success: Coping with the burden of "acting white." *Urban Review, 18,* 176–206.

Ianni, F.A.J. (1983). *Home, school, and community in adolescent education.* New York: Clearinghouse on Urban Education.

Jencks, C. & Mayer, S. (1988). *The social consequences of growing up in a poor neighborhood: A review.* Unpublished manuscript. Evanston, IL: Northwestern University Center for Urban Affairs and Policy Research.

Kohn, M.L. (1977). *Class and conformity: A study in values* (2nd ed.). Chicago: University of Chicago Press.

Lamborn, S., Mounts, N., Steinberg, L., & Dornbusch, S. (1991). Patterns of competence and adjustment among adolescents from authoritative, authoritarian, indulgent, and neglectful homes. *Child Development, 62,* 1049–1065.

Lewis, C. (1981). The effects of parental firm control. *Psychological Bulletin, 90*, 547–563.

Maccoby, E.E. & Martin, J.A. (1983). Socialization in the context of the family: Parent-child interaction. In E.M. Hetherington (Ed.), *Handbook of child psychology: (Vol. 4). Socialization, personality, and social development* (pp. 1–102). New York: Wiley.

Patterson, G.R. & Stouthamer-Loeber, M. (1984). The correlation of family management practices and delinquency. *Child Development, 55*, 1299–1307.

Schaefer, E. (1965). Children's reports of parental behavior: An inventory. *Child Development, 36*, 413–424.

Steinberg, L. (1989). Communities of families and education. In W. Weston (Ed.), *Education and the American family: A research synthesis* (pp. 138–168). New York: New York University Press.

Steinberg, L. (1990). Autonomy, conflict, and harmony in the family relationship. In S.S. Feldman & G.R. Elliot (Eds.), *At the threshold: The developing adolescent* (pp. 255–276). Cambridge: Harvard University Press.

Steinberg, L. & Brown, B.B. (1989). *Beyond the classroom: Family and peer influences on high school achievement*. Invited paper presented to the Families as Educators special interest group at the annual meeting of the American Educational Research Association, San Francisco.

Steinberg, L., Dornbusch, S., & Brown, B. (1992). Ethnic differences in adolescent achievement in ecological perspective. *American Psychologist, 47*, 723–729.

Steinberg, L., Lamborn, S., Dornbusch, S., & Darling, N. (1992). Impact of parenting practices on adolescent achievement: Authoritative parenting, school involvement, and encouragement to succeed. *Child Development, 63*, 1266–1281.

Steinberg, L., Mounts, N.S., Lamborn, S.D., & Dornbusch, S.M. (1991). Authoritative parenting and adolescent adjustment across various ecological niches. *Journal of Research on Adolescence, 1*, 19–36.

Sue, S. & Okazaki, S. (1990). Asian-American educational achievements: A phenomenon in search of an explanation. *American Psychologist, 45*, 913–920.

3
Youth Organizations, Hobbies, and Sports as Developmental Contexts

Reed Larson

In the late 19th century social reformers invented a new set of contexts intended specifically to foster adolescents' development. These reformers initiated and promoted hobbies, youth organizations, and sports as valuable and healthful parts of adolescents' lives. In the United States the Boy and Girl Scouts, 4-H, the YMCA and YWCA, Little League, and numerous recreational centers, hobby clubs, and eventually in-school extracurricular activities were launched by community activists who wanted to improve the lot of developing youth. These activists believed that, with proper adult guidance, such organized activities could promote initiative, build character, discourage delinquency, and provide "laboratories for training in citizenship."

Now, more than 100 years later, these activities are still promoted by schools and communities, yet limited research has been done to evaluate the ambitious claims about their developmental potential. There is some developmental research on the psychological benefits and costs of athletics, but remarkably little on hobbies and youth organizations. These activities are mentioned sometimes in sociological accounts of the social organization of adolescents' lives (e.g., Coleman, 1961; Rosenbaum, 1976) and several investigators have used extracurricular activity participation as a measure of adolescent mental health (Achenback & Edelbrock, 1986; Simmons, Burgeson, Carlton-Ford, & Blyth, 1987). But few studies have looked directly at these activities as developmental contexts.

One important claim is that these activities provide a vehicle of *social integration*. Participation in organizations, hobbies, and sports creates points of contact between adolescents and other adults, the community, a peer group, and possibly their own families. In a sense, they are not separate contexts, but arenas through which ties to community, peers, and family are promoted. But it is not just the contact per se that is important. These activities are deliberately structured to provide a set of operational procedures, values, and subcultural mores that teach and encourage prosocial behaviour. How effective these activities are in achieving this socially integrative function is the topic of Part I of this article.

In addition to social integration, it is claimed that sports, hobbies, and organizations serve personal developmental functions. In the language of the early reformers, these activities were thought to redirect aggressive instincts, teach mental hygiene, and promote "ethical character." In the more recent jargon of developmental psychopathology we might hypothesize that they are "protective" or that they define a "pathway" of positive mental health. The hypothesis that they promote an adolescent's *psychological integration* is the topic of Part II of this article. First, I examine findings on the relationship of extracurricular activities to self-concept. Then I review evidence for my theory that the narrative structure of participation in some activities provides a unique opportunity for development of intrinsic motivation and personal agency.

Since past research is limited, my attempt to evaluate these activities is of necessity fragmentary and incomplete. The objective is a modest one of providing an overview of the topic in hopes of stimulating more attention to this neglected, yet important, segment of adolescents' daily lives. For lack of a better word, I will use the term "extracurricular activities" to refer to these activities, with the intent of including both school-related and nonschool-related participation in sports, organizations, and hobbies.

Extracurricular Activities as Vehicles of Social Integration

I will consider two criteria of social integration: First, do extracurricular activities foster social relationships; second, do, they promote behavior consistent with prosocial membership in the community?

Fostering Relationships

With Adults

In most cases extracurricular activities are established and maintained by adults, and adolescents' participation involves regular interaction with these sponsors, coaches, and leaders. The activity may also bring a teenager into contact with other members of the community such as fans, fellow hobbyists, civic leaders, or clients of a service organization. Since contemporary adolescents have remarkably few opportunities for interactions with adults other than family members and teachers (Csikszentmihalyi & Larson, 1984), such contact is probably beneficial just because of the pure exposure it provides. Extracurricular activities offer one of the rare chances they have to get to know other adults. Nonetheless it is useful to ask about the quality of these relationships.

These adult sponsors, it is hypothesized, serve as role models, mentors, and sources of social support (Schafer, 1969). Indeed, Werner (1987) shows that having a close relationship with an adult outside the family, such as a group leader, can be a decisive protective factor that insulates at-risk youth from some of the consequences of stress. Research suggests, however, that adolescents' relationships with group leaders are not always positive. When teenagers are asked who is significant to them or who has had an important effect upon them, coaches and other adults known through organizations are mentioned occasionally, but not in great numbers (Blyth, Hill, & Thiel, 1982; McCormack, 1984). Furthermore, research on coaching suggests that these adults are sometimes perceived as being too autocratic or arbitrary and are actively disliked (Carron & Chelladurai, 1978; Chalip, 1980). In sum, extracurricular activities bring adolescents into contact with other adults, but the relationships formed are not always close and positive.

With Peers

The relationships that extracurricular activities engender with peers may be their strongest effect. Inasmuch as activities determine who an adolescent spends time with, they provide a basis for the formation of friendships and peer groups (Coleman, 1961). Chess players, dancers, cheerleaders, debaters tend to hang out with each other. Indeed, the names given to peer crowds—"jocks," "brains," "nerds"—often allude to the extracurricular activities these crowds take part in. Experimental studies by Sherif and Sherif (1953) indicate that propinquity and a common goal are all that is needed for a peer group to form. A hobby, organization, or sport links an adolescent to a set of like-minded peers; it interweaves the schedule of their day and provides a common set of experiences, goals, and gossip that is a basis for friendship.

In some cases friendships or peer group membership may precede and determine organization membership. Several studies have found that adolescents perceive youth organizations to be controlled by cliques (Hedin & Simon, 1980; Long, Buser, & Jackson, 1977). We also know that organization membership is greater among higher socio-economic status and upper-ability-tracked students (Coleman, 1961; Spady, 1970; Yarworth & Gauthier, 1978); therefore, in many cases these activities may be simply providing another setting for like-minded individuals to hang out together. Yet there is evidence that such activities can and do create ties between peers, including between peers of different ethnic groups who would otherwise not have associated (Holland & Andre, 1987).

With the Family

The teenage years are a period when many parents and adolescents find less common ground with each other, and extracurricular activities provide an added avenue of connection. Parents and other family members come to games, concerts, and other events related to extracurricular activities; the activity also provides a much-needed topic of conversation between parents and adolescents (Larson & Richards, in press). In some cases the parents may be or may have been involved in the activity, thus it is a vehicle of intergenerational sharing: the father and son who collect stamps, the mother and daughter who love softball. For better or worse, sports or organizational membership may also transmit and reinforce the family's class, ethnic, and gender identification (Kleiber & Kirshnit, 1990; Spady, 1970).

Of course, like other avenues of connection between parent and child, extracurricular activities may be an opportunity for renegotiation of autonomy, or a battleground for suppression of it. On the one hand, such activities provide teenagers a legitimate opportunity to do something on their own: to excuse themselves from the living room to go draw in the bedroom or to take the bus downtown for ballet classes. They also provide a chance for the adolescent to receive recognition and support for this independence. Dubas and Snider (in press) report one study in which 4-H participation was found to create greater communication and understanding within families. On the other hand, a parent's attempt to control the activity may be a source of conflict. Parents exert influence over the activities their children choose (Kirshnit, 1989; Medrich, Roizen, Rubin, & Buckley, 1982), and in some cases parent involvement takes the form of coercion. We do not know how many parents force their children to take music lessons nor how this force affects the value of the activity or alters the relationship between parent and child. But there is some evidence that the attitudes some parents adopt as spectators, such as encouraging winning or achievement at all cost, can be destructive (McEwin, 1981). In sum, the linkages that activities provide between the adolescent and the family, like those to coaches and sponsors, are potentially positive but may in some instances have a negative side.

A Subculture

The above findings suggest that extracurricular activities often engender relationships to specific individuals. Several longitudinal studies demonstrate that they also engender an enduring relationship with a community of participants. Adolescents who participate in an activity are often still connected to that activity and its subculture in adulthood. Hanks and Eckland (1978) found that high school participation in extracurricular activities predicted membership in adult voluntary associations at age 30, even with controls for educational achievement, occupation, and income. DeMartini (1983) found that participation in political organizations in high school was associated with political activism later in life. Bloom (1985) found that high school participation in the arts predicted continued participation in adulthood. And high school participation in sports has been found to predict sports participation in adulthood (Howell & McKenzie, 1987). Most of these findings appear to be fairly specific: Participation in an activity predicts more of that activity in adulthood. Yet given that many adolescents are alienated and detached from adult society, this process of integration into a subcommunity may be a particularly valuable function. Adolescent participation initiates one into a subcultural enclave which provides a reference group and set of mores that one carries (or that carries one) through the transition into adulthood.

Extracurricular Activities and Prosocial Behavior

Extracurricular activities and organizations are often set up with a deliberate mission of inculcating a specific set of adult values. The Little League, for example, has a written mission statement and the father-coaches take seriously their role of teaching fair play, teamwork, and other prosocial values (Fine, 1987). In Scotland, hundreds of jazz bands have been established for early adolescent girls with a deliberate goal of providing a stabilizing influence on these girls' lives (Grieves, 1989). In some cases these organizations have sought to inculcate values that we in the late 20th century may question. One thinks of the deliberate attempt of the early Boy Scouts to cultivate masculine values (Hantover, 1978), the objective of "Americanizing" immigrant youth that motivated many early youth clubs, the goal of the Soviet Pioneer Youth to make good Communists, or, more extremely, the goal of the Hitler Youth to create good Nazis. Yet even though there are instances where we question the specific values promoted, it is useful to recognize that these organizations, and many others, appear to have been quite effective in integrating youth into an adult community and an adult set of values.

I will focus here upon one measure of prosocial values, or rather its lack thereof: delinquent behavior. Hirschi (1969) argues that delinquency is emblematic of an adolescent's lack of social integration into the community and the adult world. If extracurricular activities are successful at integrating youth, we would expect participants to engage in less delinquent behavior. Indeed, several studies have found a modest cross-sectional negative correlation between extracurricular activity participation and delinquency (Agnew & Petersen, 1989; Hirschi, 1969; Landers & Landers, 1978; Schafer, 1969); however, no one has determined whether absence of delinquency preceded or was directly·attributable to activity participation. It could be that these activities attract more conforming youths.

Prior findings also suggest the need to separately examine relationships for athletics, for which the correlations are weaker, from other extra-curricular activities that yield stronger associations (Osgood & Young-Min, 1990). I also think it important to separate arts and hobbies, which can be solitary, from organization participation, which is necessarily more social. Data that I collected with Maryse Richards of Loyola University permit examination of these issues.

A Longitudinal Study of Extracurricular Participation

We obtained information from a sample of middle- and working-class American 5th to 8th graders (Larson & Richards, 1989) and then studied them again 2 (Time 2) and 4 (Time 3) years later. Sample size for the Time 1 to Time 2 computations is 263 and sample size for the Time 2 to Time 3 computations is 166. Activity participation was measured at all three data collections and delinquency at Time 2 and Time 3. Students completed a 13-item measure of delinquency (Elliot & Voss, 1974) used to obtain a total score. Information on activity participation was obtained from the first page of the Achenbach Youth Self-Report, which asks for a list of the sports, hobbies, and organizations in which a person is involved and also asks for ratings of how often the adolescent participates in each activity (Achenbach & Edelbrock, 1986). I used these time estimates to compute a weighted score for level involvement in three categories of activities: athletics, arts and hobbies, and youth organizations.[1]

Regressions were used to evaluate the longitudinal relationships as-sociated with each of the three activities. In these regressions, sex differ-ences in participation rates and delinquency were partialled out prior to the analyses in order to avoid a sex artifact. I also felt it important to separate the younger from the older students, so that effects related to specific age periods could be isolated. "Cohort 1" includes the Time 1

---

[1] *Athletics* includes participation in organized and informal physical activities, excluding gym class. This category includes noncompetitive physical activities such as dance, ice-skating, and bike riding, but competitive sports constitutes by far the largest proportion of activities here, especially among boys (69%, vs. 60% among girls). *Arts and hobbies* includes music, art, and various crafts, excluding activities done for a class. For boys, the most frequent activities here are collecting (21%) and making models (19%), activities that diminish substantially with age, being partly replaced in frequency by interests in cars and music. Among girls the most frequent activities here are reading (26%), collecting (14%) and band (14%) (both of which fall off with age), and music (10%) (which increases with age). Theoretically I felt it important to differentiate these from youth organizations, because they are more often private activities done alone. *Youth organizations* includes participation in school and nonschool clubs and organizations, from student council to band to church youth groups. There is a strong age trend here with school clubs increasing and Scouts decreasing among the older adolescents.

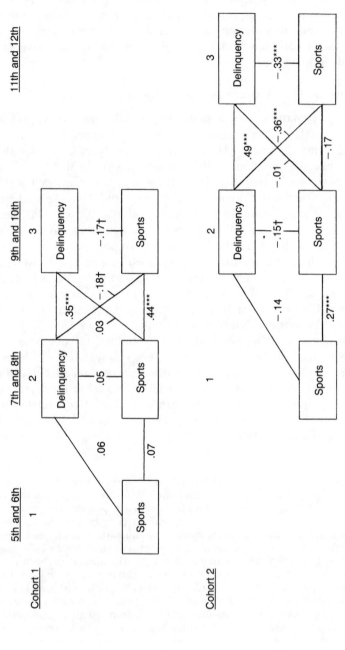

FIGURE 3.1. The association of delinquency with athletic participation.
† $p < .10$; * $p < .05$; ** $p < .01$; *** $p < .001$

Note: Vertical lines show the cross-sectional correlations between delinquency and athletic participation. Horizontal and diagonal lines show the beta coefficients for the longitudinal paths. Effects of sex were removed prior to the analyses.

fifth and sixth graders and "Cohort 2," the Time 1 seventh and eighth graders.

Athletics

A first finding of these analyses is that the cross-sectional negative correlation between delinquency and sport, which others have found for senior high school (SHS) students, is not present at the junior high school (JHS) ages (Figure 3.1). Delinquency and sport participation appear to coexist readily in the junior high years, perhaps partly because delinquency is often less severe at this age. However, the combined findings for the two cohorts suggest that the strength of the negative correlation increases with age and is strongest in the 11th–12th grades. Apparently delinquency and sports become more incompatible with age.

Does this mean sports suppresses delinquency? The data suggest the opposite: that delinquency suppresses sports participation. For Cohort 2 there is a highly significant path coefficient between 9th–10th grade delinquency and 11th–12th grade sport participation, but no reciprocal path from sports to delinquency. Likewise, for Cohort 1, seventh–eighth grade delinquency has a close-to-significant negative association with 9th–10th grade sports, with no indication of a reciprocal path. Separate analyses by sex suggest that both of these trends are stronger for boys than for girls. This path from delinquency to sports may have a simple explanation: When an athlete is caught for delinquent activities, he or she is often kicked off the team (Schafer, 1969). Alternately, high school athletics may preselect for youth who are conformers (Schafer, 1969).

But what is important here is not this finding, but the absence of the alternate path. There is no indication that participation in sports is successful in the mission of promoting generalized prosocial behavior—or specifically, surpressing antisocial behavior. This may not be surprising, given that the world view of sports does not encourage identification with a single social whole but rather separates society into us versus them. Other activities with less emphasis on competition appear to be more successful in this prosocial mission.

Arts and Hobbies

For participation in arts and hobbies there is a modest negative cross-sectional relationship across all age periods ($r = -.14$ to $r = -.29$), suggesting these two types of activities are modestly incompatible regardless of age. Do arts and hobbies suppress delinquency as advocates predict? We do see the predicted pattern of cross-lag associations for Cohort 2, though not for Cohort 1. Adolescents who report greater participation in arts and hobbies in the 9th–10th grades report less delinquency in the 11th–12th grades ($\beta = -.18$, $p = .082$). Separate analyses by sex indicated that this trend was significant for boys, but not for girls.

No evidence was found of the reverse direction of causality from delinquency to arts and hobbies. In sum, these findings suggest that participation in arts and hobbies may reduce delinquency during the SHS years.

Organizations

The pattern of associations between delinquency and participation in youth organizations is almost identical to that for arts and hobbies, only the relationships are a little stronger (Figure 3.2). First, organization participation is inversely correlated with delinquency for senior high cross-sectional correlations (but not during the one junior high correlation).

Second, there is evidence that organization participation diminishes delinquency. For Cohort 2, there is a strong negative association between organization participation in the 9th–10th grades and delinquency in the 11th–12th grades. In separate analyses by sex this path is significant for both girls and boys. The Cohort 1 path from 7th–8th grade organization participation to delinquency is also significant for boys ($\beta = -.37$, $p = .015$). None of the paths from delinquency to organization participation are significant. These findings suggest that participation in youth organizations may reduce delinquency during the SHS years.

Conclusion

In sum, existing evidence provides preliminary proof that participation in extracurricular activities promotes the social integration of adolescents. Findings by other researchers suggest that these activities create, or at least reinforce, relationships with others and establish a pattern of social relatedness to a subculture that continues into adulthood. My findings suggest that youth organizations, arts, and hobbies inculcate a resistance to delinquent behavior. Further research might attempt to look at a wider array of outcome variables: For example, do they encourage prosocial, altruistic behavior as well as discourage antisocial behavior?

Given these findings, however, the next step might be to shift from focusing on outcome to process: What happens in these settings that leads to social integration? What experiences differentiate those adolescents who benefit from those who do not? And do these activities simply promote conformity to society's standards or do they provide opportunities for self-generated learning about the "social contract" and the value of prosocial behavior? These processrelated questions arise again when we consider the role of extracurricular activities in promoting psychological integration.

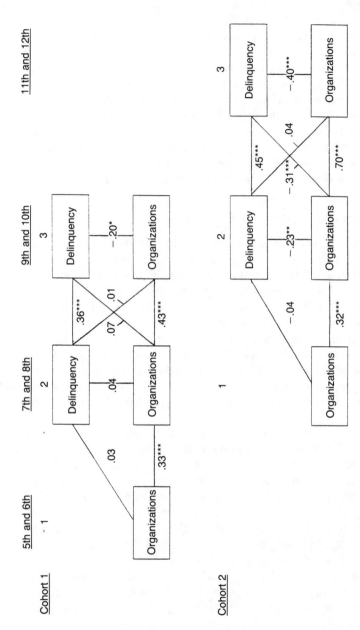

FIGURE 3.2. The association of delinquency with organization participation.

Extracurricular Activities and Psychological Integration

In addition to facilitating adolescents' social integration, extracurricular activities have often been credited with facilitating their personal development and well-being. This latter function, of course, is not separate: By connecting adolescents with a community and socializing them into a set of prosocial values, activities also provide a reference group and a set of norms that may shape their self-concepts. Research to date, however, does not allow us to examine the interconnecting links; therefore, in this section I will focus on the relationship between participation and psychological functioning as if it were distinct. First I will look at relationships between extracurricular participation and self-concept, a topic that has received some research attention; then I will look at relationships to motivational systems, a topic I believe deserves further thought.

Self-Concept Development

The argument that extracurricular activities promote self-concept development is so straightforward as to require little elaboration. In addition to providing a reference group for self-definition (à la Sherif & Sherif, 1964), these activities provide an opportunity for an adolescent to experiment with different selves and experience the feeling of competence. In theory, the chance to succeed in a domain that is self-chosen and removed from the critical grading system of schools seems like it should be an ideal environment for identity development for a wide range of youths. Indeed, when adolescents are asked to describe their personal strengths, many mention their interest in a hobby or their participation in sports (Benson, 1991; Otto & Healy, 1966; Williams & McGee, 1991).

At the same time, however, for some adolescents these activities acquire an achievement orientation that is little different than that of school, and possibly more intense. Sports in particular are often experienced as highly competitive, and, since one side always loses, for many adolescents, sports may have a zero-sum net effect on their self-esteem. Adopting the constructs of Nicholls (1984), several researchers have found that many athletes (especially males) become "ego-involved," they see competition against others as a measure of their self-worth; and thus, when they lose or do poorly, athletics has negative effects on their self-evaluation (Danish, Kleiber, & Hall, 1987; Duda, 1988). These researchers, however, find another set of adolescent athletes who are "mastery-oriented," who use their past performance, rather than winning and losing, as their standard of comparison; for these adolescents athletics are more likely to have a net positive effect. Of course, the attitude of coaches and parents may also affect whether a teen athlete adopts one or the other orientation (Danish et al., 1987).

The inclusion of both ego-involved and mastery-oriented participants within typical research samples may account for the finding that extracurricular participation is only modestly and inconsistently related to measures of self-concept. Yarworth and Gauthier (1978) found that both sports participation and nonathletic extracurricular participation were positively associated with measures of self-concept, although the magnitude of the associations after other variables were controlled were quite small (see also Winne & Walsh, 1980). Phillips (1969) found a significant correlation between participation and self-concept for boys but not for girls. Nonetheless, Waterman and Archer (1979) found that among girls the practice of poetry writing was associated with higher identity status. Kleiber and Roberts (1990; in press) found that sports involvement per se was not associated with a measure of identity achievement, nor was an adolescent's number of extracurricular activities; but a measure of perceived sports ability did show a modest correlation and number of hobbies was also related.

In addition to finding inconsistent and modest correlations, these studies are limited by their cross-sectional nature. They do not allow us to determine whether the self-esteem associated with participation is a cause or an effect. My literature search turned up three longitudinal studies that looked at whether participation was related to an increase in self-esteem. A study of high school sports participation for girls found no independent effect on self-esteem (Melnick, Vanfossen, & Sabo, 1988), a finding corroborated in a second study, which *did* show an effect for boys (Caldwell & Smith, 1989). Third, a study of the transition form sixth to seventh grade found a positive association of all activity participation on self-esteem for boys, mediated through grade point average (GPA), and a positive effect for girls, mediated through reduced social problem behavior but partly suppressed by the victimization experiences which these city girls were more likely to have from staying late after school (Simmons & Blyth, 1987).

Our data from the longitudinal study reported above provided another opportunity to examine these relationships over time; however, the findings are not very definitive. The data include Rosenberg's (1965) self-esteem scores at all three points in time as well as the measures of activity participation. I employed the same regression strategy. For athletic participation there were cross-sectional correlations across all age groups ranging from $r = .12$ to .32, but no significant longitudinal paths between participation and self-esteem. For arts and hobbies and organization participation there was little indication of cross-sectional or longitudinal associations.

In sum, I would conclude that the causal relationship between extracurricular activities and self-esteem is at best extremely small. The fact that some studies find a cross-sectional correlation and some do not suggest that the impact of these activities may vary by the activity, qualities of the coach or adult leader, and predispositions that participants bring to an activity, such as an ego-involved versus mastery orientation. A striking illustration of the variability in the effects that participation might have on self-evaluation is provided by Malmisur's (1976) finding that college athletes lagged *behind* other students in ego development. Positive effects on the self cannot be assumed.

Development of Agency

This focus on self-concept neglects another dimension of personal growth that I feel may be more important. Early promoters drew upon the educational philosophy of John Dewey and argued that extracurricular activities promote "self-reflection, self-direction, and initiative" (Roemer, Allen, & Fretwell, 1926, p. 4). The argument is that these activities provide a special environment for the development of qualities associated with agentic behavior, that they redirect the natural, intrinsic motivation of adolescents into a pattern of activity that has an adultlike structure (Briggs, 1922).

My research with colleagues has substantiated some pieces of this hypothesis. First, we found that when adolescents are engaged in extra-curricular activities they report a unique combination of mental states consistent with the hypothesis. On the one hand, they report intrinsic motivation: When interrupted during participation they report wanting to be doing what they are doing more so than when interrupted during most other daily activities (Larson & Kleiber, 1993). On the other hand, they also report feeling highly challenged and concentrating deeply. Levels on these dimensions resemble those experienced when taking a test in school (Larson & Kleiber, 1993). This combination—intrinsic motivation with challenge and deep attention—has lead us to think of these activities as 'transitional," on the theory that they provide a developmental bridge between the positive motivational states experienced in childhood free play and the structure and challenge of adult obligatory activities (Csikszentmihalyi & Larson, 1984; Kleiber, Larson, & Csikszentmihalyi, 1986).

A second part of the hypothesis is that these activities provide a special opportunity, not just for experiencing deep attention, but for learning to control it. As a preliminary test of this prediction I interviewed fifth to nineth graders about a time when they were paying attention deeply and asked them to describe their control of and other features of the experience. A striking finding was that close to 50% of the students spontaneously chose an extracurricular activity as their example of a time when they were concentrating deeply. Contrary to my prediction, they did not report more insights about attentional processes in these than in the other activities they chose (Larson & Kleiber, in press). Nonetheless, the sheer frequency with which extracurricular activities were mentioned suggests that they are an important context for learning about control of attention.

A third part of the hypothesis, one about which I do not yet have data, is that extracurricular activities provide adolescents with a unique opportunity to learn about the extension of their actions over time (Larson & Kleiber, 1993). They involve what Henry Murray called "serials" or what Little (1983) has called "projects." In some of these activities adolescents make plans, monitor the progress of their plans, employ feedback to modify their actions, and, in the long-term, produce something large from their efforts. The skills developed from such an activity might include learning to endure the frustrations and disappointments that such projects inevitably entail, learning to coordinate one's actions with others', and learning to deal with a wide range of emotions that might arise. Our argument here is similar to that of Oerter (1986) and Silberesen, Eyferth, & Rudinger (1986), who assert that self-appropriated or leisure contexts, because they are voluntary, provide special opportunities for the adolescent to be the producer of his or her own development. By engaging in a project, by experiencing and overcoming the obstacles involved in doing something large, we hypothesize that such efforts promote development of important adult skills to create and modify one's environment.

Adolescents rarely get the opportunity for this kind of self-controlled cumulative work in school; rarely do students receive school assignments that are directed to long-term goals (Larson, 1982). And at their jobs adolescents do not take opportunities for personal initiative (Dittmann-Kohli, 1986). Of course, even in extracurricular activities there may be much variation as to whether an adolescent has the opportunity and uses the chance for this kind of self-controlled initiative. Without good coaching, for example, many athletes focus primarily upon the immediate moment—shooting a basket, hitting the volleyball (Danish et al., 1987). We suspect that the adolescent who is collecting baseball cards, painting a picture, or working on the school newspaper may be more likely to organize their activity in a projectlike structure.

While there is no direct data that looks at development of agency or skills within extracurricular activities, three longitudinal studies suggest that participants are more motivated at later stages in their lives. These studies controlled for school grades, parents socio-economic status, and other factors that might create artifactual findings, but still found a relationship between high school activity participation and subsequent achievement. Spady (1970) found associations between participation in organizations and level of subsequent college education. Glancy, Willits, and Farrell (1986) found associations with occupational attainment 24 years later. And Otto (1976; Otto & Alwin, 1977) found associations with educational attainment, occupational achievement, and income 15 years later. Of course, these studies do not rule out the possibility that preexisting personality qualities underlay both the high school participation and the latter success. It is also limiting that they provide measure of achievement in very conventional activities; thus we do not know whether they provide evidence of intrinsic or extrinsic motivation. Nonetheless, they provide encouragement to future research with more careful controls.

Conclusion

Every few months or so the *New York Times* prints a story on a group of at-risk youth whose lives have been transformed by participation in an extracurricular activity. One month it was a girls' basketball team within an economically depressed Navaho reservation. A new coach got the team winning, which led not only to dramatic improvement of life opportunities for the girls, but also a revitalization for the local community whose members would drive hundreds of miles to proudly watch the team play (Starsen, 1991). In another *Times* story, a chess master became coach of a chess club in a Harlem junior high school. Club members, who had been alienated from school and tempted by life on the streets, began living and breathing chess, an involvement that led to their winning the national junior high championship. The students also described adopting their strategic chess thinking to the rest of their lives, a carryover that had positive effects on their school work and increased their resistance to the traps of street life (Tierney, 1991).

Partly these kinds of stories just make good press copy. Obviously the great majority of youth involved in these activities do not win championships—nor do I think competitive winning is the end to be emulated (Larson & Kleiber, in press). Nonetheless, I propose that there is something to the psychological experience of living the compelling day-to-day narratives within these activities that is beneficial and probably transfers to other contexts.

The thesis of this paper is that sports, organizations, and hobbies potentially serves a double function in adolescents' lives. First, they integrate adolescents into a social world: they connect them to a community and a prosocial set of norms. The findings show that extracurricular activity participants, particularly those involved in arts, hobbies, or youth organizations, engage in less delinquency. Longitudinal studies indicate that high school participation sets a pattern of participation that continues into adult life.

To some extent these activities may be only reinforcing social patterns that already exist. They integrate adolescents who are already integrated. While organizations and hobbies appear to play a small role in promoting prosocial behavior, my data suggests that for sports the association is entirely a matter of selective participation. Ironically, the youth who might benefit most from extracurricular activities—lower-achievement-tracked and delinquency-prone students—are those who participate least. This irony, unfortunately, is inherent in the enterprise, as leaders of such activities well know. The presence of adult leaders and the prosocial mission of the activity—which we judged to be positive factors—are often exactly what scare away some adolescents (Hendry, 1983; Hyde, 1978). For youth who have experienced a long history of being told they do not matter, resistance and opposition to adult authority becomes a part of their self-definition (Willis, 1977). The conundrum faced by advocates of such activities becomes how to entice their participation without badly compromising the mission, a task which often puts these leaders in unmanageable binds. Further research on factors related to entrance and exit from activities, such as that being done with sports participation (e.g., Kirshnit, Ham, & Richards, 1989), would be helpful. We need to understand the Tao of engaging all youth in these types of activities.

In addition to social integration, I have proposed that extracurricular activities can serve as a vehicle for personal integration. The research we reviewed suggests that the effects of such activities on self-concept and self-esteem are modest and inconsistent; yet it may be naive to approach a context with a single measure and expect to understand the developmental processes occurring there. Researchers need to study these activities with a wide range of methods and measures, such as those used in studies of teenagers' work experiences (Greenberger & Steinberg, 1986; Mortimer, this volume). Some of this research is being done for sports, such as Fine's (1987) excellent ethnographic study of the Little League, but little has been done for youth organizations and hobbies. I think it would be particularly useful for researchers to employ measures that capture the sequence of adolescents' involvement in an activity in order to understand their experience of acting over time, of being agents.

Inevitably we will find it necessary to make finer-grained distinctions among types of participants and types of activities. Kleiber and Kirshnit's (1990) lucid paper suggest that sports may be a different kind of developmental context for girls than for boys. It may also be naive to group together the wide range of activities I have grouped here. I have assumed there is a common core of experience that stamp collection, ballet, and student government share. But just as we are discovering that it is inappropriate to ask about the impact of divorce or child care without examining the specific circumstances of a child's experiences, it may be inappropriate to try to reach conclusions about the aggregate effect of so many different activities. As with other developmental contexts, it is crucial to look at the process that occurs for each adolescent: What is the day-to-day and month-to-month narrative that an adolescent experiences in the activity and how does he or she interpret and learn from being an active participant in that narrative?

Acknowledgments. This research was supported by NIMH grant number 38324, awarded to Reed Larson and Maryse Richards.

References

Achenbach, T. & Edelbrock, C. (1986). *Manual for the teacher's report form and teacher version of the Child Behavior Profile*. Burlington: Department of Psychiatry, University of Vermont.

Agnew, R. & Petersen, D.M. (1989). Leisure and delinquency. *Social Problems*, *36*, 332–350.

Benson, P.L. (1991). *The troubled journey: A profile of American youth*. Minneapolis: Search Institute.

Bloom, B. (1985). *Developing talent in young people*. New York: Ballantine.

Blyth, D., Hill, J., & Thiel, K. (1982). Early adolescents' significant others: Grade and gender differences in perceived relationships with familial and nonfamilial adults and young people. *Journal of Youth and Adolescence*, *11*, 425– 450.

Briggs, T.H. (1922). Extra-curricular activities in junior high schools. *Educational Administration and Supervision*, *8*, 1–9.

Caldwell, L.L. & Smith, E.A. (1989). Longitudinal analysis of the effects of high school sports participation. Unpublished manuscript. University of Waterloo. Waterloo, Ontario, Canada.

Carron, A.V. & Chelladurai, P. (1978). *Canadian Journal of Applied Sports Sciences*, *3*, 50–53. Psychological factors and athletic success: An analysis at coach-athlete interpersonal behavior.

Chalip, L. (1980). Social learning theory and sport success: Evidence and implications. *Journal of Sport Behavior*, *3*, 76–85.

Coleman, J.S. (1961). *The adolescent society*. New York: Free Press.

Csikszentmihalyi, M. & Larson, R. (1984). *Being adolescent*. New York: Basic Books.

Danish, S., Kleiber, D., & Hall, H. (1987). Enhancing motivation in the context of sport. In M. Maehr & D. Kleiber (Eds.), *Enhancing motivation*. Greenwich, CT: JAI Press.

DeMartini, J. (1983). Social movement participation: Political socialization, generational consciousness, and lasting effects. *Youth and Society*, *15*, 195–223.

Dittmann-Kohli, F. (1986). Problem identification and definition as important aspects of adolescents' coping with normative life tasks. In R.K. Silbereisen, K. Eyferth, & G. Rudinger, (Eds.), *Development as action in context: Problem behavior and normal youth development*. New York: Springer-Verlag.

Duda, J. (1988). The relationship between goal perspectives, persistence and behavioral intensity among male and female recreational sport participants. *Leisure Sciences*, *10*, 95–106.

Elliott, D. & Voss, H. (1974). *Delinquency and dropout*. Lexington, MA: D.C. Heath.

Fine, G.A. (1983). *Shared fantasy: Role-playing games as social worlds*. Chicago: University of Chicago Press.

Fine, G.A. (1987). *With the boys: Little league baseball and preadolescent culture*. Chicago: University of Chicago Press.

Glancy, M., Willits, F.K., & Farrell, P. (1986). Adolescent activities and adult success and happiness: Twenty-four years later. *Sociology and Social Research*, *70*, 242–250.

Greenberger, E. & Steinberg, L.D. (1986). *When teenagers work: The psychological and social costs of adolescent employment*. New York: Basic Books.

Grieves, J. (1989). Acquiring a leisure identity: Juvenile jazz bands and the moral universe of "healthy" leisure time. *Leisure Studies*, *8*, 1–9.

Hanks, M. & Eckland, B. (1978). Adult voluntary associations and adolescent socialization. *The Sociological Quarterly*, *19*, 481–490.

Hantover, J.P. (1978). The boy scouts and the validation of masculinity. *Journal of Social Issues*, *34*, 184–195.

Hedin, D. & Simon, P. (1980). *Minnesota youth poll: Youth's views on leisure time, friendship and youth organizations*. St. Paul, MN: Center for Youth Development and Research.

Hendry, L.B. (1983). *Growing up and going out: Adolescents and leisure*. Aberdeen, Great Britain: University of Aberdeen Press.

Hirschi, T. (1969). *Causes of delinquency*. Berkeley: University of California Press.

Holland, A. & Andre, T. (1987). Participation in extra-curricular activities in secondary school: What is known, what needs to be known? *Review of Educational Research*, *57*, 437–466.

Howell, F. & McKenzie, J. (1987). High school athletics and adult sport-leisure activity: Gender variations across the life cycle. *Sociology of Sport Journal*, *4*, 329–346.

Hyde, T.F. (1978). Youth-adult relationships and early adolescent male participation in organized leisure activity. In J. Hinchcliff (Ed.), *The nature and meaning of sport in New Zealand*. Auckland: Centre for Continuing Education.

Kirshnit, C.E. (1989). Athletic involvement during early adolescence. Unpublished doctoral dissertation. Loyola University of Chicago.

Kirshnit, C.E., Ham, M., & Richards, M. (1989). The sporting life. *Journal of Youth and Adolescence*, *18*(6), 601–615.

Kleiber, D., Larson, R., & Csikszentmihalyi, M. (1986). The experience of leisure in adolescence. *Journal of Leisure Research*, *18*(3), 165–176.

Kleiber, D. & Kirshnit, C.E. (1990). Sport involvement and identity formation. In L. Diamant (Ed.). *Mind-body maturity; The psychology of sports, exercise, and fitness* (pp. 193–211). New York: Hemisphere.

Kleiber, D. & Roberts, G. (1990). *Extra-curricular activity, academic orientation and personal development among high school students*. Unpublished manuscript, University of Illinois, Urbana-Champaign.

Kleiber, D. & Roberts, G. (in press). Extra-curricular activity and identity formation in high school students.

Landers, D. & Landers, D. (1978). Socialization via interscholastic athletics; its effect on delinquency. *Sociology of Education*, *51*, 299–301.

Larson, R. (1982). The high school research project: Promoting skills in autonomous learning. Unpublished paper.

Larson, R. & Kleiber, D. (in press). *Changes in the experience of "paying attention" during early adolescence. Society and Leisure*.

Larson, R. & Kleiber, D. (1993). Free time activities as factors in adolescent adjustment. In P. Tolan & B. Cohler (Eds.), *Handbook of clinical research and practice with adolescents* (pp. 125–145). New York: Wiley.

Larson, R. & Richards, M. (Eds.) (1989). The changing life space of early adolescence [Special issue]. *Journal of Youth and Adolescence, 18*(6), 501–626.

Larson, R. & Richards, M. (in press). *Divergent realities: The daily lives of mothers, fathers, and their young adolescent children.* New York: Basic Books.

Little, B.R. (1983). Personal projects: A rationale and method for investigation. *Environment and Behavior, 15*, 273–309.

Long, R., Buser, R., & Jackson, M. (1977). *Student activities in the seventies.* Reston, VA: National Association of Secondary School Principals.

Malmisur, M. (1976). Ego development of a sample of college football players. *Research Quarterly, 47*, 140–153.

McCormack, J. (1984). Interpersonal influences and the channeling of goals in adolescence. Unpublished doctoral dissertation, University of Chicago.

McEwin, C.K. (1981). Interscholastic sports and the early adolescent. *Journal of Early Adolescence. 1*, 123–133.

Medrich, E.A., Roizen, V.R., Rubin, V. & Buckley, S. (1992). *The serious business of growing up.* Berkeley: University of California Press.

Melnick, M.J., Vanfossen, B.E., & Sabo, D.F. (1988). Developmental effects of athletic participation among high school girls. *Sociology of Sport Journal, 5*, 22–36.

Murray, H.A. (1938). Explorations in personality. New York: Oxford Press.

Nicholls, J.G. (1984). Achievement motivation: Conceptions of ability, subjective experience, task choice, and performance. *Psychological Review, 91*, 328–346.

Oerter, R. (1986). Developmental task through the life span: A new approach to an old concept. In P.B. Baltes, L. Featherman, & R. Lerner (Eds.), *Lifespan development and behavior, Vol 7.* pp. 233–249. Hillsdale, NJ: Lawrence Erlbaum.

Osgood, D.W. & Young-Min, S. (1990). Activities and deviant behavior during late adolescence and early adulthood. Unpublished manuscript.

Otto, H.A. & Healy, S.L. (1966). Adolescents self-perception of personality strengths. *Journal of Human Relations, 15*, 483–490.

Otto, L. (1976). Social integration and the status attainment process. *American Journal of Sociology, 81*, 1360–1383.

Otto, L. & Alwin, D. (1977). Athletics, aspirations and attainments. *Sociology of Education, 50*, 102–113.

Phillips, R.E. (1969). Students activities and self-concept. *Journal of Negro Education, 38*, 32–37.

Roemer, J., Allen, C., & Fretwell, E. (1926). *Extra-curricular activities in junior and senior high school.* New York: D.C. Heath.

Rosenbaum, J.E. (1976). *Making inequality: The hidden curriculum of high school tracking.* New York: Wiley.

Rosenberg, M. (1965). *Society and the adolescent self-image.* Princeton NJ: Princeton University Press.

Schafer, E.E. (1969). Participation in interscholastic athletics and delinquency: A preliminary study. *Social Problems, 17*, 40–47.

Sherif, M. & Sherif, C. (1953). *Groups in harmony and tension: An integration of studies on intergroup relations.* New York: Harper Row.

Sherif, M. & Sherif, C. (1964). *Reference groups: Exploration into conformity and deviation of adolescents*. Chicago: Henry Regnery.

Silbereisen, R.K., Eyferth, K., & Rudinger, G. (Eds.). (1986). *Development as action in context: Problem behavior and normal youth development*. New York: Springer-Verlag.

Simmons, R.G. & Blyth, D.A. (1987). *Moving into adolescence: The impact of pubertal change and school context*. New York: Aldine de Gruyter.

Simmons, R.G., Burgeson, R., Carlton-Ford, S., & Blyth, D.A. (1987). The impact of cumulative change in early adolescence. *Child Development, 58,* 1220–1234.

Spady, W. (1970). Lament for the letterman: Effect of peer status and extra-curricular activities on goal and achievement. *American Journal of Sociology, 75,* 680–702.

Starsen, M. (1991, February 25). A team spawns pride in a land of despair. *The New York Times*, pp. B9, B10.

Tierney, J. (1991, April 26). Harlem teen-agers checkmate a stereotype. *The New York Times*, pp., A1, A16.

Waterman, A. & Archer, S. (1979). Ego identity status and expressive writing among high school and college students. *Journal of Youth and Adolescence, 8,* 327–341.

Werner, E.B. (1987). Vulnerability and resiliency in children at risk for delinquency: A longitudinal study from birth to young adulthood. In J.D. Burchard & S.N. Burchard (Eds.), *The prevention of delinquent behavior*. Beverly Hills: Sage.

Werner, E.B. (1990). Protective factors and individual resilience. In S.J. Meisels & S.P. Shonkoff (Eds.), *Handbook at early childhood intervention* (pp. 97–116). Cambridge Press. Cambridge.

Williams, S. & McGee, R. (1991). Adolescent self-perceptions of their strengths. *Journal of Youth and Adolescence, 20,* 325–337.

Willis, P. (1977). *Learning to Labor: How working class kids get working class jobs*. New York: Columbia University Press.

Winne, P.H. & Walsh, J. (1980). Self-concept and participation in school activities reanalyzed. *Journal of Educational Psychology, 72,* 161–166.

Yarworth, J. & Gauthier, W. (1978). Relationship of student self-concept and selected personal variables to participation in school activities. *Journal of Educational Psychology, 70,* 335–344.

4
The Developmental Context of Adolescent Life-styles

Leo B. Hendry, Anthony Glendinning, Janet Shucksmith, John Love, and Jeanette Scott

Introduction

This chapter sets out to explore ideas about life-styles, and the personal, social, educational, occupational, and leisure transitions which relate to their development in adolescence. The concept of life-styles is examined in a variety of ways to set the scene for the utilization of findings derived by a series of factor and cluster analyses of data from a 7-year longitudinal study of British adolescents. The results of these analyses are used to describe how a variety of personal, social, educational, and occupational influences interact in the development of life-styles across the adolescent years.

Adolescent Transitions

From the physiological and bodily changes that herald the teenage years, the adolescent has various "tasks" to achieve:

1. The establishment of personal significance and self-esteem;
2. The establishment of a personal philosophy and values;
3. The establishment of and adjustment towards independence;
4. Relationships with adults and authority figures;
5. Relationships with peers, and with the opposite sex; and
6. Engagement in an occupational (or unemployed or non-employed, domestic) role.

There are, however, no symbolic "rites of passage" in Western society, so the adolescent's route towards adulthood is not marked out by clearly defined signposts that indicate progress in a desired direction. It is perhaps remarkable that so many arrive at their adult destination emotionally and psychologically unscathed.

Psychosocial Transitions

Coleman (1979) has presented a "focal theory," arguing that the transition between childhood and adulthood cannot be achieved without substantial adjustments of both a psychological and social nature. The fact is that, despite the amount of overall change experienced, most young people are extremely resilient and appear to cope with adjustments without undue stress.

Coleman's focal theory offers a reason or rationale for this apparent contradiction. In it he proposes that at different ages, particular sorts of relationship patterns come into focus, in the sense of being most prominent, but that no pattern is specific to one age only. Thus the patterns overlap, different issues coming into focus at different times, but simply because an issue is not the most prominent feature at a particular age, it does not mean that it may not be critical for some individuals. These ideas, in association with empirical findings, combine to suggest a symbolic model of adolescent development where each curve represents a different issue or relationship. This is illustrated in Figure 4.1.

Coleman suggested that concerns about gender roles and relationships with the opposite sex decline from a peak around 13 years; concerns about acceptance by or rejection from peers are highly important around 15 years; while issues regarding the gaining of independence from parents climb steadily, to peak beyond 16 years and then to begin to tail off. Such a theory may provide some resolution between the amount of disruption and crisis implicit in adolescence and the relatively successful adaptation among most adolescents. The majority of teenagers cope by dealing with one issue at a time. Adaptation covers a number of years, with the adolescent attempting to solve one issue, then the next. Thus any stresses

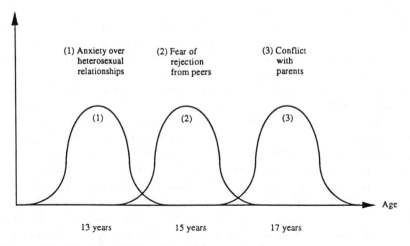

FIGURE 4.1. The "Focal Theory" model.

resulting from the need to adapt to new models of behavior are rarely concentrated all at one time. Those who, for whatever reason, do have more than one issue to cope with at one time are most likely to have problems of adjustment.

Coffield, Borrill, and Marshall (1986) have commented, however, that Coleman's focal model makes no attempt to examine social issues such as disadvantage and deprivation. Coffield et al. are right to draw attention to the social circumstances of the individual, for these will obviously contribute in a substantial way to each adolescent's psychological adjustment. Gaining independence from parents has sociological and financial implications—as in unemployment—as well as being a psychological issue. Thus the focal model hypothesizes that in situations of economic hardship it will be more difficult to manage the adolescent transitions in a satisfactory manner. This suggestion has already been made by Hendry (1983) in his argument that ecological factors are as important as psychological ones in understanding the young person's development.

Educational-occupational Transitions

Just under half of all Scottish young people leaving school do so at the minimum school-leaving age of 16 years (Hendry, Shucksmith, & Love 1989; Raffe & Courtenay, 1988), though the trend through the 1980s and into the 1990s has been towards more young people staying on at school beyond the minimum age and going on to further and higher education. National data sets confirm that more middle-class young people stay on to gain better qualifications than working-class adolescents. The association between duration in (secondary) education and post-school careers, however, suggests that "more" does not necessarily mean "better" in terms of life chances. A combination of structural arrangements within the youth labor market and wider normative constraints, especially in relation to gender, serve to mitigate the potential effects of additional years in school. Thus for some young people the opportunity to take up an apprenticeship is forfeited in staying on at school an "extra" year, and on leaving school such youngsters find themselves in a weaker position in the labor market as a result. For others, staying on at school leads to "downward status mobility" (in terms of eventual post-school careers) with many moving from "academic school courses to non-advanced further education . . . [or] from school to Youth Training Schemes" (Raffe & Courtenay, 1988) or to low status clerical and shop work (Dex, 1987).

Until the last decade the majority of young people traveled along well signposted trajectories. Their home background and educational streams enabled them to anticipate their initial occupations and, realistically, the types of adult employment to which these early jobs would lead. Now for those who leave school and move towards adult society, youth schemes have replaced jobs in many early school-leavers' immediate prospects. So the British government's responses to youth unemployment addresses an alleged mismatch between school-leavers' capabilities and occupational requirements in the service and high-technology sectors which, it is claimed, contain the best hopes for future job creation. Hence the case for Britain's Technical and Vocational Education Initiative, the Youth Training Scheme (now called Training, Enterprise and Education) and the Sixteen to Eighteen Action Plan.

However, attempts to tighten the bonds between schooling and job requirements and to strengthen young people's vocational orientations seem problematic. Educational solutions to the disappearance of jobs for adolescents produce diminishing returns (Bates et al., 1984) and the vocational skills of today may well be outdated for use in future society (Holt, 1983). Coleman and Husen (1985) have pointed out that these new educational practices are helping to create a new underclass. They claimed that, within secondary schools, a small group of students abandons hope and effort, and sometimes attendance, long before the official leaving date. The majority of young people now leave school with some qualifications, so the "failures" are a disadvantaged minority. Beyond secondary school the ultimate effect of youth unemployment may be to disrupt the adolescent's psychosocial transition to adulthood (Coleman & Hendry, 1990).

Leisure Transition

Loss of producer roles, and the inability of education and training to guarantee lifetime vocations, make young people more dependent on ascribed statuses, sometimes derived from gender and ethnicity, in establishing adult identities and independence. Current social trends may make young people more dependent on leisure activities and contexts to sustain preferred identities, independence, and emotional stability. They also enable the establishment and maintenance of relationships that allow other aspects of the transition to adulthood to proceed despite the difficulty of stepping directly from full-time education to stable employment. Thus leisure may grow in importance as a positive source of development in young people's life-styles when most other aspects of society change rapidly and are beyond the individual's control.

In the case of Hendry's (1983) focal theory of leisure, he pointed out that the adolescent's leisure focus generally shifts from adult-organized clubs and activities, through casual leisure pursuits, to commercial-based leisure; and that these transitions may occur roughly at the ages where the main relational issues proposed by Coleman—namely, sex, peers, and parents—come into focus. Further, Hendry argued that the differential effects of sex and social class on these general leisure patterns could be explained in relation to a dynamic interplay of factors. It is, therefore, necessary to stress the variability among adolescents in aspiration, motivations, attitudes, and in the values they place on their leisure interests and pursuits within their developing life-styles.

These transitions in adolescence—in educational and occupational trajectories, in social and leisure roles—are clearly subject to broader societal constraints but they are also linked to degrees of self-agency, self-efficacy, and locus of control at the level of the individual. Because there is so much change during adolescence, and these changes to self require effective adjustments on the part of the individual, the processes involved in this period of the life span are also likely to be those needed to respond to challenges throughout life. Furthermore, if adolescence differs from earlier years in the nature of the challenges encountered and in the capacity of the individual to respond effectively to these challenges, then adolescence will be the first phase of life requiring, and presumably stimulating, mature patterns of functioning and the development of a clear-cut personal and social identity that persists throughout life. Conversely, failure to cope effectively with the demands of adolescence may reflect deficiencies in the individual's self-concept, which will have negative consequences for subsequent development.

Life-styles and Ecologies

In relation to life-styles, Ansbacher (1967) attempted a typology in which he distinguished: individual life-style; group life-style; and life-style as a generic term. Aaro, Wold, Kannas, and Rimpela (1986), for example, have suggested that life-style is the relatively stable pattern of behavior, habits, attitudes, and values that are typical of groups, while Wenzel (1982) has outlined the life-style of an individual as: "the entirety of normative orientations and behaviour patterns which are developed through the processes of socialisation." This implies that understanding life-style consists not only of gauging behavior but also includes understanding the values and attitudes of the individual interrelated into a developing pattern of living. These characteristics are closely linked to the individual's social and physical surroundings, and thus life-style is also related to socioeconomic circumstances and to the material and cultural resources available to the individual.

Starting from a clear theoretical framework Abel and McQueen (1992) operationalized the concept of life-style as a complex patterning of three basic elements: behaviors, orientations, and resources. These basic dimensions interact to form an individual's way of life. However, structural constraints at a societal level affect these complex interactions among behaviors, orientations, and resources. Hence the interplay of structurally rooted "life chances" and individual "life conduct" results in the emergence of life-styles as collective phenomena; which allow for social differentiation within and between groups.

In understanding adolescent life-styles it is also important to clarify the function of roles in the socialization process. This includes a consideration of the psychological idea of "role-taking" as well as the sociological view of roles as the major mechanisms linking people to social structures. Social structure shapes the roles a young person is expected to learn. For example, different role expectations are linked to age and gender and these role expectations influence the role-taking behavior of young men and young women at different ages (Bronfenbrenner, 1979).

From an ecological perspective, the groups a person belongs to are of vital importance. Young people belonging to families with higher socioeconomic status are exposed to different types of role models than working-class young people. This may also pertain to habits and behaviors associated with "taking on" life-style patterns. For instance, Rosenstock, Strecher, and Becker (1988) have argued that during the socialization process children learn to adopt many health-related habits and practices that will permanently influence their adult behavior. Further, these patterns of adjustment cannot be fully explained without some understanding of self-efficacy and peer group interaction. For example, adolescents evaluate and involve themselves in health risk-taking practices in a functional manner as tangible, accessible, and culturally suggestive requisites in the development of life-styles.

Linked to these ideas of social roles and relationships, the importance of locality is central to an ecological perspective on adolescent life-styles. From the background of sociology Giddens (1984) attempted to deal systematically with the question of locality *and* social space. The work of Goffman (1971) is of particular relevance here since it gives emphasis to the spatial contexts in which interactions take place. The interactions in which Goffman was interested, however, consisted not only of the verbal kind but of the nonverbal, expressive kind (e.g., styles of dress, homes, domestic commodities) with which people choose to surround themselves. Through these means individuals supply impressions of themselves to others and, in return, seek information on the status and attitudes of others with whom they interact.

Spencer, Blades, and Morsley (1989) have lamented the lack of an ethnography of adolescent life, which would explore the complex ways in which young people use and perceive their leisure environments in an expressive mode. The work of urban anthropologists such as Gans (1968) and urban planners such as Banerjee and Lynch (1977) have indicated that though adolescents range further afield, physical settings continue to be important for providing meeting places and contexts for social learning and social experimentation. Spencer et al. (1989) described the "alternative scripts" in use by adolescents who inhabit adult spaces but for different reasons. They are theaters for self-display, observation points for assessing the roles of others and of oneself, meeting grounds for establishing and maintaining solidarity with one's group. Marsh, Rosser, and Harre (1978), for example, have looked at the finely regulated behavior of those football supporter groups away from the match which, to other eyes, appears chaotic or anarchic; and Anthony (1985) has described adolescents' use of shopping malls where they capitalize to the full on what the planners euphemistically label "public space," yet their very presence is often seen as subversive and threatening.

Van Vliet (1983) has coined the term "the fourth environment" to describe such local contexts where aspects of growing up take place. This fourth environment appears to fulfill important developmental functions for young people, yet surprisingly little is known about home range extensions and their importance as contexts for adolescent development.

To summarize, our understanding of the development of adolescent life-styles needs to take account of a complex "network" of interdependent factors. These include the individual's behaviors, orientations, and resources along with his/her socialization process and present personality as well as his/her immediate surroundings. It also includes the individual's social and economic environment. Thus objective conditions and subjective perceptions are contained within one model. In particular, consideration of the interconnections among this complex network of factors is essential to the understanding of adolescent life-styles.

Young People's Leisure and Life-styles Project

An ongoing longitudinal research project (see Hendry et al., 1989, 1993) is studying young people's leisure and life-styles over an extended period. The project has been designed to operate at two complementary levels. There is a survey element and this has involved a sampling frame of 126 schools to represent a nationwide sample of Scottish young people. An initial survey of 10,000 young people from 10 to 20 years of age, comprising six cohorts, was carried out in 1987. This first survey was conducted using a self-completion questionnaire and aimed to provide a broad and general picture of young people growing up in modern Scotland. This was followed by two further large scale questionnaire-based surveys of adolescents' socialization and leisure in 1989 and 1991. The content of the questionnaires was modified for each of the three survey sweeps to reflect the changing circumstances of the sample. Nevertheless there remained a substantial core of questions in common.

The second element of the project is a smaller, more intensive examination of a subsample of 250 young people living in 11 different sociogeographical areas of Scotland. This ecological approach is intended to examine some of the implications of social environment on young people's life-styles and leisure patterns by a variety of illuminative, interpretative research techniques. The areas chosen for study include rural market towns, inner-city areas, new towns, and middle-class suburban settlements.

The overall purpose of the research project has been—and is—to develop an explanatory picture of young people growing up in modern society by the use of a variety of research techniques and styles. Here we focus on the first two sweeps of the large scale longitudinal study, and attention is restricted to a group of roughly 350 adolescents. Young people from this group were aged 15–16 years in 1987 and 17–18 years in 1989. In 1987 these young people were still attending secondary school (but at the end of statutory state education); by the time of the survey in 1989, they had left school and had begun the transition to adult society. During the first sweep in 1987 the survey questionnaires were completed at school under the guidance of a field-worker: In 1989 a subsample were recontacted via a postal questionnaire. Ninety percent completed the

15-16 years, 1987				17-18 years, 1989		
Factor	% variance explained	Characteristics		Factor	% variance explained	Characteristics
1	10%	Visit friends and visited by friends often Spend a lot of spare time with best friend Go to dancing and discos often Hang about in street with friends		1	15%	In full-time education Stayed on at school Gained good qualifications From professional or intermediate social classes
2	10%	To be earning money, having an enjoyable job, having friend and a good time and my family are important		2	12%	Go to pubs and discos with friends regularly
3	7%	Spend most money on sports goods View self as athletic and competitive Participate in competitive sport regularly		3	10%	Out-going and make friends easily
4	6%	Intend to go to college or university before getting a job View this as important		4	7%	Thought well of by others Unstressed Content Disapprove of drugs
5	5%	Get on well with mother Confident about finding a job Spend little spare time alone Unstressed		5	5%	Spend a lot of spare time with a steady boy-friend Drink alcohol with boy-friend regularly Boy-friend smokes cigarettes
6	5%	Spend most money on entertainments and in particular go to cinema regularly Much spare time with boy-friend		6	5%	Spend much of spare time with colleagues and with best friend
7	5%	Family conflict Get bored in spare time Vandalism and theft can be ok Don't avoid getting into trouble				
8	5%	Disapprove of alcohol and drugs Spend little spare time with the opposite sex				

FIGURE 4.2. Summary of results of principal components analyses for young women.

school-based questionnaire and 50% responded to the postal questionnaire 2 years later.

The survey questionnaires are based around a number of major topics
such as education, employment, health, leisure, and family relations.
Rather than adopt a thematic approach and consider each of these topic
areas in turn, we prefer to examine the interrelationships among these
differing aspects of young people's lives. By doing so we are able to
identify major factors underlying adolescent socialization and leisure
transitions, and we are also able to identify differing types of adolescent
life-styles. The underlying dimensions were established using principal
components analysis, and the typology of adolescent life-styles was developed using cluster analysis. The variables used in these analyses were
guided by the conceptions of life-style discussed in the previous section on

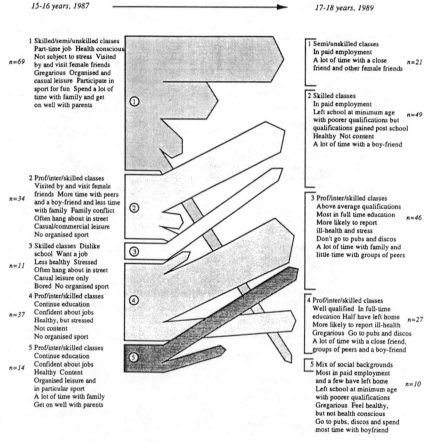

FIGURE 4.3. Young women's developing life-styles—results of cluster analyses in
abridged form. The percentage exchange between clusters (as represented by the
arrows) are drawn to scale.

life-styles and adolescent transitions. These included data on: locality; socioeconomic background; family structure; living arrangements; educational qualifications and attitudes; economic activity status; disposable income and consumer spending; organized, casual, and commercial leisure activities, including sports involvement and attitudes; self-assessed physical and mental health, health behaviors and attitudes, and health behaviors of family and peers; self-concept and self-esteem; life priorities; views on "getting into trouble" and perceptions of authority figures; and finally, relationships with family and peers.

Separate analyses were conducted for young women and young men using 1987 data and once again using 1989 data. Figures 4.2 and 4.4 briefly describe the results of the principal components analyses. A measure of the adequacy of the method was derived from the Kaiser-Mayer-Olkin statistic. This measure of sampling adequacy was greater than 0.8 for all four analyses. The factors extracted were subjected to an orthogonal varimax rotation. Only rotated factors with eigenvalue greater than 1.25 are reported in Figures 4.2 and 4.4.

Figures 4.3 and 4.5 describe the results of the cluster analyses in abridged form. All variables used in the cluster analyses were dichotomous (dummy variables were created were necessary). The metric used was the Hamman similarity measure (Statistical Package for the Social

15-16 years, 1987 ⟶ *17-18 years, 1989*

Factor	% variance explained	Characteristics	Factor	% variance explained	Characteristics
1	15%	Intend to go to college or university before getting a job View this as important Positive attitude towards school From professional or intermediate social classes	1	19%	In full-time education Stayed on at school Gained good qualifications From professional or intermediate social classes
2	10%	Don't spend money on cigarettes Disapprove of drug use Have a hobby	2	12%	Go to pubs and discos with friends regularly
3	7%	Positive attitude towards sport Health conscious View self as athletic and competitive	3	9%	Smoke cigarettes Friends and girl-friend smoke
4	5%	Get on well with father No family conflict	4	7%	Out-going and make friends easily Unstressed
5	5%	Out-going and content	5	6%	Spend a lot spare time with a steady girl-friend Drink alcohol with girl-friend regularly
6	5%	Participate in competitive sport Go to a sports club regularly	6	5%	Some close friends use drugs Don't disapprove of drug use Spend a lot of spare time alone
7	5%	Hang about in street with friends Go to dancing and discos often Don't disapprove of alcohol			

FIGURE 4.4. Summary of results of principal components analyses for young men.

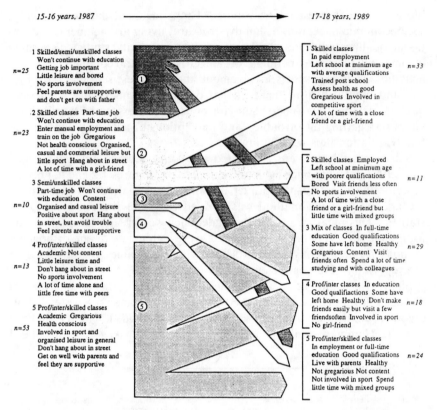

FIGURE 4.5. Young men's developing lifestyles—results of cluster analyses in abridged form. The percentage exchange between clusters (as represented by the arrows) are drawn to scale.

Sciences, 1990) and the clustering method employed was complete linkage (farthest neighbor). A cluster solution was chosen by examination of the agglomeration schedule and the associated dendrogram.

Figures 4.3 and 4.5 also indicate the longitudinal connections between the clusters obtained from 1987 data and those obtained from 1989 data.

Understanding the Development of Life-styles in Adolescence

In what ways do the principal components and cluster analyses help us to gain some general understanding of young people's developing life-styles in adolescence? In order to focus on particular aspects of the adolescent transition in some detail, we consider the findings for young women aged 15–16 in 1987. The reader will recall that these young women were still at school in 1987, and so we were able to follow them from compulsory secondary education to adult society and the world of work in 1989.

The factors associated with 15–16-year-old women can be regarded as the dimensions underlying our "description" of adolescence for these young people (see Figure 4.2). In general, these factors reflect the elements of adolescent development discussed in the earlier sections of this chapter. They are: (a) "close" relationships with female friends; (b) life values and priorities; (c) involvement in sport; (d) intended educational or employment trajectories; (e) psychological well-being and adjustment; (f) commercial leisure and boyfriends; (g) perceptions of family conflict and "trouble"; and (h) disapproval of drugs and alcohol. Essentially these are the elements that interrelate to produce the clusters that form the basis for our identification of different adolescent life-styles.

If we look at the clusters for young women at 15–16 years of age it is clear that adolescent life-styles are characterised in terms of social class differences. These differences are an amalgam of the social class of origin (i.e., parental occupation), parents' experience of education beyond school (i.e., parental education), and the type of residential neighborhood or locality as characterised by the ACORN classification (i.e., parental residence) (Shaw, 1984). These interrelated social and ecological aspects of living conditions produce a clear "class-based" differentiation of adolescent life-styles. As can be seen from Figure 4.3, Clusters 1 and 3 can be labeled as "working class" while Clusters 4 and 5 can be labeled as "middle class." Cluster 2 is more varied and can be viewed as a mix of social backgrounds. Brake (1980) has argued that we are born into particular social settings possessing distinct ways of life. Thus young people influence and are influenced by the perceptions, values, and behaviors of these social groups. Within these complex patterns of social relations and meanings, individual adolescents begin to form a personal identity and a life-style. Also Giddens (1984) has identified locality as a vital social context pertaining to interactions, habits, and behaviors by which life-style patterns develop. Put simply, there are both class-based differences and ecological differences associated with the development of young women's life-styles in adolescence.

But considerations of social class alone do not account for the five clusters obtained. Differences in life-styles also emerge within social class boundaries. For example, if we were to look at these young women's involvement in sports in terms of social class of origin *alone*, we would find *no* class-based differences. Yet it is clear from Figure 4.3 that variations in levels of sports participation do exist among the five clusters. These variations only become apparent once we begin to distinguish between different working-class life-styles and different middle-class life-styles. For the two middle-class clusters, individuals in Cluster 5 are particularly involved in sports—they spend money on sports goods, they are members of sports clubs, attend sports fixtures, and play sports competitively—whereas those in cluster 4 have little interest or involvement in sports. If we had not differentiated between those two groups we would have been in danger of concluding that middle-class young women are not particularly involved in sports, and certainly no more so than working-class women. In summary, there are also clear differences in life-style development within social classes, and we need to take account of these in any real understanding of the contexts of adolescent development.

Importantly, some life-styles are common to both middle-and working-class young women. For example, Cluster 2 seems to fit one archetypal view of adolescent young women as spending a lot of time with a close girlfriend, hanging about the neighborhood in groups, being interested in finding a boyfriend, being in conflict with the family, and spending money on entertainments and fashion. It is interesting to note that this life-style pattern cuts across class boundaries in its adherence to "youth culture" values (e.g., Brake, 1980).

When we look at the longitudinal transitions made by young women between the period when they are still at school (i.e., 15–16 years of age) and when they have left school and moved into adult society (i.e., 17–18 years of age), we begin to note identifiable life-styles emerging. For young women aged 17–18 years in 1989 there are once again clear-cut middle-class and working-class clusters, with one small cluster from a mix of social backgrounds (see Figure 4.3). Additionally, it can be seen that the development of these clusters over time represents an exchange between clusters within social class boundaries, and in terms of fragmentation across class boundaries the exchange is fairly minimal. Between 1987 and 1989 the class basis of these clusterings of young people is relatively stable over time. Thus the migration of individuals from one type of life-style to another is predominantly within social class boundaries. For example, young women from Clusters 4 and 5 in 1987 move into Clusters 3 and 4 in 1989. Hence these different groupings of young women are differentiated by their own occupational status and educational attainments as much as by their social class origins. Thus we can conclude that the social context has a powerful impact on their life-style development.

Young people in higher education, working youth, and those young people on government training schemes or the non-employed do have different life-style patterns. Different kinds of experiences help to mold developing life-styles—there can be pressures in aspiring towards higher education, in being unemployed, or on a relatively uninspiring youth training scheme, of living in poor housing conditions, or getting involved in drugs misuse. Yet it is necessary to point out that, in general terms, academic and working youth do appear to have "healthier" life-styles than those on training schemes, the unemployed or those who are non-employed.

When we look at young men in the 15–16-year-old cohort in 1987, and again in 1989, we find some similarities with young women's life-styles— but equally we see differences emerge (see Figures 4.4 and 4.5). Somewhat similar underlying factors to those for young women differentiate groupings of young men, and this is equally true of the clusterings for 15–16-year-old males. But we see a greater differentiation of life-style patterns at 17–18 years of age, and upon examining Figures 4.3 and 4.5, gender differences do emerge. For instance, young women in middle-class groupings appear to be more outgoing and gregarious in overtly social ways than young men of similar social class background and academic standing.

Health-related behaviors such as smoking, drug usage, and drinking, together with involvement in sports and physical activities, do act as important differentiators in the variations seen within both male and female adolescents' life-style development. These in their turn are linked to perceived mental and physical health statuses and may suggest the development of adolescent life-styles that have certain important implications for later life.

The psychosocial transitions across adolescence alluded to in the opening sections of this chapter interact to distinguish particular life-styles that emerge across the adolescent years. These changing patterns of life-style development do not necessarily relate directly to Coleman and Hendry's (1990) focal theory, though it is possible to note a combination of life events, relational issues, values, attitudes, and leisure interests that interact as the focal theory suggests. This allows us to consider not only social class and gender differences, but also important life-style variations within social class boundaries as young people make the transition towards adulthood. Such constellations of factors may be particularly relevant within leisure, and it is possible to perceive life-style developments that are differentiated by adolescents' involvement in organized, casual, or commercial leisure; by participation in smoking, drinking, and drug taking; by those young people who are particularly involved with a network of friends or with a special boy or girlfriend, or those who are somewhat isolated and alone; and by those who are concerned about relationships with peers or parents. It is therefore possible using cluster analyses to gain clearer insights into the various aspects of attitudes, meanings, and behaviors that make up more conventional adolescent life-styles within social class boundaries, and to acknowledge the variations within social classes that produce more "youth culture"–oriented living patterns. Additionally, "achievement-oriented" life-styles do seem to comprise of different types of psychological stress, social relationships, and life events between working-class and middle-class adolescents.

However, this is an unfinished story—the 1991 survey will, in its turn, be added to our data bank and will enable us to extend the scenarios of developing adolescent life-styles as young people move into their early

20s. In this way we will be able to refine our picture and so develop a better understanding of the manner by which adolescent life-styles emerge and consolidate in both conventional and less conventional ways as young people move towards early adulthood.

References

Aaro, L.E., Wold, B., Kannas, L., & Rimpela, M. (1986). Health behaviour in school-children. A WHO cross-national survey. *Health Promotion, 1*(1), 17–33.

Abel, T. & McQueen, D. (1992). *The formation of health lifestyles: A new empirical concept.* Paper presented to the BSA & ESMS Joint Conference on Health in Europe. Edinburgh, Scotland, 18th–21st September.

Ansbacher, J.L. (1967). Lifestyle: A historical and systematical review. *Journal of Individual Psychology, 23*(2), 191–212.

Anthony, K.H. (1985). The shopping mall: A teenage hangout. *Adolescence, 20,* 307–312.

Banerjee, T. & Lynch, K. (1977). On people and places: A comparative study of the spatial environments of adolescence. *Town Planning Review, 48,* 105–115.

Bates, I., Clarke, J., Cohen, P., Finn, D., Moore, R., & Willis, P. (1984). *Schooling for the dole.* London: Macmillan.

Brake, M. (1980). *The sociology of youth culture and youth subcultures.* London: Routledge & Kegan Paul.

Bronfenbrenner, U. (1979). *The ecology of human development: Experiments by nature and by design.* Cambridge: Harvard University Press.

Coffield, F., Borrill, C., & Marshall, S. (1986). *Growing up at the margins.* Milton Keynes: Open University Press.

Coleman, J.C. (Ed.). (1979). *The school years.* London: Methuen.

Coleman, J.C. & Hendry, L.B. (1990). *The nature of adolescence* (2nd ed.). London: Routledge.

Coleman, J.S. & Husen, T. (1985). *Becoming adult in a changing society.* Paris: OECD.

Dex, S. (1987). *Women's occupational mobility.* London: Macmillan.

Gans, W.J. (1968). *People and places: Essays on urban problems and solutions.* New York: Basic Books.

Giddens, A. (1984). *The constitution of society.* Oxford: Polity.

Goffman, E. (1971). *The presentation of self in everyday life.* Harmondsworth Middlesex, England: Pelican.

Hendry, L.B. (1983). *Growing up and going out: Adolescents and leisure.* Aberdeen, Great Britain: Aberdeen University Press.

Hendry, L.B., Shucksmith, J., & Love, J.G. (1989). *Young people's leisure and lifestyles project: Report of Phase I, 1985–1989* (Research Report No 11). Edinburgh Scotland: Scottish Sports Council.

Hendry, L.B., Shucksmith, J., Love, J.G. & Glendinning, A. (1993). *Young people's leisure and lifestyles.* London: Routledge.

Holt, M. (1983). Vocationalism: The new threat to universal education. *Forum, 25*(3), 84–96.

Marsh, P., Rosser, E., & Harre, R. (1978). *The rules of disorder.* London: Routledge & Kegan Paul.

Raffe, D. & Courtenay, G. (1988). 16–18 on both sides of the border. In D. Raffe (Ed.), *Education and the youth labour market* (pp. 12–39). London: Falmer Press.

Rosenstock, I.M., Strecher, V.J., & Becker, M.H. (1988). Social learning theory and the health belief model. *Health Education Quarterly, 15*(2), 175–183.

Shaw, M. (1984). Sport and leisure participation and lifestyles in different residential neighbourhoods: An exploration of the ACORN classification. London: Sports Council.

Spencer, C., Blades, M., & Morsley, K. (1989). *The child in the physical environment. The development of spatial knowledge and cognition.* Chichester Sussex, England: Wiley.

Statistical Package for the Social Sciences Reference Guide (1990). S.P.S.S. Inc., Chicago.

Van Vliet, W. (1983). Exploring the fourth environment. An examination of the home range of city and suburban teenagers. *Environment and Behavior, 15*(5), 567–588.

Wenzel, R. (1982). *Health promotion and lifestyles: Perspectives of the WHO Regional Office for Europe, Health Education Programme.* Paper presented to the 11th International Conference on Health Education. Hobart, Tasmania, 15th–20th August.

5
The Development of Interests during Adolescence: Social Context, Individual Differences, and Individual Significance

Eberhard Todt, Ralf Drewes, and Sigrid Heils

Introduction

The development of relatively enduring interests is not only an important developmental task for adolescents, but it is also a requirement for coping with other developmental tasks including:

- specialization in school
- selection of vocational training or college education
- satisfying arrangement of free time
- establishment of satisfying friend- and partnerships
- development of one's own identity—especially restructuring gender identity
- further development of cognitive competencies.

The development of relatively enduring and behaviorally relevant interests depends in a complex manner on the context.

- It requires a cognitively competent individual who actively explores his or her environment.
- It also requires a physical and social context which allows a competence-related and competence-supporting use of this context. Family, peers, school, residential areas, recreational opportunities, occupational structure, and values of the society have to be regarded as the context for the development of interests.
- As development of interests continues, physical and social context is used more and more selectively, and this selection increasingly determines the self-concept or identity of the individual.

Although there is good empirical evidence suggesting that development of interests is significant for coping with important developmental tasks during adolescence (Ausubel, 1954; Todt, 1984), it is difficult to prove and to differentiate empirically that development of interests depends on the context. Therefore, after defining interests, and context the attempt is made, on the basis of some empirical studies, to contribute to the clarification of the development of interests related to context during adolescence.

Defining Interests and Context

According to psychological literature, the term *interests* has diverse connotations:

- activation, attention, curiosity, flow, emotion, intrinsic motivation
- attitude, value, need, motivation by content, self-concept.

These connotations have partly state and partly trait characteristics. Thus, English and English (1958) qualify "interest" as "a term of elusive meanings" (p. 271):

- "an attitude or feeling that an object or event makes a difference or is of concern to oneself;"
- "a striving to be fully aware of the character of an object . . . a tendency to engage in an activity solely for the gratifications of engaging therein;"
- "the feeling without which a person is said to be unable to learn."

In the field of motivational psychology interests have to be assigned to linguistically based motives and emotions (Buck, 1988). They refer to different linguistically distinguishable subjects: music, arts, sports, biology, physics/technology, and so on. Buck (1988, p. 6) writes about his model:

the systems for the activation and direction of behavior exist at a number of levels of organization. Biologically based motivational systems are organized in a hierarchical manner, with the phylogenetically older and newer structures at different levels. The farther up the hierarchy, the "newer" the system and the more it is open to influence from the organism's experience, that is, from learning and cognition.

Context as a substitute for the rather static concepts "situation, setting, environment" gains increasing significance in developmental psychology (Cohen & Siegel, 1991). However, not only the definition from Cohen and Siegel but also the developmental contextual model of person-context interactions (generated by Lerner & Tubman, 1991, p. 196) reveals the complexity of this term. Cohen and Siegel (1991, p. 18) define:

Context is a melding of person and environment. Context includes the consideration of persons (conceptualized as active, constructive information processors, replete with a past history and current sets of agenda, goals, expectations etc.) as embedded within sets of social relationships (proximal and distal), and within a physical setting (offering behavioral opportunities and constraints) all developing over time.

Such a complex definition and its methodological implications establish new standards for empirical research, which are still difficult to achieve. Therefore, at this time we can present only empirical studies regarding the relationship between development of interests and context, which mark only the beginning of such a complex analysis.

Phenomenons in Development of Interests during Adolescence

English and English (1958, p. 148) define *development* as

a sequence of continuous change in a system extending over a considerable time; specifically, such change, or related and enduring particular changes, as follow one another in an organism from its origin to maturity or to death ... The changes may be in structure, function, or organization, they may be in size, differentiation, complexity, integration, or efficiency.

Since the concept of development is also conceptualized in such a complex way, only particular aspects of development of interests during adolescence can be more closely examined:

- development of the factorial structure (differentiation)
- development of the average level of interests
- development of hierarchies of interests
- development of sex differences
- development of stability of interests.

These aspects are used as structured guidelines for the empirical findings presented in the following. Other aspects of development including function, integration, and efficiency, would be interesting as well; for this, we are not aware of any empirical studies.

Development of the Factorial Structure of Interests

Considering the intercorrelation among interests for the various subjects (sports, arts, music, biology, physics, etc.), a systematic decrease of intercorrelation upon scale and item level can be observed regarding the 10- to 18-year-olds. On scale level the median of these intercorrelations diminishes for boys and girls over this time from approximately .45 or .50 to .20 or .15 (Todt, 1978).

Accordingly, relatively undifferentiated factor structures for 10-year-olds (Hengstenberg, 1990) and highly differentiated factor structures for about 18-year-olds (Todt, 1990a,b) are found, provided that the amount of explained common variance is comparable.

The Hengstenberg's study reveals two factors for the 10-year-olds that explain 52% of common variance, and in Todt's study of the 18-year-olds, two factors explain merely 32% of common variance but with 11 factors 59% are explained.

Although the sex variable has been controlled statistically, the two-factor solution for the 10- and the 18-year-olds has very much in common with the observable sex-typed interests, respectively Snow's two cultures (Snow, 1959):

Factor I: mathematics and technology
Factor II: literature, arts and music

This structure is not as distinct for 10-year-olds as it is for 18-year-olds (see also Gati, 1979).

Since empirical data are not available to the same extent for all areas of a differentiated interest-structure in adolescent development, we limit our analysis in the following on the socially and individually important interests in physics and technology.

Development of Average Level of Interests in Physics and Technology

An extensive cross-sectional ($N = 4043$) and longitudinal ($N = 250$) study including 10- to 16-year-old students of both sexes was conducted in cooperation with the Institute for Sciences Education (IPN) between 1984 and 1989 (Hoffmann, Lehrke, & Todt, 1985, description of the

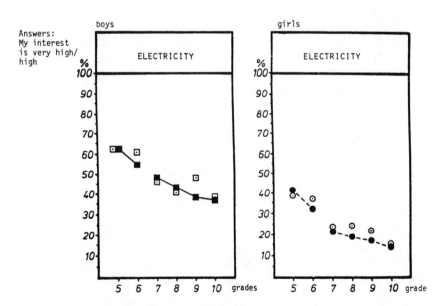

FIGURE 5.1. Adolescents' interest in physics topics Institute for Science Education (IPN), 1984–1989. Longitudinal ■ ●, cross sectional □ ○, m = □, f = ○.

questionnaire in Häussler, 1985). We found that interests in physics and technology systematically decrease during this age period. This is true for the cohorts of the longitudinal study as well as for the age cohorts of the cross-sectional investigation. And one can find the same results for boys as well as for girls. Figure 5.1 shows these exemplary results for the topic of electricity.

So far, numerous international studies (such as Lehrke, Hoffman, & Gardner, 1985) have reported similar results.

Development of Hierarchies of Interests

In a further investigation we applied a questionnaire referring to interests in physics (Todt, Arbinger, Seitz, & Wildgrube, 1974) to approximately 10,000 students between the ages of 10 to 15. We made the remarkable observation that the rank order of preference of single items within different interests-in-physics scales (for instance, mechanics) remains completely invariant (Todt, 1978). The rank correlations for the item-mean-rank order yield coefficients between .86 and .99 (16 items) for boys and girls.

We also obtained similar results from the study of the IPN as well, using the cross-sectional and longitudinal designs.

Development of Sex Differences

The results exhibited in Figure 5.1 are typical for all other results we found concerning sex differences in physics and technology: The sex differences in interests are certainly varying from topic to topic but remain invariant within the explored age period.

The sex differences in these interests are obviously established before adolescence and remain unchanged afterwards.

Development of Stability of Interests

In this case, the Pearson-Bravais correlation between interests reactions in studies that were repeated in a 1-year interval represents stability. In the longitudinal study of the IPN, for boys and girls this stability (responses to items) systematically increases within the ages of 10 to 16. The median of the stability coefficients for different scales, each containing 11 items, was approximately .25 for grades 5–6 and approximately .45 for grades 9–10. The first canonical correlations between the 11 items of the different scales increased from approximately .50 to .70. Results from other studies confirmed these findings.

Context and Development of Interests in Physics and Technology

So far, particular aspects of the development of interests during adolescence have been presented. The following considerations attempt to establish a relationship between this development and the context significant for development.

The complexity of the term *context* was already described above. Furthermore, Cohen and Siegel (1991, pp. 5–16) distinguish different facets of context for the science of development:

- Context as social systems: In this case, among others, they refer to Bronfenbrenner (1979) and separate proximal (here and now) from distal (removed in time and space) social systems.
- Context as physical environment: In this case, they refer to Barker (1968) and analogously cite (p. 9): "it is interesting that the behavioral differences among inhabitants of a behavior setting are fewer than the behavioral differences of a single person across behavior settings."
- The individual in context: In this case, they refer to the characteristics of the actor who actively constructs reality.
- Context as evolving over time: With this they express that the three described facets of context are not static, but may change over time.

Especially with regard to these facets of context, our knowledge concerning the development of interests is restricted. But we can report some results from studies we conducted.

Context as Social Systems

According to our findings it seems that distal social systems have greater impact than proximal social systems on level and structure of interests in physics and technology. The invariances described for sex differences in interests and for hierarchies of the average level of interests in relatively specific topics suggest an influence of social expectations, which are already effective in early childhood.

As an explanation for these findings, one can draw on different theorists (Gottfredson, 1981; Kohlberg, 1967), who established a close relationship between the development of sex-related self-concept and the evaluation of sex-related objects, experiences, and activities. And in accordance with this assumption it is observed that in most societies, physics and technology are male domains. In this sense, one can conclude that expectations in society and the establishment of the self-concept show a developmentally interdependent relationship. On the other hand, the proximal social system "family" contributes surprisingly little to the explanation of the results.

Exploring pairs of same-sex siblings, Grotevant, Scarr, and Weinberg (1977) reported correlations of .37 for biological siblings (75 pairs) and −.21 for adopted siblings (23 pairs) using Holland's "investigative" interest style. The same authors reported for the interest style "investigative" correlations of .09 for biological father-son pairs ($N = 108$) and .08 for adoptive father-son pairs ($N = 81$).

In our own research (Todt, Arbinger, Seitz, & Wildgrube, 1974) we performed a survey in two *Gesamtschulen*[1] including grades 6 through 10. We found maximum correlations of .22 between the scales for interests in physics and the scales for "physics-specific" stimulation by the father (perception of the son). In addition, the interests in physics and technology correlated with only .32 with the expectations of the parents as viewed by the students (male, grades 8 and 9).

The available data suggest that similar results are true for girls, although sometimes closer relationships between expectations of the parents and interests of the adolescent girls can be observed.

These relatively consistent results lead to the following explanation: Relatively early, children adjust their interests according to their observations and the communicated expectations of their further environment (peers, adults). Parents and siblings are possibly less important than persons outside the family. Upon this influence, children more or less eliminate interests that are not appropriate for their sex-role. With that, they abandon the motivation to acquire competencies in diverse kinds of cross-sex activities. As a result, they are prevented from reentering these areas of activities, as their attitudes towards sex-roles become more flexible.

The development of the previously discussed general orientation of interests—measured with the usual topic-oriented questionnaires or vocational interests questionnaires—seems to be slightly influenced by proximal social systems. This does not apply to the same extent to interests in school subjects: We conducted several studies to follow up this problem.

At this point we want to report one prototypical study (Händel, 1984).

Five hundred ninety-nine male and 532 female students (grades 7 through 10) of two Gesamtschulen were asked about their interest in physics lessons and how often certain educational conditions have been realized in these lessons. Beforehand, approximately several hundred students had marked these conditions as relevant for their interest in physics lessons, and a questionnaire was developed that included a list of those conditions. Statements made were, among others:

- that the teacher gives fair marks
- that the teacher explains the subject matter well

---

[1] *Gesamtschulen* are special types of junior and senior high schools in Germany, which are attended by all students from a specific local area without differentiating on the basis of school performance.

	boys		girls	
	R	(R^2)	R	(R^2)
School A	.70	(.49)	.73	(.53)
School B	.69	(.47)	.78	(.61)

FIGURE 5.2. Multiple correlations between frequency of realization of important conditions of being interested (students' ratings) and ratings of being interested, Grades 7 to 10. (Händel, 1984).

- that there is variation in the lesson
- that there is a positive climate between teacher and students.

Figure 5.2 shows the multiple correlations between frequency of realization of important conditions of being interested (students' ratings) and ratings of being interested in the physics lessons. Although interest in physics lessons and topic interests in physics have some common characteristics (systematic decreases during adolescence and remarkable sex differences), the context-relationships of both interests are obviously unalike.

Apparently, topic interests in physics are relatively permanently established in the self-concepts of adolescents (they also correlate high with the ability-related self-concept), but interests in physics lessons are largely dependent on concrete circumstances of teaching; therefore, they are substantially more unstable.

The Individual in Context

It was already pointed out that a relatively close relationship exists between the ability-related self-concept and interests in physics and technology. This is illustrated by Figure 5.3, using results from Todt and Händel (1988), which could be replicated similarly in other studies.

Since topic-oriented interests can be conceptualized as linguistically based motives (Buck, 1988), and since the close relationships between these interests and the ability-related self-concept presumably is less due to concrete experiences than to cognitive self-construction, such interests should change as the context of imagination is modified.

In a study including approximately 1,100 male and female students (grades 7 through 10), we presented four topics of mechanics (e.g., Archimedes' law) and four topics of electricity in different forms:

- as textbook
- as technical application
- as medical application

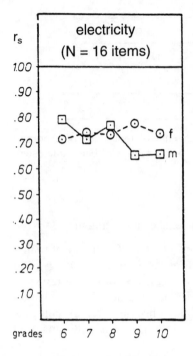

FIGURE 5.3. Rank correlations between interests and self-confidence. (ranks of sums of answers "very interested/interested", and "confidence very high/high" (Händel, 1984).

as well as other forms.

The students had to indicate how interesting the texts, particularly the applications, were for them. The results corresponded with our expectations.

While the connotations "textbook" and "technical application" show remarkable sex differences in interests, the connotation "medical application" shows none. That is, whenever girls are confronted with topics of

			grade		
Connotation		7	8	9	10
textbook	m	44	41	47	52
	f	18	19	21	17
technical application	m	53	48	53	63
	f	24	23	27	21
medical application	m	46	46	46	52
	f	48	52	45	47

FIGURE 5.4. Interests in physics in different connotations. Median of answers "very interesting" and "interesting" (percent), 8 Items.

physics related to connotations accordant with their self-concept, they are willing to attend to the topic. On the other hand, boys apparently do not lose their interest if topics of physics are embedded in connotations more appropriate for females (see Figure 5.4).

The studies existing up to now are just an initial step towards accomplishing the task of describing and explaining the development of interests during adolescence.

Perspective of Research

If the development of interests during adolescence is evaluated as relevant, as described at the beginning of this chapter, the necessity of further systematic research in development of interests cannot be denied.

The concept of context presented by Cohen and Siegel (1991) and by Lerner and Tubman (1991) might be considered as a challenge for such investigations. A model for differentiating the concept of interests compatible with the conception of English and English (1958) might be helpful. This model is shown in Figure 5.5.

In this model different aspects (general interests, specific interests, active interests) of content related (mechanical, scientific, artistic, etc.) interests refer to three diverse contexts: occupation, leisure, and school.

Numerous new challenges for further research activities will result, if the view on contexts is expanded, adding facets such as family or peers, and if the interactions between the several components of the model of interests (characteristic for a more or less dynamic system) are specified and incorporated.

In order to illustrate the above-presented model, some characteristics for the definition of interests are specified:

(a) *General interests*:
- relatively enduring (disposition)
- development dependent on cognitive development (more or less age related)
- part of self-concept (especially competence and gender)
- system characteristics
- close relationship to general valuing system (values, attitudes)
- content related
- influences by concrete experiences are small
- central ontogenetic mechanism: dropping of certain interests
- *functions*: orientation, decision making
(b) *Specific interests*:
- relatively enduring (disposition)
- compatible with but not deducible from general interests of the individual

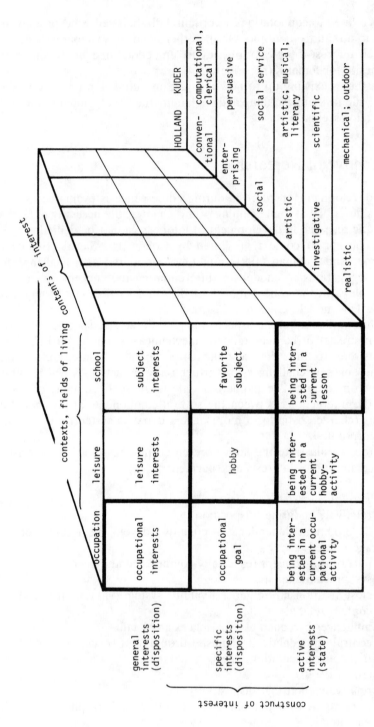

FIGURE 5.5. Model of interests.

- dependent on external hints (stimulation) and on positive experiences (cognitive learning of expectancies)
- related to relatively specific contents or activites
- related to specific non–age-related competence
- specific interests are more characteristic for individuals (are more unique) than general interests
- in certain fields specific interests can be connected with an increasing aspiration level ("need achievement")
- *functions*: self-actualization, coping with stress, compensation when satisfaction is missed in occupation, initiation of activities

(c) *Active interests* (being interested):
- positive emotional state (pleasure)
- dependent on specific characteristcs of situations (complexity, understanding, success, positive social emotional climate, etc.)
- not necessarily dependent on existing general or specific interests
- can become dispositional if stabilized by frequent repetition of certain situations (and positive consequences)
- *functions*: activates cognitive functions (attention, learning, remembering, thinking), stabilizes activities

As components of a model these features are of a heuristic nature, but they are compatible with the results reported above.

In spite of the traditions concerning psychological research about interests (Fryer, 1931; Strong, 1943), and in spite of the undeniable importance of interests in the development of children and adolescents, the knowledge in this topic of research is still limited. This is especially true when the acquired knowledge is confronted with the methodological necessities derived from the dynamic conception of development in context.

In this chapter the attempt was made to describe relevant aspects of the development of interest during adolescence and its multiple relations to different contexts or life domains. It is apparent that a psychological model of interests has to be as complex as the model for contexts. The model presented differentiating the concept of interests—combined with the context model mentioned by Cohen and Siegel and Lerner and Tubman, respectively—is in this sense an important challenge for future research in this field.

References

Ausubel, D.P. (1954). Theory and problems of adolescent development. New York: Grune & Stratton, Inc.

Barker, R.G. (1968). *Ecological psychology*. Standford, CA: Stanford University Press.

Bronfenbrenner, U. (1979). *The ecology of human development: Experiments by nature and by design*. Cambridge: Harvard University Press.

Buck, R. (1988). *Human motivation and emotion* (2nd ed.). New York: Wiley.

Cohen, R. & Siegel, A.W. (Eds.). (1991). *Context and development*. Hillsdale, NJ: Lawrence Erlbaum.

English, H.B. & English, A.C. (1958). *A comprehensive dictionary of psychological and psychoanalytical terms*. London: Longmans, Green and Co.

Fryer, D. (1931). *Measurement of interests in relation to human adjustment*. New York: Henry Holt and Co.

Gati, I. (1979). A hierarchical model for the structure of vocational interests. *Journal of Vocational Behavior, 15*, 90–106.

Gottfredson, L.S. (1981). Circumscription and compromise: A developmental theory of occupational aspirations. *Journal of Counseling Psychology Monographs, 28* (No. 6).

Grotevant, H.D., Scarr, S., & Weinberg, R.A. (1977). Patterns of interest similarity in adoptive und biological families. *Journal of Personality and Social Psychology, 35*, 667–676.

Händel, B. (1984). *Interesse und Einstellung gegenüber Physik*. [Interests in and attitudes towards physics]. Unpublished thesis, Justus-Liebig-Universität, Fachbereich Psychologie, Gießen.

Häussler, P. (1985). A questionnaire for measuring three different curricular components of pupils' interest in physics: Topic, context and action. In H. Lehrke, L. Hoffmann, & P.L. Gardner (Eds.), *Interests in science and technology education* (pp. 81–87). Kiel: Institute for Science Education.

Hengstenberg, D. (1990). *Untersuchung über die Interessen acht- bis elfjähriger Kinder*. [A Study on the interests of children between eight and eleven]. Unpublished thesis, Justus-Liebig-Universität, Gießen: Fachbereich Psychologie.

Hoffmann, L., Lehrke, M., & Todt, E. (1985). Development and change of pupils' interests in physics (grades 5 to 10): Design of a longitudinal study. In M. Lehrke, L. Hoffmann, & P.L. Gardner (Eds.), *Interests in science and technology education* (pp. 71–80), Kiel: Institute for Science Education.

Kohlberg, L. (1967). A cognitive-developmental analysis of children's sex-role concepts and attitudes. In E.E. Maccoby (Ed.), *The development of sex differences* (pp. 82–173). London: Tavistock.

Lehrke, M., Hoffmann, L., & Gardner, P.L. (Eds.). (1985). *Interests in science and technology education*. Kiel: Institute for Science Education.

Lerner, R.M. & Tubman, J.G. (1991). Developmental contextualism and the study of early adolescent development. In R. Cohen & A.W. Siegel (Eds.), *Context and development* (pp. 183–210). Hillsdale, NJ: Lawrence Erlbaum.

Snow, C.P. (1959). Die zwei Kulturen. [The two Cultures]. In H. Kreuzer (Ed.), *Die zwei Kulturen. Literarische und naturwissenschaftliche Intelligenz. C.P. Snows These in der Diskussion* (pp. 19–96). München: Deutscher Taschenbuchverlag.

Strong, E.K. (1943). *Vocational interests of men and women*. Stanford, CA: Stanford University Press.

Todt, E. (1978). *Das Interesse*. [Studies on interests]. Bern, Stuttgart, Wien: Huber.

Todt, E. (1984). Selbstkonzept und Selbstkonzeptänderung als Mittler bei der Bewältigung von Anforderungen in der Adoleszenz. [Self-concept and change of self-concept as mediators of coping in adolescence]. In E. Olbrich & E. Todt (Eds.), *Probleme des Jugendalters—Neuere Sichtweisen* (pp. 159–177). Berlin: Springer.

Todt, E. (1985). Elements of a theory of science interests. In M. Lehrke, L. Hoffmann, & P.L. Gardner (Eds.), *Interests in science and technology education* (pp. 59–69). Kiel: Institute for Science Education.

Todt, E. (1990a). Entwicklung des Interesses. [Development of interest]. In H. Hetzer, E. Todt, I. Seiffge-Krenke, & R. Arbinger (Eds.), *Angewandte Entwicklungspsychologie des Kindes- und Jugendalters (2. Auflage)* (pp. 213–264). Heidelberg/Wiesbaden: Quelle und Meyer.

Todt, E. (1990b). *Studien- und Berufswahlerfahrungen und Wünsche von Schülern und Schülerinnen der Sekundarstufe II.* [Occupational choices and aspirations of senior highschool students]. Unpublished manuscript. Research Report: Gießen: Fachbereich Psychologie.

Todt, E., Arbinger, R., Seitz, H., & Wildgrube, W. (1974). *Untersuchungen über die Motivation. Zur Beschäftigung mit naturwissenschaftlichen Problemen* [Junior highschool students' motivation to deal with problems in the natural sciences]. *(Sekundarstufe I: Klassenstufe 5–9).* Unpublished manuscript. Research Report: Gießen: Fachbereich Psychologie.

Todt, E. & Händel, B. (1988). Analyse der Kontextabhängigkeit von Physikinteressen. [Analysis of the dependency of physics interests on context] *Der mathematische und naturwissenschaftliche Unterricht, 41*(3), 137–146.

Part III

The Impact of Cultural and Ethnic Contexts

6
Culture Makes a Difference . . . or Does It? A Comparison of Adolescents in Hong Kong, Australia, and the United States

S. Shirley Feldman and Doreen A. Rosenthal

Even the most cursory examination of the anthropological literature reveals that humans are born, raised, and die in cultures that differ in ways that have important implications for individual development. Within psychology, the study of cultural variation has largely focused on documenting cultural differences and quantifying dimensions that may both underlie this variation as well as contribute to an understanding of intergroup relations. Developmental psychologists have been slow to take up the opportunities presented by cross-cultural studies as a way of elucidating developmental issues, but the past decade has seen a growing interest in the potential contribution of this research strategy. This interest has been stimulated, in part, by the emergence of several theoretical models that locate development firmly within the broader sociocultural context.

At the most general level, Bronfenbrenner (1979) proposes that development is influenced by a series of contexts, one of which, the exosystem, is represented as the society or culture in which the child is raised, and the impact of that society's rules, norms, and structures on significant others in the child's life. Other theorists such as Ogbu (1981) and Super and Harkness (1986) have focused more specifically on the contribution of culture to development. Ogbu's "cultural-ecological" model of competence and the concept of the "developmental niche" proposed by Super and Harkness take into account the idiosyncratic features of a culture in determining the precise developmental outcomes for members of that culture. Both argue that socialization practices are designed to produce children and adolescents who are able to function effectively in the society in which they are raised. To the extent, then, that different cultures and societies are organized differently, have different values, and different child-rearing practices, we should not be surprised to learn that children and adolescents from different cultures indeed differ in many ways.

In fact, recent models make it clear that a study of development across cultures has the potential to contribute to our understanding of the human condition. In particular, cross-cultural studies enable us to distinguish between what is universal or characteristic of development everywhere and what is unique to a given culture. For example, it is clear from studies of early childhood that there is universality of sequencing of stages within certain developmental domains, such as motor development, but differences in the timing of stages emerge as a function of features of a culture, such as the opportunities to perform particular behaviors or the models provided by that culture. As Segall, Dasen, Berry, and Poortinga (1990) note, the "contents" of behavior become more and more culturally marked throughout the course of development. We might expect, therefore, that at adolescence the impact of culture on developmental outcomes will be more apparent than in earlier developmental stages. It is at this period in the life span that, in addition to the family as a significant socializing force, there is an increase in the influence of peers and external, societal institutions, such as school.

The study of cultural differences in adolescent development has largely been ignored by developmental psychologists, although there has long been a view arising, in part, from the pioneering work of Margaret Mead (1928) and Ruth Benedict (1934) that adolescence as a stage of life is a cultural invention. The Western view of adolescence as a tumultuous and problematic period of life received little support from the work of early anthropologists. Yet few psychologists have taken up the challenge of examining the extent to which the adolescent experience is determined by the cultural context in which the adolescent is reared.

Cross-cultural comparisons are most useful if the dimensions of cultural variation can be described. Recent advances in this area have highlighted the centrality of individualism-collectivism as a major dimension of cultural variation (Bond, 1988; The Chinese Culture Connection, 1987). It is, for example, one of four key dimensions identified in Hofstede's ecological factor analyses of 40 world cultures (Hofstede, 1980). Other recent work has demonstrated that eight different domains of values in diverse countries can be mapped onto an individualistic-collectivistic dimension (Schwartz & Bilsky, 1987). Societies with a collectivistic orientation stress a tightly knit social framework with the rights and needs of the group as paramount. By contrast, individualistic societies emphasize individual achievement, personal growth, and the rights of the individual.

In the research reported in this chapter, we study youths from three cultures—from Hong Kong, Australia, and the United States. On the dimension of individualism and collectivism, Chinese and Western cultures vary dramatically (The Chinese Culture Connection, 1987; Hofstede, 1980, 1983; Leung & Bond, 1984), with considerable divergence between these two cultures on issues of personal freedom, conformity, and collective welfare (Bond, 1986; Hsu, 1981; Triandis, Kashima, Shimada, & Villareal, 1986). The Chinese are described as being situation-centered, valuing family and tradition, harmony, emotional restraint, conformity, and obedience to authority (Ho, 1986; Yang, 1970) while the West prizes individualism, autonomy, and original thinking (Feather, 1986; Gardner, 1989; Hsu, 1972). Chinese traditionally place greater significance upon social and moral values than upon personal values and competence in the service of individualistic goals or self-fulfillment.

The contrast between the Chinese emphasis on collectivism and the well-being of the group and the Western emphasis on individualism is seen particularly clearly in their contrasting family environments and socialization practices. The family has been described as the pivot of Chinese culture. Cohesion among family members, dependence on the family, unquestioning acceptance of parental authority, preservation of the status quo, and profound loyalty are encouraged as a means of preserving the family system (Bond & Hwang, 1986; Harrison, Serafica, & McAdoo, 1984). With its emphasis on conformity, obedience, and respect for tradition, the Chinese family has been described as demanding, structured, and authoritarian (Ho, 1986; Kriger & Kroes, 1972; Wolf, 1970). Themes of filial piety, strict discipline, proper conduct, and the acceptance of social obligations are those most often invoked in its description (Vernon, 1982). Proverbial expressions of Chinese parenting styles note that: "The stick produces a dutiful son," (Wu, 1966) and "A dull metal can be sharpened by constant grinding" (Cheng, 1946). In contrast, the Western family, with its emphasis on autonomy, individualism, and creativity, is described as accepting, moderately structured, and democratic (Baumrind, 1971; Maccoby & Martin, 1983). Unlike the Chinese family, the Western family places marked focus on assisting children to become physically and psychologically separated from their parents, and children are strongly encouraged to be self-reliant and independent (Alwin, 1988; Rosenthal & Bornholt, 1988; Steinberg & Silverberg, 1986).

It is worth noting, however, that values and child-rearing practices of the Chinese are changing—both in their homelands as well as in immigrant settings. Children and their families in Hong Kong and Taiwan are moving away from traditional Chinese practices and attitudes (Dawson & Ng, 1972; Ho & Kang, 1984; Lin & Fu, 1990). This development has been associated with industrialization, economic advancement, and higher levels of education (Martin, 1975; Mitchell & Lo, 1968). Indeed it has been suggested that in Hong Kong and Taiwan, such typically Western values as personal competence and autonomy are increasingly more important (Lau, 1988; Lin & Fu, 1990), implying a gradual shift towards individualism and self-orientation (Yang, 1986). Notwithstanding these changes, the significant contrasts between the Chinese and Western cultural contexts provides us with an opportunity to study culture as a context for adolescent development.

Most cross-cultural studies of the Chinese typically involve comparisons with American data, and the dearth of comparisons with cultures other than American has been much lamented. Our research extends the number of comparison cultures by including information from Australian as well as American youths. This extension offers an opportunity to test the generalizability of the Chinese-United States comparisons.

The two Western cultures—the United States and Australia—were selected because they share a number of common features. Both are democratic, English-speaking, industrialized, capitalistic Western nations, with a common English heritage and shared historical roots. Although there are some distinctions between the two cultures based on size, political power, and economic factors, similarities in values between the two cultures are impressive. For example, studies of Australian and American adolescents reveal the importance in both cultures of autonomy, responsibility, and honesty, and the relative unimportance of conformity to authority and social convention (Feather, 1980). In terms of family environments and practices, those of the United States and Australia seem very similar (Funder, 1991; Noller & Callan, 1991).

To examine the role of culture in adolescent development, we have selected four outcomes to study that met two or more of the following criteria: Outcomes were included if they (a) were significant behaviors or attitudes for adolescents in at least one of the cultures studied; (b) were differentially valued in the three cultures that we were investigating; or (c) previous empirical research had shown that there were significant differences among the three cultural groups. We settled on four outcomes: two positive behaviors (autonomy expectations and school effort) and two negative or undesirable outcomes (misconduct and distress).

The two positive outcomes—behavioral autonomy and school effort— are, to some extent, positively valued in each culture. However, consistent with the Western emphasis on individualism, autonomy has been defined as the central task of adolescence in Western cultures. As a result, early behavioral autonomy is more highly valued and is a more salient issue in Western than in Chinese cultures. In contrast, school effort and applying oneself in terms of scholarship is more valued in Chinese than Western cultures, especially since it is consistent with the Confucian emphasis on education as a means to developing oneself fully, serves the collectivistic aim of bringing honor to the family, and is facilitated by conformity to adult demands (Bond & Hwang, 1986; Harrison, Serafica, & McAdoo, 1984; Ho, 1986; Vernon, 1982).

The two negative outcomes—misconduct and distress—have been reported to occur with differential frequency in Western and Chinese cultures. Western children from an early age are characterized as being more aggressive and lower in restraint than Chinese children. Thus, it is not surprising that, at adolescence, when the level of misconduct increases in most cultures, misconduct and delinquency occur more often among Western than Chinese youths (Cameron, 1985; Cheng, 1946; Hong Kong Census & Statistics Department, 1988; U.S. Federal Bureau of Investigation, 1987). In contrast, it has been conjectured that since Chinese youths are less likely to "act out" their distress, they are likely to turn it inward and to feel subjectively more distressed than Western youths.

We have been guided by five major questions as we attempted to understand the role of culture in adolescent development. First, to what extent do the three cultural groups differ in adolescent outcomes? This is the most common approach to cultural differences (see the volume by Bond, 1986). Most studies documenting cultural variation in adolescent outcomes invoke putative cultural differences to explain these findings. However, it is necessary to determine empirically whether the cultures indeed differ in the ways described by previous accounts. In light of the progressive and evolutionary nature of culture and the extensive contact that Hong Kong has with Western nations, the traditional accounts of Chinese culture in Hong Kong can no longer be assumed to hold. Further, the strategy of speculating about the causes of cultural differences in adolescent outcomes is risky, for it is not known whether the presumed causes are even related to the outcomes under consideration.

Like others before us, we believe that the documentation of group differences is only the starting point in cross-cultural analyses. The real task is to "unpackage" the concept of culture (Whiting, 1976) and to specify the processes or mechanisms that underly cultural variation. A frequent approach to this task, the individual-level approach, assumes that the same variables or antecedents that account for individual differences *within* a culture also account for cross-cultural variation in outcome (Hofstede, 1980; Leung & Bond, 1989; Poortinga & Malpass, 1986; Poortinga & Van de Vivjer, 1987; Rohner, 1975). Following this reasoning, we have identified two broad classes of influences on adolescent outcomes—family environments and adolescent values—that are associated with adolescent outcomes, and that hold promise for explaining cross-cultural differences. Our second question, then, is whether youths from different cultures differ in these domains.

Until this point, our questions have focused on cultural comparisons that depend on differences in level of some outcome or some mechanism. Examining mean differences in behavior or attitudes is indeed one important way in which the impact of culture on adolescent development can be detected. However, it is not the only way. It is possible that different cultural groups are similar in level of some outcome (e.g., misconduct), but the construct (of misconduct) has different correlates and is subject to different influences in each cultural group. Thus, another way in which culture can be important is in terms of the organization (or nomological net) of a given construct. This concern leads to two additional questions. Our third question was whether the patterns of relations between adolescent outcomes, family environments, and adolescent values were similar or different across Hong Kong, Australian, and American youths.

Our fourth question was whether the influences identified—namely, family environments and adolescent values—succeed in "unpackaging" culture as it influences adolescent outcomes. Stated differently, if we partial out the effects of family and values, does culture contribute unique variance to adolescent outcomes in cross-cultural studies? Finally, our fifth question was whether there was a correspondence between the factors that account for individual differences in adolescent outcomes *within* each group and those factors that differentiate *between* the cultural groups.

To address these questions we undertook a study of middle-class adolescents from three cultures. We sampled approximately 150 tenth and eleventh graders from each culture—Chinese students from Hong Kong; Anglo-Australians from Melbourne, Australia; and Euro-Americans from San Francisco, USA. We aimed for and achieved virtual comparability of samples with respect to type of school system, age of students, gender composition, urban setting, and fathers' work status. However, the samples, reflecting accurately the populations from which they were drawn, differed with respect to birth order, mothers' work status, and fathers' education. In particular, Hong Kong students, compared to Western students, tended to come from larger families, were more likely to have mothers who were not in the paid labor force, and had fathers who had not completed high school.

The similarities and differences in the three samples point to some inherent unsolvable problems in cross-cultural research. If the samples are matched in characteristics (such as grade at school) they may not be equally representative of the adolescents in their cultures. For example, since it is normative in the United States to complete high school, high school youths are reasonably representative of all youths. In contrast, in Hong Kong, where it is not normative to complete high school, high schoolers are not representative of youths in that culture. There are similar problems when we consider fathers' education as a matching variable for the samples. If the samples are matched on fathers' education, then they are not equally representative of their culture. If representative samples (in terms of fathers' education) are used for the three cultural groups, then they will be decidedly unequal in terms of absolute amount of education. In sum, in cross-cultural and cross-national research, matching and representativeness of samples are often incompatible.

We now turn our attention to addressing the five questions that guided our research. For this task, we draw upon our published papers on cross-cultural comparisons (Feldman & Rosenthal, 1991b; Feldman, Rosenthal, Mont-Reynaud, Leung, & Lau, 1991) together with some new analyses that we carried out for this chapter. The data for the additional analyses came from a related research project of ours on the acculturation of first- and second-generation Chinese immigrants living in Australia and the United States (see Rosenthal & Feldman, in progress, for a summary).

These acculturation samples were compared to both adolescents from the culture of origin and the host culture on a diversity of outcomes (Chiu, Feldman & Rosenthal, 1992; Feldman, Mont-Reynaud, & Rosenthal, 1991; Feldman & Rosenthal, 1991b; Rosenthal & Feldman, 1991a, 1991b). Data from the three anchor samples from the acculturation studies were used to address the issues under consideration in this chapter.

Are There Cultural Group Differences in Adolescent Outcomes?

We expected that the cultural groups would differ in the extent to which they had early expectations for autonomy, invested in school, engaged in misconduct, and reported distress. We assessed these adolescent outcomes from questionnaires that were administered to students on two separate occasions. *Age expectations for autonomy* were based on a 23-item instrument that assessed at what age adolescents expected behavioral autonomy across a variety of life management domains (Feldman & Rosenthal, 1991a). *School effort* was assessed by four questions; how hard students tried in class, how much time they spent on homework, how often they cut classes, and the extent to which they paid attention in class. Each question was asked about four subject areas (Rosenthal & Feldman, 1991a). *Misconduct* was assessed by 17 items that tapped school-based misconduct, status offenses, and antisocial behavior (Feldman, Rosenthal, Mont-Reynaud, Leung, & Lau, 1991). *Distress* was assessed by a 12-item scale that measured anxiety, depression, low self-esteem, and low well-being (Chiu, Feldman, & Rosenthal, 1992).

Before considering the results, we should examine more closely the meaning of age expectations of autonomy. Two quite opposite meanings can be attributed to early autonomy. On the one hand, it may be indicative of positive growth, maturity, a willingness to fend for oneself, to take on responsibilities as well as the privileges that come with independence. On the other hand, early behavioral autonomy may be seen as a precocious and precipitous entry into the youth culture, and a premature dismissal of the restraining influence of parents. Although we intended to assess the former meaning of autonomy, it became clear to us that we had actually measured the latter, more negative, construct. We found, for example, that in all our samples adolescents who reported early autonomy expectations also reported higher levels of misconduct, both at school and at large, and significantly lower restraint than their classmates with later expectations for autonomy. Similar results are reported in other studies where early autonomy is associated with deviance and poor school performance (Dornbusch, Ritter, Leiderman, Roberts, & Fraleigh, 1987). Thus we view expectations for early autonomy as a negative adolescent outcome.

TABLE 6.1. Mean scores on adolescent outcomes, family environments, and adolescent values in three cultural groups (as described by adolesents).

	HK	Australia	USA
Adolescent outcomes[1]			
Age expectations for autonomy (1 = early)	2.9[a]	2.3[b]	2.3[b]
School effort (1 = little effort)	3.2[a]	3.6[b]	3.2[a]
Misconduct (1 = never)	1.2[a]	1.8[b]	2.3[c]
Distress (1 = low distress)	3.1[a]	2.5[b]	2.6[b]
Family environment scores[2]			
Accepting-engaged	46.2[a]	52.1[b]	51.6[b]
Demanding	49.6[a]	48.9[a]	51.5[b]
Autocratic	50.2	49.8	49.7
Monitoring	49.8	51.2	48.9
Values scores[3]			
Well-socialized behavior	53.2	52.7	52.8
Universal prosocial behavior	54.0[a]	51.8[b]	51.8[b]
Traditional behavior	43.1[a]	41.8[b]	41.3[b]
Family as residential unit	55.4[a]	46.7[b]	43.8[c]
Competence	50.5[a]	51.5[ab]	52.4[b]
Outward success	43.9[a]	48.3[b]	48.8[b]
Honors to individuals	39.2[a]	41.3[b]	42.4[b]
General individualism	51.1[a]	52.4[b]	52.8[b]

Note: Shared superscripts indicate that the groups do not differ significantly from each other.
[1] 5-point scales.
[2] z scores.
[3] The average of within-individual z scores across items.

Do youths from the three cultural groups differ in adolescent outcomes? The results, summarized in Table 6.1, show that they did. As predicted, Hong Kong youths had later expectations for autonomy, engaged in less misconduct, and felt more distressed than their Western counterparts. American and Australian students were alike in expectations for autonomy and reported distress, but Australian students engaged in less misconduct and more school effort than did American students.

It is noteworthy that adolescents from Hong Kong and the United States were alike in terms of their self-reported school effort. It is likely that students take their classmates as the reference point for defining their behavior, and that the norms for effort may vary in the three cultures studied. Thus, a subjective appraisal of "how hard they try in class" may be based on different standards in the three cultures. In one culture, trying 80% of the time may be perceived as "trying very hard"; in another culture, it may be perceived as trying "very little." Natriello and Dornbusch (1984) makes a similar point: They found that Asian students (in American classrooms) perceived that they were working less hard than did their classmates, despite the fact that they spent considerably more time on homework.

Even where the cultural differences were large, as in misconduct and expectations for autonomy, the differences were not uniform across all items or all domains. For example, in the area of misconduct, American and Hong Kong youths were similar in terms of minor school-related infractions such as tardiness, copying homework from a friend, acting up in the classroom, and reading non–school-related materials during class. They were also similar in terms of the infrequently reported antisocial behaviors such as threatening a teacher, taking items from classmates, and hurting a student on purpose. But the largest differences between the Chinese and Americans involved the more serious school-related offenses such as cutting classes and cheating on tests, as well as engaging in status offenses, such as swearing, smoking, and using drugs and alcohol. It appears from these results that American adolescents are in greater haste to enjoy adult privileges than are Chinese youths.

Similarly, the expectations for autonomy, while revealing cultural differences in virtually every item, were larger in some domains and smaller in others. The largest cultural differences arose in the sphere of peer relations. Western youths had markedly earlier timetables for attending boy-girl parties, dating, choosing own friends even if parents disapproved, and choosing to do things with friends rather than with family. The greatest similarities in timetables for autonomy among youths from the three cultural groups involved responsibilities for making own doctor and dentist appointments, and staying home alone when unwell.

Overall, however, our study, like others before it, found that culture (and all that this entails) had a significant impact on adolescent outcomes. Adolescents from Hong Kong, Australia, and the United States differed in misconduct, expectations for autonomy, and the amount of distress they reported.

Are There Cultural Differences in Family Environments and Adolescent Values?

In an effort to understand these cultural differences in adolescent outcomes, we sought to locate some mechanisms (or proximal influences) by which culture, a distal variable, would impact directly on adolescent outcomes. We settled on two domains of variables—family environments and adolescent values. There were two reasons for the choice of these domains. First, in the extant literature, these domains have been used to describe differences between cultures, especially between Chinese and Western cultures. Thus, these constructs are excellent candidates for serving as vehicles to translate distal cultural influences into more proximal influences on adolescents. Second, these domains have been linked to adolescent outcomes in one or more of the cultures.

There are reportedly cultural differences in family environments. In particular, Chinese parents have been described as more power-assertive and restrictive, and less frequently autonomy-granting and child-centered than Western parents (Kriger & Kroes, 1972; Vernon, 1982; Yang, 1986). In addition, parenting practices and family relationships are major influences in the socialization of children and youth. Despite a plethora of labels, essentially similar constructs emerge as having associations with the well-being of children. Whether studied separately or in combination, family variables such as acceptance (warmth, responsiveness), demandingness, (monitoring, control, limit setting), and child-centeredness (engaged, autonomy-promoting) have been linked positively, and autocratic parenting (authoritarian, power-assertive, punitive) has been linked negatively, to the maturity, social responsibility, and autonomy of children and youth in Western and Chinese cultures (Maccoby & Martin, 1983; Vernon, 1982; Yang, 1986).

Values–generalized and relatively enduring beliefs concerning what is desirable or undesirable–also differ across cultures. Chinese, Australian, and American cultures differ in the value ascribed to personal freedom, conformity, collective welfare, obedience and respect for parents, and maintaining harmony (Bond, 1988; Chinese Culture Connection, 1987; Feather, 1980, 1986; Poole, 1986; Rokeach, 1973; Yang, 1986). While the literature linking adolescent values to adolescent outcomes is sparse, to the extent that values are believed to guide and determine behavior on a long-term basis, such links may be expected to be found.

In the present research we assessed four dimensions of family environments and eight dimensions of adolescent values. The family scores were derived from a factor analysis of a battery of paper-and-pencil tests (Feldman & Rosenthal, 1991b). *Accepting/engaged* parenting involves family members spending time together, cohesion, acceptance of different viewpoints of family members, and authoritative parenting. *Demanding* parenting involves parental control, involvement in the adolescent's decisions, limit setting, and family organization. *Autocratic* parenting involves authoritarian mothering and fathering, and conflict in the family. *Monitoring* assessed the extent to which parents knew of the whereabouts of their adolescents at different times of the day.

Eight different value scores were derived from a factor analysis of both Chinese and Western value scales (Feldman, Mont-Reynaud, & Rosenthal, 1991). The eight value scores included the valuing of *well-socialized* behavior (e.g., polite, responsible, self-controlled behavior), *traditional values* (rites and rituals, tradition), *universal prosocial* behavior (equality, peace, justice), valuing the *family as a residential unit* (elderly parents should live with adult children, unmarried adult children should live with parents), valuing *competence* (independence, intellectual accomplishment, being logical), valuing *outward success* (wealth, power, status), attributing *honors to individuals* (rather than to the family), and *general individualism* (taking responsibility for own actions, preferring to work alone rather than cooperatively).

As expected, cultural differences were found in family environments. As shown in Table 6.1 and consistent with the previous cross-cultural literature, both American and Australian youths described their families as more accepting/engaged than did Hong Kong youths. In subsequent analyses, we have shown that the primarily contributor to this cultural difference comes from the engaged aspect of family interactions—more specifically from parents and teenagers engaging jointly in leisure time and recreational activities. The warmth or acceptance aspect did not differ between cultural groups (Chiu, Feldman, & Rosenthal, 1992). Table 6.1 also shows that, in an unexpected finding, American adolescents described their families as more demanding than did Australian or Hong Kong counterparts. Perhaps because autonomy is so much more salient to American than to Chinese youths, they are especially sensitive to actual or perceived control or restrictions.

It is also of interest that parental monitoring and autocratic parenting were described similarly by adolescents from all three cultures. The findings for autocratic parenting are particularly of note, since they accord neither with the stereotype of the Chinese family as controlling and authoritarian nor with some of the previous research findings. It has been suggested, however, that autocratic parenting is more common in Chinese parents with lower levels of education and lower socio-economic status (SES) and from rural, rather than urban, areas (see Ho, 1986). Thus, the reports in the literature of greater autocratic parenting in Chinese than Western parents may result from samples that are not comparable. In the present study, with more closely matched samples across the cultures, Hong Kong, American, and Australian youths were similar in their reports of autocratic parenting.

Among adolescents there were significant cultural differences in values, as expected. There were two patterns of results. First, the two Western groups valued outward success, competence, general individualism, and honors to individuals more, and universal prosocial behavior and tradition less, than did the Hong Kong youths. While these differences were statistically highly significant, in both cultures well-socialized outcomes and universal prosocial behaviors were very highly valued whereas outward success (wealth, power, prestige), honors to individuals, and tradition were valued less highly. Thus, although the differences between the cultures are real in magnitude, the values of the cultures differed in emphasis not in valence. In the second pattern, the valuing the family as residential unit differed across the cultures not only in emphasis but also in valence. Hong Kong youths strongly endorsed the importance of family members living together—including elderly parents living with adult children, and unmarried, adult children living with parents. In contrast, Western youths from both Australia and the United States gave this a relatively low priority.

In general, these results are in accord with previous descriptions of Chinese culture as more collectivist and Western culture as more individualistic. The results are particularly interesting in that the Chinese youths were educated, middle class, and urban, a group that in other research has been relatively high in individualism (Lau, 1988; see Yang, 1986 for a review of more than 20 studies).

Overall, it is fair to conclude that Chinese and Western youths differed in their description of family environments and adolescent values. It is tempting to speculate that the group differences in family environments and adolescent values explain the observed cross-cultural differences in adolescent outcomes—tempting, but not defensible. As a result, we have taken a different and more rigorous approach. Instead, we investigated the extent to which the patterns of relationships were similar or different across the three cultural groups.

Are There Group Differences in the Patterning of Relationships?

In American, Australian, and Chinese youths, are there similar or different nomological nets (patterns of correlations) between adolescent outcomes, adolescent values, and family environments? This question of cultural differences or similarities in organization of an adolescent outcome is quite different from the usual question addressed in cross-cultural work and, to the best of our knowledge, has not been addressed in adolescent research before. It is, however, a powerful way to consider the influence of culture.

To address the question of similarities or differences in nomological net of adolescent outcomes we used multiple regression analyses. In separate analyses, each adolescent outcome was regressed on adolescent values and family environments for each cultural group. Then we compared the slopes of the regression planes (by means of an ANCOVA). In the case of school conduct, the slopes of the regression planes were not parallel. Family environments and adolescent values accounted for significant variance in school effort for the Australian sample ($R^2 = .51$) but failed to do so for the American and Hong Kong samples. The results for the remaining three adolescent outcomes were identical. Australian, American, and Hong Kong Chinese youths did not differ in the way the adolescent outcomes were related to family environments and values of youths. Thus, despite mean differences among the cultural groups in terms of the autonomy expectations, misconduct, and distress, and despite differences among the cultural groups in terms of important aspects of family environment and adolescent values, the patterning of associations with adolescent outcomes was similar in the three cultures.

Given the similar organization of adolescent outcomes across cultural groups, it was possible to combine the samples and to examine the joint influence of family environments and adolescent values on each of the outcomes in turn. In these analyses, culture was entered as a control variable. These models accounted for significant amounts of variance in adolescent outcomes, ranging from a low of 16% of the variance in distress, to 22% for misconduct, and to a substantial 34% for expectations for autonomy. It is apparent, however, that despite the importance of family environments and adolescent values, other factors not assessed in the research also contribute in important ways to the adolescent outcomes. The results of the regression equations for autonomy expectations, misconduct, and distress are presented in Table 6.2. The results for school effort are not presented because the pattern of associations varied for each culture.

Although each of the four dimensions of family environments was individually associated with several of the adolescent outcomes, they were also associated with each other. Thus, in the regression analyses only some of the family variables contributed unique variance to the outcomes. As seen in Table 6.2, somewhat different aspects of the family environment were identified as significant predictors of each of the diverse adolescent outcomes. Parental acceptance/engagement contributed to low levels of distress, a finding consistent with the psychological literature (Harter, 1990; Hauser & Bowlds, 1990).

TABLE 6.2. Results of regression analyses with family environments and adolescent values as predictors of three adolescent outcomes.[1] Only significant beta weights are shown[2].

	Autonomy expectations	Misconduct	Distress
Family environments			
Accepting/engaged	—	—	−.36***
Demanding	.38***	—	—
Autocratic	−.12**	—	—
Monitoring	.19***	−.20***	—
Adolescent values			
Traditional	—	.10*	—
Competence	−.10*	—	—
Outward success	−.15**	.24***	—

[1] Culture was entered as a control variable.
[2] Results for school effort are not shown since the regression planes for the three groups werre not parallel.
*$p < .05$; **$p < .01$; ***$p < .001$

The other family predictors of Table 6.2 involved different aspects of control. Monitoring of the child's whereabouts by the parents was associated with both expectations for late autonomy and with low levels of misconduct. This finding is also consistent with other research in adolescent development (Pulkkinen, 1982; West, 1982), particularly with findings from the important programmatic work of Patterson (e.g., Patterson, DeBaryshe, & Ramsey, 1989). Demanding parenting was associated with late autonomy expectations whereas autocratic parenting was associated with early expectations for autonomy. In other words, it appears that it is not so much the warmth or acceptance dimensions but the family organization and control dimension that is important. When family life is structured and organized, when parents exert control that is perceived as reasonable rather than arbitrary and autocratic, when parents remain involved in adolescents' decision making, and follow through and monitor their adolescents whereabouts, youths accept parental influence on their lives and expect parental guidance to continue later into adolescence (i.e., adolescents expect to achieve behavioral autonomy at a later age) and engage in less misconduct.

Adolescent values also contributed to the prediction of adolescent outcomes, over and above that of family environments. Notably, valuing of outward success was associated with early expectations for autonomy and with misconduct. The valuing of individual competence was associated with expectations for early behavioral autonomy. Thus, those values that were manifestations of the broader construct of individualism were associated with negative developmental outcomes in teenagers. This finding fits with the suggestion that individualism, in its more marked expression, is associated with other negative behavior such as unethical behavior, selfishness, and crime (Bellah, Madsen, Sullivan, Swidler, & Tipton, 1985; Hsu, 1983; Spence, 1985; Triandis et al., 1986).

Two additional findings pertaining to values are noteworthy. First, none of the domains of values generally considered as part of collectivism (such as traditionalism, universal prosocial behavior, well-socialized outcomes and family as residential unit) predicted adolescent outcomes. We do not know whether the values associated with individualism are in general more powerful predictors of adolescent outcomes, or whether the adolescent outcomes we selected for study were themselves individualistic. Additional outcomes that are consistent with a collectivistic outlook need to be studied. Second, none of the adolescent values contributed unique variance to the prediction of distress. Since we view distress as an unintended outcome of socialization and other stresses, and therefore unrelated to the values of adolescents, we were not surprised by this finding.

In sum, many of the results that emerged from this study about the relationship between adolescent outcomes, family environments, and adolescent values are consistent with other reports in the literature. What is new, however, is the finding that the associations that have been known to hold for Western countries also hold for Hong Kong Chinese. Despite cultural differences in family environments, adolescent values, and adolescents adaptive outcomes, parental acceptance and monitoring have essentially the same effects on adolescents in Hong Kong as they do in Western nations. Similarly, the valuing of outward success has similar associations with adolescent outcomes in the individualistic West as among the collectivist Chinese of Hong Kong. Three of the four adolescent outcomes considered in this study—expectations for autonomy, misconduct, and distress—had similar patterns of correlations in American, Australian, and Hong Kong youths.

Do Family Environments and Adolescent Values Succeed in "Unpackaging" Culture as it Influences Adolescent Outcomes?

If family environments and adolescent values are the proximal influences by which culture impacts on the adolescent, then these variables should, in effect, "unpackage" culture. That is, after we have taken these influences into account, there should be no additional contribution made by culture. If, on the other hand, family environments and adolescent values fail to unpackage culture, then culture should add the same amount of variance to the prediction of adolescent outcomes as it did before we took account of family environments and adolescent values.

We assessed these predictions by using regression analyses. As shown in Table 6.3, when culture was entered first in the regression models (i.e., before it was unpackaged), it was a highly significant predictor of adolescent outcomes, and accounted for between 10 and 21% of the variance. However, after we attempted to unpackage culture by taking into account family environments and adolescent values, the amount of variance culture accounted for was markedly reduced—in each instance by 55% or more.

TABLE 6.3. The amount of unique variance that culture, family environments, and adolescent values contribute to adolescent outcomes.

		Adolescent outcomes[1]		
	Step entered	Autonomy expectations	Misconduct	Distress
Culture	1st	21%	10%	11%
Culture	last	8%	3%	5%
Family environment	last	13%	6%	10%
Adolescent values	last	5%	6%	1%

[1] Results for school effort are not presented since the regression planes were not parallel.

Thus, our attempts at unpackaging culture as it impacts on adolescents were largely, although not completely, successful. That is, part of the variance typically attributed to cultural differences can, in fact, be attributed to family environments and adolescent values—which are, of course, themselves influenced by culture. While family environments and adolescent values are clearly important, as evidenced by our studies, they do not completely account for the effect of culture. Perhaps the inclusion of additional family variables, such as parental protectiveness, enmeshment, or inconsistency may help peel away further layers of the "onion skin of culture" (Poortinga & Malpass, 1986). Or it may be that more specific parenting as it pertains to each outcome needs to be considered. For example, to fully assess the contribution of parenting to adolescents' school efforts, we may need to supplement the general measures of parenting used in this study with measures of parenting that are specifically focused on schooling. In other work (Rosenthal & Feldman, 1991a), we have assesed such things as parental involvement in school activities, parents' knowledge of what goes on in the classroom, and their reaction to both good and bad grades of their children. Alternatively, we may need to consider entirely different areas as we seek to understand the operation of culture. Candidates that seem especially salient during adolescence are the nature and extent of involvement in peer activities, the organization and atmosphere of school, and exposure to, and the messages promulgated by, the mass media.

Is There a Correspondence between Factors that Account for Within-cultural and Between-cultural Differences?

Our cross-national studies reported in this paper have clear implications for other research that compares developmental outcomes and their correlates for youths in contrasting cultures. The results of our program of research are *not* compatible with the commonly held view that those influences which account for individual differences within a group or a culture can be extrapolated to account for intergroup or cross-cultural differences. Nor are our findings compatible with the converse assumption, that those variables which differentiate among cultural groups are likely to explain individual differences within culture. To illustrate these twin points, we draw upon data from the study of misconduct of youths, although similar conclusions would hold for each of the other outcomes studied.

In the study on misconduct, those family environments and adolescent values that differed across the three cultures were, in many instances, not the same variables that accounted for individual differences within a culture. For example, Chinese and Western youths differed significantly in the extent to which their families were described as demanding, yet family demandingness did not contribute unique variance to the prediction of misconduct. Conversely, misconduct correlated negatively with parental monitoring both within cultures and in the combined analyses, yet reports of parental monitoring were essentially similar across the

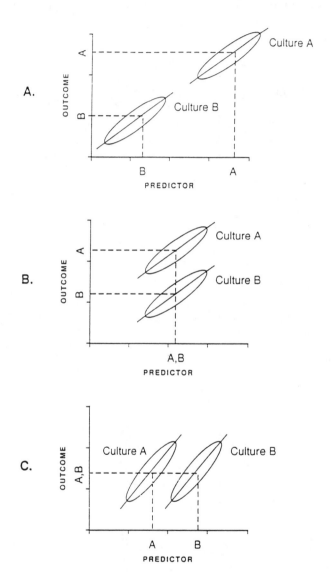

FIGURE 6.1. Hypothetical data in which the regression slopes are similar in two cultures but in which there are diverse patterns of mean differences between the two cultures in the predictor and outcome scores.

three cultural groups. Only the valuing of "outward success" and "the family as residential unit" differentiated between both the three cultural groups and contributed unique variance to individual differences in misconduct. Similar failures of the individual-level approach to cultural or ethnic differences are found in other outcomes of our research program.

Furthermore, there is no statistical reason why within-group relationships should provide information about between-group differences. In

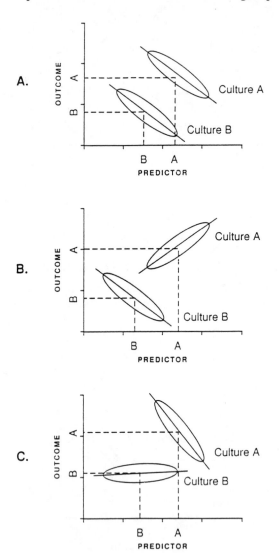

FIGURE 6.2. Hypothetical data in which the scores of culture A exceed that of culture B in both predictor and outcome scores but the regression slopes differ across cultures.

hypothetical data shown in Figure 6.1 we make this point graphically. In each of the three graphs of Figure 6.1 we begin with the assumption of similar associations between predictor and outcome (i.e., parallel regression lines across the two cultures) and show three of many possible variations in mean predictor and outcome scores for two different cultures. In each instance the two cultural groups differ on at least one variable—either the predictor or the outcome. Figure 6.1A shows mean cultural differences in both predictor and outcome. This graph, with identical intercepts for the two regression slopes, is in accord with the traditional assumption that individual differences explain group differences. Figures 6.1B and C, however, show graphs that are not consistent with the traditional assumption. Figure 6.1B shows identical predictor scores but cultural differences in outcomes; Figure 6.1C shows mean cultural differences in predictor scores but identical outcomes. Thus, Figure 6.1 shows that a common predictor of some adolescent outcome in two cultures does not support the inference that the identified predictor accounts for cultural differences in the adolescent outcome.

Figure 6.2 makes the converse point. It shows three of many ways in which consistent cultural differences in both predictor and outcome variables may be related to different patterns of organization of variables within cultures. In each instance, we keep constant that predictor A is greater than predictor B, and that outcome A is greater than outcome B. Figure 6.2A shows that in each of the cultures, the within-group relationship may be negative whereas the between-group relationship is positive. Figure 6.2B shows positive and negative slopes in two cultures. Finally, Figure 6.2C shows the absence of an association between the variables in one culture, whereas the other culture shows a negative association. In other words, both our emprical findings and our hypothetical graphs demonstrate clearly that knowledge of select factors that differentiate between youths from different cultures cannot be assumed a priori to account for cross-cultural differences in some adolescent outcome. Similarly, knowledge of factors that contribute to individual differences in some adolescent outcome cannot be assumed a priori to account for differences between cultural groups.

Conclusions

In sum, in our cross-national studies we have shown that the effect of culture on adolescent development depends on the way we frame the question. A focus on mean differences between teenagers from different nations reveals the importance of culture on adolescents. First, all four adolescent outcomes that we investigated were markedly influenced by culture. Being a Chinese adolescent in Hong Kong resulted in delayed expectations for autonomy, markedly lower levels of misconduct, but elevated levels of distress in comparison to their Western counterparts in Australia and the United States. Furthermore, even among youths from the two Western nations there were cultural differences. Australian adolescents made more effort at school and engaged in less misconduct than did American adolescents. It is reasonable to expect that many (although not necessarily all) other dimensions of adolescent behaviors would also show some effect of culture if they were investigated. Second, factors that might well be expected to account for individual differences in adolescent outcomes—namely, family environments and adolescent values—also were influenced by culture. The values and family environments of Chinese youths differed from those of their Western counterparts, although not as pervasively as a review of the literature pertaining to the traditional Chinese culture would have led us to believe.

Our efforts to unpeel the "onion skin of culture" by focusing on the two domains of family influences and adolescent values were partially successful. We demonstrated that culture operates, at least in part, by shaping the practices and environments of families and also by shaping the values that adolescents internalize. However, cultural influences encompass more than family environments and adolescent values. Future research is required to elucidate other aspects of culture as they influence adolescents.

Culture is a particularly powerful context for adolescent development because it has an impact on virtually every aspect of the adolescent's life. It shapes the settings in which adolescents are found and the people who occupy the settings. Initially, culture affects the child and adolescent in terms of the behavior of significant others, that is, those people who interact with and matter to adolescents. Indeed, the behavior and expectations of parents were shown to be influential on adolescent's functioning in each of the cultures. Almost certainly, the effects of siblings, teachers, other adults, peers, and even role models in the mass media also play a part in shaping the behavior, attitudes, and values of adolescents to fit into the cultural niche in which they are raised. Socialization agents exert their effect in many ways, including influencing the behavior of adolescents by rewards and punishments, by promoting internalization, by transmitting information about cultural standards, by modelling appropriate behavior, and by inculcating values that serve to guide adolescents in new situations and to give coherence to their lives. Further, since these same cultural influences have major effects on other children who serve as the peer group, culture comes to profoundly influence the standards available to youths for social comparison. Thus, culture influences both the internal and external standards of adolescents as well as their behavior and attitudes.

A different conclusion as to the role of culture is obtained, however, when the question of cultural influence is framed in terms of patterns of associations. When the relationships between adolescent outcomes, family environments, and adolescent values were studied, culture did *not* have a major effect for three of the four adolescent outcomes. The processes and associations that have been described for white middle-class American youths also characterized the development of other youths. The present studies found that although teenagers from Hong Kong, Australia, and the United States reported differences in adolescent outcomes (autonomy, misconduct, and distress), and differences in family environments and values, the patterning of associations between these factors was similar across the three cultures. In particular, in the three cultures, family environments were salient predictors of each of the adolescent outcomes. It appears to us that what may well be important is the perception of relative standing of one's family's practices, not a measure of absolute family practices. Indeed, adolescents' reports may not even correspond very closely to what actually happens in the family (Feldman, Wentzel, & Gehring, 1989). Family practices are embedded within a cultural context and are interpreted in light of that culture. For example, consider the case of parents' beating a child because of low school grades. A child from a culture where such behavior was sanctioned, where it occurred frequently, and where this parental behavior was regarded as a sign of parental investment in, and concern over the child's future might interpret this behavior differently than a child from a culture in which such behavior occurred infrequently, and was regarded as deviant and indicative of loss of parental control. Adolescents make social comparisons between their families and other families from within their own culture. It is the perceived departures from the cultural standard of acceptable and good parenting that may be important rather than some absolute set of behavioral practices.

Our conclusion, that culture did not influence the patterns of correlations with a variety of adolescent outcomes, is provocative and worthy of further research. The null hypothesis, however, can never be proved and our conclusion might be tempered by results from studies of additional outcomes or from studies which used more diverse predictors. Indeed, in the research reported in this chapter, culture influenced the nomological nets of one of the four adolescent outcomes—school effort. It would appear that whether of not culture influences the patterning of associations is likely to be dependent on the outcome under investigation.

Our conclusions about culture are limited by the adolescent outcomes we investigated and the cultures that we compared. The choice of variables to study may well be influenced by culture itself, and as Westerners, our selection of adolescent outcomes reflected our cultural bias. Future cross-cultural research needs to be sensitive to the issue of ethnocentrism, and other adolescent behaviors and outcomes, especially those that are salient to non-Western cultures, need both to be identified and studied cross-culturally. Additionally, to understand the role of culture it is necessary that cultures more discrepant from Western culture should be

studied. Although we chose a Chinese culture because it varied in known
and significant ways from the West, the extensive British influence on
Hong Kong, in terms of its legal, economic, educational, and govern-
mental systems, together with extensive trade and cultural contacts
with the West, may have served to diminish the differences beween the
cultures.

It is clear that culture as a context of adolescent development is worthy
of further study. Cross-cultural studies provide us with a much wider
range of variation in important developmental influences than is found by
examining individual differences within a culture. However, cross-cultural
research is complex and requires methodological rigor, shedding of
ethnocentic biases in the choice and measurement of outcomes of interest, greater sophistication in framing the questions as to how culture
comes to influence the lives of adolescents, and a comparison of many
diverse cultures. Since such research endeavors are relatively new in the
field of adolescent development, the task is challenging. The rewards, we
believe, are well worthwhile.

Acknowledgments. This chapter was supported by a grant from the Stanford
Center for the Study of Families, Children, and Youth, and from The University
of Melbourne, and was written while the first author was a Visiting Research
Fellow at the University of Melbourne. Thanks are due to Robert Canning for
data analysis.

References

Alwin, D.F. (1988). From obedience to autonomy: Changes in traits desired in
    children. 1924–1978. *Public Opinion Quarterly*, *52*, 33–52.
Baumrind, D. (1971). Current patterns of parental authority. *Developmental
    Psychology Monograph*, *4*(1, Pt. 2).
Bellah, R.N., Madsen, R., Sullivan, W.M., Swidler, A., & Tipton, S.M. (1985).
    Habits of the heart: Individualism and commitment in American life. Berkeley:
    University of California Press.
Benedict, R. (1934). *Patterns of culture*. Boston: Houghton Mifflin.
Bond, M.H. (1986). *The psychology of the Chinese people*. Hong Kong: Oxford
    University Press.
Bond, M.H. (1988). Finding universal dimensions of individual variation in mul-
    ticultural studies of values: The Rokeach and Chinese value systems. *Journal of
    Personality and Social Psychology*, *55*(6), 1009–1015.
Bond, M.H. & Hwang, K. (1986). The social psychology of Chinese people. In
    M.H. Bond (Ed.), *The psychology of the Chinese people* (pp. 213–266). Hong
    Kong: Oxford University Press.
Bronfenbrenner, U. (1979). *The ecology of human development: Experiments by
    nature and by design*. Cambridge: Harvard University Press.
Cameron, R.J. (1985). *Australia's youth population, 1984: A statistical profile*.
    Canberra: Australian Bureau of Statistics.

Cheng, C.K. (1946). Characteristic traits of the Chinese people. *Social Forces*, *25*, 146–155.

Chinese Culture Connection (1987). Chinese values and the search for culture-free dimensions of culture. *Journal of Cross-Cultural Psychology*, *8*(2), 143–164.

Chiu, M.L., Feldman, S.S., & Rosenthal, D.A. (1992). The influence of immigration on parental behavior and adolescent distress in Chinese families residing in two Western nations. *Journal of Research on Adolescence*, *2*, 205–240.

Dawson, J.L.M. & Ng, W. (1972). Effects of parental attitudes and modern exposure on Chinese traditional-modern attitude formation. *Journal of Cross-Cultural Psychology*, *3*, 201–207.

Dornbusch, S.M., Ritter, P.L., Leiderman, P.H., Roberts, D.F., & Fraleigh, M.J. (1987). The relation of parenting style to adolescent school performance. *Child Development*, *58*, 1244–1257.

Feather, N.T. (1980). Values in adolescence. In J. Adelson (Ed.), *Handbook of adolescent psychology* (pp. 247–294). New York: Wiley.

Feather, N.T. (1986). Value systems across cultures: Australia and China. *International Journal of Psychology*, *21*, 697–715.

Feldman, S.S., Mont-Reynaud, R., & Rosenthal, D.A. (1991). When East moves West: The acculturation of values of Chinese adolescents in the United States and Australia. *Journal of Research on Adolescence*, *1*, 109–134.

Feldman, S.S. & Rosenthal, D.A. (1991a). The acculturation of autonomy expectations in Chinese high schoolers residing in two Western nations. *International Journal of Psychology*, *25*, 259–281.

Feldman S.S. & Rosenthal, D.A. (1991b). Age expectations of behavioral autonomy in Hong Kong, Australian, and American youths: The influence of family variables and adolescent values. *International Journal of Psychology*, *26*, 1–23.

Feldman, S.S., Rosenthal, D.A., Mont-Reynaud, R., Leung, K., & Lau, S. (1991). Ain't misbehavin': Adolescent values and family environments as correlates of misconduct in Australia, Hong Kong, and the United States. *Journal of Research on Adolescence*, *1*, 109–134.

Feldman, S.S., Wentzel, K.R., & Gehring, T.M. (1989). A comparison of the views of mothers, fathers, and preadolescents about the family cohesion and power. *Journal of Family Psychology*, *3*, 39–61.

Funder, K. (Ed.). (1991). *Images of Australian families*. Sydney: Longman Cheshire.

Gardner, H. (1989). *To open minds: Chinese clues to the dilemma of contemporary education*. New York: Basic Books.

Harrison, A., Serafica, F., & McAdoo, H. (1984). Ethnic families of color. In R.D. Parke (Ed.), *Review of child development research 7: The family* (pp. 329–365). Chicago: University of Chicago Press.

Harter, S. (1990). Self and identity development. In S.S. Feldman & G.R. Elliott (Eds.), *At the threshold: The developing adolescent* (pp. 352–387). Cambridge: Harvard University Press.

Hauser, S.T. & Bowlds, M.K. (1990). Coping and adaptation. In S.S. Feldman & G.R. Elliott (Eds.), *At the threshold: The developing adolescent* (pp. 388–413). Cambridge: Harvard University Press.

Ho, D.Y.F. (1986). Chinese patterns of socialization: A critical review. In M.H. Bond (Ed.), *The social psychology of the Chinese people* (pp. 1–37). Hong Kong: Oxford University Press.

Ho, D.Y.F. & Kang T.K. (1984). Intergenerational comparisons of child-rearing attitudes and practices in Hong Kong. *Developmental Psychology, 20,* 1004–1006.

Hofstede, G. (1980). *Culture's consequences: International differences in work-related values.* Beverly Hills: Sage.

Hofstede, G. (1983). National cultures revisted. *Behaviour Science Research, 18,* 285–305.

Hong Kong Census and Statistics Department. (1988). *Crime and its victims in Hong Kong 1986* (A report on the Crime Victimization Survey conducted in January 1987 by the Census and Statistics Department, Hong Kong Government). Hong Kong.

Hsu, F.L.K. (1972). American core value and national character. In F.L.K. Hsu (Ed.), *Psychological anthropology* (pp. 241–261). Cambridge: Schenkman.

Hsu, F.L.K. (1981). *Americans and Chinese: Passage to differences* (3rd ed.). Honolulu: University of Hawaii Press.

Hsu, F.L.K. (1983). Rugged individualism reconsidered. In F.L.K. Hsu (Ed.), *Rugged individualism reconsidered: Essays in psychological anthropology* (pp. 402–420). Knoxville: University of Tenessee Press.

Kriger, S.F. & Kroes, W.H. (1972). Child-rearing attitudes of Chinese, Jewish, and Protestant mothers. *Journal of Social Psychology, 86,* 205–210.

Lau, S. (1988). The value orientations of Chinese university students in Hong Kong. *International Journal of Psychology, 23,* 583–596.

Leung, K. & Bond, M.H. (1984). The impact of cultural collectivism on reward allocation. *Journal of Personality and Social Psychology, 47,* 793–804.

Leung, K. & Bond, M.H. (1989). On the empirical identification of dimensions for cross-cultural comparisons. *Journal of Cross-Cultural Psychology, 20,* 133–151.

Lin, C.C. & Fu, V.R. (1990). A comparison of child-rearing practices among Chinese, immigrant Chinese, and Caucasian-American parents. *Child Development, 61,* 429–433.

Maccoby, E.E. & Martin, J.A. (1983). Socialization in the context of the family: Parent-child interaction. In E.M. Hetherington (Ed.), *Handbook of child psychology: Vol 4. Socialization, personality, and social development* (pp. 1–102). New York: Wiley.

Martin, R. (1975). The socialization of children in China and Taiwan: An analysis of elementary school textbooks. *China Quarterly, 62,* 242–262.

Mead, M. (1928). *Coming of age in Samoa.* Chicago: University of Chicago Press.

Mitchell, R.E. & Lo, I. (1968). Implications of changes in family authority relations for the development of independence and assertiveness in Hong Kong. *Asian Survey, 8,* 309–322.

Natriello G. & Dornbusch, S.M. (1984). *Teacher evaluative standards and student effort.* New York: Longmans.

Noller, P. & Callan, V.J. (1991) *The adolescent in the family.* London: Routledge Kegan & Paul.

Ogbu, J.V. (1981). Origins of human competence: A cultural-ecological perspective. *Child Development, 52,* 413–429.

Patterson, G.R., DeBaryshe, B.D., & Ramsey, E. (1989). A developmental perspective on antisocial behaviour. *American Psychologist, 44,* 329–335.

Poole, M. (1986). Perspective on the aspiration, values, and achievements of Australian adolescents. In C. Bagley & G. Verma (Eds.), *Personality, cognition and values* (pp. 24–76). London: Macmillan.

Poortinga, Y.H. & Malpass, R.S. (1986). Making inferences from cross-cultural data. In W.J. Lonner & J.W. Berry (Eds.), *Field methods in cross-cultural research* (pp. 47–83). Newbury Park, CA: Sage.

Poortinga, Y.H. & Van de Vijver, F.J.R. (1987). Explaining cross-cultural differences: Bias analysis and beyond. *Journal of Cross-Cultural Psychology, 18*(3), 259–282.

Pulkkinen, L. (1982). Self-control and continuity from childhood to late adolescence. In P.B. Baltes & O.G. Brim, Jr. (Eds.), *Life-span development and behavior* (Vol. 4, pp. 64–102). New York: Academic Press.

Rohner, R.P. (1975). *They love me not: A worldwide study of the effects of parental acceptance and rejection.* New Haven: Human Relations Area Files Press.

Rokeach, M. (1973). *The nature of human values.* New York: Free Press.

Rosenthal, D. & Bornholt, L. (1988). Expectations about development in Greek and Anglo-Australian families. *Journal of Cross Cultural Psychology, 19*, 19–34.

Rosenthal, D.A. & Feldman, S.S. (1991a). The influence of perceived family and personal factors on self-reported school performance of Chinese and Western high school students. *Journal of Research in Adolescence, 1*, 135–154.

Rosenthal, D.A. & Feldman, S.S. (1991b). The acculturation of Chinese immigrants: Perceived effects on family functioning of length of residence in two cultural contexts. *Journal of Genetic Psychology, 151*, 493–514.

Rosenthal, D.A. & Feldman, S.S. (in press). Crossing the border: Chinese adolescents in the West. In S. Lau (Ed.), *Development of Chinese children and youth.*

Schwartz, S.H. & Bilsky, W. (1987). Toward a universal psychological structure of human values. *Journal of Personality and Social Psychology, 53*(3), 550–562.

Segall, M.H., Dasen, P.R., Berry, J.W., & Poortinga, Y.H. (1990). *Human behavior in global perspective: An introduction to cross-cultural psychology.* New York: Pergamon Press.

Spence, J.T. (1985). Achievement American style. *American Psychologist, 40*(12), 1285–1295.

Steinberg, L. & Silverberg, S. (1986). The vicissitudes of autonomy in early adolescence. *Child Development, 57*, 841–885.

Super, C. & Harkness, S. (1986). The developmental niche: A conceptualization at the interface of society and the individual. *International Journal of Behavioral Development, 9*, 545–570

Triandis, H.Y.C., Bontempo, R., Betancourt, H., Bond, M., Leung, K., Brenes, A., Georgas, J., Hui, C.H., & Marin, G. (1986). The measurement of the etic aspects of individualism and collectivism across cultures. *Australian Journal of Psychology, 38*(3), 257–267.

Triandis, H.C., Kashima, Y., Shimada, E., & Villareal, M. (1986). Acculturation indices as a means of confirming cultural differences. *International Journal of Psychology, 21*, 43–70.

U.S. Federal Bureau of Investigation. (1987). *Uniform crime reports for the United States 1986.* Washington, DC: U.S. Department of Justice, Uniform Crime Report Program.

Vernon, P.E. (1982). *The abilities and achievements of Orientals in North America.* New York: Academic Press.

West, D.J. (1982). *Delinquency: Its roots, careers and prospects.* Cambridge: Harvard University Press.

Whiting, B.B. (1976). The problem of the package variable. In K.F. Reigel & J.A. Meacham (Eds.), *The developing individual in a changing world* (pp. 303–309). The Hague, The Netherlands: Mouton.

Wolf, M. (1970). Child training and the family. In M. Freedman (Ed.), *Family and kinship in Chinese society* (pp. 37–62). Stanford, CA: Stanford University Press.

Wu, Y.H. (1966). *Cong Ren Lei Xue Guan Dian Kan Mu Qian Zhong Guo Er Tong De Yang Yu Wen Ti* (An anthropologist looks at Chinese child method). *Si Yu Yan (Thought and Word)*, *3*(6), 3–7.

Yang, K.S. (1970). Authoritarianism and evaluation of appropriateness of role behavior. *The Journal of Social Psychology*, *80*, 171–181.

Yang, K.S. (1986). Chinese personality and its change. In M.H. Bond (Ed.), *The psychology of the Chinese people* (pp. 106–170). Hong Kong: Oxford University Press.

7
Economic Hardship in Polish and German Families: Some Consequences for Adolescents

SABINE WALPER AND RAINER K. SILBEREISEN

During the past decade, an increasing number of families in Germany and other Western industrialized countries had to face unemployment, downward mobility, loss in one's own business or related causes of economic deprivation. In West Germany, the unemployment rate steadily climbed from 1979 to 1983, when it amounted to 9% and remained at this high level until recently (Heinelt, Wacker, & Welzer, 1989). Issues of a "new poverty" began to be raised during this period and recent analyses show that 25% of the population experienced poverty at least once during 1984 to 1989, 10% even during 3 or more years (Habich, Headey, & Krause, 1991). Since then, economic problems even increased, foremost— and quite dramatically—in the East German states (the former GDR; see Kieselbach & Voigt, 1992). Although the "old" West German states enjoyed a short term profit from the German reunion, it is obvious that even the West German states face lean years to come. Nevertheless, the consequences of this "Quiet New Depression" for family life and children's well-being have long been neglected and only recently started to be addressed by social research (McLoyd, 1989).

Even less is known regarding to what extent effects of financial loss on families in Western economies can be generalized to countries with a different political and economic system. Economic problems are even more evident in former socialist countries such as Poland, although unemployment was not yet an issue there at the time of our research (1985–86). Compared to income loss, the more prevalent and obvious factor in financial hardship is the high inflation rate, which leaves the families' regular income far behind climbing prices and, hence, causes a problematic mismatch between financial assets and needs. Dual-earner families with parents working overtime are the necessary standard to meet the requirements of daily family life. Furthermore, even if financial assets seem sufficient, the scarce supply of goods on the market causes many daily hassles for providers.

In the following, we address these issues in a comparative study designed to investigate the effects of economic deprivation on family relations and adolescents' personality development in West Berlin as well as Warsaw. Before the recent political changes, both cities belonged to countries with quite different economic and political macrostructures and thus provide distinct contextual conditions for studying financial hardship. Most notably, in Poland but not West Germany, we can take into consideration possible strain due to marked inflation, which might hit even those families that remain stable in their nominal income but that have to cope with higher prices. So far, the psychosocial consequences of inflation have only rarely been investigated (Caplovitz, 1979; Horwitz, 1984). In addition to the cross-national comparison, this study aims at replicating earlier findings based on a small, selective sample of Berlin families (Silbereisen, Walper, & Albrecht, 1990; Walper & Silbereisen, 1987) now employing a more conclusive longitudinal design.

Economic Hardship as Stressor

Based on concepts of family stress and coping (McCubbin, Joy, Cauble, Comeau, Patterson, & Needle, 1980; Voydanoff & Donnelly, 1988) our theoretical framework is largely derived from Elder's research on the impact of the Great Depression on family life, parent-child interaction, and children's personality development (Elder, 1974; Elder & Caspi, 1988; Elder, Liker, & Cross, 1984). Using longitudinal archive data from the Oakland Growth Study and the Berkeley Guidance Study, Elder and his colleagues could compare the respective developmental trajectories of children in deprived families that were hit by the Depression, losing 30% of their income or more, with their more advantaged counterparts from families that did not face a similar income reduction. Two themes of these studies are followed here: the first pertaining to the significant role of strained family relations in mediating the effects of income loss on adolescents' psychological well-being and problem-behavior; the second pointing to the moderating influence of adaptive potential, that is, of individual and family resources in coping with economic hardship.

In line with other research (Lempers, Clark-Lempers, & Simon, 1989; McLoyd, 1989; Siegal, 1984), the findings by Elder and colleagues showed that a substantial loss of family income leads to increasing emotional strain as well as problem-behavior in children, both being largely due to the more erratic, punitive and rejecting behavior of parents. Such increased problem behavior seems to reflect a rejection of parental authority and even the adults' normative system in general, which is perceived as withholding important developmental options. As coined in the concept of transgression proneness (Jessor & Jessor, 1977), such problem behavior is a frequent response in coping with the difficulties of status discrepancies and multiple developmental tasks during adolescence.

Family Cohesion as Mediator

Deprived adolescents' impaired well-being, as indicated in low self-esteem, and their increased problem behavior proneness might either reflect a direct impact of economic loss or follow from the strained relationships in the family system which undermine children's evaluation of self. Several studies show that economic deprivation and parental unemployment do indeed cause conflict and friction between parents, between parents and children, and in the overall quality of family relationships, which at least partly mediate children's reactions to financial hardship (e.g., Angell, 1965; Elder, Liker, & Cross, 1984; Flanagan, 1990; Komarovsky, 1940; Lempers, Clark-Lempers, & Simons, 1989; Skinner, Elder, & Conger, 1990). Our focus is on family cohesion, that is, the degree of mutual support and harmony among family members that plays an important role in children's psychosocial development (Maccoby & Martin, 1983; Schneewind, Beckmann, & Engfer, 1983). Just as with parental support within the parent-child subsystem of the family, overall family cohesion can be expected to encourage high self-esteem (Cooper, Holman, & Braithwaite, 1983; Coopersmith, 1967) and protect against the development of deviance (Bahr, 1979; Elliott, Huizinga, & Ageton, 1985).

According to the first hypothesis it is expected that economic deprivation has a negative impact on family cohesion. The second hypothesis assumes that impaired family cohesion mediates the effects of income loss on adolescents' view of self and transgression proneness.

Self-derogation as Mediator

Furthermore, the relation between impaired well-being and increased transgression proneness is addressed. As pointed out by research on deviance (Kaplan, 1980; Kaplan, Martin, & Robbins, 1984), a negative view of self may provide the motivational basis for developing deviant behavior. Adolescents who feel rejected by normative groups are likely to search for alternative—typically contranormative—opportunities to enhance their view of self. This should be particularly evident if we look at adolescents' proneness to act against common rules and norms instead of their behavior itself, since deviant *behavior* may not only help to compensate for self-derogation but may cause feelings of guilt and undermine one's view of self as well, particularly among those with previously high self-esteem (McCarthy & Hoge, 1984). Here, however, our focus is on adolescents' transgression *proneness*, the motivational antecedent to factual transgressions, which should rather be a consequence than antecedent of adolescents' view of self.

According to the third hypothesis, self-derogation contributes to transgression proneness. Hence, the increased transgression proneness of deprived adolescents should firstly be mediated through reduced family cohesion, and secondly, should at least partly be due to the negative impact of family cohesion on self-esteem. As to this latter mediating influence, our assumptions are less restrictive, allowing direct effects of family cohesion on adolescents' proneness to transgress in addition to the expected indirect effects being mediated through self-derogation.

Educational Resources

As to the families' adaptive potential, the moderating influence of coping resources on how families respond to economic deprivation is addressed in a comparison of families with either high or low parental education. Research concerning the impact of stressful life events has shown that the negative effects of such changing life conditions are more devastating in the lower socioeconomic strata (Cohn, 1978; Dohrenwend, 1973; Kessler, 1979; Liem & Liem, 1978), possibly due to the lower material, personal, and social problem-solving resources. Accordingly, our fourth hypothesis claims that particularly families with lower parental education show the expected negative association of income loss with family cohesion and adolescents' self-derogation and transgression proneness, whereas families with higher educational ressources should be largely unaffected.

Cross-national Generalizability

Finally, as to the comparison of German and Polish families, our interest is twofold. First, it is asked whether the reduction of financial assets rooted in inflation has similar psychosocial consequences as loss of income. Secondly, and more generally, the main question pertains to

TABLE 7.1. Percentages and frequencies of reported income change among German and Polish two-parent families.

		Income change					
		1 High loss	2 Moderate loss	3 Stable income	4 Moderate gain	5 High gain	
Samples							Total
Berlin (West)	%	4.1	4.3	81.5	8.1[a]	2.1[a]	100.1
	(n)	(26)	(27)	(516)	(51)	(13)	(633)
Warsaw	%	4.7	4.3	40.9	43.9[b]	6.2[a]	100.0
	(n)	(25)	(23)	(218)	(234)	(33)	(533)

Note: Comparison between German (G) and Polish families (P): group G1 versus P1 and P2 combined, group G2 versus P3, and group G3 versus P4 (passive gainers only); see text for further explanation.
[a] Not included.
[b] Comprised of active gainers (98) and passive gainers (136); only the latter included.

whether the model specified so far can be generalized to families of different sociocultural and economic backgrounds. In this respect, the study is explorative, since no particular expectations concerning economic-cultural differences are set forth. Hence, according to the fifth hypothesis the same results are expected in both cities.

Design of the Studies in Berlin and Warsaw

Sample

The German sample was drawn from the Berlin Youth Longitudinal Study, which was launched in 1982. The Polish data come from a related, highly similar longitudinal study on adolescents' development in Warsaw, which was started in 1985.[1]

The present analyses refer to two-parent families only, since single-parent families may be subject to different processes and strains following financial loss. Assessing changes in monthly net household income during the years prior to parents' interviews, we distinguished loss of more than 25%, loss of more than 5% and up to 25%, changes of up to ±5%, gain of more than 5% and up to 25%, and finally gain of more than 25%. The distribution of income change among German and Polish two-parent families is given in Table 7.1.

According to our focus on the effects of economic deprivation, families reporting any gain in income (of more than 5%) were excluded from the German target sample. Among the remaining 569 families, boys and girls were about equally represented. Adolescents' mean age was 13.2 years ($SD = 1.6$), ranging from 11 to 17 years. As can be seen, high and moderate income loss was reported by about 8% of the families. Depending on the number of variables included in the analyses, the actual sample size varies. Complete data on all measures were available for 438 families.

In order to account for effects of inflation in the Polish study and provide an appropriate comparison group of stable income families, only families with high income gains of more than 25% were excluded. Such high gains exceeded the inflation rate at the time of the assessment while moderate gains did not and this merely compensated the loss of buying

---

[1] The aim of the Berlin Youth Longitudinal Study (Silbereisen & Eyferth, 1985) was to analyze the role of problem behavior in normal adolescent development. Risk and protective factors within the individual and within family, work, and leisure contexts have been investigated in Berlin (West Germany) and Warsaw (Poland). By 1989, one of the cohorts in Berlin (in all three per city) had been followed up once every year from age 11 to 18 (for short technical reference see Verdonik & Sherrod, 1984).

power due to inflation.[2] Among families who were reported to receive moderate gains (about 44% of the Warsaw sample compared to only 8% in Berlin) it seemed reasonable to distinguish between those who received a raise in wage without changes in the parents' employment ("passive gainers"), and those who actively increased their income by working more or changing to a better paid position ("active gainers"). The latter were excluded from testing the hypotheses since changes in parental employment might have additional effects on family life. Among the remaining 402 families, about half of the target adolescent children were male, half female. Adolescents' ages ranged from 9 to 17 years, with a mean of 13.4 years ($SD = 2.1$). Complete data on all variables were available for 302 of the Warsaw families.

For both samples, adolescents' data were drawn from two consecutive questionnaire assessments that were conducted during school hours in fall/winter (Berlin: 1983 and 1984, second and third wave; Warsaw: 1985 and 1986, first and second wave). For convenience, the first assessment is abbreviated by T(ime) 1, the second by T(ime) 2. Parental data, including information on income loss and family cohesion, were gathered by mailed questionnaires consisting of a household questionnaire as well as separate parts for mother and father. The parental assessment was conducted in spring between both adolescents' interviews (Berlin: 1984, second wave; Warsaw: 1986, first wave).

Variables

Changes in Family Income

In both studies, parents were asked to indicate changes in family net income during the year prior to the assessment (see Table 7.1). In the Berlin study, the sample was comprised of families with high or moderate loss, and of families with stable income. In the Warsaw study, families with high and moderate income loss were pooled, which also provides three comparison groups: families with income loss over 5%, those with no change in income, and families with moderate "passive" income gain which compensates for the inflation.[3] While no change in income implies

---

[2] As of 1985, the first measurement wave of the Polish study, unofficial estimates of the annual inflation rate were about 25%. By now, this figure has increased rapidly.

[3] In the Warsaw study reasons given for the reported income change could be used to resolve unclear cases. Families that indicated financial loss due to inflation were recoded as holding stable income. Contradictory cases were excluded from the analyses. More than a third of the cases reporting income loss indicated loss of employment of either parent, including retirement or vacation for child care. Active gain in income mostly came from adopting additional work rather than changing to a better paid position.

deprivation through inflation, moderate gain can be considered to yield stable income in terms of purchasing power. As mentioned before, "active gainers" were excluded from testing the hypothesis. They were considered, however, in analyses on the relation between reported income change and parents' occupational situation.

Educational Resources

The level of paternal schooling was used to assess high and low educational ressources. Among the Berlin families, both groups were of almost equal size, distinguishing (a) families in which the father had finished not more than the lower track of schooling (comprising 9 years *Hauptschule* n = 292), and (b) all remaining families with higher paternal school education (*Realschule* or *Gymnasium* n = 263). As might be expected, high income loss was more likely to hit families with lower paternal education (6.5% vs. 1.9%), but since the higher educated experienced somewhat more often moderate loss (7.6% vs. 2.1%), the same percentage of stable income families was given for both groups (χ^2 = 15.90, df = 2,555, $p < .001$).

For the Polish sample, fathers' matura (highest degree of schooling) had to be used as cutting point to dichotomize the sample, since Polish parents have rather high education. About 60% of the families formed the group high in education (n = 311), the remaining 40% were considered holding low education (n = 187). As in the Berlin sample, changes in family income were not equally distributed among educational groups. Families with low education were more likely to hold nominally stable income than families with higher education (56.7% vs. 36.0%), while the latter were more likely to be compensated for the high inflation rate by regular wage increases (33.1% vs. 17.6%). Both groups did not differ in the relative frequency of income loss or active gain (χ^2 = 22.79, df = 3,498, $p < .001$).

Psychosocial Variables

For the Berlin sample, *family cohesion* was assessed by parents' ratings on seven items, selected from the German adaptation (Engfer, Schneewind, & Hinderer, 1978) of Moos's (1974) family environment scales, to tap several aspects of positive emotional relations: for example, mutual support, expressiveness, egalitarian decision making, and lack of conflict. Of the four items for mothers and the three items for fathers, two were identical for both parents. The remaining items differed slightly in wording but came from the same subscales. Because of the high correlation between mothers' and fathers' mean scores ($r = .62, p < .001$), both were averaged yielding couple scores.

For the Polish sample, family cohesion was measured by mothers' and fathers' reports on 12 items, 6 answered by each parent. With few additions, the same items as in the Berlin study were used. The response format was identical. Given that mothers' and fathers' reports were highly correlated ($r = .51$, $p < .001$), both scores were again averaged.

Adolescents' *self-derogation* was measured by the same four-item scale in both the Berlin and Warsaw study taken from Kaplan's scale, which is similar to the longer Rosenberg instrument (Kaplan, 1980; see Silbereisen, Reitzle, & Zank, 1986).

Transgression proneness was indicated by four items that were formulated according to Jessor's concept (Jessor & Jessor, 1977; Silbereisen, Reitzle, & Zank, 1986).

The wording of the items and the internal consistencies (Cronbach's alpha) of the scales are given in the *Appendix*. Taking into account the small number of items per scale, the coefficients are acceptable (Nunnally, 1967). Scale scores were computed by averaging the item ratings (all ranging from *not at all* = 0 to *very much true* = 3).

While the variances of these variables did not differ between the German and the Polish sample, mean levels did. These differences were most pronounced concerning adolescents' self-derogation (*t*-tests): Warsaw adolescents clearly held a less favorable view of self than adolescents in West Berlin, among higher educated families as well as among lower educated families. Furthermore, at T1 Warsaw adolescents indicated lower transgression proneness than Berlin adolescents. Family cohesion could not be compared due to scale differences.

Risk Factors for Income Loss

Descriptive analyses were carried out for each sample on the relation of income loss to parents' occupational position and employment status. This should clarify whether reported income loss was associated with different risk factors in both countries, or whether families of lower socioeconomic standing and educational ressources were similarly more at risk for financial hardship in Berlin as well as Warsaw.

Table 7.2 shows both parents' occupational situation as related to income loss in the Berlin sample. According to the results of Chi-square–tests, fathers' but not mothers' occupational position differed significantly according to financial loss, with workers and self-employed being more prevalent among high losers. Families with income loss were also less likely to have a full-time employed father, while mothers' employment status was not related to income change. This suggests that for families in Berlin, financial loss is more likely to be attributed to fathers' occupational situation than to mothers' employment.

For Polish families, this differential "responsibility" for income change was not evident. As can be seen in Table 7.3, significant differences in the

TABLE 7.2. Parents' occupational and employment status by income change for the Berlin sample (in column %).

Status	Income change			Total	chi²-test[a]
	High loss	Moderate loss	Stable income		
Occupation father					12.99**
Worker	42.9	25.9	26.9	27.4	
Employee	19.0	41.7	42.1	41.2	
Civil servant	4.8	20.8	23.1	22.3	
Self-employed	33.3	12.5	7.9	9.1	
(n)	(21)	(24)	(484)	(529)	
Occupation mother					7.00
Housewife	21.7	24.0	37.1	35.8	
Worker	21.7	8.0	13.0	13.2	
Employee	47.8	44.0	42.2	42.5	
Civil servant	0.0	12.0	3.5	3.7	
Self-employed	8.7	12.0	4.3	4.8	
(n)	(23)	(25)	(491)	(539)	
Employment father					20.74***
Not/part-time	27.3	23.1	6.4	7.9	
Full-time	72.7	76.9	93.6	92.1	
(n)	(22)	(26)	(499)	(543)	
Employment mother					.71
Not	56.5	37.5	40.8	41.4	
Part-time	26.1	41.7	36.0	35.9	
Full-time	17.4	20.8	23.1	22.8	
(n)	(23)	(24)	(480)	(527)	

[a] Families with high and moderate income loss were pooled.
*** $p < .001$; ** $p < .01$; * $p < .05$

distribution of fathers' as well as mothers' occupational position were found for the four groups of income change. Employees were over-represented in families with income gain, while those who experienced loss or stable income were more likely to be headed by a craftsman or worker. Concerning parents' employment participation, mothers' work hours per week mattered even more for reported income change than fathers'. In families with income loss, mothers working less than full-time were much more prevalent than in families with stable income or gain, while overtime employment was most prevalent among active gainers. Neither fathers' nor mothers' work schedule was significantly related to income change (data not presented).

In sum, lower occupational position and lower employment partici-pation is a risk factor of income loss in Berlin as well as in Warsaw, but women's employment seems to be more relevant to the families' financial situation in the Polish than in the German sample.

TABLE 7.3. Parents' occupational and employment status by income change for the Warsaw sample (in column %).

			Income change			
				Gain		
Status	Loss	Stable	Passive	Active	Total	chi²-test[a]
Occupation father						35.24***
Craftsman	26.2	18.6	9.2	11.7	15.3	
Worker	23.8	41.2	24.4	26.6	32.1	
Employee	45.2	37.3	64.9	60.6	50.3	
Self-employed[a]	4.8	2.9	1.5	1.1	2.3	
(n)	(42)	(204)	(131)	(94)	(471)	
Occupation mother						36.56***
Craftsman	13.3	8.5	1.5	5.3	6.4	
Worker	20.0	24.9	12.7	18.9	19.9	
Employee	37.8	48.8	73.1	65.3	57.7	
Self-employed[a]	28.9	17.8	12.7	10.5	16.0	
(n)	(45)	(213)	(134)	(95)	(487)	
Employment father						15.49
Not	11.4	5.9	2.3	3.4	4.9	
Part-time	4.5	1.5	3.1	0.0	1.9	
Full-time	56.8	67.6	72.7	79.8	70.3	
Overtime	27.3	25.0	21.9	16.9	22.8	
(n)	(44)	(204)	(128)	(89)	(465)	
Employment mother						29.63***
Not	27.3	16.3	9.9	9.3	14.1	
Part-time	9.1	2.4	2.3	5.2	3.5	
Full-time	61.4	73.2	72.5	64.9	70.3	
Overtime	2.3	8.1	15.3	20.6	12.1	
(n)	(44)	(209)	(131)	(97)	(481)	

[a] Including housekeepers.
*** $p < .001$, ** $p < .01$, * $p < .05$

Impact of Income Change on Family and Adolescents

Income change and family cohesion were assessed in the time between the two measurements of the adolescent variables. This design allows us to study effects of differences in family income change and level of family cohesion on change in self-derogation and transgression proneness. As only one assessment was available for family cohesion, its relation with income change should not be misrepresented as indicating an impact on *change* in family cohesion.

Statistical Model

Basic to the test of our hypotheses is the following path model, as suggested by the mediation hypotheses: First, income change is predicted to relate to lower family cohesion which, in turn, relates to increased transgression proneness, directly and/or mediated through increased self-derogation. Second, transgression proneness and self-derogation need to be controlled for their levels at the previous measurement in order to assess change in these variables as caused by income change and family cohesion. Third, reciprocal effects between family cohesion and adolescents' transgression proneness are taken into account by allowing a path between earlier transgression proneness and parents' later report on family cohesion. Fourth, self-derogation and transgression proneness are controlled for differences in adolescents' age and gender (coded as 0 = male, 1 = female).

In order to represent the three categories of income change adequately in the path analyses, income change was effect-coded (Cohen & Cohen, 1975). The two dummy variables allow one to estimate effects of high income loss (vs. moderate loss or stable income) and those of stable income (vs. loss of any size) independently of each other.[4]

The path analyses were conducted using LISREL (Jöreskog & Sörbom, 1981). In testing the expected mediation effects as to how they differ for both educational groups, the most restrictive null hypothesis was assumed: Supposing that the identical model fits the data of both groups, we restricted the corresponding path coefficients to being of the same size (invariance constraint).

Results for Berlin Families

Figure 7.1 shows the resulting common model for Berlin families with either low or high paternal education. Standardized path coefficients are given for significant (solid lines) as well as nonsignificant paths (broken lines). This model yielded a good fit to the data ($\chi^2 = 48.38$, $df = 45$, $p = .34$) indicating that the same pattern and size of the paths can be assumed for high as well as low educated families.

The paths between the two assessments of self-derogation and transgression proneness were considerably high (βs = .49 and .54, $ps < .001$), indicating a fair degree of stability for these aspects of adolescents' personality. As might be expected, girls reported higher self-derogation and lower transgression proneness than boys, and the latter gender difference seemed to be accentuated across time as indicated by an additional lagged effect for the second wave (all $ps < .01$). Older adolescents showed an advantage concerning their self-esteem only at T2

---

[4] The dummy variable labeled *high income loss* received a score of 1 for the most extreme category of loss, 0 for the opposite category, and −1 for the middle category. The respective scores of the dummy labeled *stable* income were 0, 1, and −1. All Lisrel analyses were run on the covariance matrices. Concerning age and gender differences, nonsignificant paths were set to zero in order to achieve a better adjustment of the model.

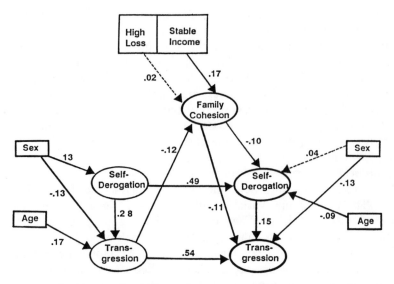

FIGURE 7.1. Berlin sample: Effects of economic deprivation on family cohesion and change in adolescents' self-derogation and transgression proneness.

$(p < .05)$, whereas their higher transgression proneness was evident at T1 $(p < .001)$.

Family Cohesion as Mediator

According to Hypothesis 1, income loss should relate to lower family cohesion. Indeed, families who held stable income were better off, reporting higher cohesion than families with either moderate or high income loss ($\beta = .17$, $p < .05$). High income loss did not seem to have any additional specific influence on family relations.

In line with Hypothesis 2, low family cohesion, in turn, contributed to increased self-derogation ($\beta = -.10$, $p < .05$) as well as transgression proneness ($\beta = -.11$, $p < .01$). Furthermore, our expectation concerning the interplay between family cohesion and adolescents' transgression proneness received support by the data: Higher levels of previous transgression proneness also seem to undermine positive family relationships ($\beta = -.12$, $p < .01$). Of course, conclusive evidence would require additional information on previous family cohesion.

Self-derogation as Mediator

Hypothesis 3 claimed that the effects of family cohesion on transgression proneness are at least partly due to the mediating influence of adolescents' self-derogation. This hypothesis is supported by a significant path between self-derogation and transgression proneness at T1 as well as T2 (T2: $\beta =$

.15, $p < .001$). Thus, family cohesion influences transgression proneness directly as well as indirectly through its association with change in adolescents' view of self.

Father's Education as Moderator

Finally returning to Hypothesis 4, as already mentioned, there was no indication of a stronger effect of income loss on family cohesion, adolescents' self-derogation, or transgression proneness among lower educated families. The only difference pertained to an age effect: that older adolescents reported a more favorable view of self at Wave 2 particularly holds for those from higher educated families. Nevertheless, the common model can be assumed for both groups and Hypothesis 4 has to be rejected.

To sum up, no substantial difference between families holding either high or low education resources could be observed while the mediation hypotheses found support. Financial loss indeed seems to undermine family cohesion which, in turn, contributes to adolescents' impaired view of self as well as their increased transgression proneness. Finally, self-derogation relates to adolescents' proneness to act against common rules and norms and hereby mediates some of the impact of family cohesion on change in transgression proneness.

Results for Warsaw Families

In the same vein, the model was tested comparing Polish families low and high in paternal education. As mentioned before, the sample of the Warsaw study differs from that of the Berlin study concerning the inclusion of families with passive (nominal) income gain, which are considered to hold stable income in terms of purchasing power. As in the Berlin study the data were effect-coded to estimate effects of income change.

The common model for both educational groups can be seen in Figure 7.2. Again, this model already yielded an adequate fit to the data ($\chi^2 = 57.23$, $df = 45$, $p = .10$), indicating no substantial differences in the pattern of relations between both groups.

The size of the stability paths for self-derogation and transgression proneness were similar to the German sample (βs = .43 and .55, respectively, both $ps < .001$). We also found the same gender difference in self-derogation, with females indicating a less favorable view of self than males, most pronounced at the later wave ($p < .01$). In contrast to the German sample, Polish adolescents did indicate higher self-derogation with increasing age ($p < .05$). As to transgression proneness, younger adolescents in general and females were less inclined to act against common rules and norms ($ps < .001$).

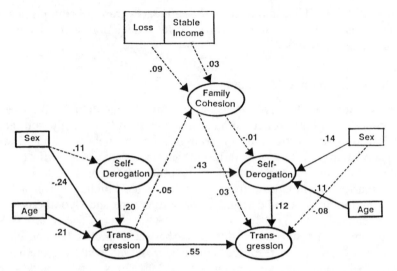

FIGURE 7.2. Warsaw sample: Effects of economic deprivation on family cohesion and change in adolescents' self-derogation and transgression proneness.

Family Cohesion as Mediator

Nonetheless, our expectations concerning the role of family cohesion as mediator between income loss and adolescents' outcome variables are not met by the data. In contrast to the Berlin sample, family cohesion was neither significantly affected by income change nor did it have any impact on adolescents' change in self-derogation. Also, parents' report about the quality of family relations was unrelated to their children's previous transgression proneness. Thus, Hypotheses 1 and 2 were not confirmed.

Self-derogation as Mediator

As a consequence, Hypothesis 3 does not quite hold for the Polish families. Since there was no impact of family cohesion on adolescents' view of self, self-derogation did not qualify as mediator between income change and strained family relations on the one hand, and adolescents' transgression proneness on the other hand. Regarding the latter link, however, a negative view of self was related to increased transgression proneness not only among German, but among Polish adolescents as well ($\beta = .12, p < .01$).

No direct impact of income change on adolescents' self-derogation or their proneness to engage in transgressions was suggested by the analyses. Thus, just as family cohesion did not seem to play any role in adolescents' functioning, financial changes per se did not emerge as any more important, either. Furthermore, as in the Berlin sample, no substantial group differences between high and low educated families were indicated. Hence, Hypothesis 4 must be rejected for Berlin as well as for Warsaw families.

Conclusions

To sum up, these findings suggest that viewing income change as a stressor to family life and adolescents' development does not similarly hold in Warsaw as in West Berlin. Among families in Berlin, income loss indeed seems to contribute to family discord and friction which, in turn, tends to reduce adolescents' well-being and their acceptance of rules and standards representing the normative adult world. However, no such predictive effects of income change could be observed among the Warsaw families. More specifically, economic deprivation neither seems to correlate with the mutual support and cohesion among Polish families, nor does this aspect of family climate have any substantial relation to change in adolescents' self-derogation or transgression proneness.

Family Relations and Adolescent Outcomes

In evaluating these findings, we first compare the evidence from the Berlin study to the results of our earlier research. Earlier analyses on a subsample of the first wave of the Berlin study utilized a different design (Walper & Silbereisen, 1987). The higher risk of socially disadvantaged families to experience income loss was accounted for by individually matching deprived families with families reporting stable income on factors related to parents' education, occupational position, and employment status.

The present results differ from our earlier ones in two respects: First, to assume that the impact of income loss on adolescents' self-derogation or transgression proneness is mediated through impaired family relations proved justified here. In the earlier study, however, it received only partial support. In addition to the mediating path, a direct effect of high loss on adolescents' self-esteem was evident among lower educated families. In line with other findings (Lempers, Clark-Lempers, & Simons, 1989), adolescents partly seemed to react to economic deprivation *per se*, irrespective of family discord and friction. While the present study emphasizes the import of cohesive relations in coping with economic deprivation, any additional direct effects of financial hardship may simply have been precluded by the relatively low incidence of income loss.

Second, in addition to the mediating influence of self-derogation, a direct impact of harmonious family relations on transgression proneness was confirmed in the present study, which was not evident in the matched sample. This suggests that the role of self-derogation as mediator between family cohesion and adolescents' transgression proneness has previously been overestimated. Due to the matching procedure, the earlier sample was more homogeneous, overrepresenting families with lower socio-economic standing in general and those with income loss in particular. Including youth from more diverse families may now have increased our chances to see different pathways to adolescents' proneness to break norms and rules.

Turning to the Polish findings, we evidence quite a different picture: Family cohesion—which was just seen to be quite relevant for Berlin adolescents' transgression proneness—showed no impact on adolescents' self-derogation or transgression proneness among Warsaw youth. As a first possible explanation, family cohesion may only seem irrelevant because Polish parents might be more likely to underreport family friction and instead draw a more favorable picture of their family. Such an attempt could fit to the traditionally high family orientation in Poland (Ziolkowsky, 1988).

Furthermore, using parents' instead of adolescents' reports to indicate family cohesion may play a role. It is well known that children's own views of family interactions and relationships are more predictive of their personality development than information from other sources (e.g., Schneewind et al., 1983). In fact, the expected relationship between family cohesion and self-derogation as well as transgression proneness can be found for Polish youth, too, if family cohesion is assessed by adolescents' reports (Walper & Wiszniewska, 1988). This suggests that Polish family members hold more divergent views on their family life than German families, perhaps due to Polish parents' longer working hours and adolescents' higher participation in institutional activities.

Why is Economic Deprivation Irrelevant for Cohesion in Polish Families?

In considering why financial loss did not show any influence on Warsaw families, several possible explanations should be mentioned. First, since the Polish economy has been very unstable and troubled by considerable scarcity in supply, changes in family income may not really be predictive of changes in household management. If even high income does not assure that basic family needs can be met, a loss of income should not have any noticeable further impact on consumption patterns. The necessary cut-down on expenditure that has been found to contribute substantially to marital conflict, impaired parenting, and distressed re-actions in other studies (Conger et al., 1989; Elder, 1974; Jahoda, Lazarsfeld, & Zeisel, 1933; Lempers et al., 1989) may not follow from deprivation in Poland, thus rendering family cohesion unaffected.

Other data from the present study, however, indicate that reported income change indeed relates to economic disadvantage and adaptive changes in the household economy of Polish families. As can be seen from the means and the results of multivariate analyses of variance shown in Tables 7.4 and 7.5, income loss significantly goes along with lower family income, with the families' less favorable perception of their socio-economic standing, and with higher financial problems. Moreover, reduced income also relates to adaptations in the household, that is, a general cut-down on the generosity of housekeeping as well as specific reductions of expenditure such as for presents and vacations. Even a good education for one's adolescent child seems less favorable if the family has to cope with lower income in Warsaw.

Of course, father's education also matters for the family's economic situation, but less so concerning *changes* in household strategies—well in line with the expectation that the level of schooling contributes to stable differences in economic assets.

Despite sufficient evidence that Polish family life changes with income loss, the necessary cut-down on expenditures does not seem to threaten mutual support and cohesion in the family system. Rather, Polish families appear to be less vulnerable to negative effects of economic loss than German families, either because of differences in conditions and consequences of income loss itself, or because of more efficient coping strategies.

TABLE 7.4. Effects of income change and father's education on Polish families' income, perceived economic position, financial problems, and changes in the household: F-values for multivariate and univariate analyses of variance.

	Effects		
Variables	Income change	Father's education	Interaction
	Multivariate		
All	3.33***	5.40***	ns
	Univariate		
Family income	12.91***	30.07***	ns
Self-rating; Poor/wealthy	6.46***	13.88***	2.89*
Mismatch; Income/needs	ns	5.37*	ns
Financial problems	6.56***	ns	ns
Changes in			
— Generosity of houshold	5.33**	ns	ns
— Regular expenditure	ns	ns	ns
— Christmas presents	4.01*	ns	ns
— Summer vacation	7.45***	ns	ns
— Fashionable clothing	5.32**	ns	3.28*
— Educational aspirations	3.80*	ns	ns

Note: Analyzed were 431 families (all except high gainers); education dichotomized with/without matura.
*** $p < .001$; ** $p < .01$; * $p < .05$

TABLE 7.5. Family income, perceived economic position, financial problems, and changes in the houshold by income change and father's education: Means.

| | Income change × Father's education | | | | | | | | |
| | Loss | | Stable | | Passive Gain | | Active Gain | | Total |
	Low	High	Low	High	Low	High	Low	High	
Family income[a]	22.3	34.0	28.7	33.8	33.3	41.7	35.5	40.5	35.0
Poor/wealthy	3.69	5.52	4.93	5.05	5.03	5.57	5.61	5.96	5.27
Income/needs[b]	1.46	1.86	1.69	1.80	1.70	2.06	1.89	1.91	1.84
Financ. probl.	2.00	1.90	1.40	1.59	1.33	1.39	1.18	1.33	1.46
Changes in[c]									
— Generosity of household	.77	.76	1.20	1.16	1.40	1.33	1.43	1.42	1.24
— Regular expenditure	3.69	3.52	3.61	3.69	3.73	3.64	3.79	3.77	3.68
— Christmas presents	.92	1.05	1.16	1.06	1.27	1.36	1.50	1.46	1.23
— Summer vacation	.54	1.14	1.50	1.35	1.37	1.73	1.79	1.75	1.51
— Fashionable clothing	.54	1.33	1.21	1.00	1.53	1.39	1.32	1.49	1.25
— Educational aspirations	2.62	2.66	2.56	2.16	2.30	2.33	3.00	2.46	2.42
(n)	(13)	(21)	(87)	(105)	(30)	(90)	(28)	(57)	(431)

[a] In thousand zloti.
[b] Income matches less than 50% of needs = 1, more than 50% of needs = 2, complete match = 3, income exceeds needs = 4.
[c] Ratings 0 through 4; stable = 2, reduced < 2, increased >2.

Several factors could explain the Polish families' lower vulnerability. First of all, conflict-prone changes in the family role system, which contribute to discord and tension among deprived German families, may not apply to Polish families, since income reductions—and even more so inflation—are as likely to affect mothers' as fathers' earnings. In earlier studies, the unemployed husband's "failure" as provider was shown to lead to his loss of status and prestige within the deprived family. If he cannot fulfill his role-obligations, the mother may take over more responsibilities as well as privileges (Bakke, 1969; Elder, 1974; Komarovsky, 1940). Previous analyses from the Berlin Youth Longitudinal Study (Walper, 1988) support that mother's increasing influence on family decision making provides a mediating link between financial hardship and impaired family cohesion.

Among Polish families, however, fathers are not more likely to lose income than mothers. Hence, economic deprivation should leave each parent's status unchanged. Further analyses will have to show whether financial hardship leads to a more focal position of mothers not only in German but in Polish families as well.

Furthermore, given the long "tradition" of financial shortage in Poland, previous experience may have fostered the development of efficient coping strategies which prevent psychological and social stress reactions. As noted by Cavan (1959) unemployment has been rather "a crisis for the common man" that is, a problem for those who are unfamiliar with financial hardship and occupational loss. In addition to the greater adaptability of experienced losers, the particular life circumstances of Polish families may have facilitated coping strategies that help to deal with conflict and tension. As mentioned above, the higher rate of maternal employment and more overtime employment of both parents suggest that family members spend less time together than members of German families. If contact is thus reduced, conflict and strained interaction may be less reinforced and hence less persistent. At the same time, families may also have been forced to develop more compromising coping strategies in dealing with intrafamily strain and preventing friction, since the ultimate escape from conflict-ridden, disharmonious families is much harder in Poland than in Germany. Even if an unhappy, hostile couple finally gets divorced, the family is often forced to stay in the same appartment due to housing problems.

Finally, Polish families may differ from their German counterparts because of the explanations available. The strong inflation suggests an external attribution of financial hardship as being caused by the political and economic structure within the country but not by individual failure. In general, attributing unemployment to external, macroeconomic factors— as it is most likely in situations of mass unemployment—seems to mitigate psychological strain (Hill, 1978; Ray & McLoyd, 1986). If, however, other family members start to blame the unemployed for family hardship, the stage is being set for tension, conflict, and even family crisis (Bakke, 1969). The widespread economic problems in Poland suggest that external causes play a more substantial role in individual and family accounts of financial hardship than is the case in West Germany.

Clearly, these findings and interpretations call for further evidence. However, a first important step has been made in showing that the meaning of economic deprivation has to be seen in the larger social context, in which such changing living conditions of families are embedded.

Acknowledgment. Parts of the results discussed in this chapter were presented at the Tenth Biennial Meetings of the International Society for the Study of Behavioural Development, Jyväskylä, Finland, July 9–13, 1989. Special thanks go to Agata Wiszniewska (Polish Academy of Sciences, Warsaw), who supervised the data gathering in Warsaw and helped with fruitful discussions, and to Helfried T. Albrecht (University of Giessen), who conducted the LISREL analyses. Last but not least, we would like to thank all families and their adolescent children who took part in the investigations.

References

Angell, R.C. (1965). *The family encounters the Depression.* Gloucester, MA: Peter Smith. (Original work published in 1936)

Bahr, S.J. (1979). Family determinants and effects of deviance. In W.R. Burr, R. Hill, F.I. Nye, & I.L. Reiss (Eds.), *Contemporary theories about the family* (Vol. 1, pp. 615–643). New York: Free Press.

Bakke, E.W. (1969). *Citizens without work. A study of the effects of unemployment upon the workers' social relations and proctices.* Hamden, CN: Archon Books.

Caplovitz, D. (1979). *Making ends meet: How families cope with inflation and recession.* Beverly Hills: Sage.

Cavan, R.S. (1959). Unemployment—crisis of the common man. *Marriage and Family Living, 21,* 139–146.

Cohen, J. & Cohen, P. (1975). *Applied multiple regression/correlation analysis for the behavioral sciences.* New York: Wiley.

Cohn, R.M. (1978). The effects of employment status change on self-attitudes. *Social Psychology, 41,* 81–93.

Conger, R.D., Elder, G.H., Jr., Lorenz, F.O., Simons, R.L., Whitbeck, L.B., Huck, S., & Melby, J.N. (1989). *Linking economic hardship to marital quality and instability.* Unpublished manuscript. Ames, IA: Iowa State University.

Cooper, J.E., Holman, J., & Braithwaite, V.A. (1983). Self-esteem and family cohesion: The child's perspective and adjustment. *Journal of Marriage and the Family, 45,* 153–159.

Coopersmith, S. (1967). *The antecedents of self-esteem.* New York: W.H. Freeman.

Dohrenwend, B.S. (1973). Social status and stressful life-events. *Journal of Personality and Social Psychology, 28,* 225–235.

Elder, G.H., Jr. (1974). *Children of the Great Depression: Social change in life experience.* Chicago: University of Chicago Press.

Elder, G.H., Jr. & Caspi, A. (1988). Human development and social change: An emerging perspective on the life course. In N. Bolger, A. Caspi, G. Downey, & M. Moorehouse (Eds.), *Persons in context: developmental processes* (pp. 77–113). New York: Cambridge University Press.

Elder, G.H., Jr., Liker, J.K., & Cross, C.E. (1984). Parent-child behavior in the Great Depression: Life course and intergenerational influences. In P.B. Baltes & G.O. Brim (Eds.), *Life-span development and behavior* (Vol. 6, pp. 109–158). New York: Academic Press.

Elliott, D.S., Huizinga, D., & Ageton, S. (1985). *Explaining delinquency and drug use*. Beverly Hills: Sage.

Engfer, A., Schneewind, K.A., & Hinderer, J. (1978). *Zur faktoriellen Struktur der Familien-Klima-Skalen nach R.H. Moos* [The factorial structure of the family climate scales according to R.H. Moos] (Technical Report No. 17 from the EKB-project). University of Munich.

Flanagan, C.A. (1990). Families and schools in hard times. In C. McLoyd & C.A. Flanagan (Eds.), *Economic stress. Effects on family life and child development. New Directions for Child Development, 46*, pp. 7–26.

Habich, R., Heady, B., & Krause, P. (1991). Armut im Reichtum—Ist die Bundesrepublik Deutschland eine Zwei-Drittel-Gesellschaft? [Poverty in wealth?—Is the Federal Republic of Germany a two-thirds-society?]. In R. Rendtel & G. Wagner (Eds.), *Zur Einkommensdynamik in Deutschland seit 1984* (pp. 487–508). Frankfurt; New York: Campus.

Heinelt, H., Wacker, A., & Welzer, H. (1989). Arbeitslosigkeit in den 70er und 80er Jahren—Beschäftigungskrise und ihre soziale Folgen [Unemployment in the 70s and 80s—employment crises and their social consequences]. *Archiv für Sozialgeschichte, 27*, 259–317.

Hill, J. (1978). The psychological impact of unemployment. *New Society, 19*, 116–120.

Horwitz, A.V. (1984). The economy and social pathology. *Annual Review of Sociology, 10*, 95–119.

Jahoda, M., Lazarsfeld, P.F., & Zeisel, H. (1933). *Die Arbeitslosen von Marienthal. Ein soziographischer Versuch* [The unemployed of Marienthal]. Leipzig: S. Hirzel.

Jessor, R. & Jessor, S.L. (1977). *Problem behavior and psychosocial development: A longitudinal study of youth*. New York: Academic Press.

Jöreskog, K.G. & Sörbom, D. (1981). *LISREL V: Analysis of linear structural relationships by maximum likelihood and least squares methods*. Uppsala: University of Uppsala.

Kaplan, H.B. (1980). *Deviant behavior in defense of self*. New York: Academic Press.

Kaplan, H.B., Martin, S.S., & Robbins, C. (1984). Pathways to adolescent drug use: Self-derogation, peer influence, weakening of social controls, and early substance use. *Journal of Health and Social Behavior, 25*, 270–289.

Kessler, R.C. (1979). Stress, social status, and psychological distress. *Journal of Health and Social Behavior, 20*, 259–272.

Kieselbach, T. & Voigt, P. (Eds.). (1992). *Systemumbruch, Arbeitslosigkeit und individuelle Bewältigung in der Ex-DDR (System transformation, unemployment, and individual coping in the former GDR)*. Weinheim: Deutscher Studien Verlag.

Komarovsky, M. (1940). *The unemployed man and his family: The effect of unemployment upon the status of the man in fifty-nine families*. New York: Dryden.

Lempers, J.D., Clark-Lempers, D., & Simons, R.L. (1989). Economic hardship, parenting, and distress in adolescence. *Child Development*, *60*, 25–39.

Liem, R. & Liem, J. (1978). Social class and mental illness reconsidered: The role of economic stress and social support. *Journal of Health and Social Behavior*, *19*, 139–156.

Maccoby, E.E. & Martin, J.A. (1983). Socialization in the context of the family: Parent-child interaction. In E.M. Hetherington (Ed.), *Handbook of child psychology*: Vol. 4. *Socialization, personality, and social development* (pp. 1–101). New York: Wiley.

McCarthy, J.D. & Hoge, D.R. (1984). The dynamics of self-esteem and delinquency. *American Journal of Sociology*, *90*, 396–410.

McCubbin, H.I., Joy, C.B., Cauble, A.E., Comeau, J.K., Patterson, J.M., & Needle, R.H. (1980). Family stress and coping: A decade review. *Journal of Marriage and the Family*, *42*, 855–871.

McLoyd, V.C. (1989). Socialization and development in a changing economy. The effects of paternal job and income loss on children. *American Psychologist*, *44*, 293–302.

Moos, R.H. (1974). *Family Evironment Scale (FES). Preliminary manual*. Palo Alto: Social Ecology Laboratory, Department of Psychiatry, Stanford University.

Nunnally, J.C. (1967). *Psychometric theory*. New York: McGraw Hill.

Ray, S.A. & McLoyd, V.D. (1986). Fathers in hard times. The impact of unemployment and poverty on paternal and marital relations. In M. Lamb (Ed.), *The father's role* (pp. 339–383). New York: Wiley.

Schneewind, K.A., Beckmann, M., & Engfer, A. (1983). *Eltern und Kinder: Umwelteinflüsse auf das familiäre Verhalten* [Parents and children: Contextual influences on family behavior]. Stuttgart: Kohlhammer.

Siegal, M. (1984). Economic deprivation and the quality of parent-child relations: A trickle-down framework. *Journal of Applied Developmental Psychology*, *5*, 127–144.

Silbereisen, R.K. & Eyferth, K. (1985). *Der Berliner Jugendlängsschnitt: Projekt "Jugendentwicklung und Drogen." Dritter Fortsetzungsantrag und die Deutsche Forschungsgemeinschaft* [The Berlin Youth Longitudinal Study: Project "Adolescent Development and Substance Use." Third renewal grant application to the German Research Council] (Berichte aus der Arbeitsgruppe TUdrop Jugendforschung 50/85). Berlin: Technische Universität Berlin.

Silbereisen, R.K., Reitzle, M., & Zank, S. (1986). Stability and change in self-concept in adolescence: Self-knowledge and self-strategies. In F. Klix & H. Hagendorf (Eds.), *Human memory and cognitive capabilities: Mechanisms and performances. Symposium in memoriam Hermann Ebbinghaus. Berlin, Humboldt University*. Amsterdam: North-Holland.

Silbereisen, R.K., Walper, S., & Albrecht, H. (1990). Families experiencing income loss and economic hardship: Antecedents of adolescents' problem behavior. In V. McLoyd & C. Flanagan (Eds.), *Risk and protective factors in children and adolescents' response to economic crises and deprivation* (pp. 27–46) (New Directions in Child Development). San Francisco: Jossey-Bass.

Skinner, M.L., Elder, G.H., Jr., & Conger, R.D. (1992). Linking economic hardship to adolescent aggression. *Journal of Youth and Adolescence, 21,* 259–276.

Verdonik, F. & Sherrod, L.R. (1984). *An inventory of longitudinal research on childhood and adolescence.* New York: Social Science Council.

Voydanoff, P. & Donnelly, B.W. (1988). Economic distress, family coping, and quality of family life. In P. Voydanoff & L.C. Majka (Eds.), *Families and economic distress: Coping strategies and social policy* (pp. 97–116). Beverly Hills: Sage.

Walper, S. (1988). *Familiäre Konsequenzen ökonomischer Deprivation* [The impact of economic deprivation on the family]. München, Weinheim: Psychologie Verlags Union.

Walper, S. & Silbereisen R.K. (1987). Familiäre Konsequenzen ökonomischer Einbußen und ihre Auswirkungen auf die Bereitschaft zu normverletzendem Verhalten bei Jugendlichen [Family consequences of economic loss and their effects on adolescents' transgression proneness]. *Zeitschrift für Entwicklungspsychologie und Pädagogische Psychologie, 19,* 228–248.

Walper, S. & Wiszniewska, A. (1988). *Consequences of income loss on family climate and adolescent personality.* Paper presented at the Research Colloquium on Youth Development in Cross-Cultural Perspective, held by the Interdisciplinary Research Group "Youth Development and Substance Use in Cross-Cultural Comparison" at the Technical University, Berlin, December 8–10, 1988.

Ziolkowski, M. (1988). Individuals and the social system: Values, perceptions, and behavioral strategies. *Social Research, 55,* 139–177.

Appendix

Internal consistencies (Cronbach's α) are given for Time 1 measurements.
Family Cohesion for the Berlin Sample (couple scores $\alpha = .82$)
Mothers ($\alpha = .74$)
   If something has to be done at home, everyone tries to get out of it (inverted)
   In our family, there is a lot of friction (inverted)
   Our family is harmonious and peaceful
   We really get along with each other very well
Fathers ($\alpha = .72$)
   At home it often happens that one helps the other only reluctantly (inverted)
   Our family is harmonious and peaceful
   In our family, there is a lot of friction (inverted)
Scale of Family Cohesion for the Warsaw Sample (couple scores $\alpha = .80$)
Mothers ($\alpha = .74$) and *Fathers* ($\alpha = .70$)
   If something has to be done at home, everyone tries to get out of it (inverted)
   In our family, everyone goes mostly his own way (inverted)
   At home there are many misunderstandings (inverted)

In difficult situations, we support each other in our family
In decision making everyone's opinion is equally important
In our family, we live in harmony and friendship
We are full of energy in what we do at home

Self-Derogation ($\alpha = .70$ Berlin, $\alpha = .57$ Warsaw)
I want to change a lot about myself
Sometimes I wish I were different
I think that I am not worth much
I am satisfied with myself (inverted)

Transgression Proneness ($\alpha = .68$ Berlin, $\alpha = .66$)
I can imagine I would steal something
I often find the rules and laws of adults bad and don't like to follow them
Sometimes I would really like to do something forbidden
Sometimes I find it funny to lie to someone

8
Racial, School, and Family Context among Adolescents

ROBERTA G. SIMMONS AND YINGZHI ZHOU

This chapter will deal with differences between African-American (black) and white young adolescents as they move into junior high school in the United States and as they are affected by their families. First, findings from earlier research relevant to the move into junior high schools will be reviewed (Simmons, Black, & Zhou, 1991), and then we will explore the effect on key outcome variables of living in a broken family and being allowed early independence from chaperonage.

In terms of racial context, over the years research has sporadically focused on minority children and youth (McLoyd, 1990a). This interest in the development of minority children has accelerated recently in response to past neglect (Bell/Scott & Taylor, 1989; Spencer & McLoyd, 1990).

Recently there has been criticism of past research for operating with a "deficit model." This deficit model was seen as emphasizing only the problems of minority members rather than the strengths or coping mechanisms (Consortium for Research on Black Adolescents, 1990; Gibbs, 1985; McKenry, Everett, Ramseur, & Carter, 1989; McLoyd, 1990a). In our comparison between African-American and white young adolescents (Simmons et al., 1991) we took a broad sweep and investigated differences in several areas, some of which turned out to show positive adjustment and others to be problematic. In no case do we attribute blame to African-American individuals, for the system of prior and present discrimination, as well as institutional racism in the United States, cannot be ignored (see Gary, 1981; Staples, 1982). Nor have we ignored the greater incidence of poverty among African-Americans. Social class as well as age are controlled in order to discover whether differences persist or disappear with these controls.

Little of the research prior to ours on African-American youth has focused on the transition from childhood to adolescence, that is, from elementary to junior high school. In the United States, young adolescents usually move into a middle-level school. We investigated the school system in one large, urban context—that is, Milwaukee, Wisconsin.

Historically in the United States, there have been dramatic changes in the school context for individuals moving out of childhood into adolescence (see Blyth & Karnes, 1981; Blyth, Simmons, & Bush, 1978; Simmons & Blyth, 1987). From 1900 to 1970, there was a marked decrease in the traditional grade structures. Traditionally there had been 8-year elementary schools followed by 4-year senior high schools. In the first seven decades of the twentieth century, this traditional system was largely, though not completely, replaced by 6-year elementary schools (ages 6 to 11–12, K-6 schools), 3-year junior high schools for young adolescents (ages 12 to 14–15), and 3-year senior high schools for older adolescents (ages 15 to 17–18). That is, elementary schools include kindergarten through 6th grade; junior high schools include grades 7–9; and senior high schools, grades 10–12. Attendance is required until age 16, after which considerable drop out occurs. After completion of senior high school, a sizeable portion of Americans go on to attend some college or university.

In the past two decades there has been a new movement into a middle school system in which the switch to a new school often precedes adolescence—that is, it occurs in grades 4, 5, or 6 (ages 9–11) (see Lipsitz, 1977). However, Milwaukee, where this study was conducted, had no middle schools. Therefore, in this research we concentrated on the junior high schools, which are large and impersonal (Simmons & Blyth, 1987).

In fact, for the cohort moving from an elementary school in grade 6 to a junior high school in grade 7 the discontinuity was severe (Benedict, 1954); that is, the change was abrupt and considerable. As Table 8.1 shows, youngsters moved suddenly from a K-6 school of 465.6 children to a junior high school close to three times as large (1307.0). In their own school there were only 59.1 students on average in grade 6, but there were between six and seven times more students in grade 7 (402.9). And, if students who are one's age and older are the most meaningful, there were over twenty times more of these students in grade 7 than in grade 6 (1307.0 vs. 59.1).

Junior high schools were not only larger, but also presented other structural changes that increased the discontinuity from an intimate to an impersonal environment. In elementary school (K-6) students typically had one teacher for most of the day and remained with the same group of students. The next year, in grade 7 of the junior high school, the schools were departmentalized: Teachers changed frequently throughout the day, and often the students in one's classroom also changed.

We predicted that this type of discontinuity into an impersonal environment from an intimate context would have negative effects on young adolescents. In fact, Simmons & Blyth (1987) have indicated that the transition to junior high school has some negative effects for white children. Work in the United States by Berndt (1989), Eccles, Midgley, and Adler (1984),

TABLE 8.1. Size and grade level composition of schools for students moving from a K-6 elementary school. To a junior high school.*

	Grade 6 Last year in elementary school	Grade 7 First year in junior high school
Mean number of students in schools (SD)	465.6 (100.9)	1307.0 (192.5)
Mean number of students in own grade (SD)	59.1 (19.1)	402.9 (70.1)
Mean number of students in own or higher grades (SD)	59.1 (19.1)	1307.0 (192.5)

*Values are summed for all schools on the relevant category and then divided by that number of schools.

and Hirsch & Rapkin (1987) has presented some congruent findings as well as some that are incongruent (see Eccles & Midgley, 1989; and Eccles et al., 1989, for a review).

The purpose of our more recent analyses (Simmons et al., 1991) is to investigate effects for African-American children as they move from elementary school to junior high school (Simmons & Blyth, 1987). Does the movement out of a school for children into a school for adolescents affect black and white students in the United States similarly or differently? The meaning of the movement into adolescence may very well differ across subcultures. Therefore, we have compared African-American and white females and males as they make the transition into junior high school. Our first task in this chapter will be to review these findings.

We examine transition changes in attitudes toward school and in five "tasks of adolescence" (Aldous, 1978; Havighurst, 1953; Simmons & Blyth, 1987). It has been posited that for the individual to be able to deal well with the transition into adulthood, certain tasks have be to accomplished during adolescence.

First, the individual needs to deal with pressures regarding conformity versus deviant behavior. Because of increased independence and increased adolescent exploration or rebellion, the teenager has a much greater opportunity to engage in deviant behavior. The adolescent is confronted with adult pressure to conform to rules and with peer and perhaps internal pressures to deviate from these rules (see Jessor & Jessor, 1977). Clearly, delinquency is one of the major problems affecting society (Simmons & Blyth, 1987). Past evidence indicates that delinquency is higher for males and that African-American males are more likely than white males to have been arrested (Bell-Scott & Taylor, 1989; Gibbs, 1984; Myers, 1989), at least partly because of discrimination in arrest patterns (Gibbs, 1990; Hawkins & Jones, 1989).

We have therefore measured problem behavior in school, academic conformity, and conflict with parents, and investigated whether these behaviors increase differently for whites and African-Americans on entry to junior high. Parent-child conflict has often been highlighted as increasing dramatically in adolescence. However, much research indicates that conflict concerns minor issues rather than major values and that change rather than conflict typifies adolescent-parent relations. Here, however, we look particularly at one indicator of conflict, the perception that parents like or dislike the adolescent's friends.

As a second task of adolescence, we consider the intensification of peer relations. This task is part of the process of disengaging from parents so that at the end of adolescence the individual can leave home and establish a new family of his or her own. An important part of this task involves the establishment of a new type of relationship with the opposite sex. We investigate whether African-American and white children move toward same-sex peer relations and toward opposite sex relationships at different paces. There is some evidence of earlier sexuality among African-Americans (Broderick, 1965; Gibbs, 1984; Hare, 1985; Phinney, Jensen, Olsen, & Cundick, 1990); we explore differences in dating behavior and values occurring as early as grades 6 and 7.

Third, on entering adolescence, because of great bodily changes and physical drives, the individual has the task of developing a revised self-image. Prior work, both by us and others, has shown that global self-image is an area of strength for urban African-American children (Hare, 1985; Hirsch & Rapkin, 1987; Johnston, Bachman, & O'Malley, 1982; Long, 1983; McKenry et al., 1989; Porter & Washington, 1979; Rosenberg & Simmons, 1972; Simmons, Brown, Bush, & Blyth, 1978). Despite prior hypotheses suggesting self-hatred among African-American children, larger-scale, representative, quantitative studies show that urban African-American adolescents have as high a global self-esteem as their white peers (Rosenberg & Simmons, 1972; Simmons et al., 1978). The mechanisms that protect the African-American child have been hypothesized to be (a) the love from parents that equals that in other groups; (b) the great number of peers who are also African-American (rather than white) for comparison; and (c) the instruction from parents that negative comments by whites may be fueled by prejudice rather than by any inferiority of the African-American child (Powell, 1979; Rosenberg & Simmons, 1972).

Therefore, we have not predicted global self-esteem differences between black and white students. However, it is not known whether on entry to junior high, African-American and white children change differently in terms of specific areas of their self-image: for example, body image and self-values (the self-domains that are cared about most).

The fourth task of adolescence is to begin establishing greater independence from parents in daily life. We explore these changes in several ways, including the holding of a part-time job. There is some evidence in the literature of less part-time work in the United States for African-

American females (Gibbs, 1985; Johnston et al., 1982). Also, among middle and older adolescents, unemployment is very high for minority members in the United States—in 1983, as high as 48%, compared with 22% for all adolescents (Gibbs, 1984). Whether this racially based unemployment affects part-time work in early adolescence remains to be seen.

Fifth, at some point adolescents need to plan for the adult future. While this is probably more of a task of late adolescence, we have investigated differential changes in educational, occupational, and marital aspirations among African-American versus white females and males in early adolescence. Most literature indicates high aspirations among African-American youngsters and their parents (Carter, 1990; Rosenberg & Simmons, 1972; Stevenson, Chen, & Uttal, 1990), although behavior aimed to the attainment of these aspirations is not equally prevalent (Carter, 1990).

In all of these areas, the question is whether African-American and white males and females change differently on entry to junior high school. African-American male youth have been regarded as an endangered species because of lower adult opportunities and the considerably greater barriers associated with poverty and past and present discrimination (Gibbs, 1984; Hare & Castenell, 1985). Does this picture emerge in early adolescence? Which areas are affected and which unaffected? In all our analyses race and gender are considered interactively—African-American males and females are compared with white males and females. It should also be noted that the group to be reported here is a cohort of the mid-to late 1970s. Obviously, differences found here may have changed in later cohorts. This issue is discussed later.

After reviewing the differences between African-American and white children upon entry to junior high school and adolescence we shall examine the effects of certain family factors that might be expected to shed some light on the process of entry into adolescence. In particular we shall look at the impact among these students, of coming from a broken versus intact family and of the degree to which parents allow independence from chaperonage in these early years. We will examine the effects of these family factors upon key outcome variables that have been identified from the first set of analyses described above.

Method

Sample

This study was conducted in the Milwaukee public school system. It is a longitudinal study following children from grade 6 to grade 10 in Milwaukee (see Simmons & Blyth, 1987). For this article we are interested only in children moving from a K-6 elementary school to a grade 7–9 junior high school.

Eight predominately white K-6 schools and 4 predominantly African-American K-6 schools were randomly drawn from the population of schools. Size of school and proportion minority were used as stratifying variables. All sixth-grade children in the sampled schools were invited to participate: 82% of the total sample provided signed parent consent. This sample is quite representative of the population from which it is drawn.

Five hundred and twelve youths were followed for these 2 years in this analysis. There was little attrition in the sample from grade 6 to grade 7. The students who were reinterviewed in grade 7 represented 89% of the original sixth-grade sample. Most of the students who were lost left Milwaukee, the public school system, or they did not make the expected type of transfer.

Of these 512 children, 88 were African-American males, 92 were African-American females, 175 were white males, and 157 were white females. Age ranged from 11 to 15 in the winter of grade 7, with a mean of 12.8 and SD of .47. The socioeconomic class of the children was based on the occupational prestige of the parent who is head of a household as coded by the Hollingshead scale. Children were split into equal thirds, with 34% in the higher, 33% in the middle, and 33% in the lower social class.

In general, this is a good representative sample of African-American and white children who made a transition into junior high school in this urban setting. Prior literature reviews have complained that samples of African-American adolescents have not been representative or sizeable.

Measures

Each year a survey interview was conducted with many identical measures across the years. Most measures were pretested among both African-American and white children of various ages. Table 8.2 lists the dependent variables in this research and classifies them according to the "developmental tasks" of adolescence (Aldous, 1978; Havighurst, 1953; Simmons & Blyth, 1987).

The first category—choosing conformity or deviance—is less strictly a task of adolescence than the other areas and more a cluster of loosely related variables. School problem behavior is investigated; we were not allowed to measure self-reports of criminal delinquency. Since, to some extent, academic success can be considered conformity to adult rules, indices of academic achievement are included in this area. Finally, conflict with parents is indexed by parental liking or disliking friends.

Finally, in addition to the five tasks of adolescence, certain attitudes toward school were measured. For exact measures for the variables in Table 8.2 see Simmons & Blyth (1987), or Simmons et al. (1991).

For analysis in the latter parts of the chapter a scale was constructed to measure the extent to which parents allow independence from chaperonage. This scale consisted of a sum of the following indicators, each of which was coded to be dichotomous:[1]

1. Do you ever go some place other than to school, in a bus, without a grownup going with you? __ Yes __ No
   (If Yes) Do you do this __ a lot+ __ a little __ or hardly ever?
2. If you wanted to go more than a block away from your home after dark, would you have to ask your parent(s) permission? __ Yes __ No+
3. If your parents aren't home, do they:
   __ Leave you all by yourself+
   __ Leave you all by yourself but with someone around if you need help, or
   __ Do they make sure someone older stays with you?
4. (The following two items are multiplied together, and a score of -1 or greater is coded as *1*, while other scores [-2 and lower] are coded as *0*.)
   (a) How much do your parents care about whether you go out with (boys/girls)?[2]
       _4_ very much
       _3_ pretty much
       _2_ not very much
       _1_ not at all
   (b) Would your parents
       _1_ like you to go out with (boys, girls), or
       _−1_ not like you to go out with (boys, girls)?

Thus, the scale ranges from *0* to *4*, with a high score representing a high degree of independence from chaperonage.

Analysis

For the first part of the findings, repeated measures of analysis of variance were used with race and sex as independent variables and each of our dependent variables studied in turn. Two points in time have been investigated—grade 6 and grade 7. We have looked for significant Race × Time or Race × Gender × Time interactions to see to what extent African-American and white males and females show different changes upon entry to junior high school. In the second part of the findings involving family effects, we use hierarchial regression and analysis of covariance.

---

[1] Any item indexed with a + is coded *1*. All other values are coded as *0*.
[2] Refers to opposite sex.

TABLE 8.2. Dependent variables—Tasks of adolescence.

1. Deal with conformity-deviance issues
   A. Problem behavior:
      Problem behavior scale
      Probations/suspensions
      Truancy
   B. Academic performance:
      GPA
      Reading achievement score
      Math achievement score
   C. Perception that adults evaluate one highly:
      Parents
      Teachers
   D. Perception of parent-peer relationship:
      Parents like close friends
      Close friends like parents

2. Intensify peer relationships:
   A. Peer popularity:
      Same sex
      Opposite sex
   B. Value popularity:
      Care about same sex
      Care about opposite sex
      Value popularity more than competence or independence
      Value opposite-sex popularity more than competence
   C. Dating behavior
   D. Others' expectation regarding opposite-sex relationships:
      Parents expect dating
      Same-sex friends expect dating
      Parents expect subject to have interest in opposite sex
      Same-sex peers expect interest in opposite sex
   E. Participation in activities:
      Total in-school clubs and sports
      Total out-of-school clubs and sports
      Coed clubs (in and out of school)
      Leadership in clubs and sports

3. Revise self-image
   A. Global self-image:
      Self-esteem
      Self-consciousness
      Self-stability
   B. Body image:
      Perceive self as good looking
      Happiness with looks
      Happiness with weight
      Happiness with height
      Happiness with figure/muscles

TABLE 8.2. *Continued*

C. Concern with body image:
   Care about looks
   Care about weight
   Care about height
D. Perceived self-competence:
   Intelligence
   School work
   Good at sports
E. Concern with competence:
   Value competence more than popularity and independence
   Care about schoolwork
   Care about being good at sports
   Care about independence from parents
F. Perceptions of gender role:
   Positive feelings about being a female or male
   Care about not acting like the opposite sex
   How often act like the opposite sex

4. Establish independence:
   A. Independence from parents:
      Take the bus without an adult
      Go places without parents' permission
      Parents' permission not required after dark
      Left home alone
      Times per month baby-sit
      Part-time job
      Perceived independence from parents
      Decision making

B. Perception that others expect older behavior:
   Parents
   Friends
   Teachers
C. Concern with independence:
   Care about independence
   Value independence more than competence or popularity

5. Plan for future:
   A. Educational, occupational, and marital aspirations:
   B. Perception that other expect career planning:
      Parents
      Teachers
      Friends

6. Attitudes toward school:
   Perceived anonymity
   Liking school
   Worry about next year

Two-tailed tests of significance were used. We present results that are significant at $p < .10$ or better. However, the reader should consider those findings that are not significant at the $p < .05$ levels as more tentative. The presentation distinguishes these levels in all cases.

Where there are statistically significant differences, we control for social class and for age to make certain differences persist. However, we recognize that perfect control for social class is not possible due to the greater poverty among African-Americans in the United States. As we shall see, there are several dramatic effects among the race/gender groups that are already present in grade 6 and which are minimally affected by the change of grade 7.

Findings: Differences among Race/Gender Subgroups

In the first section of this chapter, the main issue is whether African-American and white boys and girls change differently upon entry to junior high school. In fact, on most variables there is no significant differences among the racial groups in type of change (no significant Race × Time or Race × Gender × Time interactions.) However, in 27 out of the 71 variables there are significant or almost significant differences ($p < .10$); in 18 of 71 variables there are clearly significant differences ($p < .05$). We shall review some of the most important of these differences. (See Simmons et al., 1991, for more detail, and for the exact means on which all conclusions are based.)

Problem Behavior

One of the areas most consistently affected in our data is that of problem behavior: in specific, school problem behavior, low school grade point average (GPA), and conflict with parents.

First, in terms of school problem behavior in general and probation and suspensions in particular, African-American males (but not females) show the highest degree of difficulty (race effect and gender effect, $p < .001$ in both cases). Probation refers to the schools' punishment of a student by demanding he/she fulfill certain requirements for a specified time while attending school. If these requirements are not met, more severe punishment will ensue. Suspensions are defined as a school punishment such that the student is not allowed to attend school for a short time.

As Figure 8.1 shows, African-American males not only start out and end up with the highest level of probations and suspensions, but they demonstrate the greatest increase in these behaviors between grades 6 and 7 (Race × Time interaction, $p < .05$). Of course, it is possible that

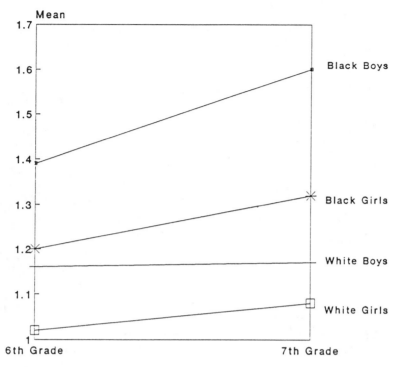

FIGURE 8.1. Probations/suspensions.

some of this racial difference is due to discrimination in punishment, with African-Americans punished more severely than whites for the same offense (Staples, 1982).

In terms of scholastic achievement or grade point average, African-Americans, especially African-American boys, score lowest at both time points (race effect, $p < .001$; gender effect, $p < .001$). (See Figure 8.2.) More importantly, while every group's grades drop at entry to the more difficult junior high school, African-American children's grades drop more sharply (Race × Gender × Time interaction, $p < .05$). Again, this finding may be due in part to different school treatment of African-Americans and whites.

Our final look at deviant behaviors versus conformity involves conflict with parents. As an indicator of this conflict, we asked the youths if parents liked their close friends. Females indicate more parental approval than do males (Figure 8.3, gender effect, $p = .001$). With the movement to junior high school, African-American males once again exhibit the most difficulty; they show the greatest decrease of parental approval of friends (Race × Time interaction, $p < .10$).

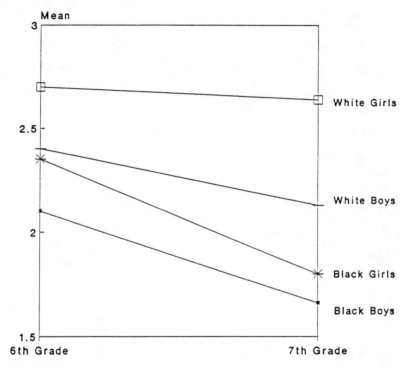

FIGURE 8.2. Grade point average. *If the student earned the highest grade or marks in school, he/she would have a GPA of 4.0, and a 4.0 is an "A;" a 3.0 is a "B;" a 2.0 is a "C." Below 2.0 is very poor.

Peer Relations: The Opposite Sex

Interest in the opposite sex is another area where the races differ and where African-American males are the most different from other groups. Parents expect African-American males to be more interested in the opposite sex than do parents of other groups both in grades 6 and 7 (Race × Gender interaction, $p < .01$). Furthermore, parents of African-American males versus white males show greater increases in this expectation (Race × Time interaction, $p < .10$).

In fact, African-American males actually date more (Figure 8.4) and care more about opposite sex popularity than do other groups both in grades 6 and 7, although they do not increase more than other groups on entry to junior high (Race × Gender interaction, $p < .001$ for both dates and opposite-sex popularity).

Interestingly, in both grades 6 and 7, black girls are the least likely of the four groups to date or to be interested in the opposite sex.

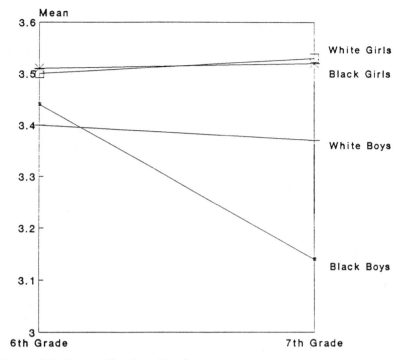

FIGURE 8.3. Parents like close friends.

Self-image

Differences in the self-image area also involve the African-American male; however, in this case he is favored. African-American males show the least "uncomfortable self-consciousness" in both grades 6 and 7 (Race × Gender interaction, $p < .001$), are the happiest with their looks (race effect, $p < .001$; gender effect, $p < .001$), are the most likely to increase this happiness with their looks in junior high school (Race × Gender × Time interaction, $p < .10$), and are the most likely to increase their positive attitude about being a member of their own gender upon entry to junior high school (Race × Gender × Time interaction, $p < .10$). While there are these significant differences primarily involving body-image and sex-role attitudes, there are, as predicted, no significant differences for global self-esteem as measured by the Rosenberg-Simmons scale (Simmons & Blyth, 1987).

Establishing Independence

Given the prior findings showing that African-American males are more likely to be involved in deviant behavior and in dating, one might expect

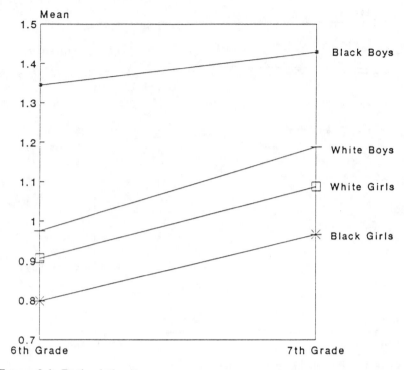

FIGURE 8.4. Dating behavior.

them to score highest in independence and increase the most in this regard on entry to junior high school. However, in terms of items measuring independence from parental chaperonage, there is no consistent evidence that African-American males score higher than white males or change more in this direction. Often, the reverse is true.

In terms of part-time work as an indicator of independence, our data show that part-time work decreases for African-American youngsters in grade 7, while part-time work increases among whites at entry to junior high (Race × Time interaction, $p < .001$). It should be noted that, at this age, part-time work in the United States involves "odd jobs"—the most common of which are yard work, delivering newspapers, paid house-work, baby-sitting, working in a store or business, running errands, and janitorial work. The sources of payment are neighbors, relatives, friends, parents, and businesses.

Plan for the Future

African-Americans also show an advantage in terms of college aspirations. It should be recalled that a substantial proportion of Americans do attend

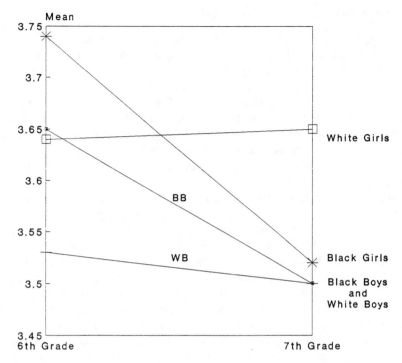

FIGURE 8.5. Liking school.

college or university and this attendance is important to securing jobs. In our data there is the discrepancy between behavior and aspirations shown in much of the literature (Carter, 1990; Johnston et al., 1982; Mickelson, 1990; Ogbu, 1989; Rosenberg & Simmons, 1972). African-Americans show the highest desire to attend college in both grades 6 and 7 (race effect, $p < .001$). While these high aspirations persist at entry to junior high school, white youngsters' aspirations decrease on average, perhaps indicating greater realism (Race $\times$ Time interaction, $p < .01$).

School Attitudes

The most important finding in terms of attitudes toward school involves the liking of school. As Figure 8.5 shows, African-American students, but not white, decrease their liking of school upon entry to junior high school (Race $\times$ Time interactions, $p = .01$). The black youngsters in grade 6, the last year of elementary school, report a relatively high level of liking school (Figure 8.5), but this positive attitude drops relatively precipitously upon entry to junior high school.

Social Class and Age Controls

Since poverty is greater in the African-American community and blacks are somewhat more likely to be older in age than whites in a grade (Simmons et al., 1991), it is important to control for age and social class to see if the reported racial and gender differences persist. With this purpose in mind, both age and social class were added as factors to the repeated measures ANOVA. For instances where we lost statistical significance, we checked to see whether the direction of findings remained the same by comparing means for the race/gender subgroups within higher-, middle-, and lower-class groups and within young, average, and older age groups.

Generally, the main effects discussed above, the effects of race and gender, remain significant. As far as differential change is concerned, in some discussed cases significance is lost: findings for suspensions and probation and parents' liking of close friends. In terms of parents' liking of friends, the direction of the relationship remains as reported above. However, the relatively greater increase in school probations and suspensions in junior high school reported above for African-American males persists in most social class and age subgroups. But this greater increase does not persist in the highest social class or youngest age. It is particularly interesting that this increase in school suspensions and probations at entry to junior high school disappears within the highest class group (when parents are white-collar status or above).

Since the direction of most findings remains the same even if significance is lost upon controlling for class and age, it is possible that the loss of significance, where it occurs, is due simply to reduced degrees of freedom.

Summary of Comparisons between Race/ Gender Groups

As noted at the beginning of this analysis, in most respects, that is, on most variables investigated (see Table 8.2), African-Americans and whites do not differ in the way they react to the entry to junior high school. For example, African-Americans and whites change similarly in their perception of parents' and teachers' evaluations, in perception of same-sex and opposite-sex popularity, in reported leadership, global self-esteem, self-stability, in self-ratings of intelligence and ability at school work and sports, in social indicators of increased independence, and in future plans concerning marriage, family, and occupations.

However, on several key variables significant differences in reaction to the junior high school transition are found. Also, there are interesting significant differences already present in grade 6 that persist into grade 7. From a life-course perspective it is valuable to know whether certain subgroups enter adolescence earlier; that is, in an earlier grade in school or a younger age. While adolescence in truth is characterized by great individual diversity, there is a cultural stereotype about what it means to be an adolescent. And it is as if African-American males change between grade 6 and 7 more in the direction of the cultural stereotype of adolescence. According to this stereotype, adolescence is a time of nonconformity, deviance and conflict, and ever increasing interest in the opposite sex. In fact, in grade 6 African-American males already show earlier adoption of many of these "typical" adolescent behaviors. It is *as if* they enter adolescence earlier. At this early age, African-American boys are involved in more problem behaviors as well as in increasing conflict with parents over friends; both African-American boys and girls appear less attached than do whites to school, earning less high marks and reducing the liking of school at entry to junior high school; and African-American males are most likely to date, to be interested in the opposite sex, and to have parents who expect this interest and behavior. However, they do not show greater perceived independence from parental chaperonage, as one might expect. Future longitudinal research should establish not only if these differences in grade 6 and differences in pattern of change in grade 7 replicate, but how early such differences occur (see Hare, 1985).

In our study, the direction of these differences almost always persists even when social class and age are controlled, although sometimes statistical significance is lost.

While some of these differences suggest negative reactions for the African-American boy, some qualifications need to be made. Negative findings in terms of GPA and problem behavior may be in part due to institutional racism and discrimination in a society in which blacks have long held lower prestige and status. While the general drop in GPA for all groups may reflect more difficult standards in junior high school, it is possible that the drop for African-Americans is more severe due to school factors—for example, (a) teachers' expectations that African-Americans will score lower (Spencer, 1985), and (b) the tracking of students in different ability groups in such a way that African-American children may be trapped in lower tracks in which high grades are not deemed appropriate.

Similarly, part of the increase in school problem behavior, and in suspensions and probations, may be due to harsher punishment by school personnel of blacks than of whites.

Also, the diversity within the African-American community must not be ignored. These findings indicate only a relative difference between African-American males and other groups. They do not mean that most African-American males of this age are involved in problem behaviors or any of the other behaviors above. That is, 40% of African-American males versus 14% of white males have experienced probation or suspension in grade 7; the majority of both groups have no such experience. Fifty-six percent of African-American males versus 37% of white males indicate high dating behavior in grade 7 (i.e., they go out alone sometimes or frequently with a member of the opposite sex).

Finally, our results do not support a "deficit model." For while there are some difficulties as indicated, on most variables there are no racial differences, and on some key variables blacks indicate greater strength. African-American males show a more favorable body-image as well as other self-image advantages. Aspirations to attend college are also very high for both African-American males and females. However, translation of these aspirations into behavior may require some help and societal change.

One of the most dramatic patterns in these findings is the difference between black boys and girls. Compared to black boys, black girls are certainly less likely to exhibit school problem behavior. They score a bit higher on GPA, like school a bit more, report less conflict with parents over choice of close friends, and are much less likely to date at this early age, to care about the opposite sex, or to perceive that their parents expect them to date (if boys date more than girls, a few girls must date many boys). It is again *as if* black girls move into adolescence more slowly than their male counterparts.

Why should African-American boys and girls differ in these regards? One factor, which we will begin to investigate in the rest of this chapter, involves differences in family socialization. McLoyd (1990b), as we did, also reviews findings that indicate more problems among African-American male children. To explain the difference McLoyd reports an old African-American adage: "Black mothers love their sons but raise their daughters" (p. 339). It is possible that some African-American mothers are stricter and more protective of their daughters, while they assume that their sons are ready to enter the typical behaviors of adolescence. They may be more likely to release their sons from control and then find these sons are more likely to become involved in trouble. (See Smith, 1982; Staples, 1982; Hare & Castenell, 1985.)

Thus, in the next section of this chapter we shall investigate whether greater relaxation of control in the form of parental chaperonage has negative results and whether these results differ for the various race/gender groups.

The Impact of Family Factors

Up to now, we have been looking at the effects of a change in school context upon children from two subcultural contexts (minority vs. majority children) and from the two different genders. For some key variables, the racial background of the student appears to affect how he or she reacts to the entry into junior high in specific, and to adolescence in general. Now, we wish to turn to the concurrent effects of the family context on these same key variables. There are two aspects of the family to be examined here. The first involves an element of family structure—that is, whether the family is intact or broken. Second, to be studied is an aspect of family socialization—the extent to which parents allow boys and girls this young to be independent from parental chaperonage. We have speculated above that the difference between black boys and black girls may be due to a tendency of their mothers to allow these boys more early independence and to protect their girls.

Dornbusch, Ritter, Leiderman, Roberts, & Fraleigh (1987) report that the most effective parenting involves both a high degree of love and high "authoritative control" or supervision. If one of these factors is absent, negative consequences ensue. That is, if there is too early independence from supervision or chaperonage, there may be negative effects in early adolescence.

The key outcome variables that emerged in our discussion above and that will therefore be examined in this analysis are: school problem behavior; GPA, conflict with parents (parents do not like one's friends), dating behavior, and liking of school. Also, we have added self-esteem to this analysis, since it has been such an important variable in our prior work (Simmons & Blyth, 1987).

The analysis will be a hierarchical regression analysis. For grade 6, race, gender, age, class, and tendency to choose extreme answers are entered into the first step along with any interactions that proved significant in a prior analysis. On the second step, broken family is entered; on the third step, independence from chaperonage (using the independence scale discussed above), and on the final step, interactions of race with broken family and/or independence. For the seventh grade, the procedure is the same except another step is added before broken family is introduced: The value of the dependent variable in grade 6 is entered. Thus our analysis allows us to see the effect of broken family, controlling for background variables, and the effect of independence controlling, for both background variables and broken family. It is also possible to determine whether the race or race/gender groups react differently from one another to a broken family or to more or less independence.

Broken family is dichotomized; children living with their own mother and father (intact) are contrasted to other children (from broken families).

Findings

As Table 8.3 shows, black children are significantly less likely to come from intact families than are white children. Seventy-six to 81% of white youngsters live with both their mother and father compared to only 58–60% of black youth ($p < .0001$). Table 8.4 indicates that girls of both races are allowed considerably less independence from chaperonage than are boys. Girls in early adolescence are more protected. Seventy percent

TABLE 8.3. Broken family status by race/gender subgroup.

	Race/gender			
	Black boys	Black girls	White boys	White girls
Broken/intact				
Live with own mother and father				
Other*	60%	58%	76%	81%
	40%	42%	24%	19%
	100%	100%	100%	100%
N	(82)	(86)	(174)	(155)

$\chi^2 = 21.65162$ $df = 3$ $p = .0001$

*Broken family is dichotomized, and children living with their own mother and father (intact) are contrasted to other children (from broken families).

to 71% of black and white girls are allowed the *lowest* degree of independence compared to only 28% of black boys and 42% of white boys ($p < .0001$).

Above and beyond race, age, gender, and class, and tendency to choose extreme answers, does membership in a broken family hurt young adolescents in terms of the key outcome variables? (For literature reviews, see Furstenberg, 1990; Hetherington, 1991.) In our data, Table 8.5 (Step 2–3) demonstrates that compared to youth from intact families, those from broken families show significantly more dating in grade 6 and 7, more problem behavior in grade 6, lower GPA's in grade 6 and 7, and less liking of school in grade 6. There are no significant differences in terms of parents liking friends, or self-esteem, in either year and also no significant differences in change upon entry to junior high school (grade 7) for problem behavior or liking school. While the results are mixed, the significant differences suggest that it is *as if* the youth from broken families enter adolescence earlier in several respects. That is, they are

TABLE 8.4. Perceived independence from chaperonage by race/gender subgroup.

	Race/gender			
	Black boys	Black girls	White boys	White girls
Independence				
Low independence	28%	71%	42%	70%
Medium independence	41%	21%	31%	24%
High independence	31%	8%	27%	6%
	100%	100%	100%	100%
N	(86)	(92)	(170)	(155)

$\chi^2 = 69.63282$ $Df = 6$ $p < .0001$

TABLE 8.5. Significant effects upon key independent variables—Standardizes Betas[1] and significant R^2 increments[2].

	Dating behavior		Problem behavior		GPA		Parents liking friends		Self-esteem		Liking school	
	Grade 6	Grade 7	Grade 6	Grade 7	Grade 6	Grade 7	Grade 6	Grade 7	Grade 6	Grade 7	Grade 6	Grade 7
Step 1[3]												
Race	ns	ns	.30**	.21*	ns	-.37*	-.32***	ns	.18*	.27*	-.33****	ns
Sex	-.46*	ns	-.31*	-.28*	.19*	.28*	ns	.18*	-.19*	-.22*	.41**	.10***
Age	.12***	ns	.10***	.08****	ns	ns	-.39**	ns	ns	ns	-.57**	ns
Class	.12****	ns	ns	ns	ns	ns	ns	ns	ns	ns	ns	ns
Extreme behavior	ns	ns	ns	ns	-.15**	-.12**	.10****	ns	ns	-.22***	ns	ns
R^2	4%*	2%****	16%*	14%*	12%*	19%*	2%***	3%**	5%*	11%*	2%****	.8%
Step 2–3												
Grade 6 dependent variable		.42*		.58*		.58*		.30*		.51*	.26%*	ns
R^2 Increment		16%*		28%*		30%*		9%*		25%*	7%*	
Broken family	.09****	.12**	.12**	ns	-.16*	-.08**	ns	ns	ns	ns	-.14**	ns
R^2 increment	.8%****	1%***	2%**	0%	2%*	6%***	0%	0%*	.3%	0%	2%**	0%
Step 3–4												
Independence	.25*	.16*	.14**	.09****	ns	ns	ns	ns	ns	ns	ns	ns
R^2 increment	5%*	2%*	2%*	6%****	2%	0%	0%	.1%	0%	0%	0%	0%
Step 4–5												
Interaction Involving race & broken family or independence	ns	ns	ns	ns	ns	ns	ns	ns	ns	ns	-.27***[4]	ns

[1] A higher score represents blacks, females, older age, higher class, more extreme answers, more problem behavior, a higher GPA, more dating, higher self-esteem, greater liking of school, a broken family, and more independence.

[2] Betas are reported from each step in turn.

[3] * $p \leq .001$ (T-test for Betas; F-text for R^2), ** $p \leq .01$, *** $p \leq .05$, **** $p \leq .10$.

[4] The significant interaction is race by broken family.

more likely at an early age to resemble the stereotype of adolescence held by the public.

Does early independence from chaperonage have negative effects or effects more in line with entry to "adolescence" as stereotyped by the public? When race, sex, gender, class, tendency to choose extreme answers, and membership in a broken family are held constant, findings (Table 8.5, Step 3–4) show that the perception that parents allow earlier independence from chaperonage is associated with more "adolescent" behaviors for two of our key variables in both grades 6 and 7—dating behavior and problem behavior. That is, children perceiving more independence are more likely to date early and to be involved in problem behavior. They are also more likely to show increases in dating and problem behavior upon entry to junior high school (grade 7). The other variables (GPA, parents liking friends, self-esteem, and liking school) are not affected by independence.

Given these findings, do blacks and whites react differently to the experience of a broken family or independence? In only 1 out of the 28 possibilities do we see a significant race interaction with broken family or independence in either grade 6 or 7 for any of the outcome variables (Table 8.5, Step 4–5). This one interaction involves liking school in grade 6, and is an interaction between race and broken family. For both black and white children those from intact families like school better, but the difference between individuals from intact and broken families is greater among blacks.

Finally, does the presence of a broken family or early independence account for the original differences among the race-gender groups; for example, for greater dating and problem behavior of black boys or the lower GPA of black youngsters? In order to answer the question, in both grade 6 and 7 we ran an analysis of covariance controlling for four covariates (age, class, broken family, and independence)[3] and another analysis of covariance controlling for only broken family and independence. The dependent variables were those upon which either of the family variables had an initial effect. We then compared the original ("observed" means) to the means adjusted for these covariates. The differences between black boys and other race/gender groups should be reduced when the covariates are controlled and the means are adjusted, if these covariates are explaining part of the difference. In fact, when either the four covariates or only the two family covariates are adjusted, the black boys in both grades 6 and 7 still date most, show the most problem behavior, and have the lowest GPA. They are also least likely in grade 7 to find parents liking their friends and to like school themselves. (The

---

[3] We already knew from prior analysis that controlling for an extreme answer did not change results very much.

race, gender or Race × Gender interaction is still significant in most cases [$p < .05$] and almost significant in the remainder [$p < .10$].)

However, the mean difference between *black boys and girls* is reduced in both grades 6 and 7 when the covariates are controlled for dating and problem behavior (not clearly for GPA, parents liking friends, or liking school). The mean difference between *black and white boys* is also reduced when these covariates are controlled in many, but not all, cases; the reduction is particularly clear in the case of grade 6 and 7 problem behavior.

Thus, the family variables (broken family and independence from chaperonage) explain some but not all of the differences between black boys and the other race/gender groups. For example, in grade 6 the difference in the unadjusted means in problem behavior between black boys and girls is .89. When broken family and independence are controlled, the difference is reduced to .49.

Conclusion

This chapter has examined the concurrent impact of three contexts on American adolescents: (a) school context and change in school context, (b) race/gender context, and (c) family context. There are many similarities among the race/gender subgroups in grade 6 and many instances in which black and white children do not differ in terms of change on outcome variables as they make a transition from an intimate elementary school to a large, impersonal junior high school. However, there are also differences on key variables, with black males almost seeming to enter adolescence early by demonstrating more deviant behavior, more reported conflict with parents, less high GPA, more dating behavior, more interest in the opposite sex, more positive body images and attitudes toward their own gender, and less positive attitudes to their new junior high school. In some cases (low GPA, lower liking of junior high school), black girls are similar to the black males, but in many cases black girls are very different from their male counterparts (e.g., dating less, less problem behavior or conflict with parents, less positive body and sex-role images). In many of these areas black males are already different in grade 6; in many, the differences expand in the same direction upon the transition to junior high school. It should be noted that the transition to junior high school in all likelihood symbolically represents entry to adolescence for many youth and their families.

At the same age and point of transition, one aspect of family structure (coming from a broken family) and one factor in family socialization (perceived independence in grade 6 from family chaperonage) has some affects on key outcome variables even a year later in grade 7. Coming from a broken family is associated with greater dating, problem behavior, and lower GPA and less liking of school in grade 6, and increases in dating and drops in GPA upon transition to junior high school. Perhaps these differences represent a faster entry to adolescence among youth from broken families. These findings certainly indicate negative associations with memberships in a broken family.

Early perceived independence from family chaperonage in grade 6 is associated with more problem behavior and greater dating among students the same year (grade 6) and increases in these behaviors the next year in grade 7. These two factors, problem behavior and dating, are particularly characteristic of entry into adolescence. These results suggest that early freedom from chaperonage may have negative effects. Tighter supervision in early adolescence may be more positive.

The initial differences between black boys and the other race/gender groups are partially, but not completely, reduced by controlling for broken family membership and allowed independence from chaperonage.

Future research on a more recent cohort should attempt to replicate these results. The causal relationship between broken family and independence, on the one hand, and negative scores on variables in early adolescence, on the other hand, should be explored more extensively. In a more recent cohort, the degree of broken families, the level of allowed independence, and the type of deviant behavior (particularly drugs) may have changed, and the changes may affect the outcomes for early adolescents. Smaller middle schools in the United States with transition points at younger ages have expanded and in many communities replaced junior high schools. Is the difficulty of school transition reduced by the more intimate environment of middle schools, and less coincidence of the school transition with pubertal changes and with change in self-definition as an adolescent? (Simmons et al., 1988). Future research also might examine the impact of minority status in general upon entry to adolescence in other nations. Are minority males allowed to enter "adolescence" faster; are minority females today still protected more than minority males?

In terms of policy recommendations, our results up to this point would suggest more supervision and chaperonage of minority males by parents. Children from broken families should be targeted for more intervention and help. In addition, transition into adolescent schools would benefit from being less abrupt and discontinuous in character. In early adolescence, more intimacy should be maintained—for example, by small "schools within schools" (Carnegie Council on Adolescent Development, 1989).

Most important, however, is enhancing adult job opportunity and equality for minority individuals, even if the policy means creating more public employment (Allen, Spencer, & Brookins, 1985; Ogbu, 1989). If minority youngsters perceive little connection between high school education and job opportunity for themselves but not for the majority, alienation from school and deviant behavior is likely to be pervasive and parents are less likely to be able to supervise their youth.

Acknowledgments. This study has been supported by the National Institute of Mental Health, grant no. 2R01MH30739; the William T. Grant Foundation, grant no. 82-0482-74; and by Western Psychiatric Institute and Clinic, University of Pittsburgh.

References

Aldous, J. (1978). *Family careers: Developmental change in families.* New York: Wiley.

Allen, W.R., Spencer, M.B., & Brookins, G.K. (1985). Synthesis: Black children keep on growing. In M.B. Spencer, G.K. Brookins, & W.R. Allen (Eds.), *Beginnings: The social and affective development of black children* (pp. 301–314). Hillsdale, NJ: Lawrence Erlbaum.

Bell-Scott, P. & Taylor, R.L. (1989). *Special Issue on Black Adolescents. Journal of Adolescent Research, 4,* 119–124.

Benedict, R. (1954). Continuities and discontinuities in cultural condition. In W.E. Martin & C.B. Stendler (Eds.), *Readings in child development* (pp. 142–148). NY: Brunner/Mazel.

Berndt, T. (1989). Obtaining support from friends in childhood and adolescence. In D. Belle (Ed.), *Children's social networks and social supports* (pp. 308–331). New York: Wiley.

Blyth, D.A. & Karnes, E.L. (1981). *Philosophy, policies, and programs for early adolescent education: An annotated bibliography.* Westport, CT: Greenwood Press.

Blyth, D.A., Simmons, R.G., & Bush, D. (1978). The transition into early adolescence: A longitudinal comparison of youth in two educational contexts. *Sociology of Education, 53*(3), 149–162.

Broderick, C.B. (1965). Social heterosexual development among urban negroes and whites. *Journal of Marriage and the Family, 27,* 200–203.

Carnegie Council on Adolescent Development. (1989). *Turning points: Preparing American youth for the 21st century.* New York: Carnegie Corporation.

Carter, C.J. (1990). Education and occupational choice. In the Consortium for Research on Black Adolescence, *Black adolescence: Current issues and annotated bibliography* (pp. 79–91). Boston: Hall.

Consortium for Research on Black Adolescence. (1990). *Black adolescence: Current issues and annotated bibliography.* Boston: Hall.

Dornbusch, S.M., Ritter, P.L., Leiderman, P.H., Roberts, D.F., & Fraleigh, M.J. (1987). The relation of parenting style to adolescent school performance. *Child Development, 58,* 1244–1257.

Eccles, J.S. & Midgley, C. (1989). Stage-environment fit: Developmentally appropriate classrooms for young adolescents. In R.E. Ames & C. Ames (Eds.), *Research on motivation in education, Vol. 3* (pp. 139–179). New York: Academic Press.

174   R.G. Simmons and Y. Zhou

Eccles, J.S., Midgley, C., & Adler, T.F. (1984). Grade related changes in school
environment: Effects on achievement motivation. In J.G. Nichols (Ed.), *Advances in motivation and achievement: The development of achievement motivation* (Vol. 3, pp. 283–331). Greenwich, CT: JAI Press.
Eccles, J.S., Wigfield, A., Flanagan, C.A., Miller, C, Reuman, D.A., & Yee, D.
(1989). Self-concepts, domain values, and self-esteem: Relations and changes at
early adolescence. *Journal of Personality, 57,* 283–310.
Furstenberg, F.F. (1990). Coming of age in a changing family system. In S.S.
Feldman & G.R. Elliott (Eds.), *At the threshold: The developing adolescent*
(pp. 147–170). Cambridge: Harvard University Press.
Gary, L. (1981). (Ed.). *Black men.* Newbury Park, CA: Sage.
Gibbs, J.T. (1984). Black adolescents and youth: An endangered species. *American
Journal of Orthopsychiatry, 54,* 6–21.
Gibbs, J.T. (1985). City girls: Psychosocial adjustment of urban black adolescent
females. *Sage, 2,* 28–36.
Gibbs, J.T. (1990). Mental health issues of black adolescents: Implications for
policy and practice. In A.R. Stiffman & L.E. Davis (Eds.), *Ethnic issues in
adolescent mental health* (pp. 21–52). Newbury Park, CA: Sage.
Hare, B.R. (1985). Re-examining the achievement central tendency: Sex differences within race and race differences within sex. In H.P. McAdoo & J.L.
McAdoo (Eds.), *Black children: Social, educational, and parental environments*
(pp. 139–154). Newbury Park, CA: Sage.
Hare, B.R. & Castenell, L.A. (1985). No place to run, no place to hide:
Comparative status and future prospects of black boys. In M.B. Spencer, G.K.
Brookins, & W.R. Allen (Eds.), *Beginnings: The social and affective development of black children* (pp. 201–213). Hillsdale, NJ: Lawrence Erlbaum.
Havighurst, R.J. (Ed.). (1953). *Human development and education.* New York:
Longmans Green.
Hawkins, D.F. & Jones, N. (1989). Black adolescents and the criminal justice
system. In R.L. Jones (Ed.), *Black adolescents* (pp. 403–422). Berkeley: Cobb
& Henry.
Hetherington, E.M. (1991). Presidential address: Families, lies, and videotapes.
Journal on Research on Adolescence, 1(4), 323–347.
Hirsch, B.J. & Rapkin, B.D. (1987). The transition to junior high school: A
longitudinal study of self-esteem, psychological symptomatology, school life,
and social support. *Child Development, 58,* 1235–1244.
Jessor, R. & Jessor, S.L. (1977). *Problem behavior and psychological development: A longitudinal study of youth.* New York: Academic Press.
Johnston, L.D., Bachman, J.G., & O'Malley, P.M. (1982). *Monitoring the future:
Questionnaire responses from the nation's high school seniors 1981.* Ann Arbor:
University of Michigan Press.
Lipsitz, J. (1977). *Growing up forgotten.* Lexington, MA: Lexington Books.
Long, S. (1983). Psychopolitical orientations of white and black youth: A test of
five models. *Journal of Black Studies, 13,* 439–456.
McKenry, P.C., Everett, J.E., Ramseur, H.P., & Carter, C.J. (1989). Research
on black adolescents: A legacy of cultural bias. *Journal of Adolescent Research,
4,* 254–264.
McLoyd, V.C. (1990a). Minority children: Introduction to the special issue. *Child
Development, 61,* 263–266.

McLoyd, V.C. (1990b). The impact of economic hardship on black families and children: Psychological distress, parenting, and socioeconomic development. *Child Development*, *61*, 311–346.

Mickelson, R.A. (1990). The attitude-achievement paradox among black adolescents. *Sociology of Education*, *63*, 44–61.

Myers, H.F. (1989). Urban stress and the mental health of Afro-American youth: An epidemiologic and conceptual update. In R.L. Jones (Ed.), *Black adolescents* (pp. 123–148). Berkeley: Cobb & Henry.

Ogbu, J.U. (1989). Cultural boundaries and minority youth orientation toward work preparation. In D. Stern & D. Eichorn (Eds.), *Adolescence and work: Influences of social structure, labor markets, and culture* (pp. 101–136). Hillsdale, NJ: Lawrence Erlbaum.

Phinney, V.G., Jensen, L.C., Olsen, J.A., & Cundick, B. (1990). The relationship between early development and psychosexual behaviors in adolescent females. *Adolescence*, *26*, 321–332.

Porter, J.R. & Washington, R.E. (1979). Black identify and self-esteem: A review of studies of black self-concept, 1968–1978. *Annual Review of Sociology*, *5*, 53–74.

Powell, G.J. (1979). Growing up black and female. In Claire B. Kopp (Ed.), *Becoming Female: Perspectives on development* (pp. 29–66). New York: Plenum.

Rosenberg, M. & Simmons, R.G. (1972). Black and white self-esteem: The urban school child. *Arnold and Caroline Rose Monograph Series*. Washington DC: American Sociological Association.

Simmons, R.G., Black, A., & Zhou, Y. (1991). African-American versus white children and the transition into junior high school. *American Journal of Education*, *99*(4), 481–520.

Simmons, R.G. & Blyth, D.A. (1987). *Moving into adolescence: The impact of pubertal change and school context*. Hawthorne, NY: Aldine de Gruyter.

Simmons, R.G., Brown, L., Bush, D., & Blyth, D.A. (1978). Self-esteem and achievement of black and white early adolescents. *Social Problems*, *26*(1), 86–96.

Simmons, R.G., Burgeson, R., & Reef, M.J. (1988). Cumulative change at entry to adolescence. In M. Gunnar (Ed.), *Minnesota Symposia on Child Psychology, 1986* (pp. 123–151). Hillsdale, NJ: Lawrence Erlbaum.

Smith, E.J. (1982). The black female adolescent: A review of the educational, career and psychological literature. *Psychology of Women Quarterly*, 261–288.

Spencer, M.B. (1985). Racial variations in achievement prediction: The school as a conduit for macrostructural cultural tension. In H.P. McAdoo & J.L. McAdoo (Eds.), *Black Children: Social, educational, and parental environments* (pp. 85–108). Newbury Park, CA: Sage.

Spencer, M.B. & McLoyd, V.C. (1990). Special issue on minority children. *Child Development*, *4*.

Staples, R. (1982). *Black masculinity: The black male's role in American society*. San Francisco: Black Scholar.

Stevenson, H.W., Chen, C., & Uttal, D.H. (1990). Beliefs and achievements: A study of black, white, and Hispanic children. *Child Development*, *61*, 508–523.

9
Comparative Analyses of Beliefs, Leisure Contexts, and Substance Use in West Berlin and Warsaw

RAINER K. SILBEREISEN, PETER NOACK, AND UTE SCHÖNPFLUG

Adolescence is a time of heightened risk for the development of substance use. However, the timing of initial use, consumption levels, and risk mechanisms may vary among persons and across contexts. In this chapter, young people's smoking and drinking are compared with samples from West Berlin (Germany) and Warsaw (Poland). The data are interpreted against the background of differences in beliefs and daily leisure contexts.

There are reasons to assume that important issues of adolescence in general and the development of problem behavior in particular can be addressed by comparing young people in West Berlin with their age-mates in Warsaw. Adolescent problem behavior, such as substance use, is influenced by normative orientations within the broader society (Marini, 1984). According to age-norms, for instance, a particular behavior may be considered appropriate or deviant and illegal, depending on the age at which the behavior is carried out by the adolescent. Norms concerning such status offenses vary within nations and among cultures. Developmental timetables concerning transitions in adolescence differ as a function of basic value dimensions such as collectivism and related family values (Feldman & Quatman, 1988).

The traditional family-orientation of Poles is well known (Höllinger, 1989). During times of economic decline in the 1980s, retreating from participation in public life into one's own private world was a dominant strategy of adaptation to the political crisis (Ziolkowsky, 1988). Concentrating on family life and devoting oneself to the children's future, both mirroring aspects of the traditional value system, gained even more importance during the economic decline (Marody, 1988). In contrast, despite problems caused by the shortage of apprenticeships and by a relatively high unemployment rate at that time, people in West Berlin lived in an affluent society, less characterized by traditional values such as family and religion.

When the Berlin Youth Longitudinal Study was designed in 1981, we planned to investigate personality development in adolescence with a particular focus on the interplay between normative behavior and problem

176

behavior (Silbereisen & Eyferth, 1986). Another key issue of the design was to study individuals within families, and not to assess youth as subjects in isolation from their contexts. Following Bronfenbrenner's (1989) plea for research on the interplay between contexts as representing a venue of its own to development, mutual influences between family and peers were on top of the research agenda.

The investigations were organized according to a cohort-sequential design, with three age cohorts each, spanning the range between 11 and 17 years of age. The results reported in this chapter rely on annual assessments of one of the cohorts between 1985 and 1987, corresponding to mean ages 14.5, 15.5, and 16.5 years. The adolescents were sampled on the basis of classes, selected mainly to represent variation in educational tracks and school districts within West Berlin and Warsaw. In about 60% of the cases at least one parent also agreed to participate. Depending on the variable and family member studied, the sample sizes vary between about 80 and 500 per national group.

The remainder of the chapter is organized into four main parts. First, beliefs held by adolescent participants are described. The results point to differences between West Berlin and Warsaw youths in terms of more individualistic versus more conformist interests. Second, research on leisure contexts is presented. Less self-direction and more adult-shaped leisure opportunities seem to be characteristic for adolescents' life in Warsaw compared to West Berlin. Third, smoking and drinking in the mid-teens are studied using comparable data from the two cities. Given the differences in beliefs and self-controlled opportunities, the cross-national variation found is interpreted as rooted in differential pathways of psychosocial development in West Berlin and Warsaw. Fourth, the results and interpretations are discussed concerning their impact for the ultimate goal of cross-national research, to substitute more explanatory concepts for "nation."

Aspects of Adolescents' Beliefs

National groups as well as individuals can be distinguished as to their relative emphasis on values that serve individualistic interests versus collectivist interests (Hofstede, 1980; Triandis, 1990). As Dornbusch (1989) put it, concern for the conformity of one's opinions to those of others is characteristic of conformist interests, while concern for the content of ideas, and a willingness or eagerness to consider seriously the diversity of ideas held by people is characteristic of individualistic interests. Below, this notion is first being explored concerning general value orientations.

The adolescents in both cities were asked to rate the import of each of 16 statements reminiscent of the Rokeach values (Smolenska & Fraczek, 1987). Statements expressing the wish to have satisfying relations with friends, to accomplish a good professional education, and to enjoy a happy family life ranked at the top in both samples. However, while Berliners favored relations with friends most, their age-mates from Warsaw endorsed a happy family life more. In both cities the occupational domain was ranked second.

At the bottom of the list, living a comfortable life without challenge had no attraction for the young in either group. Another statement rated low was the desire to exert political influence—adolescents rated this as having no interest at all for them. Furthermore, the young in Warsaw had a similar resentment against being responsible for important decisions in the work setting.

According to Schwartz and Bilsky (1987), peoples' judgments in the domains of enjoyment, achievement, and self-direction belong to individualistic interests, and those of restrictive conformity, prosocial orientation, and security belong to collectivist interests. Relying on this classification, the value statements were grouped in order to assess these aspects of belief systems. The resulting sum scales correlated at about .20 (Berlin) and .40 (Warsaw), with a diminished value across age.

As expected, ANOVAs (repeated measurement on waves of data collection) revealed that the Polish adolescents endorsed collectivist values more than their age-mates from West Berlin. The individualistic orientation, however, did not differ between the samples. Furthermore, within the age range studied no change across time was observed in the scores of the dimensions. As throughout this chapter, all effects reported are statistically significant on the .05 level or less.

Based on the preference of family over peers, and supported by the higher endorsement of collectivist values among the young from Warsaw, we expected adolescents in the two cities to differ with regard to whose advice they would trust in age-typic decisions about their future. For instance, self-satisfaction is less likely to guide adolescents' career decisions in case conformity with opinions held by the family provides the premium standard in their life.

In the beginning of the German-Polish collaboration, we were interested in research on self-attributions of prosocial motives. These attributions are viewed as rooted in a number of particular cognitive schemes which Reykowski (1982) called "evaluative standards." When conformity standards are operative, for instance, performance of prosocial behavior depends on the presence of explicit or implicit demands by an authority or reference group. As research based on this approach showed interesting commonalities and differences among samples of adolescents from West Berlin, Bologna, Phoenix, and Warsaw (Boehnke, Silbereisen, Eisenberg, Reykowsky, & Palmonari, 1989; Silbereisen, Lamsfuss, Boehnke, & Eisenberg, 1991), the notion of evaluative standards was adopted in order to investigate adolescents' decision making on important goals in life.

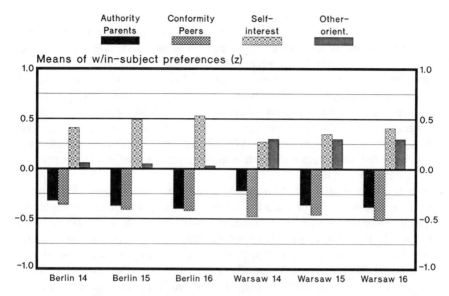

FIGURE 9.1. Standards in adolescents' life-planning. Shown are results of annual measurements of adolescents living in West Berlin (n = 473) and Warsaw (n = 263), ages 14.5 to 16.5. The mean within-subject preferences (z-scores) are depicted concerning the role of expectations and demands in decision making.

The basic idea was to let adolescents in West Berlin and Warsaw judge the role in their decisions of expectations and demands from parents, teachers, and other adults (authority standards), and of peers, students in class, and close friends (conformity). Furthermore, they rated the relevance of their own prospective life-satisfaction (self-interest), and the well-being and benefit of people more or less close to them, for whom they care (other-orientation). Two substantive domains were used, namely, the choice of an occupation, and thoughts about how to accomplish salient personal goals through one's life.

Smolenska and Silbereisen (1991) calculated the relative import of the four evaluative standards by standardization within subjects (Leung & Bond, 1989). The mean preferences and their change between ages 14 and 16 are shown in Figure 9.1. The data were analyzed using ANOVAs per evaluative standard.

In both cities and for all age-groups, relying on other's advice (parents, peers, etc.) was much less endorsed than relying on actions justified by one's own advantage (self-interest) as well as, to a lesser degree, the well-being of people close to the self (other-orientation). There was also a decrease with age for authority and conformity, and an almost linearly increasing trend with age was observed for self-interest, while the preference for other-orientation remained rather stable across the waves.

Nevertheless, there were clear differences in the pattern of preferences between West Berlin and Warsaw. German adolescents preferred conformity with peers relatively more, and focusing on their close acquaintances' point of view relatively less, than their age-mates in Warsaw. Even more impressive was the much higher premium of self-interest among the Berliners. In other words, the German adolescents presented themselves as being more independent from adults and more oriented towards their own advantage. Gender differences were more pronounced in Warsaw than in West Berlin. While Polish males endorsed self-interest more strongly than demands from acquaintances, it was quite the opposite among Polish females.

At first glance, the articulation of one's own interests among Berliners fits to expectations nourished by reports on the pronounced articulation of self-interests among West German youth (Watts & Zinnecker, 1988) and would thus point to a solid national difference. However, the similarity of age trends across samples may also indicate differences in the timing of changes as background of the national differences. Indeed, additional data, gathered at age 17, showed a further increase in the Polish group's relative import of self-interest, especially among males. The Poles' higher import of demands by close acquaintances, however, remained unchanged. Thus, while the latter (i.e., importance of close acquaintances) seems to be a stable characteristic of cultural difference, variation in self-interest reveals differential timing of change.

Adolescents and Their Leisure Contexts

After having illuminated some national differences in beliefs, we now focus on experiences in a number of daily leisure contexts. The main interest lies in national differences in the amount of autonomy and leeway taken by the adolescents.

Leisure is a special issue when considering autonomy and self-direction. More than any other aspect of daily life, adolescents exercise their growing freedom in choosing what to do in their leisure time (Larson, this volume). In previous research, we conducted systematic field observations and personal interviews in a variety of leisure locales (Noack, 1990; Silbereisen & Noack, 1988). The results showed that adolescents used these settings in order to promote their social contacts with same-sex peers and romantic friends. Thus, young people pursued age-typical developmental tasks while using malls, sports stadia, and other locales. Interestingly enough, the gist of the data resembled insights already provided in the 1930s by Muchow and Muchow's (1935; Wohlwill, 1985) seminal work on "use against the rules" of department stores as settings for self-development.

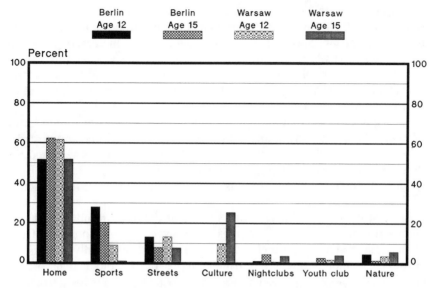

FIGURE 9.2. Most frequented leisure locales of adolescents. Shown is the share (%) of seven categories of places among the nominations of adolescents in West Berlin ($n = 454$) and Warsaw ($n = 454$). Subjects of ages 12.5 and 15.5 (cross-sections) replied to questions in an open format by specifying the concrete location. Only the first answer was coded in the present analysis.

Recently, Hendry (Coleman & Hendry, 1990) described the development of leisure activities as being characterized by a sequence of changing focal preferences. At age 13, leisure activities organized by adults are at stake, followed by a preference for casual activities at age 15, and finally a preference for commercial activities at age 17. Typical examples for the sequence are youth clubs, hangouts away from home, and discotheques. The changing preferences and their timing reflect a parallel change in focal interpersonal issues.

In comparing adolescents' most frequented and most preferred leisure locales between West Berlin and Warsaw youth, we (Silbereisen & Noack, 1990b) studied whether the basics of this approach can be generalized despite presumably quite different leisure opportunities. Swida (1987), for instance, studied Polish secondary school students and characterized close personal contacts with friends, going to the movies, and reading books as prime ways to overcome the strains of everyday life.

In line with the literature (Garton & Pratt, 1987), both aspects of adolescents' whereabouts yielded similar results. Consequently, in Figure 9.2 only the relative import (%) of the most frequented leisure locales is given. The data were analyzed by log-linear models, encompassing city, age group (12.5 vs. 15.5-year-olds), and gender as independent factors. Only the most important results are given.

The main national differences were concentrated on sports settings that scored much higher in West Berlin, and cultural settings that scored much higher in Warsaw. Sports declined with age, culture increased. Going to the movies seems to be as prototypic for young Poles as sports for young Germans. While public ice-skating rinks, indoor pools, and private sports clubs were categorized as sports, the culture category was comprised of movie theaters, concert halls, museums, and similar places.

Sports and culture may well play a functionally equivalent role in terms of their affinity to the adolescents' goals to meet peers and friends. Indeed, a check of the social company and of the activities reported for these settings provided some evidence for this expectation. Both groups of adolescents met friends and enjoyed dates at the respective settings.

In West Berlin and Warsaw, one's home or that of a friend ranked first among the most frequented settings. Moreover, a higher portion of the females claimed homes as their prime leisure setting, especially in Warsaw. However, while among the Berliners more of the older than of the younger adolescents mentioned homes, in Warsaw homes lost attraction with age.

This difference between the national samples was further investigated by addressing with whom adolescents enjoyed company at their own homes. The results showed that more of the Germans met close friends, saw their girlfriend or boyfriend, or spent time alone, while more of the Poles were together with adults and siblings. The results on the German youth are in line with Schiavo's (1987) description of the family room and adolescents' personal bedrooms in particular as offering opportunities for dealing with the chemistry of interpersonal relations. In contrast, the young Poles could not focus on visitors from outside the family.

There were also differences in the activities pursued at home (5-point self-ratings of frequency of involvement). According to the results of ANOVAs reported by Neuhof and Noack (1992), adolescents from Warsaw reported more frequent chatting, watching TV, assisting in the household, solitary and social play, and being busy doing things like needlework. In contrast, adolescents from West Berlin listened more often to music, and also felt bored more frequently. When asked about the reasons to stay at the family home, more Germans than Poles claimed they were not allowed to leave, did not have enough money, had no idea what else to do, and wanted friends visiting them.

In a nutshell, while homes were highly attractive in both cities, cultural affairs were less popular among the young in West Berlin, and sports locales were less popular among Warsaw youth. As to meeting friends and enjoying dates, sports and culture may play equivalent roles concerning their impact for development. Concerning the sequence of changing focal preferences proposed by Coleman and Hendry (1983), a clear difference turned up. The Warsaw youths' profile puts them at an earlier point in the sequence which contrasts from that of their German age-mates.

So far, differences in the attraction, company, and activities in the home were described. As a first explanatory attempt, the analyses were repeated with adolescents' degree of collectivist orientation and variation in dating experiences partialled out. These variables were chosen because they clearly revealed mean level differences between the national groups. Applying the "unpacking approach" reported by Feldman and Rosenthal (1991; Feldman & Rosenthal, this volume), the attempt was to explain parts of the effect of nation in terms of these variables. This was success-fully accomplished for 4 out of 13 leisure activities, namely, listening to music, hanging around, feeling bored, and assisting in the household. Although the variance explained by the predictors was small in absolute terms, the 50% reduction of the impact of nation was quite remarkable. As the other differences in adolescents' activities between Berlin and Warsaw remained significant, the two variables can only delineate the direction of the search for explanatory variables. Certainly, small-sized appartments have their share in precluding adolescents from meeting friends, and the traditionally higher family orientation among Poles is also a likely candidate for the further "unpacking" of the observed national differences.

With this insight into differences in leisure activities, we conclude our report on beliefs and leisure contexts in West Berlin and Warsaw. In the following, results on adolescent substance use are discussed against this background.

Smoking and Drinking in Adolescence

In their theory of problem-behavior proneness, Jessor and Jessor (1977) have stressed the instrumental role of substance use, precocious sex, and other adultlike behaviors in managing the transition to adulthood. Accordingly, young people begin to smoke and drink in order to enjoy and demonstrate what they see as a core element of adult privileges. Thus, the likelihood of substance use among the young should vary according to whether substance use is part of the concept of adulthood. Attempts to test this assumption profit from cross-cultural comparisons.

The aim of the following portion of our study (see Silbereisen, Schönpflug, & Albrecht, 1990) was to investigate the potential of some characteristics of person and context in explaining adolescent substance use: state of romantic friendships, self-esteem, clique membership, peer rejection, and parental monitoring. Obviously such a short list cannot exhaust the variance in youthful substance use. Rather, we were interested in simple markers of risk factors we and others identified in previous research.

More specifically, differences and commonalities between samples from West Berlin and Warsaw were assessed in terms of mean levels of these variables, and in terms of the relations between individual differences in these variables and change in substance use. In addition, the impact of differences between school tracks was studied as another instance of contextual variation. Lower tracks leading to several nonacademic professions were compared with the highest track, the traditional European college-bound track.

Some remarks on the import of the characteristics chosen may suffice. The formation of romantic friendships takes place in age-typical leisure contexts. Offering a cigarette or a sip of alcohol was shown to be part of widely used strategies in making friends (Evans, 1989; Silbereisen & Noack, 1988). Consequently, we expected a fostering effect of the state of friendship development on substance use.

Smoking and drinking within leisure contexts that allow "letting off steam" may help adolescents to gain self-esteem (Silbereisen & Reitzle, 1992). In turn, according to Kaplan, Martin, and Johnston (1986), negative self-evaluation is especially risky, as it may drive adolescents into contacts with problem-prone peer groups that provide models for smoking, drinking, and use of other substances. A guiding principle seems to be "like liking like" (Dornbusch, 1989), that is, future peer friends select each other on the basis of prior resemblance in a target behavior in addition to peer influence (Kandel, 1986). Adolescents who feel rejected by normative reference groups, such as schoolmates, may be especially at risk to "deviance in defense of self" to use Kaplan's (1980) phrase. Thus, both low self-esteem and rejection by normative peers are deemed as risk factors for substance use.

According to Snyder, Dishion, and Patterson (1986), parents low in monitoring tend to overlook early precursors of problem-prone peer contacts and thus put their children at risk. When monitoring, parents are engaging in procedures that allow them to know about the whereabouts of their children. Based on this research, low monitoring should increase the likelihood of early substance use.

Well-established measures were used for most of the variables (see Silbereisen, Schönpflug, & Albrecht, 1990 for details). Examples of the items follow: "How often (rarely through daily; 0–3) in the week are you away from home in the evening?" (monitoring), "Do you belong to a group of friends who meet regularly? (no, yes; 0–1)" (clique membership), "Sometimes I wish I were a different person" (self-esteem, reversed; 4-point rating of agreement), "The other students at school don't particularly like me" (peer rejection; 4-point rating of agreement). All variables refer to adolescents' judgments. In both cities, the traditional college-bound track was coded *1*, all other tracks within the school system *0*.

Our conceptualization of the state of romantic friendships, however, deserves a more detailed description (Silbereisen & Noack, 1990a;

Silbereisen, Noack, & von Eye, 1992). We were interested in the degree
to which adolescents experienced a match between the desired and the
actual state in dating. More specifically, whether an adolescent is dating
was distinguished from the hopes for the year ahead, that is, whether
having a girlfriend or boyfriend is a strong wish. Both aspects of dating
were further distinguished as to intensity of experiences and hopes, respectively. Basically, the discrepancy between desired and actual state is
used as an indication of the more or less advanced stage in the development of romantic relations. Earlier analyses at age 14 (Schönpflug &
Silbereisen, 1989) showed twice as many Berliners than Warsaw youth
who reported their hopes to exceed the reality of dating. Moreover,
about three times more of the young Poles than of the Germans experienced a match between hopes and actual state, though on a low level of
dating.

Commonalities and Differences in Group Means

In cross-national research on alcohol consumption among adults, the
Poles rank higher than West Germans (Johnston & Harrison, 1984).
Thus, assuming a higher level of substance use for the Polish adolescents
as compared to their German age-mates seems possible to justify. However, the differences in values and leisure activities reported in the previous sections warn against simply generalizing from the adult literature.
Having characterized smoking and drinking as status offenses, bearing in
mind the more traditional orientation of Polish parents, and thinking of
the differences in leisure experiences, we were in fact led to expect lower
levels of smoking and drinking among the adolescent Poles.

The results concerning self-rated annual frequencies ("How often did
you smoke cigarettes (drink beer or wine) during the past year?") are
shown in Figure 9.3. The data on smoking and drinking during the
previous years were analyzed by ANOVAs.

As expected, the Polish adolescents reported less smoking and drinking
than their German age-mates. The increase across adolescence observed
in both national groups is in line with research utilizing normal population
samples (Kandel & Logan, 1984). Adolescents' use of tobacco varied as a
function of educational track, while alcohol consumption was similar
across tracks. More specifically, in West Berlin and Warsaw, the highest
track students smoked less than their age-mates who attended lower
educational tracks.

Polish adolescents were assumed to enjoy less freedom from parental
supervision than their German age-mates do. Although the differences
were not significant, the scores were in the expected direction.

Earlier research demonstrated lower self-direction in Polish compared
to German schools (Silbereisen, Boehnke, & Crockett, 1991). Given the
likely link with self-evaluation, and bearing in mind the differences con-

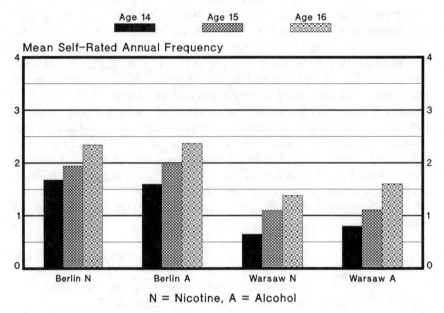

FIGURE 9.3. Substance use of adolescents. Shown are the mean self-rated annual frequencies (4 = very frequently) of adolescents in West Berlin (*n* = 351) and Warsaw (*n* = 333). The adolescents were assessed in annual waves between ages 14.5 and 16.5.

cerning leeway in leisure, the Polish adolescents were predicted to report lower levels of self-esteem. The overall difference was quite striking and confirmed the hypothesis. In contrast to what one would have expected among Germans (Schulz, 1989), in the Polish sample students of the lower tracks showed higher self-esteem. It is interesting to note that this result is in line with the results reported by Kohn, Naoi, Schoenbach, Schooler, & Slomczynski (1990), who found Polish blue-collar workers to have higher self-esteem than their managers. As known from earlier research (Alsaker & Olweus, 1986; O'Malley & Bachman, 1983), self-esteem increased through adolescence.

Concerning cross-national differences in perceived rejection by peers, specific expectations were not forwarded. In fact, Polish adolescents reported more peer rejection, but also showed a more pronounced decrease across time. This, as well as the higher rejection reported by students of the lower tracks, was in line with previous results on the German part of the studies (Silbereisen & Albrecht, 1992). With regard to membership in peer cliques, the adolescents from Warsaw and Berlin did not differ.

The Polish adolescents were assumed to report less demands for romantic friendship. Again, the reason for the prediction of this difference was seen in the more traditional value orientation of Polish parents and, generally speaking, because presumably less leeway is given for adolescents' privacy due to physical and social constraints. The rather small size of appartments, for instance, is not conducive for the development of romantic friendship. The cross-national differences found confirmed this prediction. Silbereisen and Noack (1990b) interpreted the result as indicating culture-specific differences in the "timetabling" (Feldman & Quatman, 1988) of this important aspect of the adolescent transition.

In sum, the hypotheses concerning cross-national differences in the variables were mostly confirmed. Polish adolescents reported less substance use, were less involved in issues of romantic friendship, had less unsupervised time away from their parents, and their overall self-esteem was lower. As the Polish youths' scores in self-esteem and peer rejection at the second measurement occasion resembled those of the previous assessment among the Germans, the national differences found may in part be due to differential timing of change, a recurrent topic in this chapter. Differences between tracks were alike in the two cities with one exception: Self-esteem was higher among lower track students in Warsaw.

Commonalities and Differences in Predictive Relations

Based on the results of longitudinal research reported earlier in this part of the chapter, we made the following general predictions: Concerning changes in substance use, prior self-esteem and parental monitoring were expected to show use-diminishing effects; in contrast, prior peer rejection and clique membership were predicted to have enhancing effects on future substance use, that is, effects above and beyond the stability of smoking and drinking across the period of time observed. Furthermore, more pronounced demands for romantic friendships were assumed to increase future levels of substance use.

However, earlier research led us to differentiate between smoking and drinking. In principle, alcohol consumption should show a closer association with variables indicating the intensity of age-typical interpersonal contacts, while smoking may be more related to personal well-being as indicated by self-esteem (Semmer, Dwyer, Lippert, Fuchs, Cleary, & Schindler, 1987).

Concerning cross-national differences, more than one expectation seemed plausible, and consequently the analyses are viewed as exploratory. First, national differences may influence the mean levels of the variables without affecting relationships, substance use, and psychosocial risk factors. Thus, the association of the psychosocial risk factors with change in substance use is predicted to be similar when comparing the samples from West Berlin and Warsaw, despite the already reported differences in the mean levels of some of the variables. Recent research lends support to this assumption. Feldman, Rosenthal, Mont-Reynaud, Leung, & Lau (1991; Feldman & Rosenthal, this volume) studied adolescents' misconduct in samples from Hong Kong, Australia, and the United States. The youth from Hong Kong reported less misconduct than the other adolescents, including smoking and drinking below legal age, and they also showed differences in pertinent risk factors. Despite these differences, levels of misconduct were related similarly to family variables and adolescent values. More specifically, in all samples, adolescents' valuation of outward success, an aspect of individualism, and low parental monitoring were associated with misconduct.

Second, however, there are also reasons to assume that the cross-national differences in the levels of substance use correspond to different relations among the predictor and outcome variables. In other words, when comparing the samples from West Berlin and Warsaw, different risk factors are predicted to be associated with change in substance use. If the differences in the levels actually indicate different stages in the development of substance use, level-specific risk factors are quite likely (Marlatt, Baer, Donovan, & Kivlahan, 1988; Rutter, 1988).

The analyses were conducted by ordinary regressions, using multiple-group LISREL (Jöreskog & Sörbom, 1984) in order to compare results across tracks and measurement occasions. All analyses were conducted twice: Wave 1 predicting Wave 2 scores 12 months later; and Wave 2 predicting Wave 3 scores, again 12 months later. As the previous score on the outcome measures were included among the predictors, the results indicate the import of individual differences in the risk factors in predicting change in substance use above and beyond its stability. Gender and age within cohorts were controlled. The explained variance ranged between approximately .30 and .60, depending on city, track, and substance analyzed.

We omit details on the correlations among the variables. In both national samples, peer rejection corresponded to lower self-esteem ($r = -.30$ to $-.40$, depending on sample and wave), and being a member of a clique was related to more leeway from supervision ($r = .20$ to $.36$).

Alcohol

The risk factors for change in alcohol consumption differed between West Berlin and Warsaw, but were alike across educational tracks within the cities. As the latter parallels the lack of differentiation in consumption level, similar levels seem to correspond to similar patterns of predictive relations.

In both national groups, only one variable was significant besides the stability coefficient (i.e., the coefficient corresponding to the T2 score regressed on the T1 score) of the substance. Among the Germans, change in drinking was predicted by variation in the demand concerning romantic friendship. The higher the prior mismatch between desired and actual state in this domain, the more increase in drinking frequency above and beyond the stability of alcohol consumption.

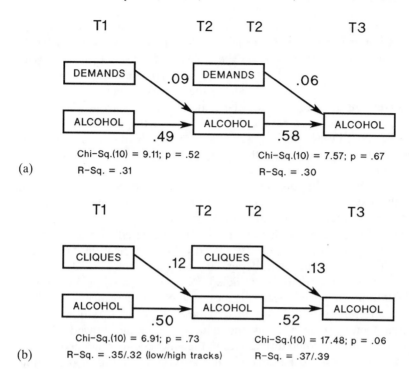

FIGURE 9.4. Predictors of change in adolescents' self-rated annual frequency of alcohol consumption: West Berlin (a) and Warsaw (b). Shown are variables with significant regression weights ($p < .05$) and goodness-of-fit statistics. Analyses for T1–T2 and T2–T3 were conducted separately. Nonsignificant predictors not shown. See text for more details.

Within the Polish sample a different pattern turned up. At both assessment periods, change in alcohol consumption was predicted by clique membership. Those who belonged to a group of friends increased their consumption more.

The results are graphically presented in Figures 9.4a and b. The size of coefficients is rather small.

In sum, risk factors specific for the national groups were observed for alcohol consumption: demands for relations with the other sex among German adolescents, membership in a peer clique among Polish adolescents. Obviously, both variables have the realm of interpersonal contacts in common. However, according to Dunphy (1963) membership in cliques marks an early step in the development of friendships.

Smoking

The risk factors for change in smoking differed not only between cities, they were also different across educational levels. Instead of going into details, an interesting commonality across samples deserves attention.

Self-esteem was central in predicting change in smoking, although at different points in time. Among the Germans, this was the case earlier in adolescence, at age 15.5. Among the Poles, self-esteem came into play later at age 16.5, that is, at a time when their consumption figures were closer to those reported by Germans in the previous year.

However, differences between the national samples seem not to be a function of consumption levels alone. Although the levels were rather similar between Poles attending schools of the lower tracks and Germans attending the highest track, the samples revealed differences in the antecedents.

Taken together, what do the results studied on alcohol and nicotine tell about the risk factors for change in substance use? Concerning overall differences between smoking and drinking, the expectations were mostly confirmed. Smoking was indeed more closely associated with self-esteem, while drinking was more closely associated with social relations. Although the results varied somewhat depending on time, track, and national group, monitoring worked as predicted concerning smoking. In contrast to expectation, however, peer rejection was of no relevance at all. The national differences found may in part be due to the variation in consumption figures. However, as the data on smoking showed, despite similar consumption some differences in the antecedents remained. While these results contrast to Feldman et al. (1991), one should bear in mind that their study was cross-sectional, and thus could not reveal commonalities concerning antecedents of change in misconduct.

Conclusions

In this chapter, beliefs held by the adolescent participants were presented first and differences were interpreted in terms of a basic facet of value orientations: individualistic versus collectivist interests. In line with the concern for the good of the in-group, characteristic of collectivist interests, close acquaintances seemed to play a more prominent role as referents in Polish adolescents' decisions on developmental tasks.

Second, leisure contexts of adolescents were surveyed. Key issues were the dominance of adults versus peers in leisure locales and activities, presumably indicating differences in the degree of self-direction. Compared to their fellows in West Berlin, the young in Warsaw were seen as living in settings less instigative for the rapid attainment of adult privileges. Taken together, the results on cross-national differences in values and self-controlled opportunities led us to propose differential timing in psychosocial development as a likely consequence.

Third, Polish compared with German adolescents reported tentatively less leeway from parental supervision, higher perceived peer rejection, a less advanced state in the development of romantic friendships, and considerably lower self-esteem. As the trends across age were mostly consistent between West Berlin and Warsaw, the differences were seen as mainly transitional, again indicating differential timing. The disadvantaged position of the young Poles in self-esteem, however, may be more than a reflection of temporarily less opportunities for self-control.

Fourth, differences were found in level and antecedents of substance use. The Polish adolescents reported less frequent smoking and drinking. This was paralleled by lower levels in well-known risk factors for substance use such as one's state in the development of romantic friendships. The antecedents of change in substance use, particularly alcohol consumption, showed some national variation. However, differential risk factors such as clique membership in Warsaw as opposed to romantic friendships in West Berlin were at least in part due to differences in the state or level of consumption.

In the following, this general pattern of results is discussed, beginning with the analyses on smoking and drinking, the last step in the reported investigations.

The assessment of substance use was accomplished by self-ratings of annual frequencies. As in many comparable studies, more objective measures were not available. However, the validity of self-ratings concerning legal substances is usually seen as adequate. Concerning socially accepted substances such as alcohol, subjects show high consistency across several reports (O'Malley, Bachman, & Johnston, 1983), and their ratings are almost unaffected under bogus physiological validation (Campanelli, Dielman, & Shope, 1987). Nevertheless, as we have no independent evidence, the possibility of underreporting by the Polish adolescents cannot be completely ruled out.

Judged from previous research, we described the Polish families as living up to a more traditional value orientation than their German fellows. Characteristic of such belief systems is a heightened emphasis on age and other status attributes, rather than on personal attributes (Beck, 1983). Behaviors seen as precocious are subject to a stricter regime and, consequently, become negatively sanctioned. As smoking and drinking represent elements of an adult life-style, parents in Warsaw should be less tolerant concerning a premature timing of such behaviors than are parents in Berlin. Consequently, Polish adolescents have or take fewer opportunities for substance use.

According to this interpretation, the differences in consumption would reflect culturally based differences concerning the appropriate timing of such behaviors. In cross-national research on adolescent drinking among the Irish and North Americans, a similar line of arguments was used. As Christiansen and Teahan (1987) reported, Irish adults have a reputation for being either abstinent or favoring problem drinking. Nevertheless, Irish adolescents scored lower than their American age-mates concerning social drinking. The normative prohibition pertinent to the Irish culture was seen as the common root of both the adolescent and the adult particularities in drinking patterns. Although strong normative prohibitions keep the level of drinking in adolescence low, they also prohibit the development of a greater range of, and less polarized, drinking styles among adults.

Despite the differences in the levels of substance use and of the psychosocial variables, the association with change in substance use showed commonalities across samples. Change in alcohol consumption, for instance, was related to social experiences—with same-sex peers among the Polish adolescents, with intimate other-sex friends among the German adolescents. Thus, the cultural differences were revealed in both position and patterning of the variables.

In our view the key to understanding the national differences lies in the notion of differential timing for some of the transitions characteristic for adolescence. According to recent research on expectations about the timetabling of developmental achievements, the kind of value orientations we studied are likely to influence the timing of development.

More collectivist cultures keep later autonomy expectations for youths. Rosenthal and Bornholt (1988) showed this for Greek-Australian as compared to Anglo-Australian families, and Feldman and Quatman (1988) demonstrated the influence for Asian-American as compared to Euro/Anglo-American families. More specifically, the age differences concerning social behaviors with peers were as large as 2 years for issues like "go to girl/boy parties" and "go out on dates." Moreover, the expectations were quite similar between generations and genders. Concerning adolescent drinking, Pulkkinen and Narusk (1987) confirmed the role of differences in belief-systems. Finnish compared to Estonian parents were much more liberal with regard to drinking prior to legal age, and this was paralleled by their less traditional value orientation.

The national variation in the demand for romantic friendships we found may be interpreted as indicating differences in the developmental timetables with regard to dating. The difference is due to a higher portion of Poles being in balance with their wishes, and a higher portion of Germans claiming more hopes than they could yet realize. Thus, although the adolescents were of the same age, for the Germans the issue of dating was more at stake than it was for the Poles. In other words, the young Berliners appear to be in greater haste than same-aged Poles to consummate the joy of romance.

This result resembles differences between European-American and African-American samples in the timing of adolescent transitions reported by Simmons and Zhou (this volume). In various indicators of youthful transitions, particularly males of the latter group behaved as if they were more advanced judged by the stereotype of adolescence. Concerning the present comparison, however, one may ask whether the concept of adolescence is similar enough to interpret national differences as related to timing rather than, for instance, to the sequence or quality of transitions.

Nevertheless, in our view several other results illuminate differential psychosocial development as well. A case in point are the leisure activities. While the young Poles seemingly started to decenter their focus from parents and siblings, youths in West Berlin were already more engaged in relations with friends and intimate affiliates. As these circumstances are known to be instigative for drinking as a means of making friends (Silbereisen & Noack, 1988), the national differences in the reported consumption figures are a likely consequence. Accordingly, we would also expect level-specific risk factors, and this is exactly what the data revealed. The risk for alcohol use was increased by peer contacts in Warsaw, while romantic contacts increased the risk for alcohol use in West Berlin. If these results can be generalized, the common thread would appear as social experiences that, in turn, are themselves graded by opportunities and culture-specific expectations as to their appropriate timing.

During the planning of the studies in West Berlin and Warsaw a decade ago, we had no clear-cut idea of the explanatory concepts required in order to understand potential cultural differences. Now that we know more, explicit tests of hypotheses are feasible. This can be accomplished by utilizing as yet unanalyzed data of two more cohorts. By introducing value orientations and other explanatory variables in structural equation models, we will investigate the quality of the national differences more directly. Furthermore, intraindividual change in substance use may be better characterized by the qualitative course from abstinence to regular use.

Adolescents' experiences in "mesocontexts" (Bronfenbrenner, 1989) such as the interplay between family and leisure are seen as inducive for the variation in psychosocial development. However, these factors themselves undergo change, and this can have an influence of its own on development (Baltes, 1987). The situation of many families with adolescent school-leavers was rather critical when the studies in West Berlin were started in 1982. Young people were confronted with a life-world characterized by unemployment of noncollege youth. In the following years this situation changed dramatically in the positive direction. The ongoing changes in Warsaw are presumably more severe, and their ultimate quality is not yet predictable. The most recent changes in Germany, however, the process of political unification, took place after we finished the last wave of data gathering.

Acknowledgments. Parts of this chapter were presented as an Invited Address to the Third Biennal Meetings of the Society for Research on Adolescence, March 22–25, 1990, Atlanta, GA, U.S.A. Much of the work reported in this chapter was supported by grants from the German Research Council (Si 296/1–1

194   R.K. Silbereisen, P. Noack, and U. Schönpflug

through 6; principal investigators: R.K. Silbereisen, K. Eyferth) and the Technical
University of Berlin (IFP 2/11; principal investigator: R.K. Silbereisen, in col-
laboration with Hans Benninghaus, Bernhard Dieckmann, and Roland Posner).
We thank the Polish team in Warsaw (principal investigator: A. Fraczek, in
collaboration with L. Kirwil and Z. Smolenska) for their support and friendship.
Special thanks go to Janusz Reykowski for his commitment and stimulation.

References

Alsaker, F. & Olweus, D. (1986). Assessment of global negative self-evaluations
and perceived stability of self in Norwegian preadolescents and adolescents.
Journal of Early Adolescence, 6, 269–278.
Baltes, P.B. (1987). Theoretical propositions of life-span developmental psychology: On the dynamic between growth and decline. *Developmental Psychology, 23*, 611–626.
Beck, U. (1983). Jenseits von Stand und Klasse? Soziale Ungleichheiten, gesells-
chaftliche Individualisierungsprozesse und die Entstehung neuer sozialer For-
mationen und Identitäten [Beyond social class? Social inequality, the societal
process of individualization and the emergence of new social formations and
identities]. *Soziale Welt, 2*, 35–74.
Boehnke, K., Silbereisen, R.K., Eisenberg, N., Reykowski, J., & Palmonari, A.
(1989). Developmental pattern of prosocial motivation: A cross-national study.
Journal of Cross-Cultural Psychology, 20, 219–243.
Bronfenbrenner, U. (1989). Ecological systems theory. In R. Vasta (Ed.), *Six
theories of child development: Revised formulations and current issues* (Annals
of Child Development, Vol. 6, pp. 187–249). Greenwich, CT: JAI Press.
Campanelli, P.C., Dielman, T.E., & Shope, J.T. (1987). Validity of adolescents'
self-reports of alcohol use and misuse using a bogus pipeline procedure. *Ado-
lescence, 85*, 7–22.
Christiansen, B.A. & Teahan, J.E. (1987). Cross-cultural comparisons of Irish
and American adolescents' drinking practices and beliefs. *Journal of Studies on
Alcohol, 48*, 558–562.
Coleman, J.C. & Hendry, L.B. (1990). *The nature of adolescence* (2nd ed.).
London: Routledge.
Dornbusch, S.M. (1989). The sociology of adolescence. *Annual Review of Soci-
ology, 15*, 233–259.
Dunphy, D.C. (1963). The social structure of urban adolescent peer groups.
Society, 26, 230–246.
Evans, S.T. (1989). *Nightclubbing: An exploration after dark*. Paper presented
at the BPS Scottish Branch Annual Conference. University of Strathclyde,
Glasgow.
Feldman, S.S. & Quatman, T. (1988). Factors influencing age expectations for
adolescent autonomy: A study of early adolescents and parents. *Journal of
Early Adolescence, 8*, 325–343.
Feldman, S.S., Rosenthal, D.A., Mont-Reynaud, R., Leung, K., & Lau, S.
(1991). Ain't misbehavin': Adolescent values and family environments as corre-
lates of misconduct in Australia, Hong Kong and the United States. *Journal of
Research on Adolescence, 1*, 109–134.

Garton, A.F. & Pratt, C. (1987). Participation and interest in leisure activities by adolescent schoolchildren. *Journal of Adolescence, 10*, 341–351.

Hofstede, G. (1980). *Culture's consequences: International differences in work-related values*. Beverly Hills: Sage.

Höllinger, F. (1989). Familie und soziale Netzwerke in fortgeschrittenen Industriegesellschaften. Eine vergleichende empirische Studie in sieben Nationen [Family and social networks in highly industrialized societies. An empirical comparison among seven nations]. *Soziale Welt, 4*, 513–537.

Jessor, R. & Jessor, S.L. (1977). *Problem behavior and psychosocial development: A longitudinal study of youth*. New York: Academic Press.

Johnston, L.D. & Harrison, L.D. (1984). *An international perspective on alcohol and drug use in adolescence* (quoted from Silbereisen, R.K. & Kastner, P. [1987]). Jugend und Problemverhalten [Adolescence and problem behavior]. In R. Oerter & L. Montada (Eds.), *Entwicklungspsychologie* (pp. 882–919). München: Psychologie Verlags Union.

Jöreskog, K.G. & Sörbom, D. (1984). *LISREL VI: Analyis of linear structural relationships by maximum likelihood, instrumental variables, and least square methods*. Mooresville, IN: Scientific Software.

Kandel, D.B. (1986). Processes of peer influence in adolescence. In R.K. Silbereisen, K. Eyferth, & G. Rudinger (Eds.), *Development as action in context: Problem behavior and normal youth development* (pp. 203–228). New York: Springer.

Kandel, D.B. & Logan, J.A. (1984). Patterns of drug use from adolescence to early adulthood: I. Periods of risk for initiation, stabilization and decline in drug use from adolescence to early adulthood. *American Journal of Public Health, 74*, 660–666.

Kaplan, H.B. (1980). *Deviant behavior in defense of self*. New York: Academic Press.

Kaplan, H.B., Martin, S.S., & Johnston, R.J. (1986). Self-rejection and the explanation of deviance: Specification of the structure among latent constructs. *American Journal of Sociology, 92*, 384–411.

Kohn, M.L., Naoi, A., Schoenbach, C., Schooler, C., & Slomczynski, K.M. (1990). Position in the class structure and psychological functioning in the United States, Japan, and Poland. *American Journal of Sociology, 95*, 964–1008.

Koralewicz, J. (1987). Changes in Polish social consciousness during the 1970s and 1980s: Opportunism and identity. In J. Koralewicz, I. Bialecki, & M. Watson (Eds.), *Crisis and transition: Polish society in the 1980s* (pp. 3–25). Oxford: Berg.

Leung, K. & Bond, M.H. (1989). On the empirical identification of dimensions for cross-cultural comparisons. *Journal of Cross-Cultural Psychology, 20*, 133–151.

Marini, M. (1984). Age and sequencing norms in the transition to adulthood. *Social Forces, 61*, 229–244.

Marlatt, G.A., Baer, J.S., Donovan, D.M., & Kivlahan, D.R. (1988). Addictive behaviors: Etiology and treatment. *Annual Review of Psychology, 39*, 223–252.

Marody, M. (1988). Antinomies of collective subconsciousness. *Social Research, 55*, 97–110.

Miller, K.A., Kohn, M.L., & Schooler, C. (1986). Educational self-direction and personality. *American Sociological Review, 51*, 372–390.

Muchow, M. & Muchow, H. (1935). *Der Lebensraum des Großstadtkindes* [The life space of the urban child]. Hamburg: Martin Riegel Verlag.

Neuhof, A. & Noack, P. (1992). *Leisure-time activities of adolescents in Berlin (West) and Warsaw.* Poster presented at the Fourth Biennial Meetings of the Society for Research on Adolescence, Washington, DC, March 19–22, 1992.

Noack, P. (1990). *Jugendentwicklung im Kontext. Zum aktiven Umgang mit sozialen Entwicklungsaufgaben in der Freizeit* [Adolescent development in context: On the role of leisure for the mastery of developmental tasks concerning social behavior]. München: Psychologie Verlags Union.

O'Malley, P.M. & Bachman, J.G. (1983). Self-esteem: Change and stability between ages 13 and 23. *Developmental Psychology, 19,* 257–268.

O'Malley, P.M., Bachman, J.G., & Johnston, L.D. (1983). Reliability and consistency in self-reports of drug use. *International Journal of the Addictions, 18,* 805–824.

Pulkkinen, L. & Narusk, A. (1987). Functions of adolescent drinking in Finland and the Soviet Union. *European Journal of Psychology of Education, 2,* 311–326.

Reykowski, J. (1982). Development of prosocial motivation: A dialectic process. In N. Eisenberg (Ed.), *The development of prosocial behavior* (pp. 377–394). New York: Academic Press.

Rosenthal, D. & Bornholt, L. (1988). Expectations about development in Greek and Anglo-Australian families. *Journal of Cross-Cultural Psychology, 19,* 19–34.

Rutter, M. (1988). Longitudinal data in the study of causal processes: Some uses and some pitfalls. In M. Rutter (Ed.), *Studies of psychosocial risk: The power of longitudinal data* (pp. 1–28). Cambridge: Cambridge University Press.

Schiavo, R.S. (1987). Home use and evaluation by suburban youth: Gender differences. *Children's Environments Quarterly, 4,* 8–12.

Schönpflug, U. & Silbereisen, R.K. (1989). *Handlungsstrategien und Entwicklung im Jugendalter. Bericht über den IFP 2/11 "Jugendentwichlung und Drogen im Kulturvergleich"* [Action strategies and development in adolescence]. Unpublished manuscript. Berlin: Technical University of Berlin.

Schulz, J. (1989). *Selbstwert und Übergänge in der Schullaufbahn: Kulturvergleichende Betrachtungen* [Self-esteem and transitions within secondary schools: Cross-cultural perspectives]. Unpublished master's thesis, Technical University of Berlin.

Schwartz, S.H. & Bilsky, W. (1987). Toward a universal psychological structure of human values. *Journal of Personality and Social Psychology, 53,* 550–562.

Semmer, N., Dwyer, J.H., Lippert, P., Fuchs, R., Cleary, P.D., & Schindler, A. (1987). Adolescent smoking from a functional perspective: The Berlin-Bremen Study. *European Journal of Psychology of Education, 2,* 387–402 (Special Issue on Adolescent Substance Use and Human Development, R.K. Silbereisen & N. Galambos, Eds.).

Silbereisen, R.K. & Albrecht, H.T. (1992). Peer and family effects on adolescent self-evaluation. In H. Remschmidt & M.H. Schmidt (Eds.), *Developmental psychopathology,* Vol. 2: Child and youth psychiatry, European perspectives (pp. 150–164). Lewiston, NY: Hogrefe & Huber Publishers.

Silbereisen, R.K., Boehnke, K., & Crockett, L. (1991). Zum Einfluß von Schulmilieu und elterlicher Erziehungshaltung auf Rauchen und Trinken im mittleren Jugendalter [On the impact of school milieu and parental attitudes on smoking and drinking in mid-adolescence]. In R. Pekrun & H. Fend (Eds.),

Schule und Persönlichkeitsentwicklung: Ein Resumée der Längsschnittforschung (pp. 272–293). Stuttgart: Enke.

Silbereisen, R.K. & Eyferth, K. (1986). Development as action in context. In R.K. Silbereisen, K. Eyferth, & G. Rudinger (Eds.), *Development as action in context: Problem behavior and normal youth development* (pp. 3–16). New York: Springer.

Silbereisen, R.K., Lamsfuss, S., Boehnke, K., & Eisenberg, N. (1991). Developmental patterns and correlates of prosocial motives in adolescence. In L. Montada & H.W. Bierhoff (Eds.), *Altruism in social systems* (pp. 82–104). Göttingen: Hogrefe.

Silbereisen, R.K. & Noack, P. (1988). On the constructive role of problem behavior in adolescence. In N. Bolger, A. Caspi, G. Downey, & M. Moorehouse (Eds.), *Persons in context: Developmental processes* (pp. 152–180). Cambridge: Cambridge University Press.

Silbereisen, R.K. & Noack, P. (1990a). Adolescents' orientations for development. In H. Bosma & S. Jackson (Eds.), *Coping and self-concept in adolescence* (pp. 112–127). Berlin: Springer.

Silbereisen, R.K. & Noack, P. (1990b). *Nutzen gegen den Strich: Vergleichende Analysen zu Freizeitkontexten Jugendlicher in Berlin (West) und Warschau* [Use against the rules: Comparative analyses of adolescents' leisure contexts in Berlin (West) and Warsaw]. Paper presented at the 37th Kongress Deutsche Gesellschaft für Psychologie, September 23–27, Kiel.

Silbereisen, R.K., Noack, P., & von Eye, A. (1992). Adolescents' development of romantic friendship and change in favorite leisure contexts. *Journal of Adolescent Research, 7*, 80–93.

Silbereisen, R.K. & Reitzle, M. (1992). On the constructive role of problem behavior in adolescence: Further evidence on alcohol use. In L.P. Lipsitt & L.L. Mitnick (Eds.), *Self-regulatory behavior and risk taking: Causes and consequences* (pp. 199–217). Norwood, NJ: Ablex Publishing.

Silbereisen, R.K., Schönpflug, U., & Albrecht, H.T. (1990). Smoking and drinking in mid-teens: Prospective analyses in German and Polish adolescents. In K. Hurrelmann & F. Loesel (Eds.), *Health hazards in adolescence* (pp. 167–190). Berlin/New York: De Gruyter/Aldine de Gruyter.

Smolenska, S. & Fraczek, A. (1987). Life-goals and evaluative standards among adolescents: A cross-national perspective. In J. Hazekamp, W. Meeus & Y. te Pool (Eds.), *European contributions to youth research* (pp. 131–144). Amsterdam: Free University Press.

Smolenska, S. & Silbereisen, R.K. (1991). *Cultural differences in adolescents' decision making.* Poster presented at the Eleventh Biennial Meetings of the International Society for the Study of Behavioral Development, July 3–7, 1991, Minneapolis, MN.

Snyder, J., Dishion, T.J., & Patterson, G.R. (1986). Determinants and consequences of associating with deviant peers during preadolescence and adolescence. *Journal of Early Adolescence, 6*, 29–43.

Swida, H. (1987). (quoted from Koralewicz, 1987).

Triandis, H.C. (1990). Cross-cultural studies of individualism and collectivism. *Nebraska Symposium on Motivation, 37*, 41–133.

Watts, M.W. & Zinnecker, J. (1988). Youth culture and politics among German youth: Effect of youth centrism. In J. Hazekamp, W. Meeus, & Y. te Pool

(Eds.), *European contributions to youth research* (pp. 93–100). Amsterdam: Free University Press.

Wohlwill, J.F. (1985). Martha Muchow and the life space of the urban child. *Human Development, 28,* 200–209.

Ziolkowski, M. (1988). Individuals and the social system: Values, perceptions, and behavioral strategies. *Social Research, 55,* 139–177.

Part IV
The Family-Work Nexus

10
The Gender-differential Significance of Work and Family: An Exploration of Adolescent Experience and Expectation

PHAME M. CAMARENA, MARK STEMMLER, AND ANNE C. PETERSEN

To the young adolescent, work is something that parents do to pay for life's necessities. Work is also what one has to do while at or as a consequence of school. Family is likely to be a secure base of operations for an ever expanding exploration of the larger social world. To the older adolescent beginning the move toward adult roles, while school may still be an important source of work, the distinctions between schoolwork and employed work have probably become firmly established parts of one's social reality. In fact, the potential for better work in a rewarding occupation or career begins to loom larger as an incentive for good work in school (for grades and diploma) and the formal workplace (for recommendations or advancement). Likewise, while family may still be a homebase for older adolescents' operations, family has also likely become a salient goal—something to be established apart from one's original family for the happiness and security it will presumably bring.   Though not descriptive of all adolescents, these general distinctions are useful in illustrating the idea that the concepts of "work" and "family" have significance or meaning for the lives of adolescents in a number of diverse yet related ways. That is, while at one level work and family represent important contexts critical to the shape of adolescents' developmental experience, at another level, they stand as expectations or desirable goals marking the transition out of adolescence and into adult roles (Bronfenbrenner & Crouter, 1982). The significance of work and family as both an expectation and an experience is not, however, the same for all adolescents. For at least in contemporary American society, work and family have profoundly different significance for the lives of girls and boys making the transition from childhood to adulthood (e.g., Katz, 1986).

The key to this gender-differential significance lies at the interaction between the worlds of family and work. In order to illustrate this issue, literature related to adolescent development in the United States is briefly reviewed and data from a longitudinal study of adolescent mental health are explored. The principles applicable across cultural contexts within the United States as well as cross-nationally are then highlighted.

Gender-differential Experiences in Work and Family Contexts

For most adolescents in the United States, direct exposure to formal contexts of work does not begin until middle or later adolescence in the form of part-time employment. Although some variation exists across social class, when adolescents do enter the part-time labor force, gender differences are generally evident in a number of key dimensions. Specifically, boys are more likely to begin working at an earlier age and to work longer hours than girls (Greenberger & Steinberg, 1986). Additionally, while both boys and girls are likely to be employed performing tasks requiring little initiative or creativity, the nature of responsibilities is often divided along gender-stereotypic lines (Nilson, 1984).

As the primary context for adolescents' work activities across the entire period of adolescence, the American school system also continues to differentially shape the experiences of girls and boys. As suggested in recent reviews of the area, the nature of education as a physical context (e.g., rules, organization of curriculum, allocation of resources) and as a social process (e.g., student-teacher interactions, social norms and models) have generally been found to be more facilitative of healthy development during adolescence of boys than of girls, both with regard to current experience and as a preparation for success in future adult work (Carelli, 1989; Entwistle, 1990).

Similarly, the body of research on family influences has demonstrated a number of ways in which adolescent girls and boys experience aspects of their family relationships differently across the adolescent years. For example, studies have identified differences in the ways that adolescent boys and girls interact with family members, respond to family stressors, and conceptualize autonomy from family (Richardson, Galambos, Schulenberg, & Petersen, 1984; Steinberg, 1981; Youniss & Smollar, 1985). Importantly, mothers and fathers are consistently identified as playing different roles in the life of the family, providing gender-typed models for family behavior (Grotevant & Cooper, 1983; Youniss & Smollar, 1985).

This issue of gender-typed roles for parents is prominent at the intersection of work and family. That is, while most children and adolescents are likely to have a parent or parents who are employed outside of the home, the significance attached to the parents' outside employment is largely prescribed by gender (Fitzgerald & Betz, 1983; Hoffman, 1984, 1989). Fathers are more likely than mothers to take the major role as financial provider and are given greater opportunities to explore work as a context for personal advancement and growth. Even in the face of national trends toward the "feminization" of the workplace, when mothers are the primary providers they are most likely to be so in the absence of an in-home father figure. Finally, regardless of social class, mothers' paid employment outside the home does not appear to substantially alter demands for work inside the home. For many contemporary women especially, the complex interactions between work and family roles provides significant personal challenge (Crouter & Perry-Jenkins, 1991).

Gender-differential Expectations for Work and Family Roles

Key to all of these gender differences are role-specific expectations that are pervasively filtered through all levels of the social context at all stages of development (Katz, 1986). Primary to these traditional roles is the expectation that work will be the central domain of men while family will be the central domain of women. Furthermore, because traditional models within American culture, including American scholarship, have defined "work" in terms of "gainful employment," the "housework" and "family-work" associated with women's roles have been both ignored and devalued (Delphy, 1984; Sapiro, 1986).

Now, as greater numbers of women enter the U.S. labor force, these traditional roles and resultant expectations are coming under increasing challenge, especially for girls. For example, findings from Monitoring the Future (Johnston, Bachman, & O'Malley, 1991) reveal that while two-thirds of 1974 high school seniors said it was not acceptable for both parents to work with preschool children in the home, by 1989 this proportion had dropped to half. These same 1989 seniors reported that even if they had "money to live as comfortably as they liked," they would still prefer to work. Most importantly, more girls (79%) than boys (67%) reported that they would not want to give up paid work!

The problem remains, however, that even as greater numbers of young women begin to aspire to success in labor force worlds traditionally dominated by men, there has not been the same corresponding investment in family work on the part of young men. Likewise, there have not generally been significant increases in the institutional supports that provide for the life of the family in the absence of the mother. How these new work and family expectations can be successfully negotiated remains to be explored. Importantly, however, this negotiation appears to have primary significance for adolescent girls and young women. That is, while adolescent boys negotiating the transition into adult work and family contexts can look forward to "parallel" and "complimentary" activities (Sapiro, 1986), the "conflict" between the demands of paid work and the family may well be the primary challenge facing current cohorts of American adolescent girls (Archer, 1985).

Experience and Expectation

The evidence from past research clearly reveals a number of ways in which cultural expectations for adult roles differentially shape the experiences of girls and boys. However, as suggested by research demonstrating important patterns of interindividual differences, developmental experiences within the work and family contexts can substantially mediate the pervasive influence of these gendered expectations. That is, while cultural norms (and resultant experiences, opportunities, and constraints) provide the overall social blueprint for adolescents' expectations, it is individual experiences within these contexts that shape the final form of any particular adolescent's actual orientation towards work and family roles.

The idea that work and family as contexts are embedded in larger social worlds and that adolescents' experience in these contexts act to shape their understanding and orientation toward young adult transitions is consistent with Silbereisen's conception of "developmental orientation" (Silbereisen & Noack, 1990). That is, as a function of social expectations, developmental experience, and practical constraints, work and family come to have a different significance, salience, or meaning in the lives of adolescent boys and girls. As a key link to adolescents' expectations, this subjective significance provides the direction for what is valued and how effectively it is pursued.

For the young adolescent, the significance of work and family may be manifested in choices made about the investment in schoolwork or compliance at home. For the middle adolescent, this significance may be evident in plans for future education and investment in part-time work. For the older adolescent, the significance of work and family may be manifested in choices of vocational track or the timing of marriage. At any time in development, however, these issues and the choices that follow have the potential to shape the path of developmental trajectories. Understanding the ways in which these work and family issues are significant in the lives of adolescent boys and girls is, therefore, a worthwhile goal.

Evidence of Gender-differential Patterns from the Adolescent Mental Health Study

Although not designed explicitly as an examination of work and family roles, the longitudinal data from the Adolescent Mental Health Study provides an excellent opportunity for exploring these issues across the decade of adolescence. This cohort-sequential longitudinal study was initially begun as an examination of gender-specific adjustment patterns across the developmental transitions of early adolescence (see Petersen, 1984).

The randomly selected sample was originally followed with both extensive personal interviews and group administered pencil-and-paper questionnaires across the sixth-, seventh-, and eighth-grade school years (roughly ages 11–14 years). Data were also collected from approximately half of the sample 4 years after the last early adolescent assessment. Finally, all study participants who could be located were asked to participate in a young adult follow-up of the early adolescent study when the sample was roughly 21 years of age. Approximately 75% of the original sample participated in this young adult follow-up. Of these 245 study participants, 147 had complete data to be included in this current set of longitudinal analyses. So far, there has been no evidence to suggest that this subsample is biased.

Sample

With regard to the focus of the present study, it is important to note that this sample has been characterized as being "resource rich" and "high achieving" (Sarigiani, Wilson, Petersen, & Vicary, 1990). Fathers were well educated (50% with postgraduate training) and were typically employed in white-collar occupations. Mothers also had strong educational backgrounds (55% with a college degree) and roughly two-thirds were employed out of the home either part- or full-time.

Although the nature of this sample somewhat limits the generalizability of results, it provides an interesting opportunity to examine the influence of gender in a context where *both* boys and girls were encouraged and given the resources to achieve in the world of work. These community standards for success are evident by the fact that in early adolescence, 95% of the boys and 98% of the girls reported that they expected to complete 4 or more years of college.

Measures

A brief summary of variables and measures included in the present study are outlined in Table 10.1. Additional details on measures are presented below.

Longitudinal Experience

Measures that were administered at both the early adolescent and young adult stages of the study provide a reference from which to understand the differences and changes in work and family experience across the period of the study. Where available, the average scores on measures across the early adolescent years were used as a more reliable indicator of

TABLE 10.1. Adolescent mental health study: Constructs and measures.

Early adolescence (EA)

  Mother work status (Mom Work) (mother self-report: none, part-time, full-time)

Longitudinal: Early adolescence to young adulthood (Early adolescence values are 3-year mean)

  Family relations scale (SIQYA: "my parents are usually patient with me")

  Course grades (GPA)

  Emotional tone scale (SIQYA: "I feel nervous most of the time")

  Attitudes toward women scale for adolescents (ATWSA: "Girls should be more concerned with becoming good wives and mothers than desiring a professional or business career")

Young adulthood (YA)

  Family expectations

    Marriage importance ("happy marriage" importance for future life satisfaction)

    Child importance ("having children" importance for future life satisfaction)

    % Child care (% of child care responsibility anticipated)

  Work expectation

    Work importance ("work success" importance for future life satisfaction)

    Prestige at 30 (NORC Rated prestige of job expected at age 30)

    % Income (% of income responsibility anticipated)

---

early adolescent experience. The young adult data therefore roughly represent a 10-year follow-up.

Family Experience

The adolescents' subjective evaluation of the family context was assessed with the Family Relations Scale of the Self-Image Questionnaire for Young Adolescents (SIQYA; Petersen, Schulenberg, Abramowitz, Offer, & Jarcho, 1984). High scores on this variable (means of three early adolescence reports) indicate a positive evaluation of self in the family context.

School Experience

The choice to examine school experience was predicated on the notion that education is the primary work of early adolescence and the primary preparation for later adult paid employment. The total grade score in early adolescence represents the average grade in required courses across the three years of assessment. In young adulthood the total grade represents the self-report of cumulative college grade point average (95% of participants reported a college GPA at the young adult follow-up). Although these represent somewhat different assessment techniques, the general awareness of a cumulative GPA among most American students helps make this self-report a robust assessment of academic success.

Mothers' Work Status

Although not asked at young adulthood, mothers' self-reported work status (none, part-time, full-time) provides an index of early adolescent exposure to a model of a working mother. Note that mother's work status is from mothers' self-report and comes from data collected in the last year (8th grade) of the early adolescence phase of the study.

Attitudes toward Women's Roles

The Attitudes Toward Women Scale for Adolescents (ATWSA; Galambos, Petersen, Tobin-Richards, & Gitelson, 1985) was used as an assessment of traditionality toward gendered roles in general and women's roles specifically. Higher scores on this variable indicate a more open acceptance of alternate roles for women.

Overall Experience

The Emotional Tone Scale of the SIQYA was used as a general index of subjective well-being (Petersen et al., 1984). The total score on this variable (mean of early adolescence) represents an assessment of emotional well-being with higher scores indicating positive experience.

Young Adult Expectations

Drawing from data collected in phone interviews, several aspects of young adults' expectations for work and family roles were assessed.

Family Expectations

Participants were asked to rate (7-point scale) the importance of various dimensions of life that they expected would promote overall life satisfaction. Two items from this list were used as an assessment of future orientation to family:

- Finding the right person to marry and having a strong marital relationship
- Having children

Family expectations were also assessed through young adults' reports of what percentage of "child care" they believed they would provide in their future family.

Work Expectations

The nature of work expectations was drawn from three different sources. The first was the life satisfaction expected to come from "being successful in your line of work." The second came from reports of the percentage of family income one expected to contribute to his or her future family. The last was based on the prestige rating associated with the occupation "expected when you are 30 years old" (Stevens & Hoisington, 1987).

Analysis and Results

It is important to note that the variables chosen for this set of analyses represent a small portion of available data relevant to work and family issues. The goal, however, is to illustrate only the gender-differential nature of work and family experiences and expectations across adolescence, not to exhaustively consider all possible influences or outcomes.

To that end, three sets of empirical analyses were completed and are reported here. The first set examines gender differences in levels and correlations of the longitudinal work and family variables. The second explores the nature of gender differences in young adult's expectations for future roles. The third explicitly tests for gender-differential patterns in the effects of early adolescent experiences on young adult expectations. Finally, themes drawn from an earlier qualitative analysis of the young adults' subjective reflections on their psychological well-being across adolescence are used to frame the issue of gendered orientations to future expectations.

Gender-related Patterns of Change over Time

Levels

Mean levels of Family Relationships and GPA across time serve as a general frame of reference from which to understand gender differences in orientations to work and family roles. Changes in mean levels on the Attitudes Toward Women Scale for Adolescence across the same period provide insights into the degree to which traditional attitudes toward work and family roles are being internalized. With regard to each set of analyses, the expectation is for evidence that highlights gender-differential patterns of experience, with indications of greater conflict between work and family domains for girls as compared to boys.

An examination of mean levels of Family Relationships and GPA across time reveal striking patterns of similarity for both boys and girls. Results from Repeated Measures ANOVAs (Sex × Time) indicated that there were no significant sex or Sex × Time effects for either Family Relations or GPA. Although the time effect for GPA was statistically significant ($F[1, 136] = 38.3, p < .05$), this increase for both girls and boys may simply reflect inflation due to self-reporting of grades. In either case, the mean scores from family and academic work alone do not provide any indication of gender-differential experience across adolescence.

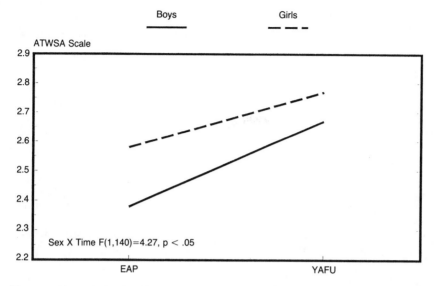

FIGURE 10.1. Attitudes Toward Women's Roles by gender and time of measurement.

In contrast, the repeated measures test for the Attitudes Toward Women scale revealed a statistically significant Sex × Time interaction ($F[1, 140] = 4.27, p < .05$) indicating a gender-differential pattern across time. An examination of the means presented in Figure 10.1 indicates that boys' attitudes changed more than did girls'; however, girls had more positive or open attitudes toward women's roles across both times of measurement. These findings suggest that the young men's attitudes were extended or broadened across the adolescent years to more closely approximate the attitudes of the young women.

Correlations with Emotional Tone

Another way to understand the significance of family and school experience across time is to examine how family relations and school success correlate with assessments of well-being. The results from correlational analysis and comparisons are presented in Table 10.2. As expected, Family Relations and GPA were generally correlated with Emotional Tone at both times for both boys and girls. Comparisons of correlations using Fisher's r-z transformation indicated that there were no reliable differences between the correlations of girls and boys. However, these comparisons did confirm that the decreasing association of both Family Relations and GPA with Emotional Tone for boys was statistically significant. There was no corresponding change for the girls. These findings

TABLE 10.2. Correlations of family relations and GPA with emotional tone across time by sex.

| | Emotional tone | | Change |
	EA	YA	(zEA-YA)
Family relations			
Boys	.65*	.37*	.437*
Girls	.46*	.41*	.061
GPA			
Boys	.31*	−.03	.351*
Girls	.20	.25*	−.052

*p < .05

reveal that, relative to girls, emotional well-being became more independent of family and school experience across time for boys.[1]

Gender-related Patterns in Young Adults' Expectations

Levels

MANOVAs were used to test for sex differences in the set of work and family expectations. Significant MANOVA effects were found for both family expectations ($F[3, 143] = 31.1$, $p < .05$) and work expectations ($F[3, 143] = 55.5$, $p < .05$).

The effect sizes (Eta) for mean sex differences on individual variables are presented in Figure 10.2. Two striking patterns in these differences are evident. First, the direction of all effects is consistent with gender stereotypes for work and family roles. Second, the largest differences for both men and women are associated with expected role performance (e.g., % of income or child care provided). In contrast, the smallest and nonsignificant differences were associated with the ratings of anticipated subjective importance of these life domains. These findings suggest that while both young men and women expected satisfaction to come from similar life domains, they actually anticipated performing in these domains differently according to gender prescriptions.

---

[1] Analyses of the link between emotional tone and employment patterns during high school were not included due to insufficient longitudinal data. It is interesting to note, however, that correlational analysis of the longitudinal subsample available (32 boys, 32 girls) revealed consistent gender-differential patterns. That is, the pattern of correlations between emotional tone and employment experiences during 12th grade were reversed for boys and girls (i.e., emotional tone with: hours part-time work, .26 for boys and −.21 for girls; hours of expected summer work, .44* for boys and −.57* for girls; *p < .05).

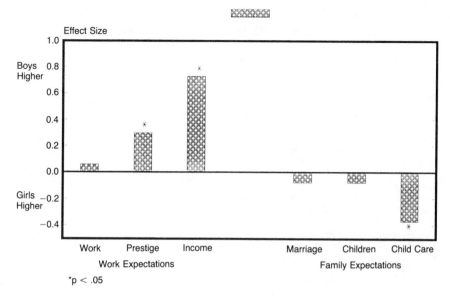

FIGURE 10.2. Effect sizes for mean sex differences on work and family expectation variables.

Correlations among Work and Family Variables

Although the general pattern of correlations between work and family variables was suggestive of an overall difference in the relationship between work and family domains (e.g., number of statistically significant correlations, direction of sign), statistically significant differences were found only in the association between anticipated child care demands and dimensions of work expectations (see Table 10.3). Specifically, young women's expectations for work and child care were in direct conflict with each other, whereas young men's expectations were generally not in conflict.

Because study participants also rated how confident they were that they would "achieve the level of each [dimension] that they desired," it was also possible to directly test the issue of conflict by examining the association between desire and expectation. Table 10.4 contains the correlations between rated importance and confidence in each of the three life dimensions assessed (work success, happy marriage, having children). These findings revealed that while importance and confidence were generally correlated for both women and men, the magnitude of the association varied by both gender and domain. The association between importance and confidence for men was consistent and strong. In contrast, the pattern for women was variable with the strongest correlation found in importance and confidence for having children. This correlation was, in

TABLE 10.3. Correlations of work and family expectation variables.

	Work	Prestige	Income		Marriage	Child	Child care
Work							
importance		.18	.20		.17	.04	−.25*
Prestige							
at 30	−.07		.17		−.10	−.16	−.25*
% Income							
provide	−.01	.04			−.16	−.26*	−.57*
							Girls
Marriage							
importance	.27*	−.01	.01			.51*	.23*
Child							
importance	.20	.05	.06		.63*		.21*
% Child care							
provide	.19	.14	−.23		.02	.07	
				Boys			

Girls are above and boys are below the diagonal.
Horizontal and vertical separates work and family constructs.
Pairs of underlined correlations are different for boys and girls ($p < .05$).
*$p < .05$

fact, significantly different from women's corresponding correlations for both marriage ($z = .34$, $p < .05$) and work ($z = .57$, $p < .05$). Note also that the sex difference between the correlations for work success was also significant ($z = .40$, $p < .05$). As a whole, these findings support the contention that young women anticipate substantial conflict in attaining both valued work and family roles, conflict that is not anticipated by young men.

Early Adolescent Effects on Young Adults' Expectations

Overall Differences

The two previous sections have identified gender-specific patterns in both the experiences and expectations of adolescents. This section examines the connection between the two by testing for gender-differential patterns in the link between early adolescent experiences in work and family contexts and young adults' future expectations or orientations toward work and family roles.

TABLE 10.4. Correlations between importance and confidence.

	Men	Women	Difference (z)
Work success Importance/confidence	.52*	.17	.40*
Happy marriage Importance/confidence	.52*	.38*	.18
Having children Importance/confidence	.47*	.63*	−.23

For women, "children' is higher than both "marriage" ($z = .34$) and "work" ($z = .57$).
*$p < .05$

TABLE 10.5. Early adolescent effects on young adult expectations: Summary of tests for sex interactions.

Early adolescence group	Young adult expectations
Sex × family	Work importance
Sex × GPA	Marriage importance
	Children importance
Sex × mother work	% Income provided
	Marriage importance
	Children importance

Sex × group interaction ($p \leq .10$)

For these analyses, Family Relations was used as an index of early adolescent support in the family context, GPA was used as a marker of success in early adolescent "work," and mothers' employment status was used as an indication of exposure to a nontraditional work/family model in early adolescence. In order to facilitate an examination of group differences, Family Relations and GPA were trichotomized into low, medium, and high groups. Mothers' employment had already been coded into three approximately equal groups corresponding to: no employment, part-time employment, and full-time employment (Kavrell & Petersen, 1984).

To explicitly test for gender-differential patterns of effects, a set of MANOVAs on family and work expectations was run separately for each sex, group, and Sex × Group interaction (see Table 10.5). Because of the difficulty in identifying significant interaction effects in groups with moderately small cell sizes, an a priori decision was made to establish $p \leq .10$ as the criteria for statistical significance.

Consistent with expectations for evidence of gender-differential patterns, a substantial number of statistically significant interaction effects were identified. In fact, 33% of the possible interaction effects were significant at $p \leq .10$ (10% might be expected by chance). Interestingly, a smaller number of main effects were also found.

Group Interactions within Gender

Similar to the expectation for overall sex interactions, it was presumed that the interaction of Family, GPA, and Mother Work Groups would have gender-differential significance as effects for young adult work and family expectations. Specifically it was hypothesized that because of the conflicting nature of girls' and women's work and family roles, there would be a greater proportion of significant interactions between groups (i.e., Family, GPA, Mother Work) for girls as compared to boys. The criteria for significant interactions was again set at $p \leq .10$.

TABLE 10.6. Early adolescent effects on young adult expectations: Summary of tests for group interactions by sex.

EA Groups	YA Expectation	Men	Women
Family × GPA			
	Work importance		
	Prestige at 30		
	% Income		
	Marriage importance		X
	Children importance		
	% Child care		X
Family × mother work			
	Work importance		X
	Prestige at 30		
	% Income		
	Marriage importance		
	Children importance	X	
	% Child care		
Mother work × GPA			
	Work importance		
	Prestige at 30		X
	% Income		
	Marriage importance		
	Children importance		X
	% Child care		

Interaction between groups $p \leq .10$

MANOVAs testing for interaction effects in pairs of groups (i.e., Family-GPA, Family–Mother Work, GPA–Mother Work) were run separately by sex. A summary of the significant interactions by sex is presented in Table 10.6. Consistent with the hypothesis, the interactions for girls outnumbered those for the boys five to one. This 27% of possible significant interactions ($p < .10$) far exceeds the 10% expected by chance.

Both of these sets of analyses are critical in that they each confirm the degree to which girls' experiences in adolescence are differentially reflected in young adult expectations 10 years later as compared to boys. This is not to imply causation; rather, it is to convey the potential for long-term longitudinal patterns and the special nature of challenge confronted by this sample of adolescent girls. Although space limitations preclude any additional detailing of specific effects and patterns, it is clear from these analyses that the relationships between work and family experiences and expectations are substantially more complex for girls than for boys. These results also indicate the need for additional exploration of the data in this area.

The Significance of Gender Differences in Personal Stories

Up to this point, the gender-differential significance of work and family has been inferred from patterns of differences in levels and associations of relevant variables. In each set of analyses, it appeared as though the girls faced a more complex set of challenges in negotiating the balance between work and family domains. Implicit in this perspective is the assumption that these statistically significant findings are reflective of subjective differences in the salience or meaning of work and family in the lives of adolescent boys and girls. Alternately, the significance of work and family issues can be explored through an explicit comparison of the ways in which adolescent boys and girls, in their own words, reflect on their past experiences and future expectations for work and family. With this idea in mind, all young adult participants were asked to reflect on their personal experience of psychological well-being in the past, present, and into the imagined future.

The required charting, labeling, and explanation tasks of this final assessment of young adults formed the basis of a previously completed qualitative analysis of major themes associated with women's and men's "personal stories" (Camarena, 1990). These themes, generated through the use of "grounded theory" methods (Glaser & Strauss, 1967), provide important insights into the ways in which adolescent girls and boys differentially interpret their experiences to frame their expectations for the future. The significance of these personal stories generally as an interpretive frame for adolescents' orientations toward adult roles is nicely stated in the words of one of our study participants. She explains:

Regardless of our upbringings—whether it be pleasant or unpleasant, most important is to develop the understanding and memory of our past that is most helpful in allowing us to be happy with ourselves and to achieve in other areas as adults. What I am saying is that my understanding of my past is an understanding which has allowed me to move on and achieve as an adult. I am very grateful for this marvelous advantage.

It is important to note that, along with peer/romantic relationships, experiences in the family and school contexts dominated the events and issues of both men's and women's stories. How these experiences connected to the larger themes of psychological well-being was, however, generally different for women and men. For the men, the experience of psychological well-being was more likely to be understood as *stability* and *perspective*, especially in the face of family and school/work disruptions. An extreme illustration of these themes is provided by one young man who experienced the death of several family members in a fire during early adolescence. He explained that, when you are faced with problems, you need to "cope with them rationally . . . if a tragedy comes along—big or small . . . deal with it and [don't] let it affect your life too much." In contrast, women were more likely to talk about psychological well-being in terms of *learning* from challenges and *accepting self* independent of others. For example, one woman, whose story revolved around the conflict between parents' standards and success in school and career, explained that psychological well-being comes from the realization that "every person is important and worth-while and that we all have faults." She concluded by saying that "loving oneself is very important—regardless of how I compare to others."

The specific ways in which these gender-typed themes frame women's and men's orientations is suggested in a number of cases where a particular orientation toward the future is explicitly connected to one's understanding of past and present experiences. For both men and women, past success in adjusting to life experiences is manifested in confidence about the future. The nature of this confidence, however, varies in ways that are consistent with the major themes associated with each gender.

For men, the degree of past success with coping and maintaining stability is reflected in a "perspective" that frames the future consistent with past experiences. For example, a number of men who reported very little distress across adolescence simply indicated that they looked forward to the "routine" and "stability" of future work and family roles after they "made it through medical school" or "adjusted to new job demands" after college. In contrast, the men with somewhat "rockier" stories tended to frame the future in terms of the need to maintain perspective in the face of future challenge or uncertainty. An excellent example of this is found in one man's reflection on what he described as a stressful adolescence and a very uncertain future. He explained his perspective on the future this way:

One must be able to look ahead at things; to be able to look to the future. This may sound optimistic, but that's how I am. And I think it's a good thing to be a bit optimistic. It seems I talk to a lot of my friends and it's like they are always down on themselves and their lives. That's bullshit, cuz it doesn't get them anywhere. Yes, I have had really horrible things happen and they bum me out and I still think of them, but life goes on. . . . You can die and the whole world won't even bat an eye. It's dismal almost but it doesn't get me down cuz that's just how it is. So I'm pretty much having fun while I'm able to. You [*sic*] got to.

In contrast, women's connections of past to future focused more on a developing confidence and assertion that came from learning the value and worth of oneself. Although this transformation in self was expressed in a number of different ways, one woman perhaps best exemplifies this general trend. This particular participant had confronted a number of major family stressors (parent divorce, mother's remarriage, brothers' psychiatric hospitalization, brother's suicide). She reported that after several years of avoiding family issues, travel abroad provided her with an opportunity to "reevaluate" her life. This "most enlightening and character building endeavor" helped her understand that "once you learn to love yourself, others will like you too." Her evaluation of the prospect for the future reflected this newfound strength of self:

I'll meet someone special, do well at my job, climb the ladder of success, be in good physical condition. I'll age well and get more attractive. I'll be well educated, financially secure, get married in my mid to late twenties and have children when I am thirty, go back to school when I'm forty. Family will be a priority, I'll be a great wife and mother. I feel I'll be well-equipped to handle the rough inevitable periods because I've overcome a lot of obstacles. I feel lucky to have had the opportunity because I know I can handle any situation I'm faced with. It's all downhill from here. Things will get better and better.

All of these examples illustrate the great interindividual variability possible in subjective experience and interpretation of experience. However, although there was evidence of the link between personally constructed stories and young adult expectations, the nature of the link appeared to be strongest for the subjective evaluation or feelings about future roles and transitions. That is, while many of the stories described how experiences can lead to changes in attitudes such as "optimism," "confidence," or "excitement," few specifically acknowledged links to changes in expected family and work role performance.

Summary and Conclusions

This exploration began as an overall assessment of the ways in which cultural prescriptions, individual differences in experience, and developmental time act to differentially shape adolescent boys' and girls' orientations towards work and family, both as contexts of experience and expectations for future roles. Overall, the results revealed a generally consistent pattern of gender-related differences that reflect contemporary American cultural norms for work and family role performance.

This reflection of contemporary norms was evident on at least two different levels. At one level, there were a number of findings of differences between levels and associations consistent with traditional notions of work as a central feature of boys' experience and family as a central feature of girls' experience. At another level, women's increasing entrance into the labor force and the resultant challenges of balancing work- and family-related demands was also consistently identified.

The conflict between the traditional and the contemporary was also manifested in the consistent pattern of discrepancies between what is desired versus what is anticipated. That is, although both men and women said they valued work and family roles, the actual expectation for role performance remained highly stereotypical and was largely resistant to influence as assessed with both empirical tests of early adolescent effects and qualitative explorations of young adults' personal stories.

That is not to say that personal experience was an unimportant influence on the developmental orientations of adolescent girls and boys. To the contrary, the number of significant early adolescent effects on young adult expectations clearly revealed that individual experience was a critical component in the development of motivation for work and family. That is, experiences in early adolescence do have significance for later young adult expectations. Additionally, the fact that there was such a large proportion of interaction effects indicative of gender-differential patterns also demonstrated how pervasive an influence cultural definitions of gender can be on the significance of these personal experiences.

Significance of Findings for Alternate Contexts

Certainly, the specific findings of this present study are bound by the American middle-class nature of the particular sample described; however, a number of key principles are illustrated that have application to the work and family-related development of boys and girls across other United States and cross-national samples. Primary among these is the recognition of multiple work-related contexts across the adolescent period and the potential for special challenges for girls and women at the intersection of work and family contexts, especially during the transition into adulthood.

Even as family systems change, the family is likely to remain a major force shaping all experiences of the individual across the entire period of adolescence. In contrast, the nature of work-related contexts found in different societies and subcultures are more likely to demonstrate remarkable variability across individuals and developmental time. For example, chores begun in the home signal the start of the gender-differentiated assignment of tasks and may be reflected in later attitudes toward adult working roles. Experiences of success and failure in an educational context may differentially prepare girls and boys for later vocational development. The opportunity for part-time work or work training programs may also vary for boys and girls across adolescence. Finally, the models of parents' balance of work and family context demands will likely provide different messages for girls and boys confronting the challenge of negotiating the dual entrance into both adult work and family roles.

In this vein, it is important to note that while conflict between the demands of work and family are not the exclusive concern of women, where conflict between these demands is likely to occur, girls and women will disproportionately carry the burden for the resolution of these competing demands. As long as cultures continue to define housework and family-work as a feminine domain, even when women are encouraged to enter the paid labor force and adolescent girls are prepared for vocations and careers, they will also likely be left with the major responsibility for the work in the home (Sapiro, 1986). The generally low value placed on work in the home by most societies further complicates the situation.

The need to examine both of these issues in alternate contexts is essential. Within the United States as well as in many other industrialized countries, women are increasingly entering the labor force. The need to adequately prepare both adolescent boys and girls for the potentially competing demands of family and work roles requires significant changes in the work and family contexts that model and prepare adolescents for these later adult roles. In addition, societies need to examine what is valued and important, and design social policies accordingly.

It also needs to be acknowledged that the relationship between the larger social contexts and the developmental orientations of adolescents is reciprocal in nature. As increasing numbers of adolescent girls continue to aspire and prepare for the working world, the institutions of the working world must respond. The degree to which various societies have provided institutional supports for these kinds of changes varies considerably (Tierney, 1989). Cross-national comparisons that examine the importance of these institutional supports are possible and would provide important insights into the links between social structure and individual experience.

Additionally, although the challenge of balancing work and family demands is currently the burden of women, current generations of boys and men are also now growing up with the realization that their roles may well have to alter to more effectively match the roles of their future spouses. Remember that in this study, it was the boys' attitudes toward the traditional roles of girls and women that changed the most over the adolescent years.

Finally, in many ways, the results from this current investigation are consistent with previous findings of the Adolescent Mental Health Study in illustrating the special conflicts and challenges facing adolescent girls, not only in our current social-historical context but in other contexts as well. In this light, the findings of the qualitative analysis also provided some perspective on the resilience of girls and women confronted with special challenges making the transition into adult roles. That is, while there may be extra challenge integrating competing life demands, for those girls who learn from these challenges, there may also be an increasing sense of empowerment that can lead to success in both the worlds of work and family, producing change for the generations to follow:

I have had more to cope with than many of my peers making me strong, independent and worthy of myself. . . . Now I can look back and can reflect on my mistakes and my accomplishments knowing that they all had their purposes in developing an assertive and individualistic person. I figure the pain then is now turning around for my gain. [Now] I feel pretty sure of myself and know that I can overcome anything.

Acknowledgments. This research was supported by grant MH 30252/88142 from the National Institute of Mental Health to Anne C. Petersen.
Phame Camarena's work on this paper was supported by NIMH grant MH 38142-08S1.

References

Archer, S.L. (1985). Career and/or family: The identity process for adolescent girls. *Youth and Society*, *16*, 289–314.

Bronfenbrenner, U. & Crouter, A.C. (1982). Work and family through time and space. In S.B. Kamerman & C.D. Hayes (Eds.), *Families that work: Children in a changing world* (pp. 39–83). Washington, DC: National Academy of Sciences.

Camarena, P.M. (1990). *Scientific and personal stories of psychological well-being across adolescence: An exploration of gender and mental health*. Unpublished doctoral dissertation, Pennsylvania State University.

Carelli, A. (1989). *Sex equity in education*. New York: Charles Thomas.

Crouter, A.C. & Perry-Jenkins, M. (1991). Working it out: Effects of work on parents and children. In M.W. Yogman & T.B. Brazelton (Eds.), *In support of families* (pp. 93–108). Cambridge: Harvard University Press.

Delphy, C. (1984). *Close to home: A materialist analysis of women's oppression*. Amherst: University of Massachusetts Press.

Entwistle, D.R. (1990). Schools and the adolescent. In S.S. Feldman & G.R. Elliot (Eds.), *At the threshold: The developing adolescent* (pp. 197–224). Cambridge: Harvard University Press.

Fitzgerald, L.F. & Betz, N.E. (1983). Issues in the vocational psychology of women. In W.B. Walsh & S.H. Osipow (Eds.), *Handbook of vocational psychology* (Vol. 1, pp. 83–159). Hillsdale, NJ: Lawrence Erlbaum.

Galambos, N.L., Petersen, A.C., Tobin-Richards, M., & Gitelson, I. (1985). The attitudes toward women scale for adolescents (AWSA): A study of reliability and validity. *Sex Roles*, *13*, 343–354.

Glaser, B. & Strauss, A. (1967). *The discovery of grounded theory*. Chicago: Aldine.

Greenberger, E. & Steinberg, L.D. (1986). *When teenagers work*: *The psychological and social costs of adolescent employment*. New York: Basic Books.

Grotevant, H.D. & Cooper, C.R. (Eds.). (1983). *Adolescent development in the family*. San Francisco: Jossey-Bass.

Hoffman, L.W. (1984). Work, family, and the socialization of the child. In R.D. Parke (Ed.), *Review of child development research* (Vol. 7, pp. 223–282). Chicago: University of Chicago Press.

Hoffman, L.W. (1989). Effects of maternal employment in the two-parent family. *American Psychologist*, *44*, 283–292.

Johnston, L.D., Bachman, J.G., & O'Malley, P.M. (1991). *Monitoring the future: Questionnaire responses from the nations' high school seniors*. Ann Arbor: Survey Research Center.

Katz, P.A. (1986). Gender identity: Development and consequences. In R.D. Ashmore & F.K. Del Boca (Eds.), *The social psychology of female-male relations* (pp. 67–84). Beverly Hills: Sage.

Kavrell, S.H. & Petersen, A.C. (1984). Patterns of achievement in early adolescence. In M.L. Maehr & M.W. Steinkamp (Eds.), *Women and science* (pp. 1–35). Greenwich, CT: JAI Press.

Nilson, D. (1984). The youngest workers: 14 and 15 year olds. *Journal of Early Adolescence, 4*, 189–197.

Petersen, A.C. (1984). The early adolescence study: An overview. *Journal of Early Adolescence, 4*, 103–106.

Petersen, A.C., Schulenberg, J.E., Abramowitz, R.H., Offer, D., & Jarcho, H.D. (1984). A self-image questionnaire for young adolescents (SIQYA): Reliability and validity studies. *Journal of Youth and Adolescence, 13*, 93–111.

Richardson, R.A., Galambos, N.L., Schulenberg, J.E., & Petersen, A.C. (1984). Young adolescents' perceptions of the family environment. *Journal of Early Adolescence, 4*, 131–153.

Sapiro, V. (1986). *Women in American society*. Mountain View, CA: Mayfield Publishing.

Sarigiani, P.A., Wilson, J.L., Petersen, A.C., & Vicary, J.R. (1990). Self-image and educational plans of adolescents from two contrasting communities. *Journal of Early Adolescence, 10*, 37–55.

Silbereisen, R.K. & Noack, P. (1990). Adolescents' orientations for development. In S. Jackson & H. Bosma (Eds.), *Coping and self-concept in adolescence* (pp. 112–127). Berlin: Springer.

Steinberg, L.D. (1981). Transformations in family relations at puberty. *Developmental Psychology, 17*, 833–840.

Stevens, G.S. & Hoisington, E. (1987). Occupational prestige and the 80's labor force. *Social Science Research, 16*(1), 74–105.

Tierney, H. (1989). *Women's studies encyclopedia: Views from the sciences* (Vol. 1). Westport, CT: Greenwood Press.

Youniss, J. & Smollar, J. (1985). *Adolescent relations with mothers, fathers, and friends*. Chicago: University of Chicago Press.

11
The Two-earner Family as a Context for Adolescent Development

Nancy L. Galambos and David M. Almeida

A few years ago a prominent story in *Time* magazine featured a glimpse at the lives of five children growing up in the United States. The author of this story wrote that

The role of mother is being rewritten, and that of father as well. . . . Childhood has become a kind of experiment. . . . Cant phrases, such as "quality time," have found their way into the vocabulary. A motif of absence—moral, emotional and physical—plays through the lives of many children now. . . . To support a family, buy a house and prepare for a child's future education, two incomes become essential. (Morrow, 1988, p. 27)

Although these observations about the lives of children growing up in two-earner families are unduly pessimistic, the author correctly asserts that the family context has undergone considerable change. This change is reflected in the steady and substantial rise of married women joining the labor force in industrialized nations since World War II. In Canada in 1991, 61% of married women were employed outside of the home (Statistics Canada, 1991). This movement of women into the labor force has had important implications for the ways in which families live. For example, in 1961, the single-earner family (i.e., married couples in which the husband is the sole income earner) comprised 65% of all family types in Canada; the comparable figure for two-earner families (i.e., both spouses employed) was 14% (Dominion Bureau of Statistics, 1964). By 1981, 49% of all families were two-earner families and 16% were single-earner families (Statistics Canada, 1985). This transformation in the proportion of two-earner families has meant that more children now than ever before grow up in households where both parents have paid jobs.

In conjunction with this transformation, a growing interest among developmental psychologists in the multiple contexts in which individual development occurs (Baltes, Reese, & Lipsitt, 1980; Bronfenbrenner, 1986; Elder, 1974; Silbereisen, Eyferth, & Rudinger, 1986) leads us to consider more specifically the context of two-earner families. The experiences associated with growing up in a family in which both parents are employed undoubtedly help to shape the child's behavior and development (Bronfenbrenner & Crouter, 1982). Recognition that parents' work is important in the lives of children is present in the history of research comparing children of employed mothers with those of nonemployed mothers on a variety of cognitive, psychological, and social characteristics (see e.g., Bronfenbrenner & Crouter, 1982; Gottfried & Gottfried, 1988; Hoffman, 1989; Lerner & Galambos, 1991). Indeed, the intricate dependencies between work and family life have been revealed in case studies of two-earner families (Piotrkowski, 1979; Rapoport & Rapoport, 1976). Moreover, a number of studies have examined the relationship between women's work and their psychological well-being (e.g., Baruch, Biener, & Barnett, 1987; Kandel, Davies, & Raveis, 1985; Kessler & McRae, 1982). Although these bodies of research have contributed to our understanding of work and family, our knowledge about children in two-earner families is incomplete because most studies have focused almost entirely on the experiences of one or the other parent (usually the mother), and rarely on the relation between the parents' work experiences and child development (for exceptions see Crouter & Crowley, 1990; Crouter, Perry-Jenkins, Huston, & McHale, 1987; Greenberger & Goldberg, 1989). Thus, there is a strong need for research examining the lives of *both parents and children* in two-earner families.

Based on a broad conceptual model for viewing how parental work situations might influence the behavior and development of children, this chapter examines selected family processes in a sample of two-earner families with adolescent children. Longitudinal data collected on this sample allow us to observe the possible ways in which parental work situations have an impact on the parents, the parent-adolescent relationship, and the young adolescent as he or she negotiates the transition to adolescence.

Our Conceptual Model

Figure 11.1 presents our model for conceptualizing the ways in which parental employment is linked to adolescent development. The model is a mediational one, in which it is assumed that the influences of a parent's work situation (e.g., long work hours) on the adolescent are indirect. That is, the adolescent's behavior is linked to parents' work through other variables that mediate between parents' work conditions, on the one hand, and adolescent behavior, on the other. In this way the mediating variables describe the mechanisms through which parents' work conditions ultimately have an impact on adolescent behavior. For the purpose of understanding this model, it is useful to distinguish between first- and second-order mediators. *First-order mediators* are those variables that are proximately linked to the exogenous variable of parents' work; these first-

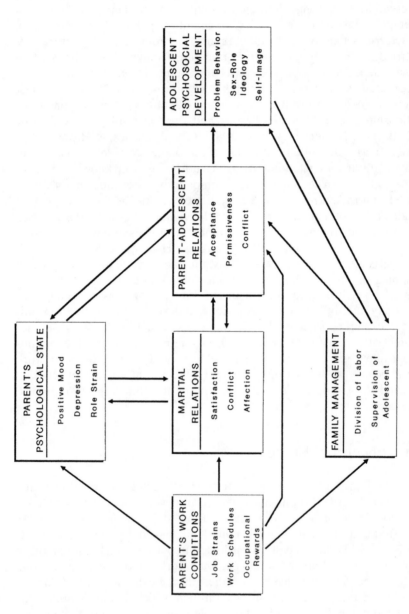

FIGURE 11.1. Conceptual model of the processes by which parent's work conditions may influence the adolescent.

order mediators (e.g., parent's psychological state) are influenced directly by parental work conditions. *Second-order mediators* mediate between these first-order mediators and the endogenous variable of adolescent behavior; second-order mediators are functionally more distal from parents' work and at the same time more proximal to adolescent behavior. The present model contains one second-order mediator that is a critical link between parents' work and adolescent development: parent-adolescent relations.

In our model, we consider three first-order mediators: (a) the parent's psychological state; (b) the quality of marital relations; and (c) family management practices. A parent's *psychological state* is presumed to depend partly upon activities, events, and roles in the workplace. Thus, inflexible work schedules, job rewards, and the quality of social interactions are examples of workplace conditions that may very well influence parental reports of current mood, depression, and role strain. Work conditions may also influence *marital relations*. Some of this influence may be directly related to work, for example, when time constraints, scheduling of hours, and shift work interfere with the amount of time available for spousal interactions (Moen, 1982). Marital relations might also be related indirectly to work conditions through the impact of work on one's psychological state. Thus, in our model, work conditions are connected to marital relations directly and also indirectly through psychological state (note that the model also accounts for the potential impact of marital relations on psychological state). Parents' work conditions may also influence *family management*, which refers to the ways in which household chores and tasks are completed and children are supervised (cf. Patterson, 1982). Naturally, time and energy constraints stemming from occupational conditions might influence supervision of the adolescent and the division of labor among the spouses and children.

This mediational model eschews a direct relationship between a parent's work and the adolescent's behavior; rather, parental work is assumed to shape the experiences of the adolescent through parental feelings and behavior. We believe that the quality of *parent-adolescent relations* is the primary vehicle (i.e., the second-order mediator) through which parental satisfactions and stresses are carried to the adolescent, although it is not the only way (e.g., family management practices may have a direct impact on the adolescent's experiences). In this regard, then, we believe that a parent who has a happy work life is more likely to be in a positive mood; this positive mood, in turn, may spill over into pleasant parent-adolescent interactions (Piotrkowski, 1979), with subsequent implications for the adolescent's behavior.

Also portrayed in this model is the potential influence of adolescent behavior on family management practices and parent-adolescent relations. Characteristics and behaviors of the adolescent undoubtedly have an impact on family interactions and on parental beliefs about how much the adolescent needs to be supervised. For example, the well-adjusted, independent adolescent might be granted more autonomy by parents than the adolescent with a history of making poor decisions and engaging in problem behavior.

Work Conditions and the First-order Mediators

What evidence is there to support the processes portrayed in the above conceptual model? Reviews of the literature have concluded that there is a clear link between work conditions and the worker's psychological well-being (Baruch et al., 1987; Repetti, Matthews, & Waldron, 1989; Rodin & Ickovics, 1990). For example, occupational demands such as excessive work time, shift work, psychological demands, and physical noxiousness of the work environment are associated with stress, role strain, and depression in male and female workers (Kandel et al., 1985; Keith & Schafer, 1980; Mott, Mann, McLoghlin, & Warwick, 1965; Pearlin, 1975; Pleck, Staines, & Lang, 1980). There is also some evidence demonstrating a link between work conditions and marital relations. Demanding and stressful jobs, for example, are associated with lower sexual activity, less time available to spend together, withdrawal, and strained relations in couples (Barling, 1984; Barling & Rosenbaum, 1986; Burke, Weir, & DuWors, 1980; Galambos & Silbereisen, 1989; Hochschild, 1989; Repetti, 1989). Clearly, individual psychological states and marital relations are closely aligned with what is happening in the work domain.

With respect to how work affects family management, husbands appear to share more in household and child care responsibilities when their wives are employed (Hoffman, 1984), although employed wives still carry far more of this burden than do husbands (Hochschild, 1989). Adolescents whose mothers are employed also have more responsibility for household chores than do those in traditional, single-earner households (Montemayor, 1984; Propper, 1972). Elder's (1974) study of families experiencing economic hardship in the early 1930s illustrated how income loss led to changes in the division of labor; some mothers entered the work force and adolescents took on a larger share of home maintenance duties. Another way in which parents' work may affect family management is through its impact on the supervision of children. With both parents in dual-earner families typically at work after school, it becomes a major task to monitor the activities of youth. Research has shown that poor monitoring is related to the adolescent's higher susceptibility to antisocial peer pressure and greater participation in deviant activities (Patterson & Stouthamer-Loeber, 1984; Steinberg, 1986).

The evidence supports the notion that parental work sets the stage for events in the family context: Work seems to influence the first-order mediators of psychological state, marital relations, and family management practices. Due to the correlational nature of most of the above research, however, we cannot be certain that the primary direction of influence is from work to home. After all, problems at home can and do affect the worker's experiences at work (Bolger, DeLongis, Kessler, & Wethington, 1989; Crouter, 1984). Our conceptual model, however, views the effects of work on the family as stronger than the effects of the family on work. This assumption stems from two considerations. First, the kind of work conditions that are of interest to us are features of the work situation that are not particularly subject to change (e.g., hours spent at work, type of work environment, supportiveness of coworkers), unless one leaves that job. Second, research on disruptive job events (e.g., being downgraded) demonstrated that these events resulted in subsequent changes in depression and self-esteem in men and women (Pearlin, Menaghan, Lieberman, & Mullan, 1981). Thus, the direction of influence was from work conditions to the manifestation of stress. If we assume, then, that work conditions may have an impact on psychological state, marital relations, and family management, can we find evidence that these first-order mediators lead to changes in the quality of parent-adolescent relations?

Parent-adolescent Relations as a Second-order Mediator

The nature of the parent-adolescent relationship is seen as critical to the adolescent's behavior and development. Numerous sources identify warm, sensitive, and moderately controlling parenting behaviors as primary predictors of cognitive, social, and behavioral competence in children and adolescents (Maccoby & Martin, 1983; Patterson, 1982; Perlmutter, 1984; Steinberg, 1990). Moreover, many writers argue that parent-adolescent relations comprise the link between parental stress, on the one hand, and adolescent development, on the other (Belsky, 1984; Bronfenbrenner, 1986; Bronfenbrenner & Crouter, 1982). Indeed, investigations showed that conflicted mother-adolescent relations were more likely to occur when the mother was depressed (Patterson, 1980) or when marital relations were strained (Margolin, 1981). Accordingly, we view parent-adolescent relations as the primary mechanism through which the consequences of parents' work conditions influence adolescent development.

Several studies have shown links between aspects of parents' work and interactions with their children. For instance, Heath (1976) found that fathers who were highly absorbed in their occupations were psychologically unavailable and less sensitive to the needs of their children. Piotrkowski (1979) observed that family interactions were affected by the worker's positive and negative experiences on the job, as well as by energy depletion resulting from job demands. In a pioneering study of work conditions, Kohn (1977) demonstrated that levels of supervision and

independent thinking in fathers' jobs were related to their values regarding obedience and conformity in children. Greenberger and Goldberg
(1989) discovered that mothers with high commitments to parenting *and*
work were more authoritative than other mothers.

Other studies have examined the impact of part- or full-time scheduling
of mothers' employment on parent-adolescent relations. In this regard,
Montemayor (1984) observed that adolescent girls and boys spent less
time with their mothers if she was employed full-time. Research has
also found that the mother's employment in lower-income families was
associated with strain in the father-son relationship (Douvan, 1963;
McCord, McCord, & Thurber, 1963; Propper, 1972). These findings
were attributed to the adolescent's view of the father as an inadequate
economic provider (Bronfenbrenner & Crouter, 1982). Indeed, studies of
the 1930s depression illustrated the adolescent's declining regard for the
father as income loss and unemployment occurred (Elder, 1974).

Recently, researchers have begun to focus their attention on the
mediational role of parent-adolescent relations. Patterson (1986) presented convincing evidence in this regard by showing that stressors such
as divorce, "bad days," and medical problems led to coercive parenting
behaviors and disruptions in discipline. These parental behaviors, in turn,
increased the child's rate of problem behavior. Research on economic
hardship and income loss provides further evidence for the pivotal nature
of parent-adolescent relations. Elder, van Nguyen, and Caspi (1985)
found that economic deprivation resulted in the father's rejection of the
adolescent daughter. Rejection, in turn, was associated with lower social
competence and more moodiness in these daughters. Galambos and
Silbereisen (1987) reported that the father's life outlook was more
pessimistic as income loss increased, and a pessimistic life outlook was
related to lower expectations for job success in adolescent girls.

Although the discussion of how parental work conditions operate to
influence family processes has burgeoned in recent years, no study has
adequately linked parents' *jobs* to adolescent behavior through the
parent-adolescent relationship. Greenberger and O'Neil (1991) have
made some progress, however, in linking parents' job conditions (e.g.,
job complexity) to parenting and to perceptions of young children. The
remaining part of this chapter is devoted to describing a study designed to
examine adolescent development in two-earner families.

The Two-earner Family Study

Features of the Sample

The Two-earner Family Study (Galambos & Maggs, 1990, 1991) is a
longitudinal study of young adolescents (mean age in January 1988 [grade
6]: 11 years, 7 months) in two-parent families in which both parents were

employed on a part- or full-time basis. Data were collected from the mothers, fathers, and adolescents in these families on four occasions (Winter, 1988; Summer, 1988; Winter, 1989; Summer, 1990). On the first occasion 112 families participated (60 girls and 52 boys). By the fourth occasion 2.5 years later, 68% of the sample remained.

The schools from which the subjects were drawn were small (with one or two classrooms of sixth graders) and were located in primarily suburban areas of a city in Canada. Sixth graders were targeted because the focus of the study was on parental work, family stress, and the transition to adolescence.

The primary mode of data collection was through questionnaire. On the first three occasions, questionnaires were mailed to each parent and child individually. Family members were requested not to discuss the questionnaires with one another and were given separate return envelopes. On the fourth occasion, some families agreed to be interviewed and audiotaped during a family interaction task; questionnaires were left with these families to complete. The families who did not participate in the interviews were mailed questionnaires. On each occasion, each family member received a token payment for participation.

Table 11.1 presents demographic characteristics of the families in the sample when the adolescents were in grade 6. The parents were distributed evenly across the working and middle classes, had a relatively small number of children, and the majority had at least a high school education. Most fathers worked full-time (72% worked 31 or more hours); among mothers, 28% worked for 20 hours or less, 18% worked between 21 and 30 hours, and 54% worked 31 hours or more.

TABLE 11.1. The two-earner family study: Characteristics of the sample in grade 6.

Demographic characteristic	M	SD
Mother's work hours (per week)	30.9	11.2
Father's work hours (per week)	42.0	10.3
Mother's years employed[a]	6.5	5.4
Father's years employed[a]	17.2	7.4
Mother's occupational prestige[b]	48.7	10.9
Father's occupational prestige[b]	50.0	15.2
Mother's age	37.4	3.9
Father's age	40.0	5.5
Mother's education (Years)	13.1	2.2
Father's education (Years)	13.8	3.1
Number of children	2.4	.9
Years married	14.7	4.5

[a] Number of years employed continuously (without more than a 6-month break in employment).
[b] Blishen and McRoberts (1976) occupational index for Canadian samples; real estate sales = 50.1; secretary = 52.45.

Measures

The approach to measuring variables in the Two-earner Family Study was to use established measures with known reliability and validity. For each element in the conceptual model (e.g., parent's work conditions), we used measures focusing on somewhat different dimensions. Following is a summary of the measures used, often at all four waves of data collection.

Parent's Work Conditions

Pearlin and Schooler (1978) was the source for four subscales measuring work strains: noxiousness of work environment; depersonalization in the work environment; role overload; and inadequate rewards. Detailed work schedules were obtained as well. There were also measures of work schedule inflexibility (the Job-Family Management Scale; Bohen & Viveros-Long, 1981) and occupational status (Blishen & McRoberts, 1976).

Parent's Psychological State

Global and work-related stresses and satisfactions tapped various dimensions of the parent's psychological state. The Center for Epidemiological Studies Depression Scale (CES-D) assessed depression (Radloff, 1977); Spielberger, Gorsuch, and Kuhlenschmidt's (1970) State Anxiety scale measured anxiety; Windle and Lerner's (1986) Dimensions of Temperament Survey-Revised was used to assess current mood. With respect to work-related affect, we used Pearlin and Schooler's (1978) occupational stress measure; Bohen and Viveros-Long's (1981) Job-Family Role Strain Scale; and Greenberger and Goldberg's (1989) Work Commitment scale.

Marital Relations

Spanier's (1976) Dyadic Adjustment Scale measured wives' and husbands' perceptions of the quality of marital relations. The subscales were occasionally combined to form a global measure of marital adjustment.

Family Management

Steinberg's (1986) measure of after-school situations was used to measure where and with whom adolescents were spending out-of-school time. To assess the spousal division of labor for household tasks, Bird, Bird, and Scrugg's (1984) measure was used. Data on weekly hours spent on household chores and child care were also collected (Pleck, 1983).

Parent-adolescent Relations

Parents and adolescents completed several scales assessing the nature of their relationship. Schaefer's (1965) Children's Reports of Parental

Behavior Inventory (CRPBI) measured acceptance, firm control, and psychological control. Prinz, Foster, Kent, and O'Leary's (1979) Issues Checklist was used to measure the intensity and frequency of conflict.

Adolescent Psychosocial Development

Problem behavior was assessed with a 25-item scale of minor and major infractions (Brown, Clasen, & Eicher, 1986; Kaplan, 1978). Peer involvement (Brown et al., 1986) and deviant peers were also measured. The Self-Image Questionnaire for Young Adolescents (SIQYA) was used to assess the adolescent's emotional tone, mastery and coping, and impulse control (Petersen, Schulenberg, Abramowitz, Offer, & Jarcho, 1984).

Results from the Two-earner Family Study

According to our conceptual model, the first step in tracing the influences that parental work may have on adolescent development involves examining linkages between parents' work conditions, on the one hand, and parents' psychological state, marital relations, and family management, on the other. Given the complexities inherent in exploring any one of these links, separate studies have been undertaken to explore one relationship at a time.

Parents' Work and Psychological State

Among dual-earner couples, the necessity of combining two work schedules has been noted as a likely source of family stress. Thus, in one study (Galambos & Walters, 1992) we were particularly interested in examining *work schedule strains*. Based on previous research, two work schedule strains stood out as important: (a) the total number of hours the parent devotes to work in one week; and (b) work schedule inflexibility, or the extent to which the job constrains the opportunity to accomplish tasks such as running errands, shopping, and scheduling appointments. Our hypothesis was that longer work hours and more inflexible work schedules would be positively associated with self-reports of stress, in particular, depression, anxiety, and role strain (which is defined as feelings of discomfort, pressure, or worry associated with adequately accomplishing family and work obligations; Bohen & Viveros-Long, 1981). In addition to exploring how each spouse's strains were associated with *his or her own* psychological state, Galambos and Walters examined how each spouse's work schedule strains were associated with the *other's* psychological state. The purpose here was to shed light on crossover from one spouse's work-related strains to the other spouse's level of stress (cf. Bolger et al., 1989).

As expected, husbands' schedule inflexibility and longer work hours were associated with their higher scores on depression, anxiety, and role strain (median $r = .29$, $p < .05$). Wives' schedule inflexibility was related to their role strain ($r = .48$, $p < .05$), as were longer work hours ($r = .35$, $p < .05$), but there were no direct links between wives' schedule strains and depression and anxiety. Subsequent path analyses, however, suggested that among wives, role strain is a mediator between scheduling strains and global indices of stress such as depression and anxiety. Consistent with Kandel et al. (1985), the first response to work-related stress may be a specific stress such as role strain, which may then lead to global feelings of stress.

With respect to the issue of crossover, husbands' work schedule strains were not associated with their wives' psychological states; thus, wives did not appear to feel more distressed when their husbands worked longer hours or had inflexible work schedules. It was found, however, that wives' longer work hours predicted husbands' higher depression and anxiety. One post hoc explanation for this crossover from wives' work hours to husbands' psychological state involves the traditional supportive role that wives play in their husbands' lives; wives tend to be emotionally supportive of their husbands and respond to husbands' work stresses by assuming larger proportions of household and child care duties (Bolger et al., 1989; Repetti, 1989). Such support may not be present in families where the wife is overburdened by work, and this absence may be reflected in husbands' poorer psychological state.

Parents' Work and Marital Relations

In another study from the Two-earner Family data set, we have attempted to examine a process that links wives' work conditions to their own and their husbands' perceptions of marital adjustment (Sears & Galambos, 1991, 1992). One aspect of this work was to capture several dimensions of women's work experiences using multiple measures for each dimension; this was important because the study of women's jobs has focused typically on a few limited variables (e.g., employment status, occupational prestige). Principal components analyses of seven indicators were conducted, resulting in the identification of three general aspects of women's jobs in the Two-earner Family Study: (a) *work overload*, which was defined by high loadings on role overload, total work hours, and work schedule inflexibility; (b) *low rewards*, which was composed of inadequate job rewards (e.g., low pay, little job security) and depersonalization in the work environment (e.g., being treated with little respect); and (c) *low work status*, which was indicated by low scores on occupational prestige and high scores on noxiousness of the work environment (i.e., whether it was dangerous, dirty, or noisy).

Using structural equation modeling, Sears and Galambos (1992) modeled a process in which (a) women's work conditions were hypothesized to influence their work-related stress (i.e., stress pertaining particularly to the job and to job-family role strain); (b) work-related stress, in turn, was hypothesized to influence their global stress (a composite score indicated by depression, anxiety, and negative mood); and (c) global stress was hypothesized to mediate between women's work-related stress, on the one hand, and women's and men's perceptions of their marital adjustment, on the other. The first part of this model was confirmed, with each of the three work conditions (work overload, low rewards, and low work status) directly linked with women's work-related stress. The second part was also supported with a direct link between work-related stress and global stress. (There was also an unexpected direct link between women's low work status and their global stress). The third part of the model was supported only for *women's* perceptions of marital adjustment; women who experienced higher work-related stresses scored higher on global stress, and global stress, in turn, was linked directly with their perceptions of poorer marital adjustment. Men's perceptions of marital adjustment, however, were not linked directly with their wives' global stress as predicted; rather, men's marital adjustment was associated significantly with their wives' perceptions of marital adjustment. Sears and Galambos (1991) found a similar process operating in the men in the Two-earner Family Study; men's stress mediated between their work conditions and their perceptions of marital relations. The wives' perceptions of marital relations were not associated directly with husbands' work conditions or levels of stress.

The conclusion to be drawn from the above studies is that there is a link between one's work conditions and perceptions of the marital relationship, but it is probably through the impact of work conditions on stress that this link is forged. Moreover, there does not seem to be a direct link between one spouse's work conditions and stress and the other spouse's evaluation of marital adjustment, at least as measured in this study. Clearly, it is through a complex set of processes that work influences the marital relationship, and we are just beginning to gain some insights into these processes.

Parents' Work and Family Management

Another set of analyses from the Two-earner Family Study was designed to measure the impact of mothers' work hours on family management. In particular, Almeida, Maggs, and Galambos (in press) wanted to determine the extent to which mothers' employment hours were predictive of mothers' and fathers' performance of child care and household chores at three times across a one-year period. Participation in child care was assessed through mothers' and fathers' responses to three self-report measures: a) *hours* per week spent in child care; b) *frequency* of child care in past week; and c) *proportional responsibility* for completion of child care tasks, relative to the spouse's. With respect to household chores, three similar measures assessed hours in, frequency of, and proportional responsibility for household chores.

The concurrent results indicated that the more hours a mother was employed the less she participated in child care (4 out of 7 correlations were significant) and household chores (3 out of 7 correlations were significant). Mothers' employment hours were predictive of husbands' contribution to child care and household chores on only 3 out of 14 measures. Given that 2 of these 3 measures assessed proportional responsibility, the results are consistent with Pleck's (1983) argument that the appearance of fathers performing a greater share of family work as a result of maternal employment may be primarily explained by decreased maternal participation in family work.

Results from longitudinal analyses, however, suggested that some fathers may be responsive to changes in the number of hours their wives are employed. These analyses examined whether changes in mothers' paid work hours across a 6-month period were related to changes in mothers' and fathers' participation in household chores and child care. Husbands whose wives increased their employment hours increased their responsibility for child care ($r = .21$, $p < .05$) and also increased the number of hours they engaged in child care ($r = .20$, $p < .05$) and household chores ($r = .45$, $p < .05$) (see Figure 11.2). For mothers, an increase in the number of employment hours was associated with a decrease in the number of hours they engaged in household chores ($r = -.33$, $p < .05$).

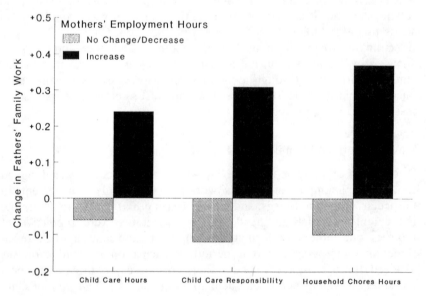

FIGURE 11.2. Change in father's participation in family work (standard scores) as a function of change in mother's employment hours over a six-month period.

A possible explanation for the apparent discrepancy between the concurrent and longitudinal findings is that changes in mothers' paid work hours may represent a period of adaptation in the family during which responsibility for family management is shifted. During transition periods fathers may increase their family work as a "help" to their wives. It remains to be seen whether the division of labor will return to its original balance once the period of transition is past.

Parent-adolescent Relations as a Mediator

The conceptual model guiding our work on the Two-earner Family Study views parent-adolescent relations as a critical vehicle through which parents' work may have an impact on adolescent development. Thus, if parents are working under strained conditions, they will more likely feel distressed, and this distress, in turn, may be evidenced in strained interactions with children. Of course, strained interactions may set the stage for adolescents to act out and feel unappreciated.

Galambos, Sears, Almeida, and Kolaric (1991) investigated and supported such a spillover process, although the second-order mediators (i.e., aspects of the parent-adolescent relationship) in this process were different for mothers and fathers. The results of a series of hierarchical regression analyses examining mothers and adolescents showed that first, mother's work overload (i.e., having too much work to do) was associated with higher levels of stress. Second, higher levels of maternal stress were associated with lower levels of acceptance of the adolescent (as measured by the combined reports of mothers and adolescents). Higher levels of maternal stress were not associated with the general level of conflict between parents and adolescents (as measured by the combined reports of mothers, fathers, and adolescents). Third, lower levels of maternal acceptance were associated with higher levels of problem behavior, controlling for earlier scores on problem behavior. Thus, mother's work overload was linked to higher levels of problem behavior in adolescents, but only indirectly through her lower acceptance of the adolescent.

With respect to fathers, it was found that work overload was linked to their higher stress. Higher stress, in turn, was associated with higher levels of parent-adolescent conflict but not to lower father acceptance of the adolescent. Parent-adolescent conflict, though, predicted higher levels of adolescent problem behavior, controlling for earlier scores on problem behavior. This set of results, then, suggests that parents' work overload may have an impact on adolescent behavior and development, but it is an indirect one, with some aspects of parent-adolescent relations more important than others.

Although the above study documents the ways in which stressful conditions at work (and the absence of them) may set the stage for adolescent behavior, it would be unfortunate to emphasize a potentially more negative side of parents' work in the face of other evidence suggesting that some aspects of parents' working are potentially beneficial.

In this regard, as discussed above, Almeida et al. (in press) showed that when mothers increased the number of hours they worked, fathers seemed to compensate by increasing their share of the child care and household work. In fact, fathers' greater involvement with their children may be a side effect of mothers' working more hours, but what impact does this involvement have on the children? In a study examining father involvement (operationalized as participation in child-care tasks), Almeida and Galambos (1991) found that father involvement was associated positively with father and adolescent reports of father acceptance of the adolescent. Indeed, an examination of longitudinal data (data collected 6 months apart) found that fathers who were more involved with their adolescents at Time 1 became more accepting of them by Time 2; higher involvement preceded warmer relations. Moreover, in families where fathers were more involved with their children, they were as accepting of their children as were mothers. This is interesting in light of other research showing that fathers are typically less warm and accepting than mothers (Youniss & Smollar, 1985). This research confirms what others have speculated; that is, parental differences in parent-adolescent relations may be due to fathers' relatively low level of involvement in their adolescents' lives. The evidence as a whole, then, is consistent with the notion that one consequence of a mother's longer work hours is that the father becomes more involved with children, and this higher involvement is associated with more acceptance of those children.

What does it mean for adolescents if their fathers are accepting? Almeida (1991) showed that over time, father acceptance of adolescents in the Two-earner Family Study predicted a more positive self-image, as measured by a composite score consisting of impulse control, mastery, and emotional tone. Put together, these results point to the indirect ways in which parents' involvement in work may affect family relations and adolescent behavior, and provide evidence that parent-adolescent relations mediate those effects.

The Context of Self-care

Another goal of the Two-earner Family Study, stimulated by interest in the context created by the dual-earner situation, was to explore the implications of self-care in early adolescence. Self-care after school is not uncommon among young adolescents whose parents work outside the home. Accordingly, Galambos and Maggs (1991) examined how well the out-of-school care situation predicted peer experience (problem behavior, peer involvement, and deviant peers) and self-image (impulse control, mastery, and emotional tone) concurrently and longitudinally. Results revealed no differences between adolescents in adult-care and those in

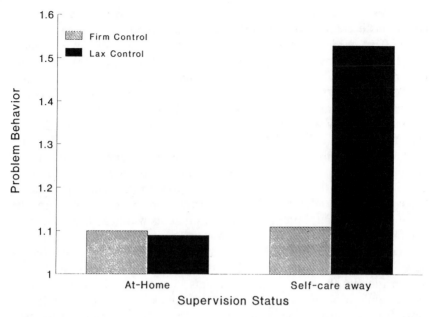

FIGURE 11.3. The buffering effect of firm control on problem behavior in girls in self-care away from home.

self-care at home. Self-care girls who were away from home, however, reported more problem behavior and contact with more deviant peers, relative to other girls and to boys. Parental acceptance and firm control mitigated this effect. Figure 11.3 shows the buffering effect of firm control (e.g., consistent rule setting) on the association between self-care away from home and girls' problem behavior. Self-care girls away from home who were in families expressing firm control were no more likely to engage in problem behavior than girls in at-home care situations. This study shed light on how the dual-earner context in concert with parent-adolescent relations can have consequences for the behavior of children.

Conclusions

The prevalence of dual-earner families in many societies in conjunction with scientific interest in the multiple contexts of development makes it particularly timely to study adolescents growing up in dual-earner families. The Two-earner Family Study and other research efforts have shown that work conditions, scheduling difficulties, occupational rewards, and supervision of children can contribute to our understanding of adolescent behavior. The question is not *whether* the dual-earner context influences adolescent behavior but rather *how* this context and the conditions it creates impact on the lives of adolescents.

The Two-earner Family Study addressed this question by examining (a) the conditions created by the dual-earner context, (b) behaviors important to adolescent development, and (c) explanatory mechanisms (first- and second-order mediators) that explain the linkages between work conditions and adolescent behavior. The most obvious set of conditions created by the dual-earner context involves the characteristics and activities of parents' work. As we have pointed out, noxious and stressful work conditions may affect mothers' and fathers' psychological health and perceptions of the marital relationship. Poorer psychological health, in turn, may place the adolescent at higher risk for engaging in problem behavior. This is only one side of the picture, however. For instance, the set of family demands present when both parents work can lead to a more equitable division of labor in the home. This may mean, in particular, that fathers become more involved in child care. Such involvement on the part of fathers was shown to be linked to adolescents' more positive self-image. Finally, the results on adolescents in self-care demonstrated how parent-adolescent relations moderated the association between self-care away from home and higher levels of problem behavior in girls; acceptance and firm control of the adolescent mitigated this relationship.

We believe that aspects of the parent-adolescent relationship such as acceptance and firm control are extremely important to adolescents, and that the study of context is incomplete without considering how the parent-adolescent relationship mediates or moderates the influence of that context on adolescents. Parents can and do have optimal relations with their children despite considerable stress, and poor relations with children can emerge even in the best of times. To the extent that parental interactions with children are controllable, the parents' work context need not create the emptiness and chaos that the media portrays as typical in the life of two-earner families. The mediational model in the present study provides initial insights into understanding adolescent development within the dual-earner context. Many questions, however, remain.

In this regard, there are three general directions that future research might follow in attempting to provide a more complete picture of adolescents in two-earner families. First, it is important to further specify those aspects of the work context that are important for parent-adolescent relations and adolescent development. For example, based on our results, we think that mother's work overload may be one of the most important aspects of her job insofar as it affects family functioning. There is some suggestion that the job satisfaction of mothers and fathers may be important as well (Barling, 1986; Barling & Van Bart, 1984; Richards & Duckett, 1991). Second, it would be wise to begin focusing on the relation between specific features of parents' jobs and adolescent vocational development. This issue has been studied only rarely (e.g., Mortimer, 1976), yet decisions about careers comprise a major developmental task in adolescence, and it is a task that is likely to be related to parents' work history and values. Third, it may be important to attempt to discern how parents' work operates in conjunction with other adolescent contexts (e.g., school, peers, and community) to influence adolescent development. As we can see from the other chapters in this volume, the adolescent moves through many different contexts, and adolescent behavior would probably best be described by understanding the system of relations among them. Before pursuing this goal, however, we need to pinpoint what it is about each specific context that is important for adolescent development. It is hoped that the Two-earner Family Study has begun to demonstrate significant features of the parents' work contexts that help us to understand adolescents.

Acknowledgments. The Two-earner Family Study was funded by University of Victoria Faculty Research grants and Social Sciences and Humanities Research Council of Canada grants to N. Galambos. The authors are grateful to the families who participated in this study.

References

Almeida, D.M. (1991, August). *Competing models linking father involvement, father acceptance, and adolescent self-image.* Paper presented at the Annual Convention of the American Psychological Association, San Francisco.

Almeida, D.M. & Galambos, N.L. (1991). Examining father involvement and the quality of father-adolescent relations. *Journal of Research on Adolescence, 1,* 155–172.

Almeida, D.M., Maggs, J.L., & Galambos, N.L. (in press). Wives' employment hours and spousal participation in family work. *Journal of Family Psychology.*

Baltes, P.B., Reese, H.W., & Lipsitt, L.P. (1980). Life-span developmental psychology. *Annual Review of Psychology, 31,* 65–110.

Barling, J. (1984). Effects of husbands' work experiences on wives' marital satisfaction. *The Journal of Social Psychology, 124,* 219–225.

Barling, J. (1986). Fathers' work experiences, the father-child relationship and children's behaviour. *Journal of Occupational Behaviour, 7,* 61–66.

Barling, J. & Rosenbaum, A. (1986). Work stressors and wife abuse. *Journal of Applied Psychology, 71,* 346–348.

Barling, J. & Van Bart, D. (1984). Mothers' subjective employment experiences and the behaviour of their nursery school children. *Journal of Occupational Psychology, 57,* 49–56.

Baruch, G.K., Biener, L., & Barnett, R.C. (1987). Women and gender in research on work and family stress. *American Psychologist, 42,* 130–136.

Belsky, J. (1984). The determinants of parenting: A process model. *Child Development, 55,* 83–96.

Bird, G.W., Bird, G.A., & Scruggs, M. (1984). Determinants of family task sharing: A study of husbands and wives. *Journal of Marriage and the Family*, *46*, 345–355.

Blishen, B.R. & McRoberts, H.A. (1976). A revised socio-economic index for occupations in Canada. *Canadian Review of Sociology and Anthropology*, *13*, 71–79.

Bohen, H.H. & Viveros-Long, A. (1981). *Balancing jobs and family life: Do flexible work schedules help*? Philadelphia: Temple University Press.

Bolger, N., DeLongis, A., Kessler, R.C., & Wethington, E. (1989). The contagion of stress across multiple roles. *Journal of Marriage and the Family*, *51*, 175–183.

Bronfenbrenner, U. (1986). Ecology of the family as a context for human development: Research perspectives. *Developmental Psychology*, *22*, 723–742.

Bronfenbrenner, U. & Crouter, A.C. (1982). Work and family through time and space. In S.B. Kamerman & C.D. Hayes (Eds.), *Families that work: Children in a changing world* (pp. 39–83). Washington, DC: National Academy of Sciences.

Brown, B.B., Clasen, D.R., & Eicher, S.A. (1986). Perceptions of peer pressure, peer conformity dispositions, and self-reported behavior among adolescents. *Developmental Psychology*, *22*, 521–530.

Burke, R., Weir, T., & DuWors, R.E., Jr. (1980). Work demands on administrators and spouse well-being. *Human Relations*, *33*, 253–278.

Crouter, A.C. (1984). Spillover from family to work: The neglected side of the work-family interface. *Human Relations*, *37*, 425–442.

Crouter, A.C. & Crowley, M.S. (1990). School-age children's time alone with fathers in single- and dual-earner families: Implications for the father-child relationship. *Journal of Early Adolescence*, *10*, 296–312.

Crouter, A.C., Perry-Jenkins, M., Huston, T.L., & McHale, S.M. (1987). Processes underlying father involvement in dual-earner and single-earner families. *Developmental Psychology*, *23*, 431–440.

Dominion Bureau of Statistics. (1964, July). *Census of Canada, 1961: Households and families*. Ottawa: Minister of Supply and Services.

Douvan, E. (1963). Employment and the adolescent. In F.I. Nye & L.W. Hoffman (Eds.), *The employed mother in America* (pp. 142–164). Chicago: Rand McNally.

Elder, G.H., Jr. (1974). *Children of the Great Depression*. Chicago: University of Chicago Press.

Elder, G.H., Jr., Van Nguyen, T., & Caspi, A. (1985). Linking family hardship to children's lives. *Child Development*, *56*, 361–375.

Galambos, N.L. & Maggs, J.L. (1990). Putting mothers' work-related stress in perspective: Mothers and adolescents in dual-earner families. *Journal of Early Adolescence*, *10*, 296–312.

Galambos, N.L. & Maggs, J.L. (1991). Out-of-school care of young adolescents and self-reported behavior. *Developmental Psychology*, *27*, 644–655.

Galambos, N.L., Sears, H.A., Almeida, D.M., & Kolaric, G.C. (1993). *Parents' work overload and problem behavior in young adolescents*. Unpublished manuscript, University of Victoria, BC.

Galambos, N.L. & Silbereisen, R.K. (1987). Income change, parental life outlook, and adolescent expectations for job success. *Journal of Marriage and the Family*, *49*, 141–149.

Galambos, N.L. & Silbereisen, R.K. (1989). Role strain in West German dual-earner households. *Journal of Marriage and the Family*, *51*, 385–389.

Galambos, N.L. & Walters, B.J. (1992). Work hours, schedule inflexibility, and stress in dual-earner spouses. *Canadian Journal of Behavioural Science*, *24*, 290–302.

Gottfried A.E. & Gottfried, A.W. (Eds.). (1988). *Maternal employment and children's development: Longitudinal research*. New York: Plenum.

Greenberger, E. & Goldberg, W.A. (1989). Work, parenting, and the socialization of children. *Developmental Psychology*, *25*, 22–35.

Greenberger, E. & O'Neil, R. (1991, April). *Characteristics of fathers' and mothers' jobs: Implications for parenting and children's social development*. Paper presented at the Biennial Meeting of the Society for Research in Child Development, Seattle, WA.

Heath, D.B. (1976). Competent fathers: Their personality and marriages. *Human Development*, *19*, 26–39.

Hochschild, A. (1989). *The second shift*. New York: Avon Books.

Hoffman, L.W. (1984). Work, family, and the socialization of the child. In R.D. Parke (Ed.), *Review of child development research* (Vol. 7, pp. 223–282). Chicago: University of Chicago Press.

Hoffman, L.W. (1989). Effects of maternal employment in the two-parent family. *American Psychologist*, *44*, 283–292.

Kandel, D.B., Davies, M., & Raveis, V.H. (1985). The stressfulness of daily social roles for women: Marital, occupational and household roles. *Journal of Health and Social Behavior*, *26*, 64–78.

Kaplan, H.B. (1978). Deviant behavior and self-enhancement in adolescence. *Journal of Youth and Adolescence*, *7*, 253–277.

Keith, P. & Schafer, R. (1980). Role strain and depression in two-job families. *Family Relations*, *29*, 483–488.

Kessler, R.C. & McRae, J.A., Jr. (1982). The effect of wives' employment on the mental health of married men and women. *American Sociological Review*, *47*, 216–227.

Kohn, M.L. (1977). *Class and conformity: A study in values* (2nd ed.). Chicago: University of Chicago Press.

Lerner, J.V. & Galambos, N.L. (Eds.). (1991). *Employed mothers and their children*. New York: Garland.

Maccoby, E.E. & Martin, J.A. (1983). Socialization in the context of the family: Parent-child interaction. In E.M. Hetherington (Ed.), *Handbook of child psychology: Vol. 4. Socialization, personality, and social development* (pp. 1–101). New York: Wiley.

Margolin, G. (1981). The reciprocal relationship between marital and child problems. In J.P. Vincent (Ed.), *Advances in family intervention assessment and theory* (Vol. 2, pp. 131–182). Greenwich, CT: JAI Press.

McCord, J., McCord, W., & Thurber, E. (1963). Effects of maternal employment on lower-class boys. *Journal of Abnormal and Social Psychology*, *67*, 177–182.

Moen, P. (1982). The two-provider family: Problems and potentials. In M.E. Lamb (Ed.), *Nontraditional families: Parenting and child development* (pp. 13–43). Hillsdale, NJ: Lawrence Erlbaum.

Montemayor, R. (1984). Maternal employment and adolescents' relations with parents, siblings, and peers. *Journal of Youth and Adolescence*, *13*, 543–557.

Morrow, L. (1988, August 8). Through the eyes of children. *Time*, pp. 26–45.

Mortimer, J.T. (1976). Social class, work and the family: Some implications of the father's occupation on familiar relationships and sons' career decisions. *Journal of Marriage and the Family, 38,* 241–256.

Mott, P.E., Mann, F.C., McLoghlin, Q., & Warwick, D.P. (1965). *Shift work: The social, psychological, and physical consequences.* Ann Arbor: University of Michigan Press.

Patterson, G.R. (1980). Mothers: The unacknowledged victims. *Monographs of the Society for Research in Child Development, 45,* (5, Serial No. 186).

Patterson, G.R. (1982). *Coercive family process.* Eugene, OR: Castalia.

Patterson, G.R. (1986). Performance models for antisocial boys. *American Psychologist, 41,* 432–444.

Patterson, G.R. & Stouthamer-Loeber, M. (1984). The correlation of family management practices and delinquency. *Child Development, 55,* 1299–1307.

Pearlin, L.I. (1975). Sex roles and depression. In N. Datan & L.H. Ginsberg (Eds.), *Life-span developmental psychology: Normative life crises* (pp. 191–207). New York: Academic Press.

Pearlin, L.I., Menaghan, E.G., Lieberman, M.A., & Mullan, J.T. (1981). The stress process. *Journal of Health and Social Behavior, 22,* 337–356.

Pearlin, L.I. & Schooler, C. (1978). The structure of coping. *Journal of Health and Social Behavior, 19,* 2–21.

Perlmutter, M. (Ed.). (1984). *Parent-child interaction and parent-child relations in child development: The Minnesota Symposia on Child Psychology* (Vol. 17). Hillsdale, NJ: Lawrence Erlbaum.

Petersen, A.C., Schulenberg, J.E., Abramowitz, R.H., Offer, D., & Jarcho, H.D. (1984). A self-image questionnaire for young adolescents (SIQYA): Reliability and validity studies. *Journal of Youth and Adolescence, 13,* 93–111.

Piotrkowski, C.S. (1979). *Work and the family system.* New York: Macmillan.

Pleck, J.H. (1983). Husbands' paid work and family roles: Current research issues. In H.Z. Lopata & J.H. Pleck (Eds.), *Research in the interweave of social roles and family jobs* (pp. 251–333). Greenwich, CT: JAI Press.

Pleck, J.H., Staines, G.L., & Lang, L. (1980, March). Conflict between work and family life. *Monthly Labor Review, 103*(3), 29–32.

Prinz, R., Foster, S., Kent, R., & O'Leary, K. (1979). Multivariate assessment of conflict in distressed and non-distressed mother-adolescent dyads. *Journal of Applied Behavioral Analysis, 12,* 691–700.

Propper, A.M. (1972). The relationship of maternal employment to adolescent roles, activities, and parental relationships. *Journal of Marriage and the Family, 34,* 417–421.

Radloff, L. (1977). The CES-D scale: A self-report depression scale for research in the general population. *Journal of Applied Psychological Measurement, 1,* 385–401.

Rapoport, R. & Rapoport, R.N. (1976). *Dual-career families re-examined.* New York: Harper and Row.

Repetti, R.L. (1989). Effects of daily workload on subsequent behavior during marital interaction: The roles of social withdrawal and spouse support. *Journal of Personality and Social Psychology, 57,* 651–659.

Repetti, R.L., Matthews, K.A., & Waldron, I. (1989). Employment and women's health: Effects of paid employment on women's mental and physical health. *American Psychologist, 44,* 1394–1401.

Richards, M. & Duckett, E. (1991, April). *The effects of parental employment and satisfaction on young adolescents' daily experience*. Paper presented at the Biennial Meeting of the Society for Research in Child Development, Seattle, WA.

Rodin, J. & Ickovics, J.R. (1990). Women's health: Review and research agenda as we approach the 21st century. *American Psychologist, 45*, 1018–1034.

Schaefer, E. (1965). Children's reports of parental behavior: An inventory. *Child Development, 36*, 413–424.

Sears, H.A. & Galambos, N.L. (1992). Women's work conditions and marital adjustment in two-earner couples: A structural model. *Journal of Marriage and the Family, 54*, 789–797.

Sears, H.A. & Galambos, N. (1991, May). *A process model of husbands' work conditions and marital adjustment*. Paper presented at the Annual Convention of the Canadian Psychological Association, Calgary, AB.

Silbereisen, R.K., Eyferth, K., & Rudinger, G. (Eds.). (1986). *Development as action in context: Problem behavior and normal youth development*. New York: Springer.

Spanier, G.B. (1976). Measuring dyadic adjustment: New scales for assessing the quality of marriage and similar dyads. *Journal of Marriage and the Family, 38*, 15–28.

Spielberger, C.D., Gorsuch, R.L., & Kuhlenschmidt, S.L. (1970). *Manual for the state-trait anxiety inventory*. Palo Alto, CA: Consulting Psychologists Press.

Statistics Canada. (1985, March). *Women in Canada: A statistical report, 1971 and 1981*. Ottawa: Minister of Supply and Services.

Statistics Canada. (1991, February). *The labour force*. Ottawa: Minister of Supply and Services.

Steinberg, L. (1986). Latchkey children and susceptibility to peer pressure: An ecological analysis. *Developmental Psychology, 22*, 433–439.

Steinberg, L. (1990). Autonomy, conflict, and harmony in the family relationship. In S.S. Feldman & G.R. Elliot (Eds.), *At the threshold: The developing adolescent* (pp. 255–276). Cambridge: Harvard University Press.

Windle, M. & Lerner, R.M. (1986). Reassessing the dimensions of temperamental individuality across the life span: The Revised Dimensions of Temperament Survey (DOTS-R). *Journal of Adolescent Research, 1*, 213–230.

Youniss, J. & Smollar, S. (1985). *Adolescent relations with mothers, fathers, and friends*. Chicago: University of Chicago Press.

12
Looking Forward in Troubled Times: The Influence of Social Context on Adolescent Plans and Orientations

GLEN H. ELDER, JR., ANN HAGELL, LAURA RUDKIN, AND RAND D. CONGER

> Ten years ago we had everything going our way, well, maybe eleven or twelve years ago. Thought you knew it all, you knew how to farm, you knew how to make money, and you were financially secure, and you paid your own bills, and twelve years later you're borrowing the money to make ends meet. You kinda feel like you're going backwards.
>
> Displaced Iowa farmer, 1989, father of two.

Across successive generations of the 20th century, American youth have decided in large numbers to leave the countryside for a future in towns and cities. Periods of economic decline have reinforced this out-migration, a drama played out most recently in the agricultural heartland of the United States, especially during the farm crisis of the 1980s in the state of Iowa. From 1980 through 1984, the demographic figures show "many more declining counties in the central and southern Corn Belt of the Midwest than there had been in the 1970s" (Fuguitt, Brown, & Beale, 1989, p. 30), a change reflecting the agricultural crisis of this era and the loss of nonfarm job opportunities and wages. Personal accounts, such as that used to open this chapter, illustrate how life has changed for the people of the Midwest during these years. By the end of the last decade, over 1 out of 10 residents in the agricultural counties of Iowa had moved elsewhere. The state and Midwest region as a whole had become a very different place for young and old.

Rural studies have long expressed an interest in the future intentions of rural youth. In the 1950s and 1960s, research addressed the actual and expected educational and occupational attainments of children who grew up in rural families, and investigated factors related to whether or not they were likely to become farmers in the near future (see, for example, Burchinal, 1965; Elder, 1963). In most cases, the aim was to understand migration and assess the future of rural life-styles in the United States. These studies declined in the 1980s, and few researchers have addressed such issues in reference to the changing economic climate of the 1980s (see Buttel, Larson & Gillespie, 1990). This period of economic change has dramatically altered the opportunities of children who were born during the heady, growth-oriented atmosphere of the 1970s (Friedberger, 1988, 1990).

The rural crisis may have had different effects on various segments of the rural population, from the children of farmers to the children of other rural residents. Among the sons of farmers, however prosperous, the crisis cast serious doubt on the feasibility of farming as a career. Even the most industrious efforts did not ensure a reasonable chance for economic success or, at least, survival. Moreover, the difficult times have, no doubt, prompted some to wonder whether they actually wanted to "work as hard as father." Daughters on the farm have never had much of an option in agricultural production, such as the management of a sizeable farm, and recent trends can only reinforce their preferences for a life-style based in the city. Yet, little is known about the direct effects of the crisis on the orientations and psychological well-being of adolescents who are coming of age in different types of rural setting.

Familiarity with the farming way of life and the familial bonds of farm families undoubtedly orient some adolescents to a future in the rural community, at least, more so than life in a nonfarm rural family. Nevertheless, many children of farmers and other rural families have few compelling alternatives other than leaving home for opportunities in other parts of the country. How do these children feel about the feasibility of an agrarian life? In terms of economic and social issues relating to farming, the context in which adolescents make decisions about their future is obviously important.

For most young people, adolescence is a period of orientation, a time for deciding directions and goals, a period of learning about and coming to terms with the various opportunities and restrictions that their lives are likely to offer. The literature suggests that mid-adolescence is a time when childhood aspirations and practical expectations begin to converge, and a phase when young people begin to think more realistically about the paths that their futures might take (Nurmi, 1989). Viewing these issues from a life-course perspective, we suggest that the intentions or inclinations of adolescents are likely to be influenced by the various contexts in which they function, such as family, school, or community. Future orientations develop in the social and cultural context. Our central focus specifically concerns the effects of different rural contexts on the residential preferences of adolescents. What factors account for a youth's preference to make a life in the rural community? Do these factors differ by rural context?

We examine both contextual influences and correlates of this preference among Iowa boys and girls in early adolescence, in their eighth grade of school. Rural orientation specifically refers to a stated desire among rural adolescents to live in one's home community, on a farm, or near relatives. The concept has particular relevance to children in early adolescence who are some years away from the realities of higher education and an occupation. Data for the study come from the Iowa Youth and Families Project, a panel study of farm and small-town families in north central Iowa, launched in 1989.

To set the stage for the analyses, we turn to the meaning of rural context and orientation, with emphasis on influences and correlates. What are the implications of rural ecologies for the correlates of residential preferences such as academic ability and self-esteem? A description of the sample and key variables follows these considerations.

Living in Rural America: Its Meaning for Youth and Their Futures

Rural society and its implications for those who grow up in the countryside have been a topic of continuing research interest over the years. This level of interest reflects the high regard of and almost mythical status given to farming as a way of life in American society. Americans tend to see farming as an embodiment of the core values of American society, such as hard work, self-sufficiency, family ties, and a close connection with the land (Barlett, 1993; Bealer & Willits, 1988; Kohn, 1988; Willits, Bealer, & Timbers, 1990). The hopes and intentions of the next generation of rural inhabitants are essential considerations for the future of rural society.

"Rural" can imply a variety of life-styles apart from the agricultural, and we argue that more fine-grained distinctions in rural contexts are sometimes ignored, given the usual emphasis on rural-urban differences. In the Iowa sample, important distinctions are made between farm families, families that previously farmed, and those families that are not directly involved in agricultural production. We hypothesize that the intention of young adolescents to remain in their rural community will depend in part on how closely associated they are with farm life.

Studies on the aspirations of rural youth (e.g., Dunne, Elliott, & Carlsen, 1981; Elder, 1963; Falk & Salter, 1978; Jackson & Meara, 1977; Murray, Keller, McMorran, & Edwards, 1983) suggest that rural adolescents generally lag behind their urban counterparts in terms of opportunities to achieve, preparation for college, and levels of expectations of reaching certain goals (Elder, 1963). However, these studies rarely make distinctions among different types of rural living—for example, between living on a farm or living in a small town.

Rural studies of aspirations tend to focus on educational and occupational plans, to the neglect of residential goals and intentions to leave the community (e.g., Looker, 1991; Schwarzweller, 1978; Schwarzweller & Lyson, 1974). When they do address residential issues, such studies are often narrowly restricted to questions of rural youths' intention to live on farms. Very few studies have addressed the issue of general orientation to a rural way of life. In this study, we extend the notion of rural orientation beyond these limitations. This is important because future aspirations regarding job, family, and residence are likely to be closely related to each other—occupational choice to a farm child is also associated with the decision about whether or not to leave the home community (see Looker, 1991).

Our empirical measure of rural orientation focuses on preferences for rural residence, in terms of the importance of remaining in the community and living close to relatives, as well as living on a farm. In addition, we investigate the extent to which rural orientation is correlated with other values that are traditionally associated with a general commitment to rural life-styles. The traditional agrarian life-style has been described as antimaterialistic, with emphases on self-sufficiency, kinship ties, and being a good neighbor (Barlett, 1992; Bealer & Willits, 1988; Bunce, 1981; Kohn, 1988). Given the limited range of occupational opportunities available to the young person in a rural community, we anticipate that a preference for rural living will include greater commitment to family, community, and traditional values than to material gain. Clearly, all members of the rural community do not hold a stereotypical rural ideology (see, for example, Salamon, 1987). Furthermore, some adolescents may not see aspirations for material gain as being in conflict with plans for family. In any case, we expect a desire to stay in the community to reflect a greater attachment to that community, kin, and tradition.

As a final comment concerning rural orientation, it is worth briefly considering developmental issues with respect to the growth of ideas about the future in young adolescents (Spenner & Featherman, 1978). Certainty concerning future goals may develop into late adolescence, but there is little strong evidence to suggest that such ideas change dramatically over this period. Poole (1983) found clarity of job choice to be higher among 17-year-olds when compared to 14-year-olds, with about 10% more students of both sexes having a definite knowledge of their job choices in the older age group. However, the same number of both sexes (one third) remained undecided at both age 14 and age 17. Similarly, Nurmi (1989), in a series of interviews with adolescents of various ages, concluded that planning for the future increased with age.

The Influences of Social Ecology, Family Attachment, and Gender

What is the role of social ecology and family attachment in the evolution of psychological orientations? Mortimer, Lorence, and Kumka (1986) identify relationships within the family of origin as a central mechanism that mediates the effect of socioeconomic position on subsequent occupational aspirations and achievements. Both class origins and family relationships are influential in shaping future orientations (e.g., Howell, Ohlendorf, & McBroom, 1981; Sewell & Hauser, 1976). For example, families of higher status in rural communities have traditionally placed their offspring in positions of socioeconomic advantage, and the identification of sons with parents has tended to increase the probability of this achievement among sons (Jackson & Meara, 1974, 1977; Jackson, Meara, & Arora, 1974). However, little is known about whether or not family effects vary according to the broader context of rural children, particularly in the harsher economic conditions of the 1980s farm crisis. We address this issue with respect to the importance of family identification for future orientations in different rural settings.

Gender is central to any discussion of the world of work (e.g., Looker, 1991), but it is especially so in rural America. Opportunities are different for men and for women, and their career expectations vary accordingly. However, the gender gap between the aspirations of boys and girls appears to be narrowing. Dunne, Elliott, and Carlsen (1981) reported higher educational aspirations among female college students than among college men, but the women's occupational aspirations lag behind (see also Kammer, 1985). There is evidence that, for boys, a commitment to higher educational and work goals is also associated with high levels of commitment to family, whereas for girls, higher occupational goals may conflict with family values (Stevens, Puchtell, Ryu, & Mortimer, 1990). Other studies also indicate that the future holds quite a different meaning for girls than for boys; for example, Nurmi (1989) reports that boys' optimism increased throughout adolescence, whereas girls became more pessimistic.

The world of rural America also offers very different prospects for boys and girls, since family farming is largely a male-oriented business, and the most able of either sex generally seek their futures in more prosperous parts of the country. Out-migration from rural areas is selective, drawing the better educated and a greater proportion of young females than males. Consistent with the male-oriented farm community and its sex ratio, the bright lights of more urban opportunities for young women are likely to be expressed in a stronger rural preference among Iowa boys than among girls.

The Psychology of Rural Orientation

A general orientation to the rural way of life is likely to have different meanings and consequences for children from varying types of rural ecologies. Adolescent preferences for rural living, for example, should have more positive implications for boys in farm than nonfarm settings, since the former have greater access to agricultural opportunities. Thus, it may be those children who are well aware of the situation, yet who are still determined to take up the family business and feel competent enough to do so, who decide to stay. Such preferences may also be coupled with higher feelings of self-esteem, mastery, and constructive behavior.

Low levels of aspirations and goals are usually associated with higher levels of psychiatric symptomatology. Poor school achievement and lower levels of cognitive ability are correlates of negative thoughts about the future (e.g., Sarigiani, Wilson, Petersen, & Vicary, 1990). Moreover, low self-esteem tends to characterize children with lower occupational goals (e.g., Chiu, 1990; Nurius, 1991). In more behavioral terms, childhood behavior difficulties or conduct problems are predictors of poor adult outcomes such as delinquency, maladjustment, and general psychosocial well-being (e.g., Robins, 1978; Rutter, 1989). Some writers have suggested that rurality is associated with negative affect and poorer psychological health (Murray et al., 1983).

However, psychological correlates of this kind would only be related to rural orientation if the latter is construed as unconstructive or negative future planning. We argue that whether or not a desire to remain in the rural community is a good or a poor aspiration will be determined in part by the nature of adolescents' rural experiences. We suggest that blanket assertions concerning the positive or negative value of rural orientations are inappropriate, and that the correlates of such values will vary by context.

The Current Study: Research Objectives

By focusing on contextual differences in the rural preferences of young adolescents, we assume that the determinants and correlates of this preference vary across three ecological settings in rural America—farm, transitional, and nonfarm. Research generally fails to address issues of variations in contexts and typically assumes, for example, that the value of having high educational and occupational goals is invariant across behavior settings. Yet adolescents within specific contexts make decisions and adjust ambitions according to their perceptions of the pluses and minuses of different life options and ways of living.

The study is organized around four lines of inquiry. First, we describe the operationalization of the concept of rural orientation within our sample, and assess the extent to which it is associated with traditional aspects of rural ideology. We also outline the nature of the different rural contexts under investigation. Second, we investigate various determinants of rural orientation, specifically in relation to context, gender, cognitive ability, family relationships, and economic hardship. For example, do adolescents with greater cognitive ability have lower orientations to a rural life-style? Third, to investigate further the interactions of rural orientation with different rural contexts, we carry out parallel analyses within farm, transitional, and nonfarm settings. For example, is the effect of gender on rural orientation significantly stronger for the farm versus the nonfarm group? Is parental identification more important for children living in farm families? Finally, we conclude by focusing on the psychological meaning of rural orientation among adolescents in each of the three settings. Are efficacious youth on farms most likely to favor life in the country, and do feelings of depression take the form of a rural preference among nonfarm adolescents who have no direct avenues to farming?

Sample and Variables

Sample

We use data from the Iowa Youth and Families Project, a longitudinal study of rural families and their children currently being conducted at Iowa State University. The original sample included 451 two-parent families from eight agriculturally dependent counties in Iowa. Families selected for the study were residing on farms, in rural areas, or in small towns (with populations of less than 6,500), and thus indicate different types of rurality. To qualify for inclusion in the original sample, families had to have a child in seventh grade (the target child) and a sibling within 4 years of age.[1] Families were visited in their homes by project staff and each of the four family members filled out a set of written questionnaires that covered a wide range of topics (see Conger, Conger, Elder, Lorenz, Simons, & Whitbeck, 1992, for a more detailed description of the data collection process).

In these analyses, we concentrate on data provided by the target children in the second wave of data collection in 1989, when those respondents were eighth graders.[2] Fifty-four (12%) of the original 451 target children are excluded from our analyses: Twenty-seven families had dropped out of the study in the second year, 6 families were no longer intact, 9 families had moved out of the study area, and 12 target children had missing values on at least one of the variables of interest.[3]

---

[1] The sample included 78% of the eligible families in the region.

[2] We use data from the second wave of data collection, primarily because information on rural orientation in residential preferences was not collected in the first year of the study. Additionally, the future plans of the target children should be better formed by this year.

[3] Families who had become single-parent families and those who had left the study area since the first wave of data collection were included in the second wave. However, we do not include them in our analyses because their responses to questions regarding family and community are influenced by their new and different contexts.

All of the families in the study are white and the 1989 median family income was $37,500. Because of the selection criteria, all of the 397 families in our analyses have at least four members; the average family size is 4.8. More than half of the mothers and fathers in our sample had attended college. The median ages of the fathers and mothers are 40 and 38 years, respectively.

Variables

In the analyses that follow, we describe the construction and meaning of rural orientation, define the psychological characteristics to which it will be related, and outline the independent variables.

The Construction and Meaning of Rural Orientation

Rural orientation is measured by three questions regarding where the Iowa adolescents would like to live as adults. They were asked how important it would be for them to live on a farm, to stay in their community, and to live close to relatives. Each question was rated on a 5-point scale, from *not important at all* (0) to *very important* (4) (average inter-item correlation, $r = .27$). The responses were summed and produced a score with a range from 0 to 12. A high score denotes a strong preference for rural life.

Our conceptual definition of rural orientation extends beyond the idea of simple residential preferences to include attachment to a traditional rural life-style. To what extent is our measure of rural orientation associated with antimaterialism and commitment to community and family? To answer these questions, we correlated the index of rural orientation with items on other conceptually related goals.[4]

To measure *antimaterialism*, the adolescents were asked how important having money and getting a well-paid job would be to them. These questions were scored on a 5-point scale from 0 (*not at all important*) to 4 (*very important*). Correlational results reflect a tendency for adolescents who are high on rural orientation to be significantly less concerned about earning money ($r = -.14$, $p < .01$). However, rural orientation is not related to the teenagers' ratings of the importance of getting a well-paid job ($r = -.05$, ns). With respect to *commitment to family and community*, the adolescents were asked to rate the importance of having children, helping others, and being a community leader. Adolescents who are high on rural orientation tended to think that having children is important ($r = .13$, $p < .01$) and also that it is important to help others ($r = .13$, $p <$

---

[4] Results for all correlations of aspirations/values and rural orientation are presented for the group as a whole, but because of the disproportionate number of nonfarm children in the sample, we confirmed that there were no significant differences by rural context.

.01), but rural orientation is not related to the importance of being a community leader ($r = .03$, ns). However, the correlations are modest, and we find only partial support for an association between rural orientation and traditional rural values.

We also investigated the relationship of rural orientation to the adolescents' *educational aspirations*, and to their belief that they must leave the community for *better occupational opportunities*. Respondents were asked what level of education they hoped to complete, from *less than high school* (0) to *a Ph.D. or professional degree* (6). They were also asked how strongly they disagreed or agreed with the statement that job opportunities will be better elsewhere. Answers to both of these questions are correlated with a preference for the rural life. Rurally oriented youth have lower educational aspirations ($r = -.22$, $p < .001$), and are less likely to believe that jobs are better elsewhere ($r = -.25$, $p < .001$). We note that educational aspirations for all three groups are quite high, with roughly 90% wanting at least a bachelor's degree and almost one third aspiring to a Ph.D. or professional degree.

Two other aspects of the rural orientation measure are worth noting. First, a low score on rural orientation does not necessarily mean the adolescent feels strongly about *leaving* the community; for some individuals a low score may mean that they do not have specific goals or plans. Thus, an adolescent may respond to the constituent items in the rural orientation index by stating that it is not very important for them to (a) live on a farm, (b) live in the community, or (c) live close to relatives. However, such a rating may only mean that they are uncertain, and need not imply that they have plans to migrate to other areas.

Second, because the adolescents are only in the eighth grade, it is possible that their future plans and goals will change by the time they leave high school. To assess the stability of rural orientation, we compared the index scores for older siblings from both waves of data collection. None of the mean scores (for the six gender-rural context groups) changes significantly between the two waves of data, collected one year apart. In addition, the correlation of individuals' scores from the two time periods is fairly high ($r = .69$).

To summarize, our index of rural orientation extends beyond a simple desire to live on a farm, and includes items concerning commitment to community and relatives. However, it is only partially associated with other traditional aspects of rural ideology such as antimaterialism.

Construction of Associated Psychological Variables

In our analyses, we will be investigating the relationship of rural orientation to various psychological variables, and to do so we use data from a series of standardized instruments.

We use Rosenberg's 10-item scale (1965) to measure the adolescent's *self-esteem* and Pearlin's 7-item measure of control (Pearlin, Lieberman,

Menaghan, & Mullan, 1981) to assess *mastery*. The range for both scales is 0 to 4, with a higher score indicating a greater sense of personal worth or self-efficacy. The standardized alpha coefficient for the self-esteem scale is .84 and for the mastery scale is .73.

To measure the adolescent's levels of *depression* and *anxiety*, we use two subscales from the *SCL-90-R* (Derogatis, 1983). The 12-item depression measure and the 10-item anxiety scale both have standardized alpha coefficients of .84. Both scales range from 0 to 4 with a higher score indicating a greater intensity of depression or anxiety.

Quay's 22-item scale identifies the level of *behavioral problems* exhibited by the adolescent (Quay & Peterson, 1983). The scale relies on mother's reports of adolescents' behavior and ranges from 0 to 3, with a higher score indicating more problems. The standardized alpha coefficient is .94.

Independent Variables

Our main concern is with the importance of context in determining levels of orientation to the rural life-style. In our analyses, we refer to three context groups—farm families, nonfarm families, and families in transition from farm to nonfarm. Farm families are defined by having a father engaged in full-time farming during 1988 and 1989 (85 families). Transitional families are those in which the father was engaged in farming part-time in either 1988 or 1989, or families in which the father was previously a full-time farmer, but was not farming in 1989 (89 families). We label this group transitional because most of these families are in transition from farm to nonfarm status and family members have experienced both farm and nonfarm influences. Fathers of nonfarm families have never engaged in farming (223 families).

Context is not a proxy for the family's socioeconomic status. Parents' education and family income show little variation across our three groups, with farm families tending to fare slightly better.[5] In addition, it is worth reemphasizing that all families were living in communities of less than 6,500, and that these definitions in context essentially reflect different versions of rural society.

Economic influences on rural orientation are measured by a scale of *felt economic constraint*. The scale includes parents' responses to questions regarding whether they felt that they had enough money to afford the kind of home, clothing, car, food, furniture, medical care, and leisure activities they thought they should have. The scale ranges from 0 to 28

---

[5] Fifty-four percent of farm and transitional fathers had attended college, as had 51% of the nonfarm fathers. The mothers tended to be better educated among the farm parents—69% attended college; respective figures for transitional and nonfarm mothers were 59% and 51%. Of the three groups, farm families had the highest 1989 median family income: $39,700. The median income of transitional families was $39,543 and that of nonfarm families was $36,775.

with a high score indicating a greater degree of economic strain. The standardized alpha coefficient for the scale is .93.

We use an index of the adolescent's *identification with parents* to identify family influences on rural orientation. Four questions (each scored 0 to 4) tap the extent to which the adolescent respects and wants to be like the parents. These scores were summed, and a mean was calculated from scores for identification with mother and identification with father. The resulting variable has a range from 0 to 16. A high score indicates greater parental identification. The standardized alpha coefficient is .83.

Since studies suggest that future orientations may be systematically related to aptitude (e.g., Sewell & Hauser, 1976), we use the adolescent's Iowa *percentile rank* on a set of standardized tests (Iowa Test of Basic Skills, 1986).[6] *Gender* is also included as an independent variable.

Results

Variations in Rural Orientation

As suggested, we expect adolescents growing up on farms to have higher rural orientations than teenagers from transitional or nonfarm households, a difference that reflects their greater access to farm opportunities and a more ingrained sense of an agrarian life-style. Through past experiences with farming, adolescents from the transitional households should have a stronger rural orientation than those from nonfarm households.

Mean rural orientation scores for farm, transitional, and nonfarm adolescents are presented at the top of Table 12.1. The table confirms that, as expected, rural orientation is higher for the farm children than for either the transitional or nonfarm children (univariate analysis of variance, $F = 9.63$, df 2,394, $p < .001$). Thus, adolescents from farm households have a significantly greater desire to remain in their communities, stay on the farm, and remain close to kin. In comparing teenagers from the transitional and nonfarm families, the same can be said for children from transitional households. Rural teenagers from nonfarm households have the weakest desire to remain in their communities.

What factors could account for these contextual differences in the mean levels of rural orientation? As a preliminary step in answering this question, we compared group means for other variables of potential interest, specifically gender, cognitive ability, identification with parents, and felt economic constraint. Contextual differences on any of these factors could account, at least in part, for variations in attraction to the rural life. Interestingly, the mean levels of virtually all of these variables

---

[6] Data on test scores and rank were collected by project staff during visits to the schools.

TABLE 12.1. Means[a] for rural orientation, independent variables, and associated variables by rural context.

	Farm (n = 85)	Transitional (n = 89)	Nonfarm (n = 223)	Range	Statistics[b]
Dependent variable					
Rural orientation	5.10	4.83	4.43	0–12	$F = 9.63$ ($p = .0001$)
Independent variables					
Male	.45	.45	.51	0–1	$x^2 = 1.55$ ($p = .5$)
Test rank	66.18	63.49	58.75	1–99	$F = 2.67$ ($p = .07$)
Identification w/parents	12.27	12.03	12.01	1–16	$F = 0.35$ ($p = .7$)
Economic constraint	9.79	9.86	10.48	0–28	$F = .8$ ($p = .4$)
Associated psychological traits					
Self-esteem	2.99	3.07	3.08	0–4	$F = .81$ ($p = .4$)
Mastery	2.83	2.93	2.86	0–4	$F = .67$ ($p = .5$)
Depression	0.52	0.51	0.46	0–4	$F = .68$ ($p = .5$)
Anxiety	0.41	0.41	0.37	0–4	$F = .38$ ($p = .7$)
Behavioral problems	0.41	0.43	0.51	0–3	$F = 2.23$ ($p = .11$)

[a] The gender variable is reported as proportion male.
[b] The statistics column reports differences in group means for each variable by group.

do not differ by context. The one exception is the measure of cognitive ability, the Iowa Percentile Rank (IPR). Teenagers in the farm group tended to be ranked at a higher level on the IPR than other youth (univariate ANOVA, $F = 2.67$, $df\ 2,394$, $p = .07$). To establish that the differences in rural orientation by context are not because of group difference in ability, we carried out an analysis of covariance, assessing differences in rural orientation by context, with test rank entered as a covariate. The results show significant differences in rural orientation, even after test rank has been taken into account ($F = 4.64$, $df\ 2,394$, $p = .01$). Thus, contextual differences in rural orientation cannot be simply attributed to compositional differences across the three groups.

Moreover, mean scores on different measures of psychological functioning are not markedly different for the three groups. Levels of self-esteem and mastery, for example, are very similar across the three types of rural settings, as are rates of psychiatric symptomatology and behavior problems. That these three groups are remarkably similar on various social and psychological measures is contrary to the common assumption that farm children lag behind other children in these respects (e.g., Murray et al., 1983). It is true, of course, that we do not have children in the study who currently live in a truly urban environment and culture. The largest residential community is 6,500 and most of the adolescents live either on farms, in the open country, or in very small towns.

From the evidence at hand, the desire of Iowa youth to live on a farm, near kin, and in their community differs significantly by rural context. In addition, these variations are not because of compositional differences in gender, test rank, identification with parents, or economic constraint, nor do the groups differ with respect to a range of psychological traits such as self-esteem.

Determinants of Rural Orientation

Farm youth are clearly more attached to a rural life-style than adolescents who live in the small communities of the study region, but what does this contextual variation mean? Does it tell us something about the male-oriented culture of farm life or about contextual differences in the relative importance of family ties? At this point, we know that these factors are not related to the farm and nonfarm distinction, but do they have different consequences within each different context? Before answering this question, we must first establish the main effects of these independent variables.

With this question in mind, we turn to the issue of differences in rural orientation between boys and girls, the most capable in school and those with less ability, the adolescents who are most and least identified with parents, and youths who face economic pressure versus abundance. A set of regression analyses (ordinary least squares) tested for these effects in two nested models. The first established the main effects of context and gender (Table 12.2). In the second model, we answer whether these effects persist even with adjustments for the effects of school performance, identification with parents, and economic strain. The latter analysis also enabled us to determine the extent to which school performance, familial identification, and economic pressures affect adolescent preferences for a rural life-style. In both models, we used two dichotomous variables to measure rural context: The variables indicate membership in the transitional or nonfarm groups, with farm children as the reference category.

Confirming the pattern suggested by Table 12.1, Model 1 indicates that context is significantly related to level of rural orientation. In addition, there is a significant effect of gender. As we hypothesized, farm youth are more rurally oriented than nonfarm children, and boys are more strongly oriented to rural living than girls. Membership in a nonfarm (versus farm) family reduces the rural orientation score by nearly three-quarters of a point and being male increases the score by .82. We find that the effect of

TABLE 12.2. Regression coefficients in metric and standardized form.[a]

Antecedent factors	Model #1 ($n = 397$)		Model #2 ($n = 397$)	
	b (se)	β	b (se)	β
Intercept	7.74		5.17***	
	(.26)		(.93)	
Transitional	−.28	−.05	−.28	−.05
	(.34)		(.33)	
Nonfarm	−.73**	−.16	−.84**	−.18
	(.28)		(.27)	
Male	.82***	.18	.63**	.14
	(.23)		(.22)	
Test rank			−.02***	−.19
			(.004)	
Identification with parents			.16***	.18
			(.04)	
Economic constraint			.06**	.14
			(.02)	

[a] When comparing the effects of variables across models, use the unstandardized coefficients (b). When comparing the strengths of the effects within models, use the standardized coefficients (β).
* significant at .05 level; ** significant at .01 level; *** significant at .001 level

being in a transitional versus a farm family is not significant. In both families, the young share a common exposure to farm life. The effects of gender and context are basically unchanged in the expanded model, Model 2, when all independent variables are included in the analysis.

Test rank has a significant negative effect on rural orientation, implying that adolescents with more ability do not feel as strongly about staying in the community. This is additional evidence for the selective migration process. In addition, boys and girls who feel closer to their parents are more likely to plan on staying in the community. Felt economic constraints significantly increase the strength of a rural orientation. We interpret this to mean that adolescents from families under economic strain are less likely to perceive residential alternatives to their own community.

Overall, school achievement, as measured by Iowa test rank scores, has the strongest effect on rural orientation, with nonfarm residence and parental identification next in order.

These analyses have confirmed the importance of context in determining rural orientation. In addition, rural orientation is significantly related to gender, school achievement, identification with parents, and economic problems. However, if interaction effects exist, these results may be influenced by the disproportionate number of nonfarm adolescents in the total sample. We turn now to potential variations within each rural setting, to determine the extent to which context interacts with other factors to influence rural orientation.

Interactions with Rural Context

Is rural orientation determined by different factors within the three different rural contexts? Although the average levels of the family and economic variables do not vary by context, their association with rural orientation may differ across contexts. Within each of the rural contexts, we estimated the basic model and then tested for interaction effects (see Table 12.3).

Family and economic influences on rural orientation do differ significantly by context in a manner consistent with our expectations. As initially suggested, the positive effect of identification with parents is stronger for farm adolescents than for either transitional or nonfarm youth. In addition, we find that the effect of economic strain is negative for the farm group, but turns positive for the other two groups. However, contrary to our initial expectations, we find no evidence that gender and test rank interact with context to affect rural orientation.[7] Both the size and significance level of the coefficients for gender and test rank vary across

TABLE 12.3. Rural orientation in interaction with rural context.[a]

Antecedent factors	Farm (n = 85)		Transitional (n = 89)		Nonfarm (n = 223)	
	b (se)	β	b (se)	β	b (se)	β
Intercept	3.22		4.74**		5.12**	
	(2.27)		(1.56)		(1.18)	
Male[b]	.74	.14	.98*	.25	.46	.10
	(.54)		(.40)		(.28)	
Test Rank[b]	−.01	−.10	−.01	−.14	−.02***	−.25
	(.01)		(.01)		(.01)	
Identification with parents[c]	.36***	.33	.12	.15	.11*	.12
	(.11)		(.08)		(.06)	
Economic constraint[c]	−.04	−.07	.08*	.22	.08**	.19
	(.06)		(.04)		(.02)	

[a] When comparing the effects of variables across models, use the unstandardized coefficients (b). When comparing the strengths of the effects within models, use the standardized coefficients (β).
[b] The coefficients do not differ significantly by context.
[c] The coefficient for the farm group is significantly different from the coefficient for the transitional and nonfarm groups. The coefficients for the transitional and nonfarm groups are not significantly different from each other.
* significant at .05 level; ** significant at .01 level; *** significant at .001 level

---

[7] For identification with parents, t(farm vs. transitional) = 2.51, $p < .05$, t(farm vs. nonfarm) = 3.27, $p < .01$. For economic strain, t(farm vs. transitional) = 2.43, $p = .05$, t(farm vs. nonfarm) 3.20, $p < .01$. The respective test statistics for gender and test rank were not significant at the $p < .05$ level.

the three groups, but the differences are not statistically significant. The nonsignificant result for the gender-context interaction is particularly interesting, given the greater economic opportunities in the community for farm boys in comparison to farm girls. We had assumed that the gender effect would be strongest in the farm group, but girls have strong ties to their communities despite the lack of economic options. Marriage and family may be more important issues in their view of the future.

Looking at the standardized coefficients within each model, we find that the most important determinant of rural orientation among farm adolescents is identification with parents. The importance of kin relationships in the farm setting is supported by statements made by members of these farm families. For example, one parent claimed that "farming is an ideal way to raise a family." Farm children are more involved in their parents' work, as one family pointed out, ". . . they know that you put so much in the feed bill and you raise these hogs. . . . They have to help get them in, and if they have trouble delivering, they have to help or watch the vet. . . . They're just much more involved out here." A displaced farmer commented "I wish we could have raised our sons on the farm, and then handed down the farm," and another wrote "I do feel our family relationships would have been closer if we could have remained on the farm." When the relationships are good, the children are more predisposed to stay in farming. In addition, there will be parental pressure to do so, since "farming is usually a family tradition." Asked what he would like to accomplish in the next few years, one farming father answered "try to influence one of them to farm, maybe."[8]

In transitional families, gender and economic strain have the strongest effects on rural orientation ($\beta = .25$ and $\beta = .22$ respectively). School achievement and economic strain emerge as the strongest determinants of a preference for rural residence among nonfarm adolescents ($\beta = -.25$ and $\beta = .19$ respectively). The most able boys and girls from nonfarm households, and those who were not limited by family hardship, were least likely to favor a life in their community.

These results illustrate the different meaning of rural orientation by context. This preference among farm boys and girls represents a positive attribute and those who feel closer to their parents generally plan to stay in the community. In contrast, the sentiment may not be positive for the transitional and nonfarm boys and girls. Those who feel more strongly about staying in the community have less ability and come from economically strained families. This suggests a general belief that future options are limited.

---

[8] Quotations are taken from comments that parents made in response to questionnaire items, or from transcriptions of video tapes made as part of the data collection process.

Psychological Aspects of Rural Orientation

The different sources of rural orientation by ecological niche may be linked as well to differing psychological correlates. For example, does an efficacious outlook characterize the psychology of farm boys who prefer life in the country? We included measures of self-esteem, mastery, depression, anxiety, and behavior problems in the correlational analyses. In Table 12.4 we present Pearson correlation coefficients between rural orientation and the psychological variables.

Again, we find that the meaning of preferences for rural life varies by social context. However, the magnitude of the variation is modest. Among farm children, rural orientation is negatively associated with depression ($r = -.22$, $p = .05$), suggesting that it is a positive concept, associated with high morale. However, among nonfarm children, strong rural orientation is linked to low self-esteem ($r = -.15$, $p = .05$), and also with conduct disorder ($r = .23$, $p = .001$), suggesting that rural orientation, within this group, has negative connotations. The results for the transitional group show a negative relationship between a rural preference and feelings of mastery and control ($r = -.27$, $p = .01$), indicating that this group resembles the nonfarm children rather than the farm group. Post hoc tests that assess the difference between correlation coefficients in different ecological groups show the association between rural orientation and mastery to be significantly different for the farm and transitional farm children ($p < .05$). The association between rural orientation and behavior problems also differs significantly between the farm and nonfarm children ($p < .05$).

These relationships between rural orientation and various psychological variables are not strong. However, the finding that the correlates of rural orientation can vary by rural context is consistent with our previous results. The meaning of youth's rural orientation varies by their context.

TABLE 12.4. Contextual comparisons of some psychological correlates of rural orientation.

	Pearson product moment correlation coefficients		
Psychological measures	Farm ($n = 85$)	Transitional ($n = 89$)	Nonfarm ($n = 223$)
Self-esteem	.02	−.05	−.15*
Mastery[a]	.09	−.27**	−.12
Depression	−.22*	−.12	−.05
Anxiety	−.06	−.07	−.11
Conduct disorder[b]	−.06	.11	.23***

[a] Correlations differ significantly between farm and transitional farm ($p < .05$).
[b] Correlations differ significantly between farm and nonfarm children ($p < .05$).
* significant at .05 level; ** significant at .01 level; *** significant at .001 level

Conclusion

Adolescents do not come of age in society as a whole, but rather in a particular community, school, and family. Nationwide events and cultural influences find expression in these settings, as seen in the economic recession of the 1980s and during the Vietnam War. The behavioral effect of any setting or context depends on its particular features and on differences among its occupants. Rural society, for example, includes farm families and a nonfarm population with no involvement in farming, a contrast that is all too often ignored despite the greater prevalence of poverty among rural nonfarm households. The latter can readily become merely an all-encompassing rural sample which obliterates social and cultural variations that make a substantial difference.

This study of Midwestern adolescents distinguishes among farm, transitional, and rural nonfarm contexts, as defined by parental socioeconomic activity, and identifies a coherent pattern of differences by ecological type in preferences for a future in rural America. Our results suggest that such preferences are strongest among farm youth, as one might expect, and they decline, on average, across the transitional group to nonfarm youth. Farm culture is male-oriented and boys generally rank higher on rural orientation than girls, but we find this difference across all settings. Rural-oriented youth in all settings are not as likely as adolescents with low scores to aspire to a college education and to value money as an end in itself (one element of the traditional agrarian ideology). However, in terms of determinants and correlates, the meaning of rural orientation varies by context.

Notable differences also appear among rural-oriented adolescents in these contexts. Not all farm youth are committed to a future in the countryside, and the same applies even more strongly to adolescents in the other settings. Among four potential determinants of a rural preference (gender, achievement score rank, identification with parents, and economic pressures or constraints), identification with parents is the only significant determinant of a strong rural orientation among adolescents in farm families. Family ties clearly matter in their residential view of the future. Rural-oriented farm youth are also more likely to be male and to rank below average on achievement, but neither of these effects is statistically significant. In the transitional group we find the strongest gender effect, with boys tending to look toward a future in the country and girls showing little interest in such a prospect. These differences parallel variations in their parents' aspirations. Despite their lack of success, fathers in the transitional group still aspire to working their own land, whereas mothers generally envision a future off the land and usually in urban centers (Conger & Elder, in press). In the nonfarm context, a future in rural America tends to appeal most strongly to the least able, followed by those under economic pressure and adolescents with attachments to parents. The common theme in this group is limited options.

These contextual variations are coupled with different psychologies. In the farm setting, psychological health co-varies with a preference for life in a rural area. Boys and girls who rank high on this preference were least likely to describe themselves as depressed and lacking a sense of mastery or self-worth. By comparison, the rural orientation of nonfarm youth is modestly coupled with a more pathogenic state. Correlates include conduct disorder, low self-esteem and mastery, personal qualities that offer no assurance of a successful transition to adulthood.

This study suggests that rural orientation is not a goal or aspiration that can be automatically assigned positive weight. Most studies simply use aspirations in an additive way, so that the higher the adolescent's goals, the better. However the social contexts of youth clearly play an important role in shaping their goals and in determining their meaning. In terms of the broader issue of the future of rural America, it is important to bear these distinctions in mind, since the out-migration of youth jeopardizes the viability of the remaining community. Our research suggests that the decision of youth to leave the rural life-style behind and the belief of some that better lives exist elsewhere is not the same for all adolescents in rural settings; it depends in part on their own internalization of the rural ideology and this is most likely to be deeply ingrained in children who were brought up on farms. Contextual issues are important in the developmental trajectories of adolescents.

Acknowledgments. This chapter is based on collaborative research involving the Iowa Youth and Families Project at Iowa State University and the Social Change Project at University of North Carolina at Chapel Hill. The combined research effort is currently supported by the National Institute of Mental Health (MH43270), the National Institute on Drug Abuse (DA05347), the John D. and Catherine T. MacArthur Foundation Program for Successful Adolescent Development Among Youth in High-Risk Settings, and the Bureau of Maternal and Child Health (MCJ-109572). In addition, we acknowledge the receipt of a Research Scientist Award (MH00567) to Elder, a Fulbright Scholarship Grant to Hagell, and a postdoctoral fellowship in demography and aging (National Institute on Aging) to Rudkin. Requests for reprints should be addressed to Rand Conger, Department of Sociology, 107 East Hall, Iowa State University, Ames, IA, 50011.

References

Barlett, P.F. (1993). *American dreams, rural realities: Family farms in crisis.* Chapel Hill: University of North Carolina Press.

Bealer, R.C. & Willits, F.K. (1988, August). *The rural mystique in American culture: Some musings.* Paper presented at the Annual Meeting of the Rural Sociological Society, Athens, GA.

Bunce, M. (1981). Rural sentiment and the ambiguity of the urban fringe. In K.B. Beesley & L.H. Russwurm (Eds.), *The rural-urban fringe: Canadian perspectives*. Ontario: Downsworth.

Burchinal, L.C. (Ed.). (1965). *Rural youth in crisis: Facts, myths, and social change*. Washington, DC: Office of Juvenile Delinquency, U.S. Department of Health, Education, and Welfare Administration.

Buttel, F.H., Larson, O.F., & Gillespie, G.W., Jr. (1990). *The sociology of agriculture*. Contributions in Sociology, no. 88. New York: Greenwood Press.

Chiu, L.-H. (1990). The relationship of career goal and self-esteem among adolescents. *Adolescence, 25*, 593–597.

Conger, R.D. & Elder, G.H., Jr. (in press). Families in a changing society. In R.D. Conger & G.H. Elder, Jr. (Eds.), *Families of the farm crisis*. New York: Aldine de Gruyter.

Conger, R.D., Conger, K.J., Elder, G.H., Jr., Lorenz, F.O., Simons, R.L., & Whitbeck, L.B. (1992). A family process model of economic hardship and adjustment of early adolescent boys. *Child Development, 63*, 526–541.

Derogatis, L.R. (1983). *SCL-90-R: Administration, Scoring and Procedures Manual-II* (2nd ed.). Towson, MD: Clinical Psychometric Research.

Dunne, F., Elliott, R., & Carlsen, W.S. (1981). Sex differences in the educational and occupational aspirations of rural youth. *Journal of Vocational Behavior, 18*, 56–66.

Elder, G.H., Jr. (1963). Achievement orientations and career patterns of rural youth. *Sociology of Education, 37*, 30–58.

Falk, W.W. & Salter, N.H. (1978). The stability of status orientations among young, white, rural women from three southern states. *Journal of Vocational Behavior, 12*, 20–32.

Friedberger, M. (1988). *Farm families and change in twentieth-century America*. Lexington: The University Press of Kentucky.

Friedberger, M. (1990). *Shakeout: Iowa farm families in the 1980s*. Lexington: The University Press of Kentucky.

Fuguitt, G.V., Brown, D.L., & Beale, C.L. (1989). *Rural and small town America*. New York: Russell Sage Foundation.

Howell, F.M., Ohlendorf, G.W., & McBroom, L.W. (1981). The "ambition-achievement" complex: Values as organizing determinants. *Rural Sociology, 46*, 465–482.

Iowa Test of Basic Skills, Teachers Guide: Multilevel Battery, ITBS. (1986). Chicago: Riverside Publishing.

Jackson, R.M. & Meara, N.M. (1974). Father identification, achievement, and occupational behavior of rural youth: One year follow-up. *Journal of Vocational Behavior, 4*, 349–356.

Jackson, R.M. & Meara, N.M. (1977). Father identification, achievement, and occupational behavior of rural youth: 5-year follow-up. *Journal of Vocational Behavior, 10*, 82–91.

Jackson, R.M., Meara, N.M., & Arora, M. (1974). Father identification, achievement and occupational behavior of rural youth. *Journal of Vocational Behavior, 4*, 85–96.

Kammer, P.P. (1985). Career and life-style expectations of rural eighth-grade students. *The School Counselor, 32*, 18–25.

Kohn, H. (1988). *The last farmer: An American memoir*. New York: Summit Books.

264   G.H. Elder, Jr., A. Hagell, L. Rudkin, and R.D. Conger

Looker, E.D. (1991). *Interconnected transitions and their costs: Gender and urban-rural differences in the transition to work*. Paper presented to the Transition to Work Conference, Toronto.
Mortimer, J.T., Lorence, J.P., & Kumka, D.S. (1986). *Work, family and personality: Transition to adulthood*. Norwood, NJ: Ablex Publishing.
Murray, J.D., Keller, P.A., McMorran, B.J., & Edwards, B.L. (1983). Future expectations of rural American youth: Implications for mental health. *International Journal of Mental Health*, *12*, 76–88.
Nurius, P. (1991). Possible selves and social support: Social cognitive resources for coping and striving. In J.A. Howard & P.L. Callero (Eds.), *The self-society dynamic: Cognition, emotion and action* (pp. 239–258). Cambridge, England: Cambridge University Press.
Nurmi, J.E. (1989). *Adolescents' orientation to the future: Development of interests and plans, and related attributions and affects, in the life-span context*. Helsinki: Finnish Society of Sciences and Letters.
Pearlin, L.I., Lieberman, M.A., Menaghan, E.G., & Mullan, J.T. (1981). The stress process. *Journal of Health and Social Behavior*, *22*, 337–356.
Poole, M.E. (1983). *Youth, expectations and transitions*. Melbourne: Routledge & Kegan Paul.
Quay, H.C. & Peterson, D.R. (1983). *Interim manual for the revised Behavior Problem Checklist*. Coral Gables, FL: University of Miami Press.
Robins, L.N. (1978). Sturdy childhood predictors of adult antisocial behavior: Replications from longitudinal studies. *Psychological Medicine*, *8*, 611–622
Rosenberg, M. (1965). *Society and the adolescent self-image*. Princeton, NJ: Princeton University Press.
Rutter, M. (1989). Pathways from childhood to adult life. *Journal of Child Psychology and Psychiatry*, *30*, 23–51.
Salamon, S. (1987). Ethnic determinants of farm community character. In M. Chibnic (Ed.), *Farm work and fieldwork: American agriculture in anthropological perspective* (pp. 167–188). Ithaca, NY: Cornell University Press.
Sarigiani, P.A., Wilson, J.L., Petersen, A.C., & Vicary, J.R. (1990). Self-image and educational plans of adolescents from two contrasting communities. *Journal of Early Adolescence*, *10*, 37–55.
Schwarzweller, H.K. (1978). Career desiderata of rural youth and the structuring of ambition: A comparative perspective. *International Journal of Comparative Sociology*, *19*, 185–202.
Schwarzweller, H.K. & Lyson, T.A. (1974). Social class, parental interest and the educational plans of American and Norwegian rural youth. *Sociology of Education*, *47*, 443–465.
Sewell, W.H. & Hauser, R.M. (1976). Causes and consequences of higher education: Models of the status attainment process. In W.H. Sewell, R.M. Hauser, & D.L. Featherman (Eds.), *Schooling and achievement in American society* (pp. 9–27). New York: Academic Press.
Spenner, K.I. & Featherman, D.L. (1978). Achievement ambitions. *The Annual Review of Sociology*, *4*, 373–420.
Stevens, C.J., Puchtell, L.A., Ryu, S., & Mortimer, J.T. (1990). *Gender, work and adolescent orientations to the future*. Paper presented at the annual meeting of the American Sociological Association, Washington, DC.
Willits, F.K., Bealer, R.C., & Timbers, V.L. (1990). Popular images of "rurality": Data from a Pennslyvania survey. *Rural Sociology*, *55*, 559–578.

Part V

The Interplay between School and Work

13
Employment Prospects as Motivation for School Achievement: Links and Gaps between School and Work in Seven Countries

Stephen F. Hamilton

Young people are motivated to work hard in secondary school by their expectations regarding the "payoff" for school achievement in the labor market. Those expectations, in turn, are shaped by institutional links between education and employment. This two-step hypothesis frames a comparison among school/work connections in seven countries: the United States, Japan, Germany, Austria, Switzerland, Denmark, and Sweden.

Cross-national comparisons are poorly suited to testing hypotheses such as this because differences among nations yield too many plausible explanations. The conclusion to this chapter will discuss one approach to testing the hypothesis more formally. However, the primary function of the hypothesis is as a framework organizing a comparative analysis.

The education-employment nexus constitutes a mesosystem in Bronfenbrenner's (1979) terms; that is, a system of systems. Meso-systems operate within the macrosystem of each country's economic, political, and social structures. Cross-national comparisons are ideally suited to identifying critical features of mesosystems and macrosystems because they highlight features that are frequently taken for granted within any single country.

School Performance and Employment Prospects

Employment prospects are not the only motivators for school perform-ance. Classroom reward structures, parental sanctions, peer assessment, and other "microsystem" factors all have a more immediate impact on the desire to do well in school. However, as they approach adulthood, adolescents' capacity to think about the future makes them increasingly susceptible to less immediate influences. The most important of these, I propose, is the perceived relationship between present behavior and the achievement of long-term future goals. Adolescents who believe their current efforts will bring them closer to a desirable future are far more likely to work hard in school and avoid self-destructive behavior than those who are either unable to think about the future or who believe their prospects are beyond their control. This hypothesis has been explored by others in broader terms as self-efficacy, which is usually treated as an intraindividual variable (Bandura, 1986). It is examined here as an aspect of the environment (an approach taken by Hamilton, 1987, 1990; Ogbu, 1974, 1978; Stinchcombe, 1964; and others).

This exercise has implications for all the countries examined, and others too, particularly Eastern European countries attempting to bring their educational systems in line with more democratic states and capitalistic economies. However, it is motivated by a chauvinistic concern for the poor school performance and high incidence of problem behavior among young people in the United States (Bishop, 1989). In previous decades, invidious comparisons between the average achievement levels of secondary school students in the United States and other countries could be dismissed as unfair because the United States educated the majority of youth to the secondary level while other countries retained only small elites in their secondary schools. This explanation has evaporated as other countries have followed the United States' lead and developed more inclusive systems.

Transparency and Permeability

Two characteristics of the nexus between labor market and educational system deserve special attention; I shall label them transparency and permeability. *Transparency* refers for present purposes to *how well youth can see through the educational system and labor market and plot a course from where they are in the present to a distant future goal*. In a transparent system, young people are knowledgeable about education and training requirements of various occupations and how to meet them. They can readily explain how a person enters a particular career. *Permeability* refers to the *ease of movement from one point in the education–labor market system to another*. In a permeable system it is relatively easy to move from one part of the educational system or labor market to another, and to change career directions.

Formal credentials or qualifications are central to both transparency and permeability. However, they have an inverse relation to each other. While the existence of specific educational qualifications for employment makes connections between education and the labor market more transparent, those same qualifications constitute barriers to easy movement within the labor market, rendering the system impermeable.

In the United States, high school students' motivation to perform well in school and otherwise behave in prosocial ways is hampered by an opaque education-career nexus. Connections between school and work are opaque in part because few jobs in the middle and lower levels of the occupational hierarchy require formal credentials. In the highly permeable American labor market, workers move rather easily among employers, and from one type of work to another. Once they are engaged in full-time employment, permeability is a great advantage to American workers. It allows upward mobility, voluntary career changes, and adaptation to economic change. Auto mechanics become chefs. Laid off factory workers become truck drivers. Hairdressers become receptionists.

Young people in the German-speaking countries face precisely the opposite conditions. Extensive credentialing marks out a clear path from education into employment. Apprenticeship, which is the primary means of obtaining jobs in the middle levels of the occupational hierarchy, concludes with a national examination having both a written and a practical component. Only by completing the schooling and on-the-job training prescribed for a specific occupation and then passing the examination can one enter any of the 370 training occupations. (Some 20,000 additional occupations also treat this training and examination as qualifications, sometimes adding further training.) This system of very strong and highly visible connections between education and employment provides a clear answer to a young person's question, "How can I become an electronics technician, dental assistant, airplane mechanic, or office worker?" The answer is, "Do as well as possible in school, then find the employer who offers the best apprenticeship in your chosen field and apply. If you work hard in your apprenticeship and part-time schooling and get a good grade on your qualifying examination, your training firm will probably hire you, and if they don't you will have good chances in other firms."

The trade-off is impermeability. A 3rd-year apprentice auto mechanic in Munich explained to me that he had decided to switch to auto body repair because it was a more creative occupation. He added that this would entail a second 3-year apprenticeship, including 3 additional years of part-time schooling. German adults who wish to change occupations, or whose occupations have been made redundant by new technology or economic change are best advised to seek training in fields that do not have apprenticeship programs. If they are unable to retrain, they face serious downward mobility because the social and economic gap between skilled and unskilled jobs is vast.

Ideally, young people would be able to envision a path for themselves from studenthood to satisfying employment and then, while following that path, find opportunities for changing their minds, adapting to changed conditions, and surpassing their original goals. However, because formal educational credentials simultaneously mark the path and place hurdles across it, transparency is purchased at the price of impermeability.

In the following analysis, I shall compare the transparency and permeability of seven countries' education-employment connections. These broad characterizations should not obscure clear and important variations within countries, and across occupational fields. In all countries, my concern is with the middle levels of the occupational hierarchies: skilled jobs but not professions; requiring post-compulsory education, but less than a university degree. This caveat is very important because connections between employment and education for university graduates entering the professions are more alike than different among these countries. All are characterized by high transparency and low permeability. For example, the educational credentials required of a physician are clearly prescribed, making the path from school to career quite transparent, but those credentials are sufficiently daunting that they prevent easy movement into the profession and discourage movement out of it.

Democracy and the Transformation of Workplaces

All of the countries included in the following comparison are dealing with two trends or pressures. One is toward greater democratization of society. In the European countries, barriers that maintain social class distinctions have been steadily lowered. More recently, nonnative workers and their progeny have been incorporated in varying degrees and with varying acceptance into formerly homogeneous countries. In the United States, where social class divisions have long been more permeable, the greatest democratization is occurring in the realms of increasing gender and racial equality and reducing barriers encountered by people with disabilities. Since the end of World War II, Japan has rapidly moved toward meritocracy, but maintains quite rigid gender roles and a sizable underclass.

Every industrialized country is currently struggling with the impacts of computer technology and of growing international competition. The Japanese are leading the way in transforming workplace organization to increase efficiency and productivity. American and European firms are making rapid strides as well. In general, routine mass production is either being automated or relegated to Third World countries with lower wages, and being replaced by "flexible specialization" (Piore & Sabel, 1984) in "self-managed work teams." The proportion of the work force dealing with things is decreasing while the proportion dealing with people and data is increasing.

Democratization and workplace transformations demand changes in educational systems and in the transition from school to career. Rigid educational systems have both mirrored and maintained rigid social structures in the German-speaking countries, making upward mobility and occupational change much more difficult than in the United States. Not only the sociopolitical press toward equality but also the realities of contemporary workplaces require greater permeability. The United States, in contrast, must increase the transparency of connections between school and work, even at the cost of reduced permeability. Allowing young people to flounder in unskilled jobs or remain unemployed is both a waste of society's human resources and an added affliction to the poor and to those who suffer from racial discrimination. The Scandinavian countries, with their dynamic economies and strong democracies, come closest to the ideal balance.

The American Model: School-based Learning

Relative to other countries, the United States has a highly permeable but opaque school/work nexus in the middle levels of its occupational hierarchy. Formal qualifications for such occupations are rare and not terribly hard to acquire. Entry into a particular occupational field often requires no special training or licensing. Movement from one field to another is frequent and easy. Permeability both reflects and allows a distinctively American work force in which management, especially "scientific management," predominates over skill. Workers are treated as interchangeable parts. They are quickly laid off in poor economic times and just as quickly replaced when times improve.

High permeability matches the individualistic ideology prevailing in the United States. Each person is considered responsible for his or her own destiny. Demanding specific training and certification for most jobs is considered an infringement on the individual's freedom to choose an occupation and the employer's right to select freely among applicants. Industrial unions frequently succeed in establishing seniority as the preeminent qualification for desirable jobs.

High permeability, in addition to matching American economic conditions and social ideology, contributes to a relatively open society. The cost is low transparency. Because requirements for occupations and jobs are not spelled out clearly and movement appears to be highly random, a young person trying to look into the future has difficulty planning. No one can tell her or him precisely what to do in order to prepare for a certain kind of employment.

There are exceptions, to be sure. Anyone anticipating a clerical career knows that keyboard skills are essential. Occupations affecting health and safety require licensing examinations, not only for health care providers but for barbers and hairdressers and for electricians and plumbers. However, a wide range of skilled blue-collar occupations such as carpenter and auto mechanic do not require specific qualifications. The growing set of occupations with "technician" in their titles may demand advanced knowledge and skill but most allow aspirants to achieve them in a variety of ways, including military training, community or technical colleges, proprietary (profit-making) trade schools, or informal on-the-job training.

Japan has evolved an education–labor market system that exaggerates the American pattern. Its greater success in motivating young people reveals another means, in addition to formal credentials, of increasing transparency; namely, employers' use of school credentials when making hiring decisions, and the creation of strong connections between individual schools and employers.

As in the United States, the Japanese secondary education system is driven by preparation for higher education, but in even more extreme form. Elementary and junior high school are compulsory in Japan. Most young people attend their neighborhood schools. Because high school enrollment is not compulsory, high schools have the right to select among applicants; they are not required to admit those who live in their localities.

Selection is accomplished by means of examinations. Each high school administers its own examinations and admits the highest scoring candidates. Competition is fierce for admission to high schools with the best records of preparing their students for university entrance. At the end of high school, the same process is repeated, with universities admitting the highest scorers on their examinations and students competing for admission to the best universities. The best universities are those that are most successful at placing graduates in good jobs with the government or with prestigious firms (Rohlen, 1983).

Japanese youth who are not involved in the competition for university admission are, unlike their American counterparts, motivated to work hard in school to improve their career prospects. They enroll in less prestigious high schools, notably vocational high schools. Although such schools lack the academic rigor of more competitive schools, many vocational and academic high schools maintain long-term relationships with specific firms in which the schools recommend their best graduates and the firms hire them. The relationship is reciprocal. If the schools begin sending second-rate graduates, the firm will stop offering jobs. If the firm refuses to guarantee employment for the school's best graduates, the school will send its prize pupils elsewhere (Rosenbaum, Kariya, Settersten, & Maier, 1990). This practice enables young people to see how they can move from school into desirable careers.

However, greater transparency, as compared to equivalent careers in the United States, is purchased by sacrificing permeability. Large firms offer lifetime employment. Status and pay are determined more by seniority than by performance. Any employee who remains with the firm and demonstrates proper loyalty and commitment, including long hours and short vacations, can count on a steady rise up the corporate escalator until age 50 or so, after which retirement is likely to be required.

This system of (abbreviated) lifelong employment, however, does not exist in all firms. Small firms cannot always make such guarantees.

Moreover, women are commonly employed even in large firms as "temporary" workers with no security or benefits regardless of how long they are actually employed.

The great strength of the Japanese system is that it motivates a remarkably high level of school achievement across a wide spectrum of the population. Japanese schools effectively impart general academic knowledge that provides a foundation for specific vocational training given by employers. From the perspective of motivation, the most striking accomplishment of the Japanese system is that the competition for desirable employment motivates school achievement even among those who have clearly lost the competition.

The German Model: Learning at Work

With respect to occupations that do not require a university degree, the German-speaking countries present the starkest contrast with the United States and Japan in terms of transparency and permeability. Germany, Austria, and Switzerland have strong apprenticeship systems that were transformed around the turn of the century to meet the demands of an industrial economy. Compulsory part-time schooling was added to on-the-job training to create what is known as the "dual system" in all three countries. Examinations were created to certify apprentices' accomplishments and qualify them for entrance into their training occupation. New occupations were added to the traditional list of crafts, including industrial, technical, and administrative occupations (e.g., machine repairer, dental lab technician, office worker). After World War II, compulsory full-time schooling was extended from grade 8 to grade 9 (in some German states, to grade 10).

Apprenticeship places the German-speaking countries at the opposite end of the continuum from the United States with regard to both transparency and permeability. However, precisely the specificity of occupational training makes career entry and movement within the labor market more difficult. One cannot, as in the United States, become a carpenter simply by getting a job as a carpenter, or an auto mechanic by learning to fix one's own car. Both occupations require specific training programs, exams, and certification.

Of the three German-speaking countries (East Germany had a similar dual system of apprenticeship combined with part-time vocational schooling), Austria has the most traditional system, traditional in the sense that it remains sharply separated from higher education. As a consequence, choosing apprenticeship tends to limit young people to a particular segment of the labor market. This problem of permeability, which is recognized as a serious current issue in Austria,[1] has been worsened by increasing enrollments in extended full-time schooling. Enrollment in the college preparatory *Gymnasium* and in post-compulsory full-time vocational schools (*berufsbildende höhere Schulen*) has increased and a larger proportion of the youth population has enrolled in full-time vocational schools, leaving a smaller proportion in apprenticeship.

Although full-time vocational schools provide an alternative path into skilled occupations and qualify graduates for further education, increasing school enrollment has two drawbacks in Austria. One is a surplus (in labor market terms) of university-educated people who cannot find jobs appropriate to their educational attainment. The second, more germane to the present analysis, is that employers prefer school-trained office and technical workers for middle-level positions in the same fields for which many apprentices are trained, reducing apprentices' prospects for upward mobility. Employers' preference for school graduates over apprentices holds apprentices in lower-level positions and blocks their rise through the occupational hierarchy.

Switzerland and Germany have recognized the desirability of advanced schooling for a larger proportion of their populations, and they have incorporated extended schooling with apprenticeship more rapidly than Austria. Interestingly, they have done so in two distinct ways.

In both countries, occupations that require higher levels of theoretical or abstract knowledge and skill (primarily administrative and technical occupations) require 1½ days of school per week, while less academically challenging occupations require only 1 day. Switzerland is moving toward making 1½ days per week standard for all occupations. Moreover, by law every apprentice who qualifies and chooses to do so may add an extra half day per week of vocational middle school (*Berufsmittelschule*), maintaining the same earnings despite spending 2 days per week off the job. Completion of this form of schooling confers the qualification required to pursue postsecondary education and training. This option establishes a direct tie between apprenticeship and higher education that is lacking in Austria.

The German answer to this same need is, surprisingly, less planful and more individualistic. It is "double qualification" (Kaiser, Nuthmann, & Stegmann, 1985). Double qualification means that a young person completes an apprenticeship *and* the comparable course of study in a full-time post-compulsory vocational school. While growing enrollment in full-time secondary education in Austria has reduced enrollment in apprenticeship, in Germany growing school enrollment has been accompanied by increased enrollment in apprenticeship because the two have increasingly

---

[1] It was Austrian concern for permeability (*Durchlässigkeit*) that first suggested to me the polarity between permeability and transparency.

been combined rather than treated as mutually exclusive. As in Switzerland, the post-compulsory school credential opens an apprentice's path to further education. But German employers do not normally prefer applicants with school qualifications over those who qualified by means of apprenticeship.

One of the most dramatic developments in recent years in Germany has been the growing proportion of young people who graduate from the *Gymnasium*, earning the *Abitur*, which qualifies them for university study, and then enroll in an apprenticeship instead. (In 1988 and 1989, about 16% of new apprentices in West Germany had earned the *Hochschulreife*. See Bundesminister für Bildung und Wissenschaft, 1990, p. 116.) These youth take the most prestigious apprenticeships, particularly in banking and insurance. Some then enroll in the university after completing their vocational training. Even without higher education, this combination of academic and vocational qualifications is highly valued by German employers. One consequence of the trend to combine apprenticeship with post-compulsory schooling is that the average age of apprentices has been rising too.

Augmenting apprenticeship with extra schooling, whether simultaneously or sequentially, makes the education-employment nexus more permeable for those who complete both forms of education and training; they have access both to further education and to higher-level occupations. However, it can simultaneously make the system less permeable for those without the added qualifications, as in Austria.

Reducing the number of different training occupations is another approach to improving permeability. Germany has taken a dramatic step in this direction, by combining related metalworking occupations into one training program. This increases the progam's flexibility because apprentices need not have made so specific an occupational choice and have a larger number of options upon completion. It also meets employers' growing need for skilled workers who are broadly trained and flexible.

Germany has an excessive number of separate occupations in part because the structure of apprenticeship reflects employers' organizations. In Germany, all occupations in large firms are controlled by the chamber of industry and commerce (*Industrie- und Handelskammer*). Essentially identical occupations practiced in small firms are controlled by the appropriate craft chamber. Thus, an apprentice auto mechanic in a large firm has a different title, curriculum, and qualifying examination than one in a small firm. Furthermore, in Germany, the large category of middle-level administrative workers (*Kaufleute*) is subdivided by sector; for example, industry, retail trade, wholesale trade, banking, insurance, advertising, real estate, etc.

Switzerland has one training program and one qualifying examination for Kaufleute in all types of firms. Lacking the number of giant firms found in Germany, Switzerland does not distinguish so sharply among related occupations.

Enhanced school qualifications and double qualification open access to postsecondary education and to the higher-level occupations that require such credentials, making the dual system more permeable. Combining related occupations into one comprehensive training program also increases horizontal permeability. However, neither of these adaptations appears to impair transparency, suggesting that a better balance between the two can be attained. Reducing the number of distinct paths from education to career seems to be an ideal adaptation from the perspective of optimizing both permeability and transparency.

Balancing Apprenticeship and Schooling: Scandinavia

Denmark, like the other Scandinavian countries, patterned its education and training system after Germany's in the 19th century, but over the past three decades has tried to increase that system's permeability, both horizontally, among occupations at the same status, and vertically, across social classes. Vocational schooling has been a major part of that effort, notably for the purpose of retraining adults.

Two recent adaptations of apprenticeship are of particular interest. One is a consolidation of what had become two parallel vocational training systems, one school-based, the other relying on apprenticeship. In contrast to the Austrian experience with such an arrangement, the Danes have concluded that the school-based system is inadequate. Therefore, they are phasing it out in favor of apprenticeship. What remains is an option for young people who may begin their vocational education either with full-time schooling or full-time work. However, after the first half-year, the two paths converge and participants in both must alternate schooling with work experience. This means that all young people in the vocational education system must obtain an apprenticeship contract by the middle of grade 11.

The second adaptation is a thorough consolidation and rationalization of training occupations. From an array of some 350 training occupations, nearly as large as Germany's, Denmark has reduced the number of training occupations to 85. This simplifies the system in several ways. Fewer occupations means a smaller number of regulations and curriculum guides. Young people can choose broader occupational areas without, for example, making fine distinctions among different types of work with metal. Specialization is postponed until the last year or two of training. The structure of occupations resembles a tree, with a thick trunk of related occupations at the base and narrower specialties branching off above. Ironically there are some occupations in which the number of specialties has actually increased because this provision for late specialization makes it possible to offer training that is narrower at the end than would be feasible if the program had to stand alone.

Because all apprentices in each of the 85 occupations receive identical training for their first 2 years, they share a common base of knowledge and skill and can change their minds about a specialty without having to begin their training again from the beginning. Similarly, if changes in the labor market require retraining, it can begin from that common base, making workers more flexible over time.

Sweden adapted to democratization and workplace transformation very differently from either Denmark or the German-speaking countries. Apprenticeship has been a common experience for noncollege youth in Sweden for decades, but it was never so thoroughly integrated with schooling as in the German dual system.

As of 1970, the Swedes abandoned the sharp distinction they had made between academic and vocational schooling and made all secondary schools comprehensive, more in line with American practice. At that time they determined that education should be the responsibility of the state, not of private businesses, and they relocated the majority of vocational training from the workplace to schools.

In principle, all secondary schools are now equal and all graduates are qualified to pursue higher education. Naturally, the formerly selective college preparatory schools (which had the same name used in Germany, *Gymnasium*) maintained some of their prestige, and former vocational schools are generally seen as less desirable. Furthermore, although it is possible for a secondary school graduate enrolled in a vocational course to enroll in higher education, they have access only to a limited number of less desirable programs. Enrollment in liberal arts or preprofessional courses is not possible for a vocational graduate without extensive added coursework.

This system is currently undergoing a new round of adaptation that, ironically, takes it back a bit in the German direction. Vocational "lines" in secondary school that formerly lasted only 2 years are being extended for a 3rd year, which is the duration of what were previously more advanced vocational lines and only 1 year short of the 4-year college preparatory line. The extra time is used both to augment academic knowledge and to add a substantial work experience component. In general, Swedish vocational high school students can expect in the future to spend half of their 3rd year acquiring on-the-job training. This approach has been tested in about 10% of schools and judged successful. Therefore, it will be extended to the remaining schools over the next few years.

Swedish vocational students are ordinarily not apprentices. They are not paid for their work. The state-run schools and not the firms are responsible for their education and training. There are exceptions, however: A few large firms maintained the apprentice schools they had before the 1970 reform. These schools are operated by private firms for the benefit of their apprentices. They teach all of the courses required by the state but add firm-specific training and experience that can be closely integrated with academic and vocational instruction.

For many Swedish youth, formal apprenticeship in the sense of being an employee as well as a student begins after secondary school graduation. In many occupations—construction is a good example—vocational training begins in secondary school, incorporates a modicum of work experience, and then continues for 2 years after graduation with a full-time apprenticeship. In these occupations, apprenticeship is continuous with vocational schooling, but there are far fewer institutional links between school and apprenticeship than in the German dual system.

The Swedish system was designed quite explicitly to enhance permeability as a matter of democratic principle. The use of modules to organize the vocational curriculum makes the Swedish vocational certification system much more flexible than the German. A module is a self-contained unit in which acceptable levels of knowledge and skill are specified. Vocational competencies may be achieved either in school or at work or both. The record of modules that a young person has completed informs an employer precisely what she or he knows and is able to do. Some graduates complete more modules than others. If an employer requires additional modules, the young person can complete them after being hired and add them to his or her credential file. The modular curriculum is ideal for adult education and retraining; indeed, the use of modules was borrowed from adult education in Denmark.

The Swedes also promote permeability with their youth centers, institutions that fulfill a distinctive obligation. Swedish schools are given responsibility for all youth until they reach age 18. Discussions are underway about raising the age to 20. That responsibility persists even when young people choose to leave school at age 16. Youth center staff are charged with maintaining contact with out-of-school youth to ensure that they have opportunities either to reenroll in school or to find employment. They do this by engaging in "door-knocking activities." That is, they are not passive, waiting for young people to get in touch; rather, they actively seek out youth, in person and by telephone, to learn what they are doing and to offer assistance and opportunities. Their capacity to do this is enhanced by the availability of fully subsidized work placements lasting up to 6 months. In addition, youth center staff members constitute a rich professional resource. They include teachers, career counselors, nurses, and psychotherapists. Career counselors are specially trained with equal amounts of psychology, sociology, and labor market economics.

There is some loss of transparency as a result of high permeability. Lower reliance on formal credentials (and less precise credentials) than in the German-speaking countries makes entry into and movement within the labor market easier. However, Swedish youth do not have crystal-clear guidelines to lead them into a specific occupation. This has not been a serious problem in the recent past because Sweden's prosperity and government policies have virtually assured the availability of well-paid employment. However, Sweden is feeling the effects of a slowing economy and growing international competition. The electoral loss of the Social Democrats reflected a perceived need to reduce social welfare benefits, the government payroll, and taxes.

In comparison with other countries, however, benefits are still generous and, combined with a welcoming labor market, they will probably continue to give Swedish youth a relatively leisurely transition from school to career. Following high school graduation, young Swedes often try out more than one occupational field and take time off for international travel. Giving older youth a chance to look around after they complete compulsory schooling is another way of increasing transparency.

Transparency versus Permeability

Future career prospects motivate adolescents to perform well in school when adolescents can see clearly what those prospects are and how to achieve them (i.e., the education-employment nexus is transparent) and when it is possible to move readily through that system, (i.e, it is permeable). Unfortunately, these two characteristics tend to be contradictory because specific educational qualifications for employment, which increase transparency by communicating precisely what is required to enter an occupational field, simultaneously decrease permeability by establishing barriers to career entry and career change.

The United States stands at one extreme among the seven nations discussed. Lacking specific qualifications for most occupations below the professional level, it has a highly permeable system. Occupational mobility is high. The cost is that adolescents who do not intend to enroll in 4-year colleges have grave difficulty seeing the value of schooling. This is exacerbated by a peculiar impermeability in the system; namely, that employers tend to use age as a proxy for worker virtues and refuse to hire teenagers for career entry positions.

Austria stands at the opposite extreme. A traditional apprenticeship system makes career paths very clear. However, the need for very specific occupational qualifications reduces occupational mobility, especially horizontally. And a traditional school system that is sharply divided from apprenticeship limits apprentices' option to continue their full-time schooling and to rise through the corporate ranks.

Japan has added transparency to an American-style school-based system by means of almost contractual arrangements between schools and specific firms, which motivate students to perform well even if they are not engaged in competition for university admission in order to gain employment recommendations from their school. Though this privilege

is available to only a minority of students, school achievement is remarkably high among Japanese adolescents.

Sweden consciously increased the permeability of its system by enrolling
nearly all adolescents in comprehensive high schools, thus enhancing their
opportunity for further education. A current move to extend vocational
studies another year and to add substantial work experience to classroom
instruction represents a step in the direction of the work-based approach
found in the German-speaking countries.

Denmark's recently reformed apprenticeship system maintains transparent connections between education and employment but increases
permeability by combining similar occupations and delaying specialization.

Germany and Switzerland are both engaged in serious efforts to increase the permeability of their systems. Germany is doing so formally by
reducing the number of separate training occupations and informally by
the popular practice of double qualification. Switzerland has more 4-year
apprenticeships and is also consolidating related occupations, though the
initial number is not so high as in Germany and the basic white-collar
administrative occupation has traditionally been unified across economic
sectors. The most promising Swiss reform is the addition of more school
time to apprenticeship, simultaneously deepening technical understanding, broadening general education, and qualifying apprentices for further
education.

Implications for the United States

I have previously argued that the United States should develop a form of
apprenticeship to enhance young people's motivation to work hard in
school by strengthening the connection between school performance and
employment (Hamilton, 1990). Adding Sweden and Japan to the comparative analysis refines this recommendation because these countries
do not have German-style dual systems, but they are much more successful than the United States at supporting the transition from school
to career. Clearly it is not apprenticeship, per se, that accounts for the
difference. Rather, I believe, it is the strength of the connection between
school performance and career entry.

This interpretation is substantiated by the fact that the part of the
American youth population that works hardest in school is also the
part that can see that connection most clearly: those who hope to gain
admission to selective colleges and universities, which, in turn, will give
them access to selective graduate and professional schools and then to
desirable careers.

The question that remains is how best to increase the transparency
of the education–labor market nexus for American youth who do not
plan to enroll in 4-year colleges, without at the same time reducing its
permeability to levels incompatible with American values, traditions, and

practices. The dimension that best differentiates among the countries examined is the extent to which work experience constitutes a major element of upper secondary education. Work experience is central to education in the German-speaking countries and Denmark and completely separate from education in Japan. Sweden drastically reduced but now is increasing the work experience component of secondary vocational education.

In the United States, work experience plays an ambiguous role in secondary education. Some vocational education programs utilize "cooperative education" (General Accounting Office, 1991), meaning that students receive credit for time spent in employment related to their vocational studies. However, there are no uniform definitions or common standards, making it impossible to know from the title just what a program entails. The best programs are similar to the Swedish approach. The least developed merely allow students to leave school earlier in the day in order to earn money.

Formal cooperative education programs constitute only a tiny fraction of the work experience acquired by American secondary school students. By far the most common form of work experience is part-time employment after school and on weekends, having no connection at all with schooling. Although there are some benefits from this type of work experience, it can also distract young people from their educational responsibilities. Not only can excessive work hours reduce time available for school, but heavy commitment to work also competes with commitment to school (Greenberger & Steinberg, 1986), reinforcing the belief that school is not important.

The case of Japan proves that it is possible to achieve high levels of motivation in a school-based educational system. But I continue to believe that the United States should move in the German direction to make the school/career connection more transparent. The most decisive argument against the Japanese approach is simply that the United States has already tried keeping all youth in school full-time through high school graduation and it has not worked. There is little basis for expecting that a Japanese-style zeal for learning can be injected in quantity into American schools, especially in the absence of key cultural characteristics that provide the context for Japanese schools' effectiveness: high respect for authority in general and teachers in particular; faith in effort; a view of achievement as reflecting on the family and other groups rather than just the individual; and mothers' near absolute devotion to their children's education.

Conclusions

My principal concern has been with improving the motivation of American youth, not only because of my citizenship but because the problem is clearly greatest there. However, the other six countries could also learn from each other. Sweden is already increasing emphasis on work-based learning, borrowing from its own past, from Denmark, and from the German-speaking countries. Germany would do well to examine some of the more progressive aspects of Swiss apprenticeship, many of which are already found in some German programs but are not yet universal. Austria's system could benefit from practices in both Germany and Switzerland, but is hampered by the dominance of small businesses, whose owners too often view apprentices as cheap labor and are unwilling to make the investment required to upgrade the quality of education, even though in the long run it would make economic sense for them.

Japan is the country with which I am least familiar. Work-based learning is highly developed there, at least among large firms, but sharply separated from school-based learning. Both high school and university graduates receive rigorous training after they are hired, but I have no detailed information on the nature of that training. The results in terms of productivity indicate that it is effective. However, Japanese critics cite the sterility of school pedagogy in Japan, which demands memorization and does not reward originality. And there is a huge gap between privileged permanent employees, who are predominantly male, and "temporary" employees, predominantly females, and males of Korean and low-caste Japanese ancestry. School pedagogy and the career prospects of low-status people might be addressed using some adaptation of work-based learning combined with formal schooling in order to render education more available and more useful.

Motivating adolescents to learn in school requires attention to immediate, short-term incentives but also to the connection between school performance and career opportunities. Finding the optimal combination of transparency and permeability is the key.

The best way to test empirically the hypothesized relationship between the opacity of the school/career nexus and poor school performance in the United States would be to create a more transparent system and then observe whether students' behavior changed in the predicted direction. My colleagues and I are engaged in such an effort, inspired by German-style apprenticeship. Several other groups are similarly engaged.

The utility of these educational reforms as experiments testing the motivational hypothesis will depend not only on research design and methodology, but also on whether any of the demonstration projects achieves an adequate scale. In order to achieve the predicted effect, youth apprenticeship must be available for all young people who prefer it over a long enough time period to become a dependable part of their prospects for the future. If this occurs, and if those young people who are eligible to become apprentices take their schoolwork more seriously and behave more responsibly in other realms, this will constitute evidence supporting the hypothesis around which this chapter has been organized.

Acknowledgments. Much of the information about Europe was obtained during the author's year in Germany as a Fulbright Senior Research Scholar and brief subsequent visits sponsored by the German Marshall Fund. Thanks are due to these organizations and to the innumerable individuals who graciously shared their knowledge. In addition to the sources cited, Paul Osterman provided information on Japan.

References

Bandura, A. (1986). *Social foundations of thought and action: A social cognitive theory*. Englewood Cliffs, NJ: Prentice Hall.

Bishop, J. (1989). *Incentives for learning: Why American high school students compare so poorly to their counterparts overseas*. (Working Paper No. 89–09). Center for Advanced Human Resource Studies, School of Industrial and Labor Relations, Cornell University, Ithaca, NY.

Bronfenbrenner, U. (1979). *The ecology of human development: Experiments by nature and by design*. Cambridge: Harvard University Press.

Bundesminister für Bildung und Wissenschaft (1990). *Grund- und Strukturdaten, 1990/91*. Bad Honnef: Bock.

General Accounting Office (1991). *Transition from school to work: Linking education and worksite training*. Washington, DC: Author.

Greenberger, E. & Steinberg, L.D. (1986). *When teenagers work: The psychological and social costs of adolescent employment*. New York: Basic Books.

Hamilton, S.F. (1987). Adolescent problem behavior in the United States and West Germany: Implications for prevention. In K. Hurrelmann, F.X. Kaufmann, & F. Lösel, (Eds.), *Social intervention: Chances and constraints*. Berlin: Walter de Gruyter.

Hamilton, S.F. (1990). *Apprenticeship for adulthood: Preparing youth for the future*. New York: Free Press.

Kaiser, M., Nuthmann, R., & Stegmann, H. (Eds.), (1985). *Berufliche Verbleibsforschung in der Diskussion (volume 1), Schulabgänger aus dem Sekundarbereich I beim Übergang in Ausbildung und Beruf*. Nürnberg: Institut für Arbeitsmarkt- und Berufsforschung der Bundesanstalt für Arbeit. *(Research on career attainment under discussion (volume 1): School leavers from the first stage of secondary school at the transition to training and career*. Nuremberg: Institute for Labor Market and Occupational Research of the Federal Institute for Work.)

Ogbu, J.U. (1974). *The next generation: An ethnography of education in an urban neighborhood*. New York: Academic Press.

Ogbu, J.U. (1978). *Minority education and caste: The American system in cross-cultural perspective*. New York: Academic Press.

Piore, M.J. & Sabel, C. (1984). *The second industrial divide: Possibilities for prosperity*. New York: Basic Books.

Rohlen, T. (1983). *Japan's high schools*. Berkeley: University of California Press.

Rosenbaum, J.E., Kariya, T., Settersten, R., & Maier, T. (1990). Market and network theories of the transition from high school to work: Their application to industrialized societies. In *Annual Review of Sociology, 16*, 263–299.

Stinchcombe, A.L. (1964). *Rebellion in a high school*. Chicago: Quadrangle.

14
Vocational Identity Development in Adolescence

Fred W. Vondracek

One of the most significant features of adolescence is that it witnesses, among other things, the transformation of child into adult, and play into work. There is evidence from both the developmental and clinical literature that those who are successful in becoming well-functioning adults are also successful in becoming well-functioning workers. Freud was not being facetious, after all, when he declared that to be able to work was one of the two major characteristics of a well-functioning person, the other being the ability to love. The focus of the present chapter will be a discussion of some of the processes that have been shown to contribute to the successful transition from being a playful child to being a hard-working and productive adult. In particular, the theoretical framework of Erikson (1959, 1963, 1968) will be examined with respect to its implications for vocational development. Using Marcia's (1966) operationalization of Erikson's identity theory, some empirical findings will be presented to demonstrate the relevance of the identity status framework for examining school- and work-related attitudes and behaviors associated with various phases of identity development.

A review of recent literature on adolescence reveals that there is a growing awareness among researchers and writers of the importance of vocational development within the overall adolescent developmental processes. Nevertheless, when compared to such areas as pubertal development, moral development, and cognitive development, vocational development seems relegated to a status of secondary importance. This certainly seems to be a curious phenomenon in view of the fact that, at least in Western societies, most adults spend about half of their waking time in the pursuit of their occupation. Moreover, anecdotal evidence suggests that most adults attribute their occupational choices to chance factors, or to features of environmental press, which they felt were outside of their control. This apparently unplanned, often accidental, or at least externally determined, avenue into the occupational world would seem to have some rather far-reaching consequences. After all, the first or second question one is asked by a new neighbor is "What do you do?"

Similarly, most of us have some curiosity about the person taking a seat next to us in an airplane, leading to the question of "Are you traveling on business?" In short, while it may be an exaggeration to say that we are what we do, few would take issue with the assertion that our occupations represent a significant and pervasive feature of our identity.

As a psychologist, and especially as one who works in the area of career development, I am not prepared to accept that important occupational choices are or should be determined by chance or environmental contingencies. Instead, I would prefer to believe that the important occupational choices individuals make throughout their adult lives have their precursors in important processes that occur in childhood and adolescence. For example, the contribution by Todt, Drewes, and Heils (this volume) represents a unique conceptualization of how the development of vocational interests represents just such a process. Glendinning, Hendry, Love, Scott, and Shucksmith (this volume) show how these individual developmental processes are shaped by the social and cultural contexts within which adolescent development occurs. My own view of how vocational development occurs may be considered "developmental-contextual" in nature (cf. Vondracek, Lerner, & Schulenberg, 1986), a view that holds that individual development has bidirectional links to the changing social context, and thus individuals actively participate in producing their own development. It is indebted primarily to the work of Lerner (1985; Lerner & Busch-Rossnagel, 1981), but also to a number of theoretical formulations in vocational psychology that have been forwarded during the past 40 years, which explicitly recognize the developmental nature of the "vocationalization process" (e.g., Ginzberg, Ginsburg, Axelrad, & Herma, 1951; Havighurst, 1964; Super, 1953). It is also consistent with many of the proposals regarding vocational development made by Erik Erikson.

Theoretical Framework

Although not generally considered among vocational psychologists, Erikson (1959, 1963, 1968) has been quite explicit about the central role of vocational development throughout the life-course. Particularly unique about Erikson's approach is his recognition that vocational development starts much earlier than is commonly assumed. Moreover, he proposed that the person's development could not be properly understood without understanding the sociocultural context within which it is occurring. As the child moves into adolescence, and as the adolescent moves into adulthood, society requires different kinds of adaptive behaviors from the developing individual. What is considered to be adaptive at one stage of life may not be adaptive at another. Importantly, Erikson asserts that within each stage a certain adaptive capacity has to be attained before the person can begin to acquire the capacities necessary to move on to the next stage.

The eight psychosocial stages of development identified by Erikson correspond to eight different capabilities the person must develop in order to meet the demands of society. Three of these are particularly relevant in the vocational development of children and adolescents. During the third of Erikson's eight stages, which may start around age 5 and is called the Genital-locomotor stage, the child finds pleasure in using tools and in caring for younger children. It is these activities which, in Erikson's view, may well sow the seeds of the child's ultimate vocational identity. Erikson's fourth stage is called the Latency stage, during which the child begins to be a worker and internalizes the work principle. Simultaneously, this allows the child to overcome feelings of inferiority and to develop a sense of industry. With the advent of puberty, children reach Erikson's fifth stage, Puberty and Adolescence, which features most prominently the task of developing an identity, a large component of which is what has come to be called vocational identity (e.g., Vondracek, 1992).

Havighurst's (1964) ideas about the development of vocational identity proceed along similar lines. He proposed that children during the period of approximately 5 to 10 years of age establish "identification with a worker" primarily through identification with parents or significant other persons. During early adolescence, the period from approximately ages 10 to 15, children acquire the basic habits of industry. Havighurst proposed that during this period children learn to do schoolwork and chores, and learn circumstances that are appropriate for work, on the one hand, and play, on the other. Following this period, during late adolescence and early adulthood, individuals acquire identity as a worker, or an occupational identity.

Super (1957) proposed a comprehensive developmental theory dealing primarily with the process of vocationalization. He asserted that the main task of the young adolescent is the crystallization of a vocational preference, which involves the formulation of ideas about work and self, and which would ultimately evolve into an occupational self-concept. He realized that the development of such a self-concept is a continuous process, changing as life experiences of the individual change. According to Super (1963), the process begins at birth with the child's awareness of self and gradually broadens to create a more elaborate and differentiated understanding of self as distinct from others. It is Super's position that the vocational self-concept is a reflection of the person's overall self-concept, but more specialized in the sense that it has implications for educational and vocational decisions.

A common theme that is reflected in these theoretical formulations is the recognition that once children have reached the requisite level of cognitive and physical maturity, they must acquire some knowledge and understanding of the world of work. In other words, they learn about the difference between play and work and they become capable of doing work. Moreover, this advance in children's understanding of work leads to the eventual realization that they, themselves, must ultimately find a role for themselves in the world of occupations. They must establish a vocational identity.

Two key questions are suggested by this:

1. What are the childhood and adolescence antecedents of the successful achievement of a vocational identity?
2. How are the processes and outcomes of the vocational identity process, especially during adolescence, related to other key processes and variables of adolescent functioning?

The answers to these questions have been elusive thus far, in part because large-scale longitudinal research would be required to even begin to arrive at any definitive answers. In addition, it is quite clear that the process of vocational identity development is more directly influenced by sociocultural, political, and economic factors than most other aspects of adolescent development. In spite of these difficulties, and without any claim to being definitive, I shall attempt to review what is known about the first question and present some modest findings from my own research program pertaining to the second.

Antecedents of Vocational Identity Achievement

The establishment of identity has become increasingly recognized as a major task of adolescence and young adulthood. As a consequence, the term *identity* has been accepted into the vernacular without, however, necessarily being confined to the original meaning intended by Erikson (1959, 1968). Thus, broadly speaking, identity has been generally accepted as meaning the accomplishment of a coherent and firm sense of self, a sense of being at home in one's own body, a sense of being reasonably comfortable with who one has become, and a sense of knowing where one is going. This process of self-definition occurs in a number of different areas, such as vocational plans, religious beliefs, political ideologies, sex-role orientation, values, and family roles (Archer, 1989b), and it does not necessarily occur in all areas at the same time. Importantly, however, Erikson (1959) reminds us that "like a 'good conscience', it is constantly lost and regained, although more lasting and economical methods of maintenance and restoration are evolved and fortified in late adolescence" (p. 118).

Chickering (1969) has compared the adolescent's establishment of identity to the task of learning to drive:

First, signals and signs must be learned and behaviors must be mastered. Despite intense concentration much goes unobserved and mistakes are made. Progress occurs in fits and starts, with much wandering from one side of the road to the other. But with time and practice change occurs. Driver and vehicle become acquainted. Peculiar requirements for starting and operating become understood, customary noises assure soundness and unusual ones prompt informed action. The ways of the road become familiar, the driver learns his own limits and those imposed by varied conditions. In time, snow, heavy traffic, and mechanical failures are met with ease and assurance. Driving becomes a pleasure, not a chore, and other things can be attended to while doing it. (p. 80)

The analogy may not be perfect but it clearly indicates the complexity of the identity development process and it hints at the difficulties one might encounter in specifying the antecedents of such processes.

Fortunately, Erikson himself offers some insight. His developmental stage model proposes that identity achievement is preceded, in most individuals, by a decision-making process that is characterized initially by a lack of identity (diffusion) which may lead to a foreclosure status when adolescents become committed to the values, beliefs, and goals of significant others. As adolescents gain more experience and cognitive sophistication, they may enter a moratorium period during which they are in an identity crisis, whose resolution culminates in the achievement of a self-chosen identity.

Even before the adolescent embarks on the difficult processes of identity formation, he or she will have more or less successfully negotiated what Erikson calls the Latency stage. Erikson, in particular, attached a great deal of psychosocial importance to the latency years. He felt that this was the stage at which children learn the basic tasks necessary for being adult members of society. These tasks could vary by society, and while they begin in our society by the child's being sent off to school, in other societies it could take the form of teaching the child to farm, hunt, fish, or keep house. Erikson stated that children, ". . . sooner or later, become dissatisfied and disgruntled without a sense of being useful, without a sense of being able to make things and make them well and even perfectly: This is what I call the *sense of industry*" (1959, p. 86). In short, the child will gain confidence in the fact that he or she knows, or is successfully learning, what it takes to be a well-functioning adult member of society. Thus, Erikson noted that it is socially a most decisive stage, because it involves doing things beside and with others, providing a first opportunity to appreciate such concepts as division of labor and equality of opportunity.

As the child acquires a sense of industry through the acquisition of a good understanding of the world of skills, childhood nears an end, youth begins, and the individual is faced with the necessity to develop identity. Before considering that major task of the adolescent, however, it may be enlightening to further explore the ramifications of successfully acquiring a sense of industry, not only for the ensuing task of identity formation, but also for the individual's long-term future. One particularly relevant and important study was reported by Vaillant and Vaillant (1981), consisting of a 35-year prospective study of underprivileged, inner-city, junior high school boys, who were subjects in a study by Glueck and Glueck (1950) designed to examine delinquency. In the original study all subjects, their parents, and teachers, were interviewed and virtually all subjects were reinterviewed at ages 25, 31, and 47. Remarkably, 392 subjects, 80% of the original group, continued in the follow-up studies. Thus, it should be clear that findings reported on the basis of such a unique and rare longitudinal study should be considered with considerable care.

In an effort to establish how well the children in this study had accomplished the tasks of Erikson's Latency stage, and had thereby established a firm sense of industry, an objective measure was devised which assessed whether the children had a regular part-time job, regularly did household chores, participated in extracurricular clubs/sports, performed adequately in school relative to their IQ, participated regularly in school activities, and displayed some evidence of ability to plan, or make the best of the environment. Scoring of these items was done on the basis of systematically recorded observations made when the boys were between 11- and 16-years-old. More than 30 years later, the 45 men who obtained the highest scores concerning these tasks of industry, when compared with the 67 who received low scores, were twice as likely to be rated as generative, twice as likely to have warm relations with a wide variety of people, five times more likely to be paid well for their adult work, and 16 times less likely to have experienced significant unemployment. On the other hand, the 67 men who had been least successful at accomplishing latency-period tasks during early adolescence, were 10 times more likely to be rated as emotionally disabled, were far more likely to manifest sociopathic behavior as adults, and were 6 times more likely to be dead.

Vaillant and Vaillant (1981) provide further interesting insight into the differences between individuals who were successful in establishing a sense of industry and those who were not. Those who succeeded were much more likely to have had family environments with many positive attributes, while those who failed were much more likely to have come from multiproblem families. Interestingly, the two groups did not differ in parental social class, they differed only modestly in subsequent educational opportunity, and they did not significantly differ in intelligence. Vaillant and Vaillant suggest that the variables of parental social class, IQ, and multiproblem family membership may carry more weight in cross-sectional studies than in longitudinal studies. Finally, they note the striking fact that among their various childhood measures the scale reflecting success in the mastering of the tasks associated with the emerging sense of industry turned out to be correlated with adult adjustment most robustly.

Another large-scale study conducted by Goldstein and Oldham (1979) to evaluate children's socialization to work concluded that early work experience was not only more common than initially assumed, but that it also facilitated the child's eventual readiness to enter the world of work. They found, for example, that children from as early as fifth grade had rather sophisticated comprehension of occupations, and that their experiences and knowledge related to work were subject to age-related increments. They concluded that children, in spite of preferring play to work, were overwhelmingly positive about their own work experiences.

These findings of positive work experiences, especially of early work experiences, are at odds with more recent research dealing with the effects of part-time work on the functioning of contemporary adolescents (e.g., Greenberger & Steinberg, 1986). The overall findings of their research paint a rather negative picture of adolescent employment. For example, they found, especially among middle-class students, that working was associated with an increase in certain forms of deviant behavior, including money-, substance-, and school-related deviance. Other researchers have reported that working had negative effects on school performance (e.g., Mortimer & Finch, 1986), that working students used drugs and alcohol more extensively (Bachman, Bare, & Frankie, 1986), and that their involvement in delinquent behavior was at least as high (Gottfredson, 1985) or higher (Ruggiero, 1984). Steinberg and Dornbusch (1991), in a large-scale study of the relationship between part-time employment and a variety of school performance, psychosocial, and behavioral variables, concluded that the apparent negative consequences of part-time work for school-age adolescents increased significantly as the number of hours worked increased. Interestingly, however, their data appear to show that those students who worked 1–10 hours per week actually showed small increases in grade point average, time spent doing homework, and family time when compared with students who did not work. On virtually all other variables they were comparable to students who did not work at all.

Recently reported findings from an important large-scale longitudinal study of work experience and adolescent development offer some additional support for the idea that moderate hours of part-time work may, indeed, have a positive effect for adolescents (Mortimer, Finch, Ryu, & Shanahan, 1991). For example, Mortimer and her colleagues reported that 9th and 10th grade students who worked less than 15 hours per week displayed less problem behavior than those who did not work at all. This "protective effect" appeared to be operative for both genders. In addition, they found that moderate hours of work enhanced girls' sense of mastery and decreased boys' level of participation in school problem behaviors. Perhaps most importantly, Mortimer et al. reported the finding that intensity of work (hours worked) may well be a product rather than a cause of the problem behaviors that have been reported to be associated with long hours of work (e.g., Steinberg & Dornbusch, 1991). Mortimer et al. found no cases in which working adolescents, regardless of number of hours worked, fared worse on a number of mental health outcome measures than did nonworking adolescents.

In explaining the apparent discrepancy between their longitudinal findings and the reports of largely negative consequences from part-time work, Mortimer et al. indicated that

youth who choose to work, those who are employed at greater intensity, and those who have what we would think of as higher quality work experiences are likely to be initially different from those who do not enter the youth labor market, from those who work fewer hours, or from those who have less salutary work experiences. To fully comprehend the effects of working, one must take into account these prior differences. (p. 24)

This perspective quite obviously takes us back to our earlier discussion of Erikson's position that a firm sense of industry must be established during the latency period for adolescents to be in a position to move on to the developmental task of developing a self-chosen identity. Quite possibly, the prior differences Mortimer and her colleagues refer to may turn out to be differences in how and whether their adolescent workers succeeded in the establishment of a sense of industry.

Exploratory Research on Vocational Identity Development

Longitudinal research is clearly needed to demonstrate any definitive links between the child's developing sense of industry (and the contextual features that foster it) and the adolescent's efforts at establishing an identity. Unfortunately, although we have some longitudinal data in this area, our research has not progressed far enough for me to be able to share the longitudinal findings with you. In the meantime, however, it will be important to learn more about the transition from the task of developing a sense of industry to the task of identity formation. Jane Kroger (1989), in her review of theoretical formulations on identity development in adolescence, concludes that all major contributors see the process of identity development as an evolutionary one in which the individual defines and redefines his/her self in relation to an expanding and increasingly complex set of interpersonal and social contexts. At the same time, she notes that:

given the evolutionary nature of the identity formation process, it is surprising that greater attention has not been directed to mechanisms involved in stage transformations; to date such important passages have been left largely to clinical observers, poets, and novelists to elucidate. (p. 188)

One apparent reason for the relative paucity of research on these critical transformations appears to be related to difficulties in the assessment or measurement of identity and related concepts. Another is the relative absence of empirical research that documents how the processes of identity development are embedded in and related to other developmental processes, on the one hand, and various salient interpersonal and sociocultural processes and contexts, on the other. It is apparent that this is an area that could benefit from the application of cohort-sequential designs such as those proposed by Baltes (1968) and by Baltes, Cornelius, and Nesselroade (1979), which facilitate the disentanglement of ontogenetic change from cohort-specific sociocultural (historical) influences.

Quite clearly, the shortcomings in research on identity development in general, lamented by Kroger, apply also to the more specific issue of identity development in the vocational area. In this connection, one should note the observation that identity development does not occur at the same time in all areas of identity (Archer, 1989a), and that the development of vocational identity may actually represent the first, and thus perhaps the most important, area of identity achievement. Of particular concern is the fact that so little is known about this area that exploratory research must be conducted to first establish variables and domains that are especially salient. This, then, brings me to the point at which I would like to share with you some findings from my study of approximately 600 students in a rural Pennsylvania school, comprising 7th through 12th grade, that is, students 13 through 18 years of age. We consider this research to be largely exploratory, designed to identify some of the intraindividual as well as contextual variables that may be assumed, largely on the basis of theory and clinical observation, to be related to the vocational identity development process. Ultimately, longitudinal research should be conducted to more definitively map and explore the complex processes of vocational identity development.

In order to accomplish our exploratory objectives and to obtain a more differentiated view of the vocational identity development process, we basically decided to classify our subjects into four identity status groups, based on Marcia's (1966, 1980) framework. Marcia developed the identity status paradigm as a methodological device designed to render Erikson's notions about identity development more readily subject to empirical study. The identity statuses are named Identity Diffusion, Foreclosure, Moratorium, and Identity Achievement, to signify different modes of dealing with identity issues characteristic of adolescents. Although Marcia introduced an interview procedure to accomplish the classification of subjects into identity statuses, this process is too slow and impractical for use with the number of subjects required for the kind of exploratory research we contemplated. Consequently, we used a self-report measure developed by Adams, Bennion, and Huh (1987), the Extended Objective Measure of Ego Identity Status-2 (EOMEIS-2).

The EOMEIS-2 was designed to facilitate the conduct of studies with larger samples and to enhance the comparability between studies and reliability and validity of findings. Following a number of preliminary versions, Adams, Bennion, and Huh (1987) produced the EOMEIS-2, which was used in the findings to be reported below. It consists of 64 items, which are rated on a 6-point scale, ranging from "strongly agree" to "strongly disagree" by subjects who are asked to indicate the degree to which a given item reflects their thoughts and feelings. Following a suggestion made by Grotevant, Thorbecke, and Meyer (1982), Bennion and Adams (1986) divided the EOMEIS-2 into two distinct sections, one measuring ideological and the other interpersonal identity. Because of time limitations in the data collection process the present study measured ideological identity only, particularly since it "refers to commitments to such things as work, and ideological values associated with politics, religion, a philosophy of living, and so forth" (Adams, Bennion, & Huh, 1987, p. 10). Bennion and Adams (1986) reported Cronbach alphas ranging from .62 to .75 for the four identity status subscales of ideological identity. In addition, they reported evidence of predictive and concurrent validity, based on correlations between the identity subscales and measures of self-acceptance, intimacy, and authoritarianism, which were generally consistent with the expectations based on the underlying theoretical framework (Adams, Bennion, & Huh, 1987). Although it is possible to score various transition states, all subjects were collapsed into four basic identity status groupings according to Adams, Bennion, and Huh (1987, pp. 98–100), and adapted to the shortened (ideological identity only) EOMEIS-2 administered as part of the present study.

For those not entirely familiar with Marcia's (1966) identity status paradigm, it will be useful to briefly review the operationalization of the identity statuses as envisioned by Adams, Bennion, and Huh (1987) in connection with the development of the EOMEIS-2:

Drawing on two of the major dimensions of Erikson's theory of identity formation, Marcia has conceptualized four types of identity formation. These two dimensions involve the presence or absence of a *crisis* period (or as more recently conceptualized by Matteson [1977], exploration period) and the presence or absence of a clearly defined and stable *commitment* to values, beliefs, and standards. This exploration or crisis period is expected of adolescents during their psychosocial moratorium (youth). Prior to recognizing a psychosocial moratorium, the youth does not experience a motivating identity consciousness. He or she, therefore, doesn't experience a compulsion to explore life alternatives and fails to establish ideological commitments. These youth are referred to as *identity diffused*. A second category of youths report stable commitments but have not experienced a true crisis period. That is, these youths have acquired commitments from others (usually parents) and have not tested their stated commitments for individual fit. Such youths merely adopt the commitments of others and make them their own, without shaping or modifying them. This process is similar to that of early childhood identifications. These youths are labeled *identity foreclosed*. The third category includes youths who are currently experiencing the identity consciousness of an identity crisis and are exploring, but have not yet arrived at their own self-defined commitments. These youths are categorized as being in *moratorium*. Finally, youths who have experienced a psychosocial moratorium and have made substantial exploration prior to identifying personal and unique ideological commitments are referred to as *identity achieved*. (p. 4)

In line with our charge of examining some aspect of the school/work interface, we decided to study the relationship between a variety of self-reported school-related variables and (ideological) identity status. In order to accomplish this we used a number of questions from the Primary Prevention Awareness and Usage Scales (Form 7) developed by Swisher (1983). The first area to be examined was self-reported school performance. As expected, Identity Diffusion subjects were more likely than any of the other groups to have a C average or lower ($\chi^2 = 28.4$, $p = .000$). Thus the students who are most advanced, from a vocational identity development perspective, were also most likely to report that they had good grades (see Figure 14.1). Next, we asked students to report on a number of school-related attitudes. Specifically, they were asked to indicate whether they disliked or enjoyed school in general, whether they found teachers to be unhelpful or helpful, and whether they considered their school subjects to be boring or interesting. All ratings were made on a 7-point Likert scale. As Figures 14.2, 14.3, and 14.4 show, the Identity Diffusion subjects were most negative and least positive, with the Identity Achievement subjects' ratings at the opposite extremes. In other words,

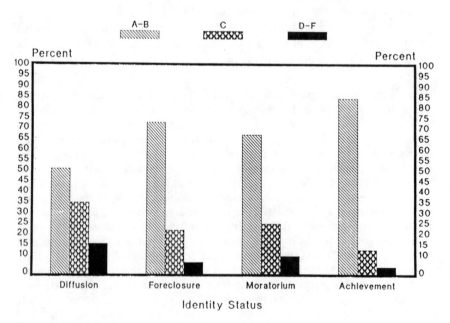

FIGURE 14.1. Identity status and grades.

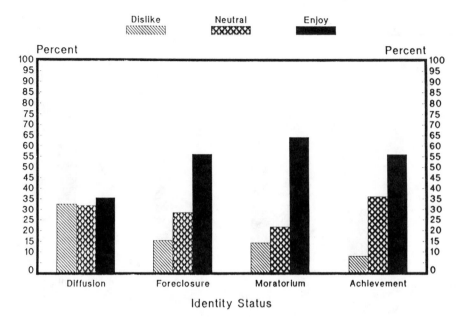

FIGURE 14.2. Identity status and feelings about school.

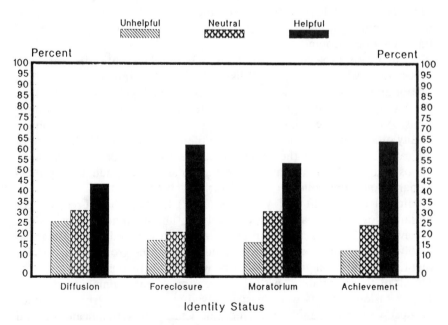

FIGURE 14.3. Feelings about teachers.

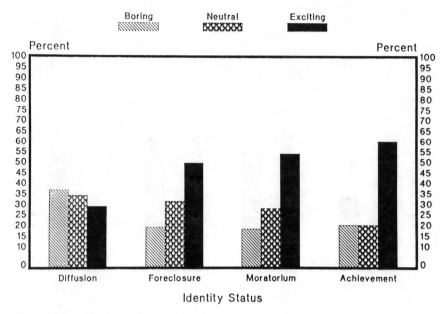

FIGURE 14.4. Feelings about subjects.

the Identity Achievement subjects felt overwhelmingly positive about school ($\chi^2 = 46.6$, $p = .000$), teachers ($\chi^2 = 18.08$, $p = .006$), and school subjects ($\chi^2 = 41.1$, $p = .000$), while the Identity Diffusion subjects, for the most part, felt negatively or, at best, neutrally about these aspects of their school environment.

As might be expected, the students' school-related attitudes were also reflected in whether they were likely to have aspirations to remain in school and to obtain a higher educational level. Figure 14.5 shows how the four identity status groups differ in terms of their educational aspirations. As can be seen, Diffusion subjects were more than twice as likely as any other subject group to terminate their education with a high school education or less. On the other hand, the Achievement subjects were almost twice as likely as any other group to aspire to graduate or professional school after college ($\chi^2 = 58.14$, $p = .000$).

Mindful of Vaillant and Vaillant's (1981) findings that successful negotiation of Latency-stage tasks involved, among other things, active involvement in extracurricular activities, we examined the differential involvement of members of the four identity status groups in entertainment, academic, religious, and extracurricular activities, and in sports. On all of these variables, with the exception of entertainment activities, the Diffusion subjects were least involved, and subjects from the other groups were much more involved (all Chi-squares significant beyond $p = .001$). Figure 14.6, regarding degree of participation in academic

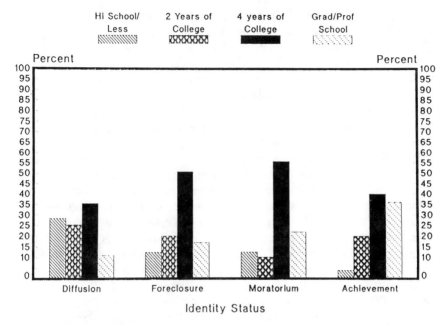

FIGURE 14.5. Educational aspirations.

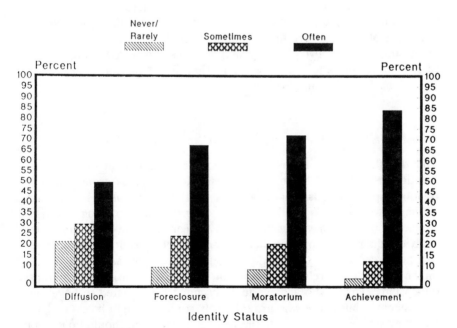

FIGURE 14.6. Participation in Academic Activities.

activities, is illustrative of the pattern of involvement in various activities by subjects from the different identity status groups ($\chi^2 = 42.9$, $p = .000$). It is noteworthy, however, that the pattern was just as clear in differentiating Diffusion subjects from, especially, Achievement subjects in the nonacademic areas as it was in the area of academic activities. What is suggested by this relationship is that students who are more advanced in terms of their vocational identity development are more involved with their context than those who are less advanced, especially those who are in the Diffusion status.

Because of conflicting evidence about adolescents' attitudes toward work we were especially eager to determine whether such attitudes could serve to distinguish adolescents at different levels of vocational identity achievement. Subjects were given a number of negative and positive statements about work, asking them to indicate which statement best described their feelings about work. Negative statements included such statements as "I hate work," and "If I had the choice, I'd never work a day in my life," while positive choices included statements such as "I could easily see myself becoming a 'workaholic'," and "I'm willing to work if I'm paid well." Subjects were then grouped into "worker" and "work-avoider" groups. Sixty-five percent of all work-avoiders were Diffusion subjects. On the other hand, 96% of the Achievement subjects were "workers" ($\chi^2 = 14.96$, $p = .002$).

In further examining relationships between identity status membership and work-related variables, we wondered whether there was a relationship between identity status and whether students held part-time jobs. No significant relationships were found, although the Moratorium and Achievement subjects, the two developmentally most advanced groups, were slightly more likely to not have a part-time job while the opposite was true of the Diffusion and Foreclosure subjects.

Identity Status, Depression, and Self-esteem

Thus far the discussion has focused on the development of vocational identity (as indicated by membership in identity status groups) and its relationship to various school- and work-related variables. Before concluding, I would like to briefly report on our exploration of two personality characteristics that have recently received considerable attention in the study of adolescence, namely, depression and self-esteem. We anticipated that adolescents, who supposedly are subject to significant mood swings, might reflect their relative success in identity establishment on those dimensions: Those who achieve identity might be expected to have high self-esteem, while those who are relatively confused might be expected to have low self-esteem. Precisely the reverse expectation should hold as far as depressed mood is concerned.

We administered two relatively simple, brief measures to our sample of 537 junior and senior high school students: The Kandel and Davies (1982) measure of self-reported depressive mood, and the Rosenberg Self-Esteem Scale (Rosenberg, 1979). Both scales were constructed specifically for use with adolescents, and their authors have reported acceptable reliability and validity for these scales. A multivariate analysis of variance (MANOVA) was performed to examine whether the level of self-reported depressive mood could serve to differentiate subjects in the four identity status groups. No significant differences were found either for identity status, gender, and grade (the main effects) or for any of the interaction effects.

Next, we performed a MANOVA to determine whether level of self-esteem was different for members of the identity status groups. There was a significant main effect for identity status ($F = 5.97$, $p < .001$), but neither gender, nor grade, nor any of the interactions were significant. Specifically, self-esteem was significantly higher for Achievement status subjects when compared with the other three identity statuses, and it was also significantly higher for Moratorium status subjects when compared with Diffusion status subjects.

Implications and Conclusions

Erikson (1959) has stated that "in general it is primarily the inability to settle on an occupational identity which disturbs young people" (p. 92). The findings that I have presented suggest that adolescents who perceive that they have not achieved a self-chosen identity or that they are confused and relatively directionless may, indeed, be more disturbed than those who have achieved an identity of their own or at least feel that they are moving toward it. These differences are most pronounced, of course, when the developmentally most advanced students (the Achievement status subjects) are compared with the developmentally least advanced students (the Diffusion status subjects). Nevertheless, those adolescents who have a sense of direction, especially in the vocational area, appear to feel better about themselves and about others than do adolescents who do not have it. They also tend to feel more positively about school and work, and they appear to subscribe more strongly to the idea that certain aspects of work represent a viable vehicle for the satisfaction of their aspirations in life.

Viewed from this perspective it seems self-evident that adolescents who successfully go through the process postulated by Erikson would be in a more desirable position than adolescents who lack vocational direction and commitment. Indeed, there is consistent evidence of positive correlations between identity achievement and various positive psychological outcomes (Archer, 1989b). Although many of these findings are correlational and/or cross-sectional in nature, they suggest the likely presence of factors in successful identity development that bode well for ultimate success in assuming adult work roles. For example, Matteson (1977), using a sample of Danish students, found that those who were most advanced toward the achievement of identity scored highest on a measure of autonomy. In a similar vein, Neuber and Genthner (1977) found that Identity Achievement and Moratorium status subjects were much more likely to take personal responsibility for their own lives than were Identity Diffusion subjects. Marcia (1989), as well as Rotheram-Borus (1989), have pointed out, however, that in some cultures identity achievement may not be the most desirable outcome, and several researchers have reported significant differences in identity processes based on gender and sex-role attitudes (e.g., Marcia & Friedman, 1970; Orlofsky, 1978).

Currently available evidence suggests, nevertheless, that the achievement of vocational identity may have demonstrable positive consequences, some of which may not be directly related to vocation or work. Moreover, especially when studying younger adolescents, a number of significant cautions must be applied. While there is a great deal of anecdotal evidence about the fact that adolescents are, in fact, occupied (if not preoccupied) with achieving an identity of their own, different individuals experience this developmental task in different ways. The various contexts within which adolescents operate can play a major role in how they cope with this experience (Glendinning, et al., this volume; Oswald & Suess, this volume). In addition, it is probably necessary to take a much closer look at moderator variables, such as locus of control orientation, social support (Sandler, 1980), temperament, parental attachment (Greenberg, Siegel, & Leitch, 1983), and parenting style (Steinberg & Darling, this volume), and how they may influence different ways of identity formation. Hamilton (1990, p. 4) has suggested that "human capital" is actually wasted in the United States by societal expectations and educational policies that "often fail to inculcate the work attitudes and behavior employers seek." According to Hamilton, adolescents growing up under those conditions may end up floundering for a prolonged period, with many ending up unemployed, underemployed, or deemed unemployable.

What emerges from these considerations is the view that the development of industry and the subsequent development of a unique identity, which are the precursors of successful career development, are complex, multiply determined phenomena that are of central importance not only to the developing individual but also to the well-being of society. As we move into the 21st century with its major sociological, demographic, and technological changes, it will become increasingly apparent that issues of vocational development cannot wait until early adulthood. Moreover, there is no theoretical, empirical, or moral basis for neglecting the *vocational* development of children and adolescents in favor of concentrating on *intellectual* or *motor* development. What may be needed, however, is a better understanding of how all aspects of development relate to all other aspects, and how development and context interact. Ultimately, this could lead to programmatic interventions designed to facilitate successful vocational identity development, and all of the benefits that this entails for the individual and for the various contexts within which the individual develops.

Several proposals have been made in recent years to facilitate the processes of vocational development and the associated transition from school (i.e., preparation for work) to work and career. Quite properly, these include, for example, school-based interventions for identity promotion in individuals (Waterman, 1989) and proposals for important structural changes in the socioeconomic contexts of adolescent development (Hamilton, 1990). Waterman sees three elements in the process of promoting identity formation: (a) stimulating the consideration of a variety of alternative goals in the various identity domains; (b) facilitating the gathering of relevant information, and (c) fostering the willingness of individuals to make commitments to the goals, values, and beliefs that best express their chosen direction (pp. 390–391). He concedes that the educational system could play an important role in promoting an environment where these elements are valued. Hamilton envisions a collaborative effort among government at all levels, the schools, employers, unions, and various social agencies, designed to develop a new kind of apprenticeship system in the United States that would create environments in which adolescents and young adults could work to learn and learn to work. The proposals made by Hamilton and by Waterman are illustrative of efforts that are feasible, at the level of individual development and the various levels of context, to facilitate vocational development. Their proposals represent further illustrations of a central feature found in all contributions to this volume: Adolescent development can be understood and modified only within a framework that fully accounts for its dynamic interaction with the contexts within which it takes place.

References

Adams, G.R., Bennion, L., & Huh, K. (1987). *Objective Measure of Ego Identity Status: A reference manual.* Laboratory for Research on Adolescence, Utah State University.

Archer, S.L. (1989a). Adolescent identity: An appraisal of health and intervention. *Journal of Adolescence, 12,* 341–343.

Archer, S.L. (1989b). The status of identity: Reflections on the need for intervention. *Journal of Adolescence, 12,* 345–359.

Bachman, J.G., Bare, D.E., & Frankie, E.I. (1986). *Correlates of employment among high school seniors.* Ann Arbor: Institute for Social Research.

Baltes, P.B. (1968). Longitudinal and cross-sectional sequences in the study of age and generation effects. *Human Development, 11*(3), 145–171.

Baltes, P.B., Cornelius, S., & Nesselroade, J.R. (1979). Cohort effects in developmental psychology. In J.R. Nesselroade & P.B. Baltes (Eds.), *Longitudinal
research in the study of behavior and development* (pp. 61–88). New York:
Academic Press.

Bennion, L.D. & Adams, G.R. (1986). A revision of the extended version of the
Objective Measure of Ego Identity Status: An identity instrument for use with
late adolescents. *Journal of Adolescent Research*, *1*, 183–198.

Chickering, A.W. (1969). *Education and identity*. San Francisco: Jossey-Bass.

Erikson, E.H. (1959). Identity and the life cycle. *Psychological Issues*, *1*, 18–164.

Erikson, E.H. (1963). *Childhood and society* (2nd ed.). New York: Norton.

Erikson, E.H. (1968). *Identity: Youth and crisis*. New York: Norton.

Ginzberg, E., Ginsburg, S.W., Axelrad, S., & Herma, J.L. (1951). *Occupational
choice: An approach to a general theory*. New York: Columbia University
Press.

Glueck, S. & Glueck, E. (1950). *Unraveling juvenile delinquency*. New York:
Commonwealth Fund.

Goldstein, B. & Oldham, J. (1979). *Children and work: A study of socialization*.
New Brunswick, NJ: Transaction Books.

Gottfredson, D. (1985). Youth employment, crime, and schooling: A longitudinal
study of a national sample. *Developmental Psychology*, *21*, 419–432.

Greenberg, M.T., Siegel, J.M., & Leitch, C.J. (1983). The nature and importance
of attachment relationships to parents and peers during adolescence. *Journal of
Youth and Adolescence*, *12*, 373–386.

Greenberger, E. & Steinberg, L.D. (1986). *When teenagers work: The psychological and social costs of adolescent employment*. New York: Basic Books.

Grotevant, H.D., Thorbecke, W., & Meyer, M.L. (1982). An extension of
Marcia's Identity Status Interview into the interpersonal domain. *Journal of
Youth and Adolescence*, *11*, 33–48.

Hamilton, S.F. (1990). *Apprenticeship for adulthood: Preparing youth for the
future*. New York: Free Press.

Havighurst, R.J. (1964). Youth in exploration and man emergent. In H. Borow
(Ed.), *Man in a world at work* (pp. 215–236). Boston: Houghton Mifflin.

Kandel, D.B. & Davies, M. (1982). Epidemiology of depressive mood in adolescents. *Archives of General Psychiatry*, *39*, 1205–1212.

Kroger, J. (1989). *Identity in adolescence: The balance between self and other*.
London: Routledge.

Lerner, R.M. (1985). Individual and context in developmental psychology: Con-
textual and theoretical issues. In J.R. Nesselroade and A. von Eye (Eds.),
Individual development and social change: Explanatory analysis (pp. 155–187).
New York: Academic Press.

Lerner, R.M. & Busch-Rossnagel, N.A. (1981). Individuals as producers of their
development: Conceptual and empirical bases. In R.M. Lerner & N.A. Busch-
Rossnagel (Eds.), *Individuals as producers of their development: A life-span
perspective* (pp. 1–36). New York: Academic Press.

Marcia, J.E. (1966). Development and validation of ego identity status. *Journal
of Personality and Social Psychology*, *3*(5), 551–558.

Marcia, J.E. (1980). Identity in adolescence. In J. Adelson (Ed.), *Handbook of
adolescent psychology* (pp. 158–187). New York: Wiley.

Marcia, J.E. (1989). Identity and intervention. *Journal of Adolescence, 12,* 401–410.

Marcia, J.E. & Friedman, M.L. (1970). Ego identity status in college women. *Journal of Personality, 38,* 249–263.

Matteson, D.R. (1977). Exploration and commitment: Sex differences and methodological problems in the use of identity status categories. *Journal of Youth and Adolescence, 6,* 353–374.

Mortimer, J.T. & Finch, M.D. (1986). The effects of part-time work on self-concept and achievement. In K.M. Borman & J. Reisman (Eds.), *Becoming a worker* (pp. 66–89). Norwood, NJ: Ablex Publishing.

Mortimer, J.T., Finch, M., Ryu, S., & Shanahan, M. (1991). *Evidence from a prospective longitudinal study of work experience and adolescent development.* Paper presented at the Biennial Meeting of the Society for Research in Child Development, Seattle, WA.

Neuber, K.A. & Genthner, R.W. (1977). The relationship between ego identity, personal responsibility, and facilitative communication. *Journal of Personality, 95,* 45–49.

Orlofsky, J.L. (1978). Identity formation, need achievement, and fear of success in college men and women. *Journal of Youth and Adolescence, 7,* 49–62.

Rosenberg, M. (1979). *Conceiving the self.* New York: Basic Books.

Rotheram-Borus, M.J. (1989). Ethnic differences in adolescents' identity status and associated behavior problems. *Journal of Adolescence, 12,* 361–374.

Ruggiero, M. (1984). *Work as an impetus to delinquency: An examination of theoretical and empirical connections.* Unpublished doctoral dissertation, University of California, Irvine.

Sandler, R.N. (1980). Social support resources, stress and maladjustment of poor children. *American Journal of Community Psychology, 8,* 41–52.

Steinberg, L.D. & Dornbusch, S.M. (1991). Negative correlates of part-time employment during adolescence: Replication and elaboration. *Developmental Psychology, 27,* 304–313.

Super, D.E. (1953). A theory of vocational development. *American Psychologist, 8,* 185–190.

Super, D.E. (1957). *The psychology of careers.* New York: Harper & Row.

Super, D.E. (1963). Self-concepts in vocational development. In D.E. Super, R. Starishevsky, N. Matlin, & J.P. Jordaan (Eds.), *Career development: Self-concept theory* (pp. 1–16). New York: CEEB Research Monograph No. 4.

Swisher, J.D. (1983). *Primary prevention awareness, attitude, and usage scales (Form 7).* University Park: The Pennsylvania State University.

Vaillant, G.E. & Vaillant, C.O. (1981). Natural history of male psychological health, X: Work as a predictor of positive mental health. *American Journal of Psychiatry, 138*(11), 1433–1441.

Vondracek, F.W. (1992). The construct of identity and its use in career theory and research. *Career Development Quarterly, 41,* 130–144.

Vondracek, F.W., Lerner, R.M., & Schulenberg, J.E. (1986). *Career development: A life-span developmental approach.* Hillsdale, NJ: Lawrence Erlbaum.

Waterman, A.S. (1989). Curricula interventions for identity change: Substantive and ethical considerations. *Journal of Adolescence, 12,* 389–400.

15
The Effects of Adolescent Employment on School-related Orientation and Behavior

Jeylan T. Mortimer, Michael Shanahan, and Seongryeol Ryu

In prior generations most adolescents in the United States did not work while school was in session, reserving paid employment for summer and other vacation periods. Now, however, simultaneous involvement in school and in the paid labor force has become the modal adolescent experience in the United States. Contemporary research shows that the vast majority of American students have worked at some time while attending high school (Marsh, 1991); this pattern is much less common in Europe and Japan. While the increasing prevalence of employment among in-school youth has generated much controversy in the United States, there has been little systematic study of the interrelations of school and work, two potentially important socialization contexts that occupy the better part of most American adolescents' waking hours.

Several national task forces have called for greater adolescent involvement in the workplace (Carnegie Council on Policy Studies in Higher Education, 1980; National Commission on Youth, 1980; President's Science Advisory Committee Panel on Youth, 1974; Wirtz, 1975) and parents' attitudes toward youth work are highly favorable (Phillips & Sandstrom, 1990). Some research points to benefits associated with adolescent work that could promote achievement in school. Greenberger and Steinberg's (1986) widely publicized study of four California high schools showed that employment was associated with self-reported punctuality, dependability, and personal responsibility (see also Greenberger, 1984; Steinberg, Greenberger, Garduque, Ruggiero, & McAuliffe, 1982); employment was also related to girls' sense of self-reliance (Greenberger, 1984). D'Amico's (1984) analysis of the NLS (National Longitudinal Study) youth data showed that employment at low intensity (less than 20 hours per week) lessened drop-out rates. He argued that both employers and schools reward personality traits that promote achievement. Self-discipline, mobilization of effort, and application to a task are necessary even in marginal jobs (Snedeker, 1982).

Nonetheless, the tone of recent scientific commentaries on youth employment is rather negative. Much of the concern about youth work arises from a belief that working may draw students away from school and reduce academic achievement. Greenberger and Steinberg (1986, p. 132) report that working adolescents are more frequently late for school and engage in more deviant behavior than those students who are not employed. Steinberg and Dornbusch (1991) also find that workers report more school misconduct than nonemployed students. Some investigators (Bachman, Bare, & Frankie, 1986; Marsh, 1991; Steinberg & Dornbusch, 1991) have linked decrements in adjustment to the number of hours of work, with adolescents working long hours particularly prone to problem behaviors such as delinquency and low achievement. Recent studies also suggest that long hours of work are linked to diminished involvement in school, as indicated by time spent doing homework, extracurricular participation, and grades (Greenberger & Steinberg, 1986; Mortimer & Finch, 1986). However, Steinberg and Dornbusch (1991) found that students who worked *moderate*, rather than long hours, reported the highest rates of school misconduct; there is a lack of consensus about the effect of employment on grades (D'Amico, 1984; Hotchkiss, 1982; Lewin-Epstein, 1981; Marsh, 1991; Schill, McCartin, & Meyer, 1985; Steinberg & Dornbusch, 1991; Steinberg, Greenberger, Garduque, Ruggiero, & McAuliffe, 1982; Steinberg, Greenberger, Garduque, Ruggiero & Vaux, 1982).

Prior research has thus considered the association between adolescent employment and a range of presumed outcomes that are of relevance to the young worker's attitudes, adjustment, and academic performance in the school context. Three analytically distinct issues are implicated in assessing the consequences of youth employment for the school setting. First, there is the question of employment status. Are there differences in school-related attitudes and behavior between students who work and those who are not employed? Second, one must consider the number of hours of work. Are the harms (and, possibly, benefits) that have been linked to employment primarily a function of work intensity? Greenberger and Steinberg (1986, p. 117) found that 10th graders who worked more than 15 hours per week had lower grade point averages. Third, there is the quality of work experience—some work may provide a wide range of intrinsic and extrinsic benefits and rewards; other jobs provide few rewards of either kind and confront the adolescent with new stressors for which coping mechanisms may be ill-developed.

Clearly, all three issues are deserving of systematic empirical scrutiny, though the first two have been given the most attention. With respect to employment status, adolescents who have paid jobs while they are in school have acquired a position in an environmental context that is entirely new to them. In this arena, they must enact an unfamiliar role that has major significance in the lives of adults. Just having a job may lead to changed self-concepts and new identities, new expectations of responsibility and independence on the part of parents (Phillips &

Sandstrom, 1990), and high status in the eyes of peers (Mortimer & Shanahan, 1991). Employment may bring the student into contact with working peers, as well as with adult workers. These coworkers may constitute new reference groups and provide models of more "grown-up" behaviors.

But, with reference to the second issue, as hours of employment increase, adolescents may experience growing difficulties in juggling the demands of work, school, and extracurricular activities, as well as commitments to family and friends. Greenberger and Steinberg (1986) warn that because work typically consumes so much time, some adolescents may miss out on a valuable "moratorium" period which should be available to allow them to explore alternative identities and to develop close interpersonal relationships. Those who are working long hours will also have less time available for homework and extracurricular activities.

The third consideration, the quality of work, may be somewhat controversial when applied to adolescent employment. The kinds of work that are most readily available to youth have been found to have the most negative psychological consequences for adults. In contrast, challenging and self-directed occupational conditions have beneficial outcomes, increasing adults' self-confidence, lessening anxiety, and fostering self-directed values (Kohn & Schooler, 1983; Slomczynski, Miller, & Kohn 1981). However, most young people work in the retail and service sectors in positions involving high turnover, low pay, little authority (Greenberger & Steinberg, 1981) and low prestige (Schill et al., 1985). They do simple repetitive tasks that require no special training or skills (Greenberger, Steinberg, & Ruggiero, 1982; Osterman, 1980). It could be argued that adolescent work is so homogeneous that investigation of the quality of youth work would have limited payoff. Yet, jobs that may seem routine from the standpoint of the adult may be viewed quite differently by a young person who is working for the first time. Adapting to the new rules and routines of the workplace environment, and building even simple job-related skills, may present quite a challenge to the young novice. When adolescents have work that enables the development of skills, provides opportunities for advancement, and allows other growth-inducing experiences, there could be a positive "spillover" effect, promoting positive school attitudes and academic achievement. However, work may also involve exposure to new stressors which are reflected in problems in the school realm. We have already shown that the quality of work experiences has significant consequences for employed adolescents' sense of internal control and depressive affect (Finch, Shanahan, Mortimer, & Ryu, 1991; Shanahan, Finch, Mortimer, & Rye, 1991) and these orientations could influence academic performance.

This research first examines 10th-grade adolescents' own views about the linkages of work and school. It then systematically considers all three issues—work status, work intensity, and work quality—in relation to the level of intrinsic motivation toward school work, school-related behaviors (time spent doing homework, time devoted to extracurricular activities, and school problem behavior), and academic achievement. We also examine whether prior school attitudes, behavior, and achievement influence subsequent employment status and the intensity of work.

Data Source

The data were obtained from the first and second waves of a 4-year longitudinal study of work experience in adolescence. The sample was chosen randomly from a list of enrolled ninth graders in the St. Paul (Minnesota) public school district. In the American school system, students enter first grade at about the age of 6, so most ninth-graders are 14 or 15 years of age. Characteristics of the sample and its representativeness, in relation to the entire student body and to American teenagers in general, are examined elsewhere (Finch et al., 1991; Mortimer, Finch, Shanahan, & Ryu, 1992). It is concluded that there is a reasonable basis for broad generalization of the findings.

While students initially filled out questionnaires in school classrooms, those who missed two in-school administrations were mailed questionnaires. Data were obtained from 1001 ninth graders and from 962 of these students one year later, yielding a retention rate of 96.1% across the two waves. As part of the first-wave data collection, mailed questionnaires were also obtained from 1,575 parents of the adolescent participants. They constituted 95% of all mothers and 90% of fathers who were living with the child. Parental attitudes toward adolescent work and information pertaining to socioeconmic status were thus obtained directly.

Measurement

Six dependent variables are the focus of this analysis: intrinsic motivation toward schoolwork, time spent in extracurricular activities, time spent doing homework, grade point average, and two measures of school problem behavior. The following items measure intrinsic motivation toward schoolwork (derived from Bachman's Youth in Transition Study, Bachman, O'Malley, & Johnston, 1978):

- I put a great deal of myself into some things at school because they have special meaning to me. (Response options for the first three items constituted a 4-point scale: *not at all true* to *very true*.)
- School helps me to improve my ability to think and to solve problems.
- I have little interest in my classes in school. (reversed)
- How often does time seem to drag for you in school? (options ranged from *never* to *almost always*)

Item loadings were derived from a confirmatory factor analysis, including both waves of data, using LISREL PC VI.3. A systematic assessment of the similarity of the measurement structure across waves, and for each sex, was performed by constraining corresponding lambda coefficients (analogous to factor loadings) to be equal across waves and groups. Goodness-of-fit tests showed that there was no significant difference between freely estimated and fully constrained (across waves and groups) models. Thus, the pattern of covariation among the items, which reflect their meaning in relation to one another, does not differ across waves and is the same for boys and girls. Therefore, we use unstandardized lambda coefficients derived from the fully constrained model (lambdas set to be equal across waves and groups) as item weights.

Students were asked how much time they spent doing homework and in extracurricular activities. On the average, these 10th-graders report 7 hours of homework per week, or about 1 hour per night. They spent 8 hours, on the average, in extracurricular activities. They also reported their current grade point averages. The first measure of school problem behavior assessed whether or not the adolescent got into any trouble at all in school (a dummy variable, coded 1 if there were any such behavior). The second expressed the frequency of such behavior. Both measures were derived from summing the following items (derived from Simmons & Blyth, 1987):

- Since the beginning of school this year, how often have you gotten into trouble for misbehaving or breaking school rules?
- Since the beginning of school this year, how often have you been sent to the principal's office or to detention because of something you have done?
  (Response options for each ranged from *never*, coded 1 to *more than 10 times*, coded 5.)

Adolescents were considered employed if working at least once a week, outside the home, for pay. Occasional sporadic employment and work done without monetary compensation do not meet these criteria. Work intensity was measured by hours of employment per week. The median number of hours worked in the 10th grade was 20 for boys and 15 for girls. Quality of work measures were obtained from several prior studies of adolescents and adults, including Bachman's Youth in Transition Study (Bachman et al., 1978), Quinn and Staines' (1979) Quality of Employment Survey, the Michigan Panel Study (Mortimer, Lorence, & Kumka, 1986), and Kohn and Schooler's (1983) national longitudinal study of American workers. Items representing similar work experience dimensions were subject to both exploratory and confirmatory factor analyses, and indices were constructed when indicated. Objective indicators of the complexity of work were derived from the Dictionary of Occupational Titles (U.S. Department of Labor, 1977).

In considering the possible effects of employment, hours of work, or the quality of work on adolescent school-related attitudes and behaviors, it is necessary to take possibly confounding factors into account. For example, if employed students of lower socioeconomic background work longer hours than those who come from more advantaged families (and we find that they do), this could fully account for the effects of hours of work. Moreover, minority students, students from more disadvantaged backgrounds, from single-parent households, or those who are foreign-born, may perhaps do more poorly in school. We thus control four background variables—socioeconomic status (an index comprised of parental education and family income), race (coded 1 if *white*, 0 if *other*), family composition (1 if *two-parent family*, 0 if *another family type*), and nativity (1 if *born in the U.S.*, 0 if born *elsewhere*).

Moreover, if students who have more negative school attitudes and behavior select themselves into employment, choose to work longer hours, or have different types of work experiences, any association between these presumed independent variables and the school-related phenomena could be attributable to processes of selection and to the stability of these variables over time. Therefore, we also control the lagged school attitudes and behaviors in our multivariate assessments of the effects of work.

Findings

Students' Perceptions of the Linkages between School and Work

We asked a series of questions about the employed students' perceptions of the connections between school and their work. There is no formal linkage between school and work for the majority of these students; very few—less than 10% in grade 10—said they were in a work-study program in the school or received school credit for their jobs. Less than one in five felt that their jobs provided information about things they were studying in school, or felt that they could contribute more to class discussion because of what they learned at work. Some reported interference between school and work—43% said that because of their jobs they had less time to do their homework. Perhaps because of this, half agreed that 'being both a worker and a student is stressful."

Still, many students perceived connections between work and school that are positive and mutually enhancing. Bronfenbrenner (1979) argues that when there is communication and mutual knowledge among the participants in various socialization settings, there is a more favorable "mesosystem" context for development than when such contexts are highly isolated from one another. As one indication of the degree of overlap we asked, "In class discussions at school, do the students ever talk about their jobs or get ideas about how to do their jobs better?" Almost half (47%) answered in the affirmative. Forty-eight percent thought that "my job has taught me the importance of getting a good education," and for almost a third, the job "has made me recognize the subjects I really like and don't like." Thirty-six percent agreed that "what I have learned in school helps me do better on my job."

When asked directly about whether they thought the job had affected their grades, the vast majority (73%) thought that it had no effect; 19% thought that their grades had gotten lower as a result of working, and 8% reported that their grades had improved. The students themselves do not appear to share the widespread view of educators and developmental psychologists that employment is detrimental to school achievement.

Work Status

Among the 10th-graders, 42% of the boys were employed, and 52% of the girls. There were no significant differences ($p < .05$) between students who were working and those who were not employed in intrinsic school motivation, time spent on homework or extracurricular activities or grade point average in the 10th grade (this was also the case in grade 9). Moreover, when each school-related variable was regressed on work status, the lagged variable, and the four control variables, employment status had no significant effect on any of them.

Examination of the distribution of school problem behavior showed that many adolescents do not report any such behavior: 34% of 10th-grade boys and 46% of the girls. Therefore, two questions are relevant. First, is work status related to engaging in school misconduct? Second, among those who do get in trouble at school, is work status associated with the frequency of involvement? There were no significant bivariate associations between work status and either participation in school problem behavior or frequency of involvement among those who participated. Moreover, work status had no effect on either of these variables when examined in a multivariate context, using logistic regression (predicting engagement) or OLS regression (predicting frequency). Thus, there is no evidence from these data that workers, in comparison to nonworkers, are less engaged in schoolwork, spend less time doing homework or in extracurricular activities, have lower levels of academic achievement, or are more apt to get into trouble at school.

It is conceivable, however, that students who are less interested in school, or who get in trouble at school, are more likely to enter the paid work force subsequently. To examine this possibility, we regressed 10th grade work status on each of the school-related variables, controlling the four background indicators, using logistic regression. We found no evidence that earlier disengagement from school increased the propensity to work. However, girls with *higher* intrinsic motivation toward school-work in grade 9 were *more* likely to be employed in grade 10 than girls with less positive attitudes toward school ($p < .05$).

Hours of Work

To assess the effects of work intensity, we first plot the relationship between work hours and the criteria. To explore the possibility that working a limited number of hours could give rise to benefits that do not accrue to students who are not employed, two sets of regression analyses were performed. In the first set, a "high hours" dummy was assigned the value of 1 if the student worked more than 15 hours per week; the "low hours" dummy was coded 1 if the student worked 15 or fewer hours (in these analyses, the reference category consists of the non-employed). This cutoff was chosen because of Greenberger and Steinberg's (1986) finding that 10th-grade students who work more than 15 hours per week have lower grades than those who work fewer hours. In the second set, the cutoff was more than 20 hours per week. After first observing the effect of the dummy hours variables considered alone, we add the lagged dependent variable and the background control variables to determine whether any significant effects of hours remain.

Figure 15.1 shows that there is no clear linear relationship between hours of work and intrinsic motivation toward school for either boys or girls. Highest motivation occurs among students who work relatively few hours (1–5). There is then a decline in intrinsic motivation as hours of work increase; but among girls working more than 25 hours, intrinsic

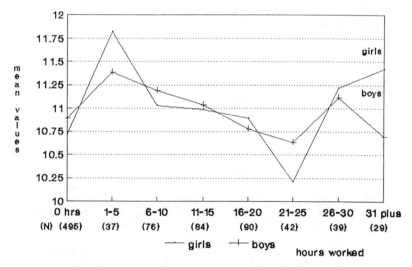

FIGURE 15.1. Intrinsic schoolwork motivation by hours worked for boys and girls.

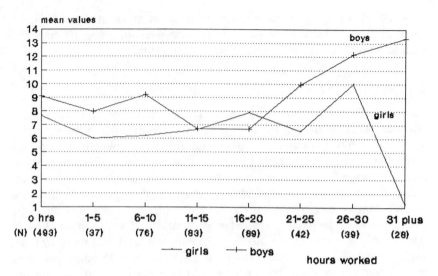

FIGURE 15.2. Extracurricular activities by hours worked for boys and girls.

motivation increases. Boys who worked at very low (1–5 hours) and at rather high (26–30 hours) intensity exhibited the highest intrinsic motivation. The analyses showed no differences between the dichotomous work intensity categories, with or without controls.

Similarly, we find no clear trend with respect to time spent in extra-curricular activities (see Figure 15.2), and no significant differences be-tween hours-of-work categories among girls. However, boys who worked

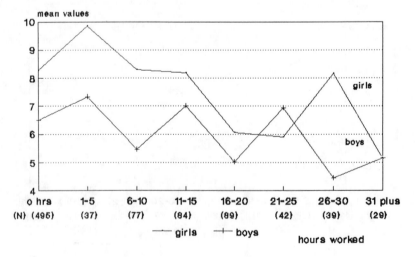

FIGURE 15.3. Time spent on homework by hours worked for boys and girls.

more than 20 hours per week had higher levels of extracurricular participation than boys who did not work ($\beta = .095$, $p < .05$); the difference
persisted with the lagged variable controlled. However, with the background variables also entered into the equation, it disappeared.

The bivariate relationship between homework time and hours of work
is presented in Figure 15.3. We see, for boys, that there is no discernible
pattern of relationship. For girls, time spent on homework is greatest
among those working a small amount of time, 1–5 hours, after which
point there is a decline in investment in homework to the 21–25 hours
interval, followed by an increase at 26–30 hours, and then further decline.

Table 15.1 shows the relationships between the low and high hours
dummy variables and time spent on homework (measured in minutes)
for girls. Girls who are employed more than 15 hours per week spend
significantly less time doing homework than students who work no hours
($\beta = -.102$, $p < .05$). When the time spent on homework during the
previous year is controlled, this effect remains ($\beta = -.086$, $p < .05$).
However, when the background variables are added (see Panel 3), the
relationship between hours of work and homework time becomes only
marginally significant ($p < .10$). (There are no significant differences
between girls who are employed more than 20 hours and those who are
not employed.) It is noteworthy that girls of higher socioeconomic status
spend more time doing homework. There are no significant relationships
between the work hours variables and time spent at homework for boys.

Academic achievement is probably the greatest concern to those who
have raised questions about youth work. Figure 15.4 suggests that work
hours may be deleterious to academic achievement. Among girls, there is
a gradual decline in grade point average from those working 1–5 hours
through the higher hours categories. Boys show a similar decline, which
becomes steeper after 30 hours.

TABLE 15.1. Effects of dichotomized hours of work on time spent on homework,
10th-grade girls.

	(1)		(2)		(3)	
	B/se	beta	B/se	beta	B/se	beta
Hours >15	−118./54.	−.102*	−100./51.	−.086*	−84.4/51.	−.076[a]
Hours ≤15	8.31/50.	.007	14.3/47.	.013	7.08/47.	.007
Homework, 9			.459/.05	.378***	.469/.06	.358***
SES					33.4/12.	.129**
Race					−5.48/50.	−.005
Nativity					120./82.	.066
Family composition					−35.8/44.	−.037
R^2		.011		.153		.160
p		.063		.000		.000
N		504		499		457

[a]$p < .10$; *$p < .05$; **$p < .01$; ***$p < .001$

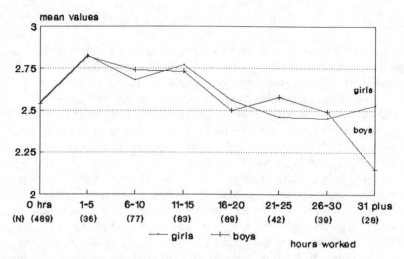

FIGURE 15.4. Grade point average by hours worked for boys and girls.

TABLE 15.2. Effects of dichotomized hours of work on grade point average, boys and girls.

	Boys					
	(1)		(2)		(3)	
	B/se	beta	B/se	beta	B/se	beta
Hours >15	−.068/.10	−.034	−.089/.08	−.044	−.100/.08	−.048
Hours ≤15	.246/.11	.107*	.104/.09	.045	.071/.09	.031
GPA 9			.613/.04	.626***	.579/.04	.584***
SES					.043/.02	.092*
Race					.121/.08	.062
Nativity					.209/.14	.062
Family composition					−.020/.07	−.011
R^2		.014		.402		.418
p		.044		.000		.000
N		440		425		394

	Girls					
	(1)		(2)		(3)	
	B/se	beta	B/se	beta	B/se	beta
Hours >15	−.042/.09	−.022	−.050/.07	−.026	−.068/.07	−.035
Hours ≤15	.182/.08	.102*	.081/.07	.045	.021/.07	.012
GPA			.647/.03	.650***	.629/.04	.631***
SES					.042/.02	.092*
Race					.059/.07	.032
Nativity					.044/.12	.014
Family composition					.047/.06	.027
R^2		.012		.432		.460
p		.048		.000		.000
N		496		482		443

$^*p < .05$; $^{***}p < .001$

Turning to Table 15.2, it is noteworthy that students who work more intensely are not disadvantaged, when compared with the nonworkers, with respect to academic achievement. None of the coefficients for the "high hours" category, representing students who work more than 15 hours per week, indicate a significant difference in grade point in comparison to those who are not employed. But boys and girls who work *fewer* hours do better in school than those who are employed (for boys, the beta coefficient for the effect of "low hours" is .107, $p < .05$; for girls it is of similar magnitude, .102, $p < .05$). However, when we control the lagged variable (Panel 2) and both lagged and background variables (Panel 3), the significant relationship between "low hours" and grades in each case disappears. (There are no significant hours coefficients in any of the equations when the 20 hours cutoff is used.)

From Figures 15.5 and 15.6 it would appear that both engagement in, and amount of, school problem behavior increases with work hours. We used logistic regression to predict engagement in school problem behavior (coded 1 if the student reported any behavioral problems at all, 0 otherwise), first examining the high hours–low hours variables alone, then with the lagged variable, and finally adding the background controls. Neither of the hours variables significantly predicted engagement in any model specification. With respect to the frequency of school problem behavior (for those who participate), there were no differences between those who work more than 15 hours, or more than 20 hours, and those who are not employed. However, boys and girls who work less than 20 hours report *less* problem behavior than those who are not employed. Table 15.3 shows that only among boys who work less than 20 hours is

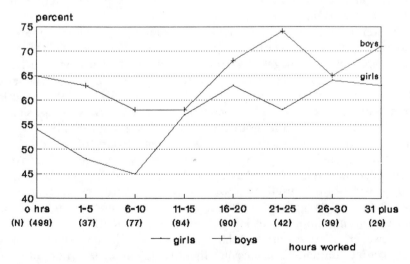

FIGURE 15.5. Percent who engage in school problem behavior by hours worked.

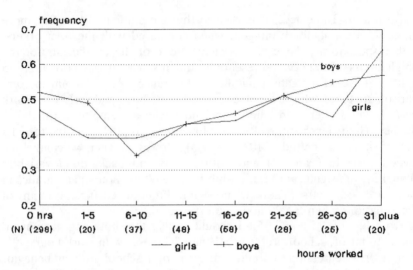

FIGURE 15.6. Frequency of problem behavior (for those who engage in such behavior).

there a significant decrease in the frequency of problem behavior (among those who engage), which persists when the controls are added.

It could be argued that these mostly null findings are due to a mis-specification of work intensity. Perhaps the true relationship between hours and the criteria is obscured by the dichotomous categorization of hours. Moreover, while we compare students who work more and less intensively with those who are not employed, there may be greater interest in whether those who work at higher intensity are different from those who work fewer hours.

Therefore, we deleted non-employed students and examined the relationships between hours of work and the criteria. For employed students, there are significant negative zero-order correlations between 10th-grade students' work hours and grades for boys ($r = -.255, p < .001$) and girls ($r = -.153. p < .05$). Work intensity is also negatively related to girls' homework time ($r = -.145, p < .05$). (Hours of work were not significantly related to intrinsic motivation in the 10th grade for either boys or girls, or to girls' extracurricular involvement. Hours of work bore a positive association, $r = .181, p < .05$, to boys' participation in extracurricular activities.) It is thus apparent that with this specification of hours, some of our results appear to be consistent with Greenberger and Steinberg's (1986) research, which links high work intensity to a lack of investment in school and to low academic achievement.

However, these bivariate relationships must also be examined in a multivariate format. First, because there is systematic selection into employment, we control a selection-to-work hazard rate (Heckman, 1976,

TABLE 15.3. Effects of dichotomized hours of work on frequency of school problem behavior, boys and girls.

| | Boys | | | | | |
| | (1) | | (2) | | (3) | |
	B/se	beta	B/se	beta	B/se	beta
Hours >20	.202/.38	.032	.222/.33	.034	.178/.35	.028
Hours ≤20	−.900/.33	−.160**	−.596/.30	−.106*	−.626/.31	−.113*
Problem behavior, 9			.428/.05	.482***	.402/.05	.445***
SES					−.081/.08	−.057
Race					.027/.30	.005
Nativity					−.820/.62	−.074
Family composition					−.325/.26	.067
R^2		.029		.258		.264
p		.015		.000		.000
N		292		286		266

| | Girls | | | | | |
| | (1) | | (2) | | (3) | |
	B/se	beta	B/se	beta	B/se	beta
Hours >20	.348/.37	.058	.155/.33	.026	.220/.36	.035
Hours ≤20	−.472/.24	−.123*	−.241/.213	−.063	−.218/.23	−.057
Problem behavior 9			.415/.05	.486***	.416/.05	.495***
SES					.100/.07	.083
Race					−.203/.26	−.047
Nativity					−.492/.53	−.052
Family composition					−.353/.23	−.090
R^2		.023		.253		.275
p		.046		.000		.000
N		273		271		248

$^* p < .05; ^{**} p < .01; ^{***} p < .001$

1979) which indicates the propensity to be employed, estimated on the basis of background variables and the timing of first employment (see Finch et al., 1991). Second, we examine the relationships controlling the lagged dependent variable. Finally, we subject the relationships to all relevant controls.

Table 15.4 shows that there is a significant negative effect of girls' work hours on time spent on homework ($\beta = -.138$, $p < .05$). However, when the lagged variable is taken into account, the effect of work intensity on homework time becomes marginally signficant. When all relevant control variables are entered, the coefficient for girls remains at this near-significant level. Thus, the pattern of findings is similar to that using the dichotomized hours specification (see Table 15.1). Moreover, as reported

TABLE 15.4. Effects of work hours on homework time and grades, 10th-grade boys and girls.

	Homework time, boys					
	(1)		(2)		(3)	
	B/se	beta	B/se	beta	B/se	Beta
Hours	−4.31/3.3	−.108	−3.48/3.29	−.088	−1.53/3.4	−.038
R^2		.012		.038		.082
p		.408		.136		.095
N		149		148		147

	Homework time, girls					
	(1)		(2)		(3)	
	B/se	beta	B/se	beta	B/se	Beta
Hours	−6.42/3.15	−.138*	−5.60/3.05	−.119[a]	−6.35/3.28	−.128[a]
R^2		.019		.124		.145
p		.128		.000		.000
N		220		218		216

	Grades, boys					
	(1)		(2)		(3)	
	B/se	beta	B/se	beta	B/se	Beta
Hours	−.020/.006	−.259**	−.011/.005	−.140*	−.010/.005	−.130[b]
R^2		.067		.438		.462
p		.007		.000		.000
N		147		143		142

	Grades, girls					
	(1)		(2)		(3)	
	B/se	beta	B/se	beta	B/se	Beta
Hours	−.012/.006	−.143*	−.004/.004	−.052	−.006/.004	−.068
R^2		.032		.451		.492
p		.031		.000		.000
N		219		212		210

[a] $p = .054$
[b] $p = .052$
(1) Each equation includes the selection to work hazard rate.
(2) Each equation includes the selection to work hazard and the lagged variable—9th grade homework time or grades.
(3) Each equation includes the selection to work hazard, the lagged variable, socioeconomic status, race, nativity, and family composition.

earlier, boys' work intensity has no significant effect on time spent doing homework.

Analysis of work intensity and grades, with the same sequence of controls, shows that grades diminish with long hours ($\beta = -.259$, $p < .01$ for boys, and $\beta = -.143$, $p < .05$ for girls). When the lagged variable is introduced, the effect disappears for girls (see Panel 2) and remains

TABLE 15.5. Effects of work hours on engagement in school problem behavior, logistic regression,[1] boys.

	Odds ratio	t	p
Hours	1.09	2.29	.022
	[1.01–1.17][a]		
Complexity data	.59	−2.03	.043
	[.359–.983]		
School problem 9	27.82	3.92	.000
	[5.26–147]		

[a] 95% confidence intervals.
[1] Controlling socioeconomic status, race, nativity, family composition and the selection to work hazard, none of which had statistically significant odds ratios.

statistically significant ($\beta = -.140$, $p < .05$) for boys. However, when all controls are introduced, there is only a near-significant coefficient for boys ($\beta = -.130$, $p = .052$). (The multivariate analyses of the effect of work hours on extracurricular activities and intrinsic motivation toward school are not presented because none of the hours coefficients were statistically significant.)

Finally, we assessed the effect of work intensity, considered as a continuous variable, on school problem behavior. Boys who worked longer hours were more likely to engage in problem behavior in school ($p < .05$), as indicated by a multivariate logit analysis (see Table 15.5),[1] but there was no evidence that girls' engagement in problem behavior was affected by work hours. The amount of problem behavior, among those who engage, was not influenced by work hours for either gender.

In summary, we find no compelling evidence that employment at higher intensity increases the risk of poor school attitudes, problem behavior in school, diminished time invested in homework or extracurricular activities, or poor school grades. The bivariate relationships between work intensity, on the one hand, and indicators of investment and achievement with respect to school, on the other, appear to be largely spurious, attributable to processes of selection. After relevant controls are introduced, these relationships generally become weak and marginally significant, or they disappear altogether. In no case were those students who were employed relatively long hours (more than 15, or more than 20) found to be disadvantaged in comparison to students who were not employed. There was no evidence that students of either gender who

---

[1] Table 15.5 includes the complexity of work with data, which was also found to influence boys' school problem behavior, as a predictor (see section on "The Quality of Adolescent Work").

worked more intensively exhibited more problem behavior than those who were not employed. But when we restrict the analysis to employed boys (see Table 15.5), we find that work intensity (measured continuously) is positively associated with the propensity to engage in problem behavior in school. As indicated in Figure 15.5, this is attributable more to the depressed rates of school problem behavior among those boys who work at low intensity than to any pronounced difference in engagement between those who work at high intensity and those who are not employed. In fact, with respect to the frequency of participation in school problem behavior, Figure 15.6 and Table 15.3 suggest that low intensity employment may have a protective effect for boys. Among those who engaged in school problem behavior, those working 20 hours per week or less reported significantly fewer instances of these problems that those who were not employed.

We then assessed whether students select themselves into employment on the basis of prior, school-related variables; that is, whether intensity of work is a product, rather than a cause, of school orientation and behavior. Deleting students who did not work in the 10th grade, we regressed 10th-grade work hours (measured continuously) on the school-related variables, measured in the 9th grade (controlling the selection-to-work hazard, socioeconomic status, race, family composition, and nativity). Ninth-grade intrinsic motivation toward schoolwork, grade point average, time spent doing homework, and time spent in extracurricular activities had no significant effects on 10th-grade work hours for either boys or girls. Ninth grade school problem behavior (those who did not participate were assigned a value of 0 in this analysis) did, however, have a near-significant positive effect on boys' work hours ($\beta = .143$, $p = .087$) and a significant effect, in the same direction, among girls ($\beta = .164$, $p < .05$). Thus, *prior* school problem behavior may lead adolescents to work at higher levels of intensity.

The Quality of Adolescent Work

In examining the effects of the quality of adolescent work on the school-related criteria, we assessed intrinsic experiences and rewards (the extent to which the job offers opportunities for skill learning and the exercise of self-direction), extrinsic experiences and rewards (advancement opportunity, pay, and the student's evaluation of his or her pay), the context of work (whether informal, in a private household; or formal, in other employment contexts), the complexity of job tasks, and the stressfulness of work (e.g., as indicated by role strain, work stress, and responsibility for things that are beyond one's control). We find evidence that opportunities for skill development increase girls' intrinsic motivation toward schoolwork. We measured job skills by an index composed of the following five items: "How much has your job helped you to develop the following abilities: to follow directions, to get along with people, to be on time, and to take responsibility for your work?"; "Do you think that the things you are learning in your job will be useful to you in your later life?" The relationship between this measure of skills learned on the job and girls' intrinsic motivation in grade 10 remained statistically significant ($\beta = .147$, $p < .05$) even when the selection-to-work hazard, the lagged psychological construct, and four background variables were controlled. While the opportunity to acquire job skills was not significantly related to boys' school attitudes, more complex work with data lessened boys' propensity to engage in school problem behavior ($p < .05$), in a logit regression including current job hours (which, as noted earlier, was also found to influence boys' school problem behavior, see Table 15.5).

Work stressors appear to have negative consequences for schoolwork. The index of work stress included time pressure, work overload, the need to work very hard, the feeling of being "drained of energy" after work, and exposure to excessive heat, cold, or noise. Work stress ($\beta = -.157$) and the responsibility for things that are seen as beyond one's control ($\beta = -.136$) diminished the time that girls spent doing homework ($p < .05$ for each, controlling the four background variables, the selection-to-work hazard, and the lagged dependent variable). Boys' job stresses are reflected in more frequent school problem behavior (among those who participate), as indicated by significant positive effects of work stress ($\beta = .205$, $p < .05$), and responsibility for things that are beyond one's control ($\beta = .261$, $p < .01$).[2] Indicators of the quality of work bore no relationship to boys' or girls' participation in extracurricular activities or to grade point average.

Conclusion

As we have seen, many youth perceive their jobs and school as mutually enhancing, reporting class discussions relevant to their jobs, or that their jobs led to greater appreciation of the value of education or a better understanding of their academic interests. Though about half the respondents indicated stress in combining their student and worker roles or indicated difficulty in getting their homework done because of their jobs, relatively few thought that their grades had actually suffered as a result of working. This perception is quite congruent with that obtained from parents, the vast majority of whom reported that their children's work

---

[2] Given moderate correlations between work stressors and responsibility for things that are beyond one's control ($.34$, $p < .001$ for girls; and $.33$, $p < .001$ for boys) their effects are assessed separately rather than pitting them against one another. When they are both included in the same equations, no significant effects on the school-related variables, for either gender, are produced.

had no effect on their grades. Many parents thought that because of working their children had, in fact, become more competent in allocating their time. They reported that their children developed greater confidence and a stronger sense of responsibility which enabled them to cope more effectively with the demands of schoolwork (Phillips & Sandstrom, 1990).

In view of the findings, we cannot conclude that working itself is deleterious at this age. In fact, comparisons of workers and nonworkers revealed no significant differences on the school-related variables. The impacts of work intensity on the outcomes were insignificant on a bivariate level or became so after the application of appropriate controls. Indeed, there was some evidence of a protective effect of low-intensity employment with respect to boys' problem behavior in school.

Little attention has been given in prior studies to the effects of the quality of adolescent work experiences on school-related attitudes and behavior. We find that when girls perceive that they are obtaining valuable skills from their jobs, their intrinsic motivation toward schoolwork increases. Boys who do more complex work with data have a weaker tendency to engage in school problem behavior than those who do less complex work. Thus, adolescent work that is challenging has favorable repercussions in the school realm.[3] However, in the face of job stressors, girls reduce the time they spend on homework, and boys, problem behavior (for those who participate) increases. These conditions of work represent environmental demands for adaptation in a new life cycle context that has growing salience (see Kellam, Rebok, Mayer, & Wilson, this volume), though the adolescent's ability to cope with these demands may be limited. Given these trends, future research should assess which contexts of employment are more or less stressful, and which lead to the perceived enhancement of job skills as students go through high school. In this way, we might gain further insight into the kinds of jobs that are most beneficial and least interfering with schoolwork.

Gender differences in these "mesosystem interrelations" (Bronfenbrenner, 1979) also deserve further scrutiny. The positive effects of work stressors on the frequency of boys' problem behavior may be linked to a general tendency for boys to "act out" when they are distressed, whereas girls may be more likely to internalize their problems. But it is unclear why the attainment of skills at work increases girls', but not boys', intrinsic motivation toward schoolwork.

Despite these findings, the analyses suggest that work is probably not a major influence on the school-related outcomes, confirming the views

---

[3] The sense of challenge and psychological engagement stimulated by work that involves complex problem solving and promotes skill acquisition would likely have other developmentally beneficial consequences as well (see Larson, this volume).

of parents and the adolescents themselves. A large body of evidence indicates the significance of the family and the peer group for school achievement and other educationally-relevant outcomes (see Steinberg & Darling and Oswald & Uwe, this volume); these contexts are probably of far greater importance than work. Our efforts to find differences between employed and non-employed youth were not successful. Neither can we confirm others' assertions that long hours of work cut into time spent doing homework or investment in extracurricular activities, or lead to a reduction in grade point average. There was evidence, to the contrary, that students who already are engaged in school misconduct chose to invest in work—by working longer hours—the following year. Moreover, most of our quality-of-work indicators were not significantly related to the criteria.

In view of this general pattern of findings, it may be useful in future studies to examine the reciprocal effects of school on work, giving greater attention to school-related orientations and behaviors that could influence students' work behavior. After all, secondary school students have spent many years in the school context, but only a relatively short time in paid employment (most American students begin to work outside the home at about the age of twelve, often in informal jobs such as baby-sitting and yard work). Prior school experiences, previously developed orientations toward education, academic performance, and other behaviors in the school context may, in fact, be the more powerful influences, affecting the adolescent's investment in work as well, perhaps, as reactions to that employment. We must consider the reasons why youth who are exhibiting problems in school choose to invest more of their time in paid work. Is it because they are looking for an alternate context in which to achieve a sense of self-esteem and efficacy, after having failed to find support for these positive self-concepts in the school environment? Do students who are having difficulties in the school context seek an "arena of comfort" (Simmons & Blyth, 1987) in the workplace? It could be that our small set of school-related variables do not represent the full range of educational orientations and behaviors that could influence the propensity to work.

We concluded earlier (Mortimer et al., 1992), on the basis of a cross-sectional analysis of the first-wave data obtained from the ninth graders, that the highly negative, even alarming, tone of some recent commentaries on adolescent work may be overdrawn. This conclusion is only strengthened by the present analysis of longitudinal data obtained from students as they move from grade 9 to grade 10. Still, it may be that deleterious effects of working come later, after the 10th grade of schooling. Based on an analysis of the nationally representative High School and Beyond data, Marsh (1991) finds that hours worked during high school have negative effects on 16 of 22 academic outcomes, including grades, time spent on homework, and getting into trouble in school and elsewhere. Of particular importance in that study, hours worked during the 10th grade had much less pervasive implications (negative effects on only 7 of 22 out-comes) than work intensity in the 11th and 12th grades. (While Marsh reports, in agreement with our findings, that hours of 10th grade work have no significant effects on grades and time spent on homework, measured in the senior year, he also notes that sophomore hours of work significantly predict senior disciplinary problems.) The juxtaposition of these two studies raises the possibility that the meaning of work, as well as its consequences, changes as adolescents grow older and acquire greater work experience. With data from the junior and senior years of high school, we will continue to monitor the effects of employment, work intensity, and the quality of work experiences on the school-related attitudes and behaviors of youth.

Acknowledgments. The research was supported by a grant from the National Institute of Mental Health (MH42843), "Work Experience and Adolescent Well-being."

References

Bachman, J.G., Bare, D.E., & Frankie, E.I. (1986). *Correlates of employment among high school seniors.* Ann Arbor: Institute for Social Research.

Bachman, J.G., O'Malley, P.M., & Johnston, J. (1978). *Youth in transition: Vol VI. Adolescence to adulthood—change and stability in the lives of young men.* Ann Arbor: Survey Research Center, Institute for Social Research.

Bronfenbrenner, U. (1979). *The ecology of human development: Experiments by nature and by design.* Cambridge: Harvard University Press.

Carnegie Council on Policy Studies in Higher Education. (1980). *Giving youth a better change.* San Francisco: Jossey-Bass.

D'Amico, R.J. (1984). Does employment during high school impair academic progress? *Sociology of Education*, 57, 152–164.

Finch, M.D., Shanahan, M.J., Mortimer, J.T., & Ryu, S. (1991). Work experience and control orientation in adolescence. *American Scociological Review*, 56, 597–1611.

Greenberger, E. (1984). Children, families, and work. In N.D. Reppucci, L.A. Weithorn, E.P. Mulvey, and J. Monahan (Eds.), *Children, mental health, and the law* (pp. 103–122). Beverly Hills: Sage.

Greenberger, E. & Steinberg, L.D. (1981). The workplace as a context for the socialization of youth. *Journal of Youth and Adolescence*, 10, 185–210.

Greenberger, E. & Steinberg, L.D. (1986). *When teenagers work: The psychological and social costs of adolescent employment.* New York: Basic Books.

Greenberger, E., Steinberg, L.D., & Ruggiero, M. (1982). A job is a job is a job . . . or is it? *Work and Occupations*, 9, 79–96.

Heckman, J.J. (1976). The common structure of statistical models of truncation, sample selection and limited dependent variables and a simple estimator for such models. *Annals of Economic and Social Measurement*, 5, 475–492.

Heckman, J.J. (1979). Sample selection as a specification error. *Econometrica*, *45*, 153–161.

Hotchkiss, L. (1982). *Effects of work time on school activities and career expectations*. Columbus: National Center for Research in Vocational Education.

Kohn, J.L. & Schooler, C. (1983). *Work and personality: An inquiry into the impact of social stratification*. Norwood, NJ: Albex Publishing.

Lewin-Epstein, N. (1981). *Youth employment during high school*. Washington, DC: National Center for Educational Statistics.

Marsh, H.W. (1991). Employment during high school: Character building or a subversion of academic goals? *Sociology of Education*, *64*, 172–189.

Mortimer, J.T. & Finch, M.D. (1986). The effects of part-time work on self-concept and achievement. In K.M. Borman & J. Reisman (Eds.), *Becoming a worker* (pp. 66–89). Norwood, NJ: Ablex Publishing.

Mortimer. J.T., Finch, M.D., Shanahan, M.J., & Ryu, S. (1992). Work experience, mental health, and behavioral adjustment in adolescence. *Journal of Research on Adolescence*, *2*, 25–57.

Mortimer, J.T., Lorence, J., & Kumka, D.S. (1986). *Work, family and personality: Transition to adulthood*. Norwood, NJ: Ablex Publishing.

Mortimer, J.T. & Shanahan, M.J. (1991). *Adolescent work experience and relations with peers*. Paper to be presented at the American Sociological Association Annual Meeting, Cincinnati.

National Commission on Youth. (1980). *The transition to adulthood: A bridge too long*. Boulder, CO: Westview Press.

Osterman, P. (1980). *Getting started: The youth labor market*. Cambridge: MIT Press.

President's Science Advisory Committee Panel on Youth. (1974). James S. Coleman, Chair. *Youth: Transition to adulthood*. Chicago: University of Chicago Press.

Phillips, S. & Sandstrom, K.L. (1990). Parental attitudes towards youth work. *Youth and Society*, *22*, 160–183.

Quinn, R.P. & Staines, G.L. (1979). *The 1977 Quality of Employment Survey*. Ann Arbor: Institute for Social Research.

Schill, W.J., McCartin, R., & Meyer, K. (1985). Youth employment: Its relationship to academic and family variables. *Journal of Vocational Behavior*, *26*, 155–163.

Shanahan, M.J., Finch, M.D., Mortimer, J.T., & Ryu, S. (1991). Adolescent work experience and depressive affect. *Social Psychology Quarterly*, *54*, 299–319.

Simmons, R.G. & Blyth, D.A. (1987). *Moving into adolescence: The impact of pubertal change and school context*. New York: Aldine de Groyter.

Slomczynski, K., Miller, J., & Kohn, M.L. (1981). Stratification, work, and values: A Polish–United States comparison. *American Sociological Review*, *46*, 720–744.

Snedeker, G. (1982). *Hard Knocks: Preparing youth for work*. Baltimore: Johns Hopkins University Press.

Steinberg, L.D. & Dornbusch, S.M. (1991). Negative correlates of part-time employment during adolescence: Replication and elaboration. *Developmental Psychology*, *27*, 304–313.

Steinberg, L.D., Greenberger, E., Garduque, L., Ruggiero, M., & McAuliffe, S. (1982). High school students in the labor force: Some costs and benefits to schooling and learning. *Education Evaluation and Policy Analysis*, *4*, 363–372.

Steinberg, L.D., Greenberger, E., Garduque, L., Ruggiero, M., & Vaux, A. (1982). Effects of work in adolescent development. *Developmental Psychology*, *18*, 385–395.

U.S. Department of Labor, Employment and Training Administration. (1977). *Dictionary of Occupational Titles* (4th ed.). Washington, DC: U.S. Government Printing Office.

Wirtz, W. (1975). *The boundless resource: A prospectus for an education/work policy*. Washington, DC: New Republic Book Co.

16
The Effects of Sponsored Mobility: Educational Careers of Adolescents in West Germany

UWE ENGEL AND KLAUS HURRELMANN

Introduction

The present analysis deals with two aspects of educational careers of adolescents to shed some light on the way contextual features of family and school interact in favoring, or even producing, developmental risks within the status transition to adulthood, namely, (a) How the probability of school failure depends on a *familial* background characteristic and the way this very characteristic is distributed within the *school* context, and (b) How educational careers involve career-, not origin-specific potentials of psychological stress if viewed diachronically in a 2- to 4-year perspective.

To make clear how these aspects and their corresponding hypotheses relate to the German situation, two things will be outlined first: (a) How the institutionalized type of educational mobility affects the distribution of collective resources and (b) How this institutionalization makes for educational careers established early on in the transition to adulthood.

The importance of the *context-interaction hypothesis* will become apparent in starting with a most prominent sociological explanation for the fact that one's status attainments do now, as before, depend largely on one's social class origin. A well-known explanation for this correlation is in terms of resources are available for supporting the adolescent's educational career and simply says: The more such resources are available, the more likely is scholastic and, in turn, occupational success.

Though such a statement will be valid on the whole, it risks falling short of fully acknowledging the variety of potential resources and, most importantly, the conditions that prevent existing potentials from becoming effective resources at all. A recently noted case in point concerns the lack of parental investments in time and effort spent that can prevent existing cultural potentialities within high-status families from being utilized as resources for the offspring's scholastic development (Coleman, 1988). Another easily overlooked case in point concerns institutional arrangements that affect basic social recruitment processes into school and hence, the within-classroom availability of what was called "free resources" (Coleman, 1972, p. 152). Consequently, only a refined explanation in terms of resources (social and cultural capital) will bear the criticism.

By affecting those recruitment processes and consolidating them afterwards, the predominant type of mobility also shapes the school context in terms of (adherence to) social values from the students' families. The resulting value context may correspond to the values learned at home, but may also contradict the students' value commitments, depending on what values dominate in the school context (due to recruiting) and whether a student (as part of this context) belongs to this local "cultural majority" or not. In sponsored mobility systems, value conflicts can arise due to reference group change; for instance, in the case of students from low-status families realizing educational upward mobility in school contexts with an above-average proportion of classmates coming from high-status families. In particular, mental health risks are due to such kinds of interacting contexts.

The Social Capital Perspective

In sociology, social capital theory represents a most prominent attempt to explain how social class reproduction takes place in modern industrial societies. Actually three concepts are involved in that attempt, namely, the concept of "social capital" as well as its twin concepts of "cultural" and "financial" capital (Bourdieu, 1983).

The *cultural capital* of a student is usually seen to consist of specific characteristics of the family context that he or she can use to achieve, for example, academic goals. Collins (1979), in referring to the Bourdieu approach, states:

The key concept is "cultural capital," a set of cultural outlooks and predispositions that children receive from their home environment and invest in formal education. This capital determines their progress through the schools and is cumulatively enhanced or diminished, according to the previous accumulation of cultural capital, at any transition point among different levels and types of schooling within the system. (p. 9)

Educational capital can be understood as cultural capital in an incorporated state and be regarded as a characteristic specific to an individual. It differs from *social capital* in that the latter is a genuinely collective (emergent) characteristic as a component in social relationships. Whereas the accumulation of educational capital can take place even without being anchored within a specific context of social relations, the acquisition of social capital is always connected to such a social network. It is precisely this capital that the individual can exploit because of his or her integration into a specific network: Being anchored in such a network of social relationships is a condition sine qua non of social capital—even when it is finally always individual or collective actors who use this capital as a resource in order to achieve particular goals. As Bourdieu, 1983, p. 191) notes: "The extent of social capital held by an individual is determined by both the size of the network of relationships which he/she can *actually mobilize* [italics added] and the amount of (economic, cultural, or symbolic) capital held by those persons with whom he/she is related".

For the adolescents, usually the parents are considered the primary persons in this respect. Only the adherence to the parental network creates the options with which the potentials within the family can be utilized effectively for one's own development. However, we cannot assume that this is always the case. Rather, the structure of the family and the amount of time and attention that parents devote to their children's intellectual development determine whether the available educational potential can be utilized as a social resource or social capital (Coleman, 1988, p. S110). But even when these investments are made, their impact can be annulled by psychological or other kinds of factors that make it difficult to approach the adolescent offspring.

Among these other and easily overlooked factors are institutional arrangements: Educational success as well as availability of privileged educational certificates, in their function as "cultural credentials" (Collins, 1979; Murphy, 1988) within the status attainment process, is more than just a simple function of the student's social class; rather, they are products of an interaction between social class characteristics and the institutionalized structure of the school system.

Youth in Germany: Sponsored Mobility to Adulthood

This interaction becomes clear from the fact that in the West German school system competition primarily does not take place as "contest mobility," but is more a form of "sponsored mobility" (Turner, 1960), realized via early allocation to one of four different tracks that vary in terms of the possibilities they entail. Such early career-influencing "branching points" take effect at the beginning of the initial secondary stage by delegating the individual students (on the basis of institutional recommendations and parents' wishes) to differently privileged forms of secondary school. These forms have been described as a "**sponsored mobility system**, in that once the branching point has been reached, the rest of the student's career is set, and the student who passes this point is sponsored through successive levels without much attrition." (Collins, 1979, p. 91). Since the tracks are differently privileged in terms of the postscholastic career chances they convey, and since there is only minor between-track mobility after first allocation, it is nothing but rational for the individual family to choose a track in such a way as to keep the

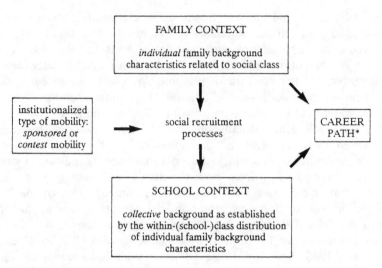

FIGURE 16.1. Institutionalized type of mobility in bringing forth interacting family and school contexts. *Including, e.g., career-specific resource pattern and mental health risks.

offspring's long-term career prospects. Consequently, this form of institutionalized mobility heavily affects the social recruitment processes into secondary school tracks and hence, permanently shapes the school context (as represented in each classroom community) in terms of those family background characteristics that underlie this very recruiting. This basic mechanism to bring forth interacting contexts simply by means of institutionally supported forms of within-(school-)class aggregation of family background characteristics is displayed in Figure 16.1 and underlies both hypotheses reported below.

The West German Secondary School Tracks

As noted above, the West German secondary school system consists of tracks that represent a clear, cumulative scale in terms of the career opportunities they convey (Max-Planck-Institute, 1983). The least opportunities are offered by the *Hauptschule* (vocational preparatory school); the *Gymnasium* (grammar school) offers the best opportunities, including university entrance qualifications; the *Realschule* (intermediate school) is situated between these two. Together, they form the traditional three-level school system to which, with the introduction of the *Gesamtschule* (comprehensive school) during the 1970s, a school type was added that is strongly track-immanent, with greater orientation toward the realization of contest mobility.

In view of the sponsored mobility type of the German school system it comes as no surprise that social class has a pronounced effect on the choice of secondary school track. For Germany, it holds by and large: The higher the family status, the greater the probability that the family's children will attend the type of secondary school offering the best postscholastic career prospects. Accordingly, the lower and middle social classes are concentrated in the lower tracks of secondary school, Hauptschule and Realschule, whereas the upper social classes let their children mainly attend the privileged Gymnasium track. Within the Gesamtschule, the social classes are more evenly distributed.

To provide an idea of the official figures involved for Germany: In 1989–1990, 31.7% of all seventh graders attended the Hauptschule, 27.1% the Realschule track, and 31.2% the Gymnasium; just 5.9% attended the Gesamtschule (4.1% were at special schools for handicapped children) (Hansen & Rolff, 1990, p. 48). As in other industrial societies, in Germany a remarkable (and still ongoing) run on higher education has taken place in the long run: The Hauptschule, which was originally conceived as a standard track, has increasingly lost favor in comparison to the Realschule and, above all, to the Gymnasium. Official statistics show that whereas in 1952/53 a total of 79.3% of all seventh graders attended the Hauptschule, this figure dropped to 31.7% in 1989/90. In the same period, the proportion of seventh graders attending the Gymnasium rose from 13.2% to 31.2% (the 1989/90 figures as indicated above).

Hypotheses

We assume that children's educational success is not only determined by the resources available in the family, but that the resources that result from the relationships to peers (e.g., classmates) also play a decisive role. In particular, we assume not only the adolecent's *individual* background to be an important factor influencing educational success. The adolescent's peers stem from specific social backgrounds too, and are therefore also "carriers" of social conditions they "bring with them into school," to use this metaphor. Within each classroom, there thus emerges a distribution of such background variables that, as contextual features, can take on the function of *collective* resources for all persons attending this class (regarding the impact of student body characteristics on achievement (growth), see Coleman et al., 1966, pp. 302–312; Coleman & Hoffer, 1987, pp. 82f.; and Lee & Bryk, 1989, pp. 182f.; for possible variations in the degree of this type of context dependence see also McPartland & McDill, 1982, p. 82; and the reply to critics by Coleman, Hoffer & Kilgore, 1982; see Gamoran, 1987, p. 142; and Raudenbush & Bryk, 1986, pp. 10f.).

Therefore, the structure of the West German school system is of some importance, inasmuch as the social classes are (as they actually are) unevenly distributed across the different tracks. For if we regard a high family status to be a resource for the children's intellectual development, then the origin-specific recruitment as such must lead to an accumulation of this (potential) resource at the top of the vertical school structure: the greater the number of children from high-status families attending the same (school-)class, the higher the collective status of this class, as constituted by the relative frequency of the involved, already favorable (in themselves) background variables.

A vertically structured school system that is oriented toward sponsored mobility contributes, by way of its underlying social recruitment processes, to the fact that the proportion of classes with high collective status increases with the quality of the respective school type: In the FRG this means from Hauptschule, over Realschule, on to the Gymnasium. Best chances would then have students from high-status families attending high-status classroom communities, since advantages accumulate in that case, as do disadvantages in the opposite configuration. Most interesting, then, are the low-high and high-low configurations referred to in Hypotheses 1 and 2 below.

Hypothesis 1

Hypothesis 1 refers to the high-low status configurations and states: In sponsored mobility systems, an in itself favorable individual social background (i.e., a given familial potential of resources) does favor the offspring's scholastic success (in terms of avoided setbacks in school progress) only if this background is predominant also as a collective resource of the (school-)class attended. Otherwise, a favorable background increases the probability of scholastic failure.

There is a major reason to be said for this hypothesis, namely that scholastic failure is rather a function of the *career path* than of more or less advantageous family backgrounds. If in the FRGs sponsored mobility system a child from a high-status family attends a low-status class, this will in many cases represent a career path with a high risk of downward mobility involved. Setbacks to academic development—that means, a decreased probability of success—can thus be immanent in this career path, not so much as a result of the family's status as such, but via the interaction of familial and school-related status. Despite a high family status, the potential "capital" contained therein cannot be utilized effectively as a resource in the adolescent's development. Even within family contexts involving a high level of educational potential, a lack of social capital can be responsible for a negative academic career.

Hypothesis 2

Hypothesis 2 addresses the question of psychological side effects of the transitional process from adolescence to adulthood and states: In sponsored mobility systems, educational careers that ultimately imply upward or downward mobility within succeeding generations involve a higher average stress potential than careers reproducing the family status.

Two reasons give way to this hypothesis: (a) Downward mobility violates parental status expectations. This leads to conflicts in the parental home and, in turn, to symptoms-of-stress reactions; (b) Upward mobility leads to exposure to conflicting social values provoked by career-related reference group changes and this, in turn, leads to symptoms-of-stress reactions.

Regarding the former reason, educational downward mobility is detrimental to parents' status expectations and is a threat not only to the adolescent concerned but in the generation line also to the social position of his or her parents. The conflicts with parents that result from the anticipated loss in final educational status (as intitiated by the choice of secondary school type) may then be a sufficient precondition of stress reactions.

On the other hand, increased symptoms-of-stress reactions are likely to arise in career trajectories that finally imply a rise in status, because such pathways do more or less involve exposure to conflicting social values provoked by career-related reference group changes.

Within the context of an underprivileged background, such an educational development can be connoted as "switching sides," for instance, inasmuch as one's own underprivileged situation is—comparable to a zero-sum game—viewed as a reaction to the privileged groups in whose ranks the young adult will find himself after having achieved upward social mobility. Achieving or striving for such positions not only results in sensitive, achievement-related comparisons with one's family of origin; but, within the family, it also vitalizes latent social class tensions that usually exist between privileged and underprivileged groups.

Within underprivileged families, the identification with a culture oriented toward success and superiority, which is a necessary prerequisite of academic success, reaches its limits because accepting this culture is compromising in that it inevitably leads to an implicit recognition of one's own social inferiority. Thus, a situation arises in which, in order to be successful, the young adult must identify with a culture that is difficult to accept for families with an unfavorable background history. If, at the same time, status-related ambitions are present within the family, and the competition for scarce status goods appears attractive, the fundamental value system becomes ambivalent: It begins both to approve of and to condemn the acquisition of privileges and higher positions.

To sum up, the German predominant type of mobility shapes educational careers early on in the transition to adulthood and in case structurally anchors upward or downward mobility at an early stage. This heavily influences career prospects and also brings forth career-specific, not origin-specific, stress potentials. This does not mean to say that the family of origin is irrelevant, but that the family background gains importance during the course of the career in which it is settled—at least in societies that promote social mobility. What counts then is group membership in terms of mobility pattern rather than of social class origin.

Data and Study Design

Sample

The data for the present analysis come from a longitudinal sample survey conducted at the University of Bielefeld's Special Research Unit 227 "Prevention and Intervention in Childhood and Adolescence." The first-wave sample consists of $N = 1,717$ adolescents aged about 12–16 (mean age = 13.9; SD = 1.3; 51% male, 49% female) and was, within a panel-cohort design, reinterviewed up to three times. For the analysis reported below, this means that the 2W (two-wave) panel analysis rests on both cohorts (of initially seventh and ninth graders), whereas the 3W- and 4W-analyses refer to the younger cohort (of initially seventh graders) only (for a complete description of the underlying longitudinal design, see Engel & Hurrelmann, 1989; and 1993). The average annual panel mortality amounts to 15%.

In statistical terms, the first-wave population is defined as seventh and ninth-grade students at all school types that provide the first stage of secondary education in the West German's Federal state of Northrhine-Westphalia (vocational preparatory school, intermediate school, grammar school, and comprehensive school). A proportionally (by grade and type of secondary school) stratified cluster sample was drawn within each of three statistical areas purposively selected from an official frame of counties in this federal state, where each area chosen represents one type of socio-ecological area as distinguished by the respective official documents. These were an inner-city, an urban, and a rural area. The sample includes a total of $k = 87$ (school-)classes. All data were obtained through a completely standardized questionaire administered in the classroom under the supervision of a member of the research team.

Data

"School failure" is operationalized by reference to the following condition: one or more occasions on which the adolescent had actually repeated a class or was transferred to a lower school type. Based on the methods proposed by Heise (1985) and Wiley and Wiley (1985) to estimate the stability and reliability of survey research items in case of single-indicator three-wave panel models, as well as—in the present case—correcting for possible school failures after Waves 1 and 2, the reliability of this measure on school failure *prior* to Wave 1 turned out to be $r = .86$.

The "educational background" is operationalized by the father's level of education; that is, "low" for unskilled worker; "medium" for skilled but lacking a high school diploma (*Abitur*); "high" for those having achieved a high school diploma or university degree. Cross-tabulated with the four tracks of secondary school reported above, 12 background-by-track configurations (times two, in the case of the model version that additionally considers the collective status of each class) resulted to be used below for classifying the implied career trajectories in terms of (a) evolving via sponsored or contest mobility, and (b) of sponsored mobility careers ultimately reproducing the family status, implying upward or downward mobility (for a more detailed description of the underlying classification scheme, see Engel & Hurrelmann, 1993).

"Symptoms of stress" is measured with a mental health scale based on the 22-item scale initially employed in the Stirling County Study Health Opinion Survey (Macmillan, 1957), a nationwide health survey in the United States (Gurin, Veroff, & Feld, 1960), the Midtown Manhattan Study (Langner, 1962) and in a whole series of subsequent studies (for a list of references, see Engel & Hurrelmann, 1989, p. 69). The present index contains the following symptoms of stress: loss of weight due to worrying, spells of dizzines, pronounced heartbeat, nausea, sleeplessness/disturbed sleep, trembling hands, loss of appetite, upset stomach, profuse perspiration, difficulties with breathing, nightmares, headaches, nervousness/restlessness, and lack of concentration (response scale for each symptom: never, seldom, sometimes, often; average within-wave reliability of the total 14-item scale, $r = .86$). The number of frequent ("often") symptoms of stress serves to analyze the probability of students with above-average (median) symptoms of stress; in the present case this means having at least one frequent symptom of stress.

As we refer to a multistage sampling device in the following analyses, the simple raudom sampling (SRS) standard errors are, strictly speaking, not applicable. To deal with this complication, we adopt the recommendation (Davis, 1985) to correct all standard errors by the factor 1.225 (thus assuming a design effect of 1.5) in order to obtain more conservative estimates of significance.

Findings

Hypothesis 1 maintains that the within-classroom distribution of individual background characteristics determines whether this characteristic would have an advantageous or disadvantageous effect on the student's academic success individually. Due to the career paths involved, one could assume a positive correlation in cases of collectively high-status classes and a negative correlation in the opposite case.

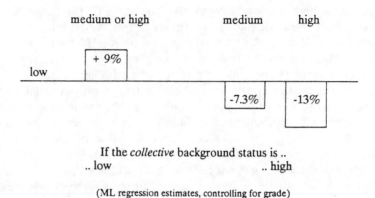

FIGURE 16.2. Estimated differences in the probability of school failure.

Figure 16.2 supports this assumption. It displays the result of a maximum likelihood (ML) regression analysis for categorical data (Table 16.1) in which the probability of school failure is analyzed as a function of three factors: the individual educational background, the collective educational background as a structural (aggregate) feature of the (school-)class, and the grade (conditional main effects model; according to a preliminary version, the collective background status showed no significant main effect).

TABLE 16.1. School failure and educational background as individual and collective resource.

Maximum likelihood estimates		
Constant	b_0	.222
Grade 9 (vs.7)	b_1	.064
Educational background status individually medium or high (vs. low) while collectively low	b_2	.090
individually medium (vs. low)	b_3	−.073
high (vs. low) while collectively high	b_4	−.130

GOF: Chi^2 = 4.43, df = 7, p = 73; N = 1,572; p < .05 for all b_k (k = 0, 1, . . . , 4; p level corrected for multistage sampling).

For classroom communities with *high* collective status, Figure 16.2 shows that the probability of school failure is reduced to the extent that the individual educational background fits into this collective framework: In the case of an intermediate level, the estimated probability of failure turns out to be 7.3%, and in the case of high individual family statuses it is 13% below the level of schoolchildren from low-status families. Thus, the greater the discrepancy between the individual background status and the predominantly high collective background, the greater the probability of failure. This means that the realization of educational upward mobility is in many cases associated with a higher probability of failure than attempts to reproduce status at a high level.

In cases of classroom communities with *low* collective status, however, the impact of family status on the probability of school failure is in the opposite direction: Here, the estimated probability of school failure in respect to intermediate or high individual family statuses is 9% *higher* than that of those with low family status (9.0% and 9.4% if the differences were estimated separately for intermediate and high family statuses, respectively). This +9% difference clearly contradicts the commonly accepted hypothesis regarding the positive relationship between social class and academic success, since for low-status (school-)classes the data suggest: The higher the family status, the lower the probability of success (or the higher the probability of failure).

Within a social capital perspective, however, this simply means that a high family status is not necessarily indicative of a correspondingly high level of developmental resources, but depends (among other things) on how the respective background status is distributed within the school context. Rather, a high family status can become a burden when the offspring's educational career is likely to fail to reproduce the family status, for instance, due to the fact that higher family statuses cannot be reproduced within the Hauptschule or Realschule tracks (three fourths of this population are in low-status classes).

To test Hypothesis 2, a longitudinal analysis should prove whether or not the temporal stability in being placed within the same school track (and hence, intergenerational mobility trajectory) would be re-expressed in a correspondingly stable symptoms-of-stress risk. To assess this risk, the ratio of having to not-having frequent symptoms of stress seems to provide a most reasonable measure. For the 2W panel analysis, this means in particular, analyzing the ratio of those having frequent symptoms of stress on both occasions to those with none such symptoms on both occasions.

Figure 16.3 displays the result of the logistic model set up to analyze this ratio as a function of sponsored mobility careers ultimately reproducing the family status, on the one hand, or involving upward or downward mobility, on the other. The model also provides an estimate for comparing contest mobility careers with corresponding sponsored mobility

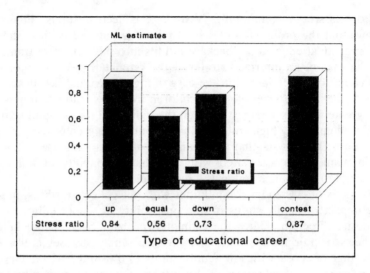

Estimated stress ratio ($f_{11} \div f_{00}$) in sponsored mobility careers ultimately...
.. reproducing family status:
$$r_0 = e^{\beta_0} = 0.56$$
.. involving upward mobility:
$$r_1 = e^{\beta_0} \times e^{\beta_1} = 0.84$$
.. involving downward mobility:
$$r_2 = e^{\beta_0} \times e^{\beta_2} = 0.73$$
Estimated stress ratio ($f_{11} \div f_{00}$) in corresponding contest mobility careers:
$$r_3 = e^{\beta_0} \times e^{\beta_3} = 0.87$$

FIGURE 16.3. Symptoms of stress in a 2-year perspective by type of educational career.

careers (at each background level, respectively). Applying the exponential function to both sides of the original equation (as shown in Table 16.2) yields the estimated stress ratios displayed in Figure 16.3. The main finding is that careers involving both upward or downward mobility in the generation line involve a significantly higher stress ratio than careers that ultimately reproduce the family status (raised by the factor 1.5 to 0.84 or 1:1.2 in the case of upward mobility and by 1.3 in the case of impending descent). And secondly, it was found that contest mobility careers involve, on average, a higher stress ratio than corresponding sponsored mobility careers (raised by about 1.6).

Extending this analysis over three to four waves supports the same conclusions. As before, two states are distinguished: State 1, "having frequent symptoms of stress," and the opposite state (0). This enables us to analyze possible stress trajectories starting with State 1 or 0 at Time 1 and then following any connecting line from left to right, as indicated in

TABLE 16.2. Psychological stress and type of educational career.

		Logistic model Maximum likelihood estimates		
		2W design[+]	3W design	4W design
1st: $\ln (f_{11} \div f_{00})$			$\ln (f_{111} \div f_{000})$	$\ln (f_{1+} \div f_{0+})$
Constant	β_{10}	$-.58^*$	$-.66^*$	$-.85^*$
Careers involving				
upward mobility	β_{11}	$.40^*$	$.26$	$.26$
downward mobility	β_{12}	$.27°$	$.39$	$.55°$
(vs. careers reproducing family status)				
Careers involving				
contest mobility	β_{13}	$.44^*$	$.14$	$.12$
2nd: $\ln (f_{01} \div f_{10})$				
Constant	β_{20}	$-.17$	Here no 2nd response	
Educational background	β_{24}	$-.19$	function analyzed	
GOF: $X^2/df/p$		15.63/18/.62	5.77/8/.67	5.73/8/.68
N		1,381	328	329

Note: "$\ln (f_{1+}/f_{0+})$" means "$\ln ((f_{111^*}$ or $f_{*111})/(f_{000^*}$ or $f_{*000}))$" (with the * substituting 1 or 0, i.e., having at least three equal consecutive values in four measurements). The 3W and 4W analyses refer to the younger cohort of initially 7th graders only; out of this cohort the sub-set of students with the above described stress trajectories is analyzed (60% and 70% of total N_t of individual trajectories [i.e., valid cases] involved, respectively).
$^* p < .06$; $°p < .09$; p level corrected for multistage sampling (all corresponding SRS p's < .05).
$^+$ Multiresponse design in case of 2W analysis.

Figure 16.4, where in the present analysis the response functions simply extend their 2W-counterpart in reflecting the ratio of being constantly stressed to non-stressed on three occasions or on at least three *consecutive* in four occasions (measurements).

The main results are as before: an increased stress ratio in careers involving upward or downward mobility when compared to careers re-producing the family status, and again (though just slight) differences between corresponding contest and sponsored mobility careers.

All this suggests that there *are* career-specific circumstances that affect the adolescent's health—most probably with transmitting factors involved. Cases in point are violated status expectations leading to social conflicts in the parental home and, in turn, to symptoms-of-stress-reactions; or value conflicts due to reference group changes provoked in cases of pupils from low-status families realizing educational upward mobility—so to speak—mainly not "among their equals," meaning, for instance, in intermediate and grammar school contexts with an above-average proportion of pupils already coming from high-status families.

This suggests a corresponding categorical data regression analysis in which, for careers that ultimately imply educational upward mobility,

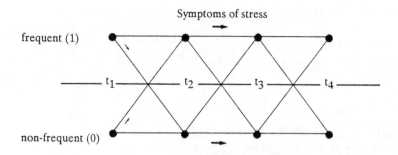

The stress ratios studied
in the 3W-analysis: $f_{111} \div f_{000}$
in the 4W-analysis: $(f_{111*} \text{ or } f_{*111}) \div (f_{000*} \text{ or } f_{*000})$
(with * indicating 1 *or* 0; i.e., having *at least* three equal consecutive values in four
measurements)

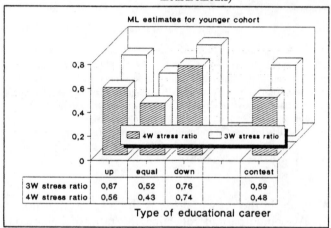

	up	equal	down		contest
3W stress ratio	0,67	0,52	0,76		0,59
4W stress ratio	0,56	0,43	0,74		0,48

Type of educational career

Estimated 3W *(4W)* stress ratio in sponsored mobility careers ultimately...
.. reproducing family status:
$$r_0 = e^{\beta_0} = 0.52 \ (0.43)$$
.. involving upward mobility:
$$r_1 = e^{\beta_0} \times e^{\beta_1} = 0.67 \ (0.56)$$
.. involving downward mobility:
$$r_2 = e^{\beta_0} \times e^{\beta_2} = 0.76 \ (0.74)$$
Estimated stress ratio in corresponding contest mobility careers:

$$r_3 = e^{\beta_0} \times e^{\beta_3} = 0.59 \ (0.48)$$

FIGURE 16.4. Symptoms of stress in a 3- and 4-year perspective by type of
educational career.

additional attention is paid to the collective (aggregate) status of the
pupil's class (as defined above), since this analysis reveals the stress ratio
to be significantly increased by the factor 1.8 in collectively high-status
classes and by just 1.2 in contexts of low-status classes (to be com-

pared to the global factor 1.5 reported above for careers implying upward mobility).

This analysis also shows the effect due to attending a contest rather than sponsored mobility track to be remarkably dependent on the collective status of the class attended, since the global risk factor of 1.6 (reported above) significantly raises up to 3.2 in case of low-status classes. If, on the other hand, the recruitment tends to become similar to that of the Gymnasium, this changes exactly those contextual conditions that otherwise would be the basis of a considerable stress risk. The fact that Gesamtschule classes, which are more or less identical with Gymnasium classes in terms of recruitment conditions, do not vary greatly in terms of stress potential, has already shown on a preliminary cross-sectional analysis based on first-wave data only (Engel & Hurrelmann, 1989, pp. 94 and 224).

In returning to the 2W model, the finding regarding the second function analyzed supports the assumption of career-specific symptoms-of-stress risks, since there doesn't exist any significant trend (see Table 16.2) in this tendency toward stress over time, when standardized on the opposing trend. Though this tendency becomes stronger the more unfavorable the educational background (this most parsimonious model already fits well), this can only be interpreted as an insignificant trend, leaving us with the career-specific effects reported above.

Discussion

During adolescence, interacting family- and school-contexts may be brought about in a multiplicity of ways, just one of them being the institutionally supported forms of social recruiting and thereby of within-(school-)class aggregating of family background characteristics. In sponsored mobility systems, with their early establishment of (rather stable) intergenerational career trajectories, this affects the adolescent's position in terms of both the developmental resources available and the risks he/she is exposed to.

In theoretical terms, this clearly suggests some need for further specification of, or even reorientation in, any attempt to explain phenomena such as differing status attainments or differential risk-expositions by sole reference to social class categories (or related characteristics). Regarding the former aspect—that is, the way social-class origin is involved in creating or keeping the offspring's career prospects—this means that any explanation by reference to a notion of social capital assumed to be simply increasing with family status must at best remain incomplete. For such an explanation fails to see that by institutionalization of sponsored mobility, a ranking system emerges that structurally anchors educational careers in terms of origin-destination (mobility) patterns early on in the status transition to adulthood—what becomes clear, if the underlying social recruitment processes into schools are taken into account. Then the actually available social capital proves to be determined not so much by the family status per se but rather by the interplay between individual and collective resources within the adolescent's career path. Depending on the pathway involved, a high family status may be more of a burden than a favorable requisite, since in meritocratic societies such background statuses not only create options but also the moral obligation to realize them.

Shifting the focus from social class origin (as a basic conceptual unit of analysis) toward the career path, of which this very origin is a part, would provide a fruitful perspective also for purposes of studying developmental risks associated with the adolescent's status passage toward adulthood. The present analysis suggests this to be the case for larger sponsored mobility systems.

For the analysis of mental health risks, this shift in focus would clearly represent a theoretical reorientation, if it is taken into account that social-class origin has been a major explanatory concept in this research field from the beginning. For such a reorientation speaks, however, the high extent to which contemporary society promotes social mobility. In Germany, for instance, a remarkable and still-ongoing run on higher education has taken place in the last decades. Though this, by and large, left unaffected the basic structure of social inequality (except partly for gender-related social inequalities), this general trend toward the top of the social structure raised the degree of competition among the social classes and thereby created an increased social pressure to submit to this broader societal trend at an earlier stage of life, namely, in school age.

Viewed on a larger historical scale, society has internally become more and more dynamical and hence, in today's society mobility patterns do count more than the once-and-for-all status pattern of static societies. Improved career chances and increasingly frequent attempts to realize upward mobility via educational channels have made the social class boundaries (and, hence, the social class relationships) less secure. Having obtained a social position secures superior status, wealth, or power only as long as the distance to all who also compete for those privileges can be maintained. In a sense, Durkheim's late 19th century "anomic society," for him a pathological type at that time, has become the rule. To refer to a recently debated hypothesis in German sociology which becomes more and more prominent in youth research too, not "individualization" and the process of structural disintegration (implied by that hypothesis) is what society undergoes, but social change that retains society's vertical structure, but at an immanently much higher level of status competition. For individuals, this increases the need for permanently renewing their investments in keeping their status positions during the life course. Thus, "career" and not so much "social class origin" seems to be most suitable as a key concept to future analyses of, e.g., mental health risks in contemporary society.

References

Bourdieu, P. (1983). Ökonomisches Kapital, kulturelles Kapital, soziales Kapital [Economic capital, cultural capital social capital]. In R. Kreckel (Ed.), *Soziale Ungleichheiten* (pp. 183–198). Göttingen: Schwartz.

Coleman, J.S. (1972). The evaluation of "equality of educational opportunity." In F. Mosteller & D.P. Moynihan (Eds.), *On equality of educational opportunity* (pp. 146–167). New York: Random House.

Coleman, J.S. (1988). Social capital in the creation of human capital. *American Journal of Sociology, 94*, S95–S120.

Coleman, J.S., Campbell, E.Q., Hobson, C.J., McPartland, J., Mood, A.M., Weinfeld, F.D., & York, R.L. (1966). *Equality of educational opportunity*. Washington, DC: U.S. Government Printing Office.

Coleman, J.S. & Hoffer, T. (1987). *Public and private high schools: The impact of communities*. New York: Basic Books.

Coleman, J.S., Hoffer, T., & Kilgore, S. (1982). Achievement and segregation in secondary schools: A further look at public and private school differences. *Sociology of Education, 55*, 162–182.

Collins, R. (1979). *The credential society*. New York: Academic Press.

Davis, J.A. (1985). Statistical inference with proportions. In R.B. Smith (Ed.), *A handbook of social science methods, Vol. 3: Quantitative Methods* (pp. 336–366). New York: Praeger.

Engel, U. & Hurrelmann, K. (1989). *Psychosoziale Belastung im Jugendalter* [Psychosocial risks in adolescence]. Berlin-New York: Walter de Gruyter.

Engel, U. & Hurrelmann, K. (1993). Was Jugendliche wagen [Risk behavior in youth]. Weinheim und München: Juventa.

Gamoran, A. (1987). The stratification of high school learning opportunities. *Sociology of Education, 60*, 135–155.

Gurin, G., Veroff, J., & Feld, S. (1960). *Americans view their mental health*. New York: Basic Books.

Hansen, R. & Rolff, H.-G. (1990). Abgeschwächte Auslese und verschärfter Wettbewerb—Neuere Entwicklungen in den Sekundarschulen [Weakened selection and strengthened competition—New developments in secondary schools]. In H.-G. Rolff, K.-O. Bauer, K. Klemm, & H. Pfeiffer (Eds.), *Jahrbuch der Schulentwicklung 6* (pp. 45–79). Weinheim und München: Juventa.

Heise, D.R. (1985). Separating reliability and stability in test-retest correlation. In H.M. Blalock (Ed.), *Causal models in panel and experimental design* (pp. 117–132). New York: Aldine Publishing Co.

Langner, T.S. (1962). A twenty-two item screening score of psychiatric symptoms indicating impairment. *Journal of Health and Human Behavior, 3*, 269–276.

Lee, V.E. & Bryk, A.S. (1989). A multilevel model of the social distribution of high school achievement. *Sociology of Education, 62*, 172–192.

Macmillan, A.M. (1957). The Health Opinion Survey: Technique for estimating prevalence of psychoneurotic and related types of disorder in communities. *Psychological Reports, 3*, 325–339.

Max Planck Institute for Human Development and Education (1983). Between elite and mass education: Education in the Federal Republic of Germany. Albany: SUNY Press.

McPartland, J.M. & McDill, E.L. (1982). Control and differentiation in the structure of American education. *Sociology of Education*, *55*, 77–88.

Murphy, R. (1988). *Social closure*. Oxford: Clarendon Press.

Raudenbush, S. & Bryk, A.S. (1986). A hierarchical model for studying school effects. *Sociology of Education*, *59*, 1–17.

Turner, R.H. (1960). Sponsored and contest mobility and the school system. *American Sociological Review*, *25*, 855–867.

Wiley, D.E. & Wiley, J.A. (1985). The estimation of measurement error in panel data. In H.M. Blalock (Ed.), *Causal models in panel and experimental designs* (pp. 133–143). New York: Aldine Publishing Co.

Part VI

The Sample Case of Aggressive Behavior

17
The Influence of Parents and Peers on Misconduct at School: Simultaneous and Synergistic Effects

Hans Oswald and Klaus-Uwe Süss

Introduction

In this chapter we contribute to the debate about the influence of parents and peers on adolescents' attitudes and behavior. The investigation deals with the misconduct of adolescents at school, measured as self-reported teacher-annoying behavior and bullying of other students. In the multiple regression model we developed for this analysis, variables from the parental, peer, and school contexts simultaneously predicted the teacher-annoying behavior. Variables from the parent and school contexts predicted the bullying of other students. We employed Bronfenbrenner's concept of synergistic effects in mesosystems to calculate interaction effects between the parent and the peer contexts. The results show a clear pattern for the teacher-annoying behavior: Students are susceptible to negative peer pressure against school authority only if their relationship to their parents is disturbed.

The Problem

The topic under investigation is the influence exerted by parents and peers on adolescent boys and girls with regard to the annoying of teachers and bullying of other students. Of special interest are both the relative impact of parental and peer influences, and the possible interactions between the two contexts.

This topic is one area of a long-standing debate around youth subculture, generation gap, and parent versus peer influence that encompasses a wide range of adolescent attitudes, values, and behavior. As many researchers (e.g., Parsons, 1942) have viewed peer-culture influence to be counteractive to the aims of the educational system, the school behavior, educational aspirations, and career plans of adolescents have constituted one of the major objects of concern in this debate.

Despite early empirical evidence which weakened the counteractive peer-culture hypothesis (e.g., Hollingshead, 1949), and theoretical arguments in support of the hypothesis of the functionality of peer groups (Eisenstadt, 1956; Piaget, 1932/1965), Coleman's landmark empirical study (1961) appeared to establish conclusively that the influence of peers outweighs that of parents, and that the culture of the leading crowd of a high school rejects academic values. However, the empirical base of Coleman's thesis has since generated a variety of intense research activity, which has refined our knowledge in several respects.

One line of research has focused on the parent-adolescent relationship and the influence of parents on their children. Replication studies proved that most adolescents had a good emotional relationship with their parents. This result has remained stable over the years (Steinberg, 1990). A good emotional relationship is usually not threatened by common and mundane conflicts about household chores, curfews, clothes, or school responsibilities. These everyday disagreements far outnumber conflicts arising from differing values or political views (Conger, 1981) and are thought to have positive functions in adolescent psychosocial development (Cooper, 1988), as well as in the transformation of the parent-child relationship from one of unilateral authority to one based on symmetric reciprocal cooperation (Youniss & Smollar, 1985).

One major set of variables within the family context which accounts for the influence of parents on adolescent behavior concerns parenting style. Several recent studies have demonstrated the effectiveness of authoritative parenting as compared to autocratic or permissive parenting. The combination of parental demand with acceptance and emotional warmth, characteristic of authoritative parenting, has been associated with higher grades in school (Dornbusch, Ritter, Leiderman, Roberts, & Fraleigh, 1987), less misconduct (Feldman, Rosenthal, Mont-Reynaud, Leung, & Lau, 1991), less psychological distress, and less delinquency in both intact and single-parent families of all social classes (Steinberg, Mounts, Lamborn, & Dornbusch, 1991). A more specific set of parental behaviors connected with higher grades is the management of the school career of students by parents (Epstein, 1990). As in the area of substance use (Silbereisen, Boehnke, & Crockett, 1991), interaction effects between school and family contexts may exist with certain types of schools calling for more parental involvement than others (Oswald, Baker, & Stevenson, 1988).

A second line of reasoning and research has been concerned with the positive influences of peers and the parent-peer interaction. Youniss states that the symmetric reciprocity in peer and friendship relations leads to cooperation and the co-construction of knowledge and therefore to social and cognitive growth (1980). Peers are necessary for healthy development. For example, clique membership is a predictor of an adolescent's psychological well-being (Hansell, 1985). Some studies show the positive effect of friends on career plans and school achievement (Brown, 1982). Brown summarizes the results of this direction of research: "Values of an adolescent's peer group are more likely to support parental values than to be in conflict with them" (1990). In addition, the influences of parents and peers seem to be domain-specific and not mutually exclusive (Kandel, 1986).

Even in those peer cultures and associations that have subcultural and deviant orientations, links exist to adult subcultures, as demonstrated, for example, by Miller's "focal concerns" (1958). Moreover, family structure and child-rearing practices may predispose children to opt for deviant peer groups (e.g., Steinberg, 1987). These findings draw attention to interaction effects which can be interpreted as synergistic effects in a "mesosystem" (Bronfenbrenner, 1989). Bronfenbrenner quotes a study conducted by Steinberg and Brown (1989) which shows that conditions in the family context moderate the influence of peers on students' academic achievement. The present chapter is devoted to the analysis of such synergistic effects in the parent-peer mesosystem on the behavior of adolescents at school.

With few exceptions, school-related research has focused on achievement and educational aspiration as dependent variables. Thus far, misconduct directed against teachers has been accorded little attention except as part of broader concepts of deviance (e.g., Dornbusch et al., 1985), or in the exceptional form of physical attacks occurring in certain parts of metropolitan areas (Hanna, 1988). As everyday harassment by students does make life very difficult for teachers, the educational literature has concentrated on suggesting suitable measures through which teachers might curtail this kind of behavior. Little attention has been given to the mundane forms of teacher-annoying behavior itself.

More effort has been devoted to the investigation of aggressive behavior toward other students because it predicts later manifestations of maladaption, such as delinquency (Farrington, 1986). The bullying, harassment, and beating of other students at school is more typical among boys than girls, and has been shown to occur at stable levels over time (Olweus, 1984a). Its relation to poor academic performance (e.g., Hirschi & Hindelang, 1977) directs attention to causes in the school context itself. In his pioneering work on bullying behavior in Scandinavia, Olweus found that poor grades do not cause aggression (1983). More evidence, in fact, is given for the hypothesis that aggression causes poor grades. However, a multivariate analysis of longitudinal data indicates that the correlation between grades and bullying behavior of boys may be spurious and caused by early family factors (Olweus, 1983). Several factors of the family context, such as socio-economic status (SES), single-parent upbringing, negativism of mother, and power-assertive discipline, are proposed as predictors of bullying behavior (McCord, 1990). Insecure attachment of the infant to the main caretaker may be one of the earliest causes of maladapted behavior (Sroufe & Fleeson, 1986). In addition, the peer context may pose risk factors. Deviant friends (Snyder, Dishion, & Patterson, 1986), low peer status, and rejection by classmates (Asher & Dodge, 1986) constitute sources of bullying behavior. Determinants in all three contexts seem to explain aggressive behavior at school.

The Research Question

In the present chapter we have selected the problem of misconduct at school for the purpose of analyzing simultaneous and synergistic effects of the parental and peer contexts on adolescent behavior. Misconduct is operationalized as self-reported "teacher-annoying behavior" and "bullying of other students." A first set of hypotheses proposes that aspects of the parent-adolescent relationship and of the adolescent's involvement in peer activities simultaneously predict misconduct at school. A second set of hypotheses proposes that conditions prevailing in the family context moderate the effects of conditions in the peer context on school misconduct. Because an independent effect of the school context itself on misconduct of students could be assumed, we have controlled for key variables of this third context, such as grades, attitudes and behaviors regarding school achievement, and educational aspiration. The aim is to predict both kinds of misconduct, the harassment of teachers and bullying of students, by the same multiple regression model.

Method

Subjects

The data analyzed in this paper were collected as part of a large-scale, representative, multi-purpose survey conducted in West Berlin in 1986. From this survey we have used two different subsets: (a) parent-adolescent dyads ($N = 264$); (b) parent-adolescent-best friend triads ($N = 130$).

The first subset consists of adult German citizens with schoolchildren aged 12 to 18 years. We interviewed 264 parents, approximately half of whom were fathers (45%) and half mothers (55%), and their 264 adolescent children separately.[1] During the interviews the adolescents were asked to give us the name of their best same-sex friend. We were able to conduct 130 interviews with best friends of the adolescents, and are thus able to analyze and compare the answers of 130 adolescent-best friend pairs from the second subset.

---

[1] An earlier paper using data from the same survey (see Oswald, Baker, & Stevenson, 1988) was based on only 238 parent-adolescent pairs, because adolescents who did not answer the track questions were excluded from the data file (see Klingemann, 1991 for a full report of the survey procedures).

The adolescent sample is almost evenly split between boys (47%) and girls (53%). The average age of the parents was 44.2 years, ranging from 31 to 71 years. The average age of the adolescents was 14.7 years and ranged from 12 to 18 years.

The head of household in the majority of families (64%) held a white-collar job of lower-middle to middle level, in 23% of the families was either a blue-collar or low-level white-collar worker, and in 14% of the families was a professional or higher-level civil servant. The sample of parent-adolescent pairs can be regarded as roughly representative of German families in West Berlin with schoolchildren between 12 and 18 years of age.

Due to the aforementioned selective sampling procedure, the same does not hold true for the sample of best friends ($N = 130$). The parents of the triad sample had slightly higher levels of education and occupation, and were slightly older than the parents of the dyad sample. Girls are slightly overrepresented. The average age of the best friends was 15.1 years.

Measures

The Dependent Variables

From Olweus' (Norway) short inventory of self-reported bullying be-havior (1984b) we selected three questions,[2] one pertaining to "annoying of teachers", and two questions which, combined, formed the scale "bullying of students." A high value on either of the scales indicates a high amount of annoying or bullying behavior, respectively. The two dependent variables were moderately correlated ($r = .22, p < .001$).

Translating questions from one language into another—necessary for a cross-cultural comparison—is always a difficult undertaking (see Kohn, 1987). In the English version of his questionnaire Olweus used the term *bullying*. Because there is no word in German corresponding exactly to this term, we chose the expression *stänkern*, which seemed to be used in Berlin in a way very similar to the term *bullying* in the United States. We defined this expression in the questionnaire as Olweus did:

"Here are some questions about bullying or annoying. In Berlin the term 'bul-lying' (= stänkern) is used if somebody says nasty or unpleasant things. It is also bullying if somebody is hit, kicked, threatenend, or locked inside a room. It is also bullying when a student is teased repeatedly. But it is *not bullying* when two students of about the same strength quarrel or fight."

---

[2] "How often have you annoyed teachers in the last three or four months?" and "How often have you bullied students in the last three or four months (since the last summer vacation?)" (7-point scales ranging from (1) *never* to (7) *several times a day*).

Though we used the same definition, connotational differences between the Berlin term *stänkern* and the original Scandinavian expression led to the determination of a far higher percentage of bullies in the Berlin sample than were found in the Scandinavian samples. In addition, we found as many female bullies as male bullies in Berlin. Discussing the matter with Olweus, we concluded that a plausible explanation for these discrepancies might lie in the fact that the Berlin interview measured both verbal and nonverbal psychological attacks, prevalent in girls' behavior, as well as physical attacks, which are typical among boys, whereas the Olweus interview concentrated primarily on physical attacks by boys.

The independent variables concern the parent context, the peer context, and the school context.

The Parent Context

The occupation of the head of household was taken as the measure of the SES of the family. The structure of the family was indicated by the variable "loss of a parent by separation, divorce or death" (coded [1] *yes*, [0] *no*). Other variables pertained to the parent-child emotional relationship and conflicts between parents and their children. There were two questions in the adolescent questionnaire and one question in the parent questionnaire about closeness between the adolescent and his/her father and mother (5-point scales coded from [1] *not close* to [5] *very close*). A further question in the adolescent questionnaire addressed the adolescent's approval of his/her parents' parenting style (4-point scale coded from [1] *no approval* to [4] *total approval*). The children were asked questions about everyday conflicts regarding helping at home, going out at night, spending Sunday afternoons with the family, and clothes and hairstyle (the latter asked separately for fathers and mothers). The answers had to be listed on 5-point scales (coded from [1] *never* to [5] *very often*). On the basis of these five questions we constructed the scale "everyday conflicts," with higher values indicating more conflicts.

Parents were asked a series of questions about their management of their adolescents' schooling (see Oswald et al., 1988). Six indicators of parental management corresponding to Epstein's (1990) Types 4 and 5 of parental involvement were obtained by asking parents if they (a) asked their children about homework every day, (b) helped their children with homework, (c) discussed the choice of school subjects with their children, (d) had ever been a school-class parent representative during their children's school career, (e) usually attended meetings of the parent-teacher association (PTA), and (f) had spoken to one of their children's teachers during the past 2 years (the dummy variables are coded [1] for *yes* and [0] for *no*).

Adolescents were asked whose advice they sought when having problems or facing trouble: "mother," "father," "both parents," "siblings," "best same-sex friend," "best opposite-sex friend," "my group," or "others." Only two sources of advice could be listed. From this information we formed the variables "mother as adviser," "father as adviser," "parents as advisers" (at least one parent named),[3] and "peers as advisers (the first variable of the peer context)."[4]

The Peer and the School Context

Besides "peers as advisers" the indicators for the degree of integration in the world of peers were "number of same-sex friends" and "number of opposite-sex friends," combined to form the scale "number of friends"; "group membership" ([1] yes, [0] no); and "going out at night during the week" (4-point scale coded from [1] very seldom to [4] very often). Additionally, we asked the adolescents how much they talked with their best friends about 16 different subjects. The answers were combined to comprise the scale "amount of talking with friends," with higher values indicating more talking.

From the interviews with the best friends, we had drawn up the scales "annoying of teachers by best friend," and "bullying of students by best friend." Both variables were constructed in the same way as the independent variables described above.

The school context was measured by (a) the educational aspiration level (low, middle, high), (b) the grade point average (GPA) in mathematics, German, and English (1 = best grade, 5 = worst grade), (c) a single question about well-being at school (5-point scale coded from [1] *not well at all* to [5] *very well*), and (d) a variable "school motivation" formed by three questions about school, performance, and homework, with higher values indicating higher academic motivation.[5]

Results

Teacher-annoying Behavior: Bivariate Analyses

Forty percent of the students questioned denied engaging in annoying behavior altogether, while 27% said they annoyed teachers "very seldom," and an additional 19% indicated they "seldom" did so. Only 13% admitted higher rates of annoying behavior. In contrast to the results

---

[3] The three variables are coded (1) *yes* and (0) *no*.

[4] Coded as (0) *no peer*, (1) *one peer*, (2) *two peers* named.

[5] The three questions comprising the "school motivation" variable were: "How much effort do you make with regard to school performance?"; "How hard do you persevere when doing your homework?"; and "How much time do you usually devote to homework?"

of the multivariate analysis presented below, self-reported annoying of teachers was not related to sex or age of the adolescents.

The hypothesis that misbehavior at school is a peer-group phenomenon was only moderately confirmed by bivariate analyses and it applied more for girls than for boys. Students who reported higher rates of annoying behavior had more opposite-sex friends ($r = .21, p < .001$) and same-sex friends ($r = .12, p < .05$), talked more with friends ($r = .20, p < .01$), more often went out at night during the week ($r = .13, p < .05$), more often preferred peers as advisers ($r = .15, p = .01$), and were more often members of a group ($r = .09, p < .10$) than students who reported lower rates of annoying behavior. In addition, these adolescents tended to have same-sex friends who also admitted annoying teachers ($r = .23, p < .01$).[6] The seven indicators for peer affiliation correlated significantly on at least the 10% level. All correlation coefficients except one were higher for the girl sample than for the total sample, amounting to $r = .32$ ($p < .01$) for the number of opposite-sex friends, as well as for having a same-sex friend who also reported annoying teachers.

In contrast, only two indicators of peer affiliation applied to boys. Boys who reported that they annoyed teachers talked more with friends ($r = .20, p < .05$) and preferred peers as advisers ($r = .18, p < .05$). The correlation between boys' teacher-annoying behavior and other indicators of the peer context did not reach sufficient levels of significance.

Characteristics of family background and of the parent-child relationship were shown to influence adolescents' behavior at school. The SES of the family was related to teacher-annoying behavior ($r = -.26, p < .001$), with students from families of higher status being better adapted to school than those from families of lower status. The impact of status on misbehavior was stronger for girls ($r = -.32, p < .001$) than for boys ($r = -.20, p < .05$). The family structure variable "loss of a parent" did not correlate with annoying behavior. Indicators of parent-child conflicts were more often and more strongly related to teacher-annoying behavior than were indicators of the parent-child emotional relationship. The reported amount of teacher-annoying behavior was related to the prevalence of everyday conflicts ($r = .26, p < .001$), the adolescents' criticism of their parents' parenting style ($r = -.18, p < .01$), and unwillingness to ask parents for advice ($r = -.21, p < .001$). Fathers of sons who admitted annoying teachers said that their relationships to their sons were not very close ($r = -.20, p < .10, N = 52$[7]). The closeness of boys to mothers and of girls to both parents was not related to annoying behavior. Addition-

---

[6] For comparing best friends we used the parent-adolescent-best friend triad sample ($N = 130$).

[7] The small sample size is due to the fact that half of the interviewed parents were fathers and half were mothers and only half of the adolescents were boys.

ally, the variable pertaining to the seeking of paternal advice correlated only with the annoying behavior of boys ($r = -.27, p < .01$) and not of girls.

One set of variables connecting the parental and school contexts concerns parents' management of their children's school career. The relationship of these parental activities to the misbehavior of students at school was negligible. Only the attendance at PTA meetings was related to the annoying behavior ($r = -.13, p < .05$), the parents of annoying students not attending such school events.

When exploring the impact of parents and peers on misbehavior at school, the influence of the school context itself must be taken into account. As would be expected, student well-being at school, attitudes towards school career, and involvement in achievement activities were all related to the amount of teacher-annoying behavior at school. However, the correlation coefficients between teacher-annoying behavior and student well-being at school ($r = -.21, p < .001$), GPA ($r = .19, p < .01$), educational aspiration ($r = -.24, p < .001$), and school motivation ($r = -.16, p < .01$) proved to be only moderate. The four correlations were very similar for both sexes.

Teacher-annoying Behavior: Simultaneous and Synergistic Effects of the Parent and Peer Context

To estimate the influence of variables of the three contexts on misbehavior at school, by controlling for other variables of all three contexts as well as for age and sex, we calculated an overall multiple regression model by jointly entering all variables described in Table 17.1.

The results for the whole sample are presented in column 1. Variables of each of the three contexts clearly had independent impacts on the annoying of teachers. The variables of the three contexts plus age and sex explained 31% of the variance in the dependent variable. Ten of 14 predicting variables had significant effects on at least the 10% level. Contrary to the result of the bivariate analysis, the multiple regression revealed that age and sex did have an influence. Teacher-annoying behavior was predicted by two variables of the peer context: the number of friends, and the amount of talking with friends. It was also predicted by the SES of the family and by three other variables of the parental context: everyday conflicts, parent nonattendance of PTA meetings, and adolescent tendency not to seek maternal advice. As in the bivariate analysis, the emotional relationship between students and their parents did not augment the explained variance significantly. When included in the equation, the family structure variable "loss of a parent" had no significant effect. In the school context, low educational aspiration and lack of well-being at school predicted annoying behavior. When included in the equation, GPA did not add to the explained variance.

TABLE 17.1. Multiple regression of "annoying teachers" on variables of the three contexts "peers", "parents", and "schools" (beta weights).

	Annoying teachers		
Variables of contexts	All	Girls	Boys
(1) Peer context			
Number of friends	.15++	.22+++	.04
Amount of talking	.17++	.12	.18+
Going out at night	.09	.22++	−.05
(2) Parent context			
Closeness to child[1]	−.02	.03	−.07
Asking mother for advice[2]	−.10+	−.14+	−.08
Asking father for advice[2]	−.10	−.01	−.20+
Everyday conflicts	.11+	.20++	.02
Attending PTA meetings[1]	−.15++	−.16++	−.08
SES[1]	−.20+++	−.26+++	−.10
(3) School context			
School motivation	−.07	−.05	−.08
Aspiration	−.14++	−.07	−.24++
Well-being at school	−.13++	−.15+	−.10
(4) Control variables			
Age	−.17++	−.21++	−.11
Sex (f = 1, m = 0)	−.14++	—	—
R	.56+++	.64+++	.52+++
R^2	.31	.41	.27
N	227	123	104

[1] Parents answers; half of the parents were fathers, half were mothers.
[2] (1) yes, (0) no.
+ $p < .10$; ++ $p < .05$; +++ $p < .01$

Annoying behavior was better predicted for girls ($R^2 = .41$) than for boys ($R^2 = .27$), and the pattern of predicting variables was very different for the two sexes. In the model for girls, 8 of 13 variables from all three contexts had significant effects on the dependent variable on at least the 10% level. Girls were more likely to admit teacher-annoying behavior if they: were younger and of lower social background; felt ill at ease at school; had many friends (especially opposite-sex friends, as the bivariate analysis makes clear); frequently went out with their friends at night during the week; and had conflicts with their parents, presumably their mothers, whose advice they no longer sought and who did not attend PTA meetings.

Among boys, only 3 of 13 variables had significant effects on the dependent variable on at least the 10% level. As the findings with girls, variables of each of the three contexts had significant effects on the dependent variable, but, unlike the findings with the girls, only one variable of each context had such an effect. Boys who talked a lot with friends, did not ask fathers for advice, and had low educational aspiration reported more often than the others that they engaged in annoying behavior. Note that annoying girls did not ask *mothers* for advice, whereas annoying boys did not ask *fathers* for advice.

The last stage of our analysis is devoted to Bronfenbrenner's concept of synergistic effects (e.g., 1989). The core of this idea is that certain conditions in one context influence the effects of conditions of another context on the outcome variable. A multiple regression model as presented in Table 17.1 reveals the simultaneous independent effects of variables of different contexts if controlled for other variables in all contexts under consideration. Thus, on the basis of the results in Table 17.1, the hypothesis may be stated that the number of friends and the extent to which the adolescent talked with them had a negative influence, irrespective of conflicts in the family, which we controlled for.

An additional hypothesis states that the influence of the peer-group affiliation is negative only if the parent-child relationship is disturbed. To explore the possibility of such synergistic effects, we designated "asking parents for advice" as the moderating variable that alters the influence of peers on teacher-annoying behavior. Seventy-five percent of all students reported that they ask at least one parent for advice (Oswald & Boll, 1992, p. 36). No gender difference was found in this respect. The 25% minority that did not report seeking advice from their parents is presumably subject to negative peer influence.

We first calculated a multiple regression equation, using as predictor variables the dichotomous variable "asking parents for advice,"[8] the three variables of the peer context, and the background variables SES, age, and sex of child. "The annoying of teachers" was the criterion variable. We then calculated the same equation again, this time including the interaction term "asking parents for advice times number of friends."[9] The effect of the interaction term on the annoying of teachers in the second model was significant (see Table 17.2). The increase of R^2 in the second model as compared with the first model was significant ($F = 4.08140$, $df = 1,242$, $p < .05$). The synergistic effect can be demonstrated

---

[8] In order to obtain a single dichotomous variable for constructing the interaction term, we have replaced the two variables that separated fathers and mothers in Table 17.1 with the variable "asking parents for advice."

[9] This combined equation is

$$y' = a + b_1 x_1 + b_2 x_2 + b_3 x_3 \ldots + b_i x_1 x_2,$$

where x_1 is a dummy variable coded (1) for *asking parents for advice* and (0) for *not asking parents for advice*, x_2 is the variable "number of friends," and b_i is the coefficient of the interaction term $x_1 x_2$. For *asking for advice* it is written as

$$y' = (a + b_1) + (b_2 + b_i)x_2 + b_3 x_3 \ldots ,$$

and for *not asking for advice* as

$$y' = a + b_2 x_2 + b_3 x_3 \ldots .$$

TABLE 17.2. Multiple regression of "annoying teachers" on variables of the "peer" context, "asking parents for advice," and a parent-peer interaction term.

	Annoying teachers		
	B	SE B	Beta
Asking parents for advice	−.29793	.28971	−.09
Interaction term*	−.02871	.01421	−.22[++]
Number of friends	.03399	.01112	.28[+++]
Amount of talking	.45391	.17536	.17[++]
Going out at night	.18857	.08839	.14[++]
Age	−.12901	.05404	−.16[++]
Sex (f = 1, m = 0)	−.40206	.16154	−.15[++]
SES	−.34900	.07250	−.27[+++]

R = .47   Standard error = 1.23640
R^2 = .22 $F = 8.72456$[+++]
N = 251

* Asking parents for advice (dummy: [1] yes, [0] no) times number of friends.
[+] $p < .10$; [++] $p < .05$; [+++] $p < .01$

by using the B's of Table 17.2: The effect of the "number of friends" variable was six times stronger in cases in which parents were *not asked* for advice (b_1 = .03399) than in those in which they *were asked* ($b_1 + b_i$ = .00528).

When calculated separately for the two sexes, the interaction term had a significant effect for girls but not for boys. Thus, the synergistic effect is true only for girls: The effect of the "number of friends" variable on the teacher-annoying variable for girls was 25 times stronger in the condition "did not ask parents for advice" (b_1 = .04280) than in the condition "asked parents for advice" (b_1 = .00173).

Seeking an explanation for these results, we hypothesized that adolescents who sought advice from their parents selected friends in accordance with parental expectations, and that in cases in which this aspect of the parent-child relationship was disturbed, adolescents chose friends with deviant tendencies. We used the parent-adolescent-best friend triad sample (N = 130) to explore this possible explanation. We calculated a small equation, regressing the teacher-annoying behavior of the target students on the variables "asking parents for advice" and "annoying of teachers by best friend," as well as on the interaction term of both.

Both the main effect of friends' teacher-annoying behavior and the interaction effect were significant (see Table 17.3). The R^2's of the models with and without interaction term differed significantly ($F = 6.27579$, $df = 1,121$, $p < .05$). The effect of the annoying behavior of best friends on the annoying behavior of the target students was more than seven times

TABLE 17.3. Multiple regression of annoying teachers on "annoying teachers by best friend," "asking parents for advice," and the interaction term.

	Annoying teachers		
	B	SE B	Beta
Asking parents for advice	.21821	.50488	.07
Annoying teachers by best friend	.52957	.15197	.53[+++]
Interaction term*	−.45556	.18183	−.49[++]

$R = .39$ Standard error = 1.28838
$R^2 = .15$ $F = 8.19232^{+++}$
$N = 125$

*Asking parents for advice (dummy: [1] yes, [2] no) times annoying teachers by best friends.
$^+ p < .10;$ $^{++} p < .05;$ $^{+++} p < .01$

higher under the condition that parents were *not asked for advice* ($b_1 = .530$) than under the condition that parents were *asked for advice* ($b_1 + b_i = .074$). This result confirms the proposed explanation that adolescents whose relationship with their parents is disturbed are likely to choose friends with deviant tendencies.

Bullying Behavior

Applying the same predicting variables as presented in Table 1, and replacing the criterion variable "teacher-annoying behavior" with "bullying behavior," we obtained the following results.

The selected variables were better suited to predict annoying behavior than bullying behavior. However, the standardized multiple regression coefficients were $R = .44$ for all students, $R = .51$ for girls, and $R = .48$ for boys. The two sexes did not differ in the amount of bullying behavior. No variable of the peer context had a significant effect on the bullying behavior, either for the whole sample or for girls or boys separately. Furthermore, the bivariate correlation between bullying behavior admitted by the students and that admitted by their best same-sex friend was not significant. Due to the sampling procedure used, we were not able to include sociometric peer status in the equation. However, when we introduced into the model a scale accounting for self-reported feelings of integration in the peer network, this variable did not have any effect. Thus, the variables of the peer context did not increase significantly the explained variance in the criterion variable.

Similarly to the variables of the peer context, the variables of the parent context were not well-suited to predict students' bullying behavior. Only the SES had an effect in the overall sample ($\beta = -.17, p < .05$) and in the girl sample ($\beta = -.34, p < .01$), but not in the boy sample. In the boy sample one additional variable, everyday conflicts, had an effect on bullying ($\beta = .17, p < .10$). Inclusion of the family structure variable "loss of a parent" in the equation significantly affected the results for the girl sample ($\beta = -.22, p < .05$), increasing the explained variance of the model from 26% to 28%. Girls who had experienced the loss of a parent tended to bully other students. This effect was found neither in the overall sample, nor in the boy sample.

The school context variables are better suited to predict bullying behavior at school than the variables of the two other contexts. Educational aspiration and comfort-level at school had significant effects on boys' bullying ($\beta = -.29, p < .01; \beta = .21, p < .05$), those with low aspiration and a low level of comfort admitting more bullying behavior than others. School motivation had significant effects on girls' bullying ($\beta = -22, p < .05$). Girls who neglected homework and performed poorly reported more bullying behavior than did conscientious and achievement-oriented girls. The addition of GPA proved relevant to the results for the girl sample only, girls with lower grades admitting more bullying behavior than girls with higher grades.

Of the variables we selected for the study, girls' bullying behavior is best predicted by SES, age, and three variables of the school context. Neither any of the remaining parental context variables, nor any of the variables of the peer context had a significant effect. Boys' bullying behavior is best predicted by age, two variables of the school context, and one variable of the parent context: everyday conflicts. The other variables of the parent context and all variables of the peer context failed to predict bullying behavior among boys.

Because of the irrelevance of the peer context with respect to bullying behavior, we determined—unlike in the case of teacher-annoying behavior—no synergistic effects between the parental and the peer contexts on bullying behavior.

Discussion

One limitation of this study is that it is cross-sectional and correlational, and thus does not allow us to determine the direction of effects. We treated the variables of the parent and peer contexts as predictors of misconduct at school. However, there are good reasons to assume that effects could work in the opposite direction. With this reservation in mind, we discuss the results reported above in the light of further information about German adolescents.

As in the United States, most adolescents in (West) Berlin have a warm, close, and trustful relationship with their parents (Oswald & Boll,

1992). At the same time, most adolescents have close relationships with friends and are members of peer groups. Peer and parental influences generally do not counteract one another.

Conflict with parents per se is not believed to have a negative impact on the behavior and development of adolescents "when it co-occurs with the subjective conditions of trust and closeness" (Cooper, 1988, p. 183). As reported elsewhere (Oswald & Boll, 1992), most adolescents in our study speak of everyday conflicts with parents, with household chores topping the list of issues of dispute. These everyday conflicts have a small but significant effect on adolescents' emotional relationship with fathers and mothers. There is a small group of up to 10% or 15% of adolescents for whom conflicts with parents are not embedded in a close and trustful relationship (see Steinberg, 1990, for similar results found in the USA).

In the analysis presented above, variables indicating conflicts with parents predicted teacher-annoying behavior, while variables indicating closeness did not. In accordance with the literature, the SES of the family is related to misconduct at school, with students of lower socioeconomic background annoying more often than students of higher socioeconomic background. Contrary to expectations based on the results of several studies (e.g. Dornbusch et al., 1985; Steinberg, 1987), the family structure variable "loss of a parent" did not predict annoying behavior. Variables indicating peer influence also had an independent effect on annoying behavior.

In order to control for effects of the school context itself on teacher-annoying behavior, such variables as educational aspiration, which is closely associated with type of school (track), school motivation, and sense of well-being at school were included in the model, and these had independent effects as well. But contrary to expectations, grade point average did not augment the explained variance significantly.

Boys annoy teachers slightly more frequently than do girls. More importantly, the pattern predicting girls' behavior differs markedly from that which predicts the behavior of boys.

If younger girls are members of large crowds that include girls as well as boys; if they often go out at night; if they have conflicts with their parents, especially with mothers whose advice they no longer seek and who do not attend PTA meetings; and if they do not feel well at school, then they tend to annoy teachers. Variables of all three contexts operate together to predict girls' behavior in a convincing model.

As in the case of girls, boys' annoying behavior is predicted by variables of all three contexts, but only one variable of each context has a significant effect; younger boys who do not ask fathers for advice, who talk with friends a lot, and who report low educational aspiration tend to annoy teachers. Despite the level of explained variance obtained through this model, the number of variables in the model that have a significant effect on boys' behavior is unsatisfactory.

Variables of the three contexts in question proved to affect annoying behavior independently. One interpretation is that these effects are additive. A supplemental hypothesis presumes interaction effects between the parental and peer contexts. Following Bronfenbrenner's concept of synergistic effects in mesosystems (e.g., 1989), we calculated such interaction effects. On the basis of the results we propose that adolescents are only vulnerable to negative peer pressure if the relationship with their parents is severely disturbed. Adolescents with a disturbed relationship with their parents tend to select friends with deviant tendencies. This applies possibly more to girls than to boys, and more to teacher-annoying behavior than to the bullying of other students.

The results thus far show that our German expression of bullying behavior covers a broader range of assertive, punitive, agonistic, and aggressive behaviors than did Olweus' Scandinavian term (1983). In contrast to results of research in Scandinavia, the students in Berlin admitted engaging in higher amounts of bullying behavior. Also unlike the Scandinavian studies, our study determined no gender difference as regards such behavior. We assume this to be due to the fact that *stänkern*, our translation of the term *bullying*, covers both psychological and physical attacks, the former being more typical for girls, the latter more so for boys.

One aim of the analysis above was to predict the bullying behavior of girls and boys by the same model used for predicting teacher-annoying behavior. The pattern of predictors was very different for the two kinds of school misconduct, and the teacher-annoying behavior was much better predicted by the parent and peer variables than was the bullying behavior. All variables of the school context, including GPA, had significant effects on bullying behavior either for girls or for boys. This is in keeping with the literature summarized in the first section of the chapter. Olweus argues that family factors, including SES, produce such relationships (1983). As in Olweus' study, SES and the loss of a parent had effects on bullying, but only for girls, whereas Olweus dealt mainly with boys. We unfortunately were not able to include variables like power-assertive discipline, authoritative parenting or parental negativism, as some scholars propose (e.g., McCord, 1990). The variables we did employ, with corresponding intent, such as closeness, the seeking of parental advice, criticism of parenting style, failed to predict bullying behavior. Only the everyday conflict scale had a slight effect on boys' bullying. As discussed by Steinberg (1990), a closer investigation of dynamics inside the family is needed in order to better understand the causes for adolescent maladjustment.

The failure to predict bullying behavior by variables of the peer context may be partly caused by the ambiguity of the term *bullying*, which covers accepted as well as unaccepted self-reported behaviors. When admitting bullying behavior, some students may have in mind legitimate forms of assertive and punitive behavior. In a qualitative study of primary school children, we observed sanctions aimed at putting another student in his or her place (Oswald, 1992). Further research is needed to disentangle different types of bullying behavior, so that the varying causes and consequences may be understood.

Despite the discussed limitations of the study, the results presented in this chapter prove the simultaneous or additive effects of three contexts, and the synergistic effects of two contexts, on adolescents' misconduct directed against teachers. Conditions at school, in the family, and in the peer group have direct effects on misbehavior that are independent of each other. In addition, conditions in the family have indirect effects: A highly conflictive situation in the family makes students vulnerable to peer influences that reinforce misconduct. We conclude that the hypothesis of the domain-specific influences of parents and peers (Kandel, 1986) has to be supplemented by the hypothesis of synergistic effects in the parent-peer mesosystem on the behavior of adolescents as proposed by Bronfenbrenner (1989). Peers can exert negative pressure successfully only if the relationship between parents and their adolescent children is severely disturbed.

References

Asher, S.R. & Dodge, K.A. (1986). Identifying children who are rejected by their peers. *Developmental Psychology, 22*, 444–449.

Bronfenbrenner, U. (1989). Ecological system theory. In R. Vasta (Ed.), *Six theories of child development: Revised formulations and current issues* (pp. 185–246). Greenwich, CT: JAI Press.

Brown, B.B. (1982). The extent and effects of peer pressure among high school students. *Journal of Youth and Adolescence, 11*, 121–133.

Brown, B.B. (1990). Peer groups and peer cultures. In S.S. Feldman & G.R. Elliott (Eds.), *At the threshold: The developing adolescent* (pp. 171–196). Cambridge: Harvard University Press.

Coleman, J.S. (1961). *The adolescent society*. New York: Free Press.

Conger, J. (1981). Freedom and commitment. *American Psychologist, 36*, 1475–1484.

Cooper, C. (1988). Commentary: The role of conflict in adolescent-parent relationships. In M. Gunnar (Ed.), *21st Minnesota symposium on child psychology* (pp. 181–187). Hillsdale, NJ: Lawrence Erlbaum.

Dornbusch, S.M., Carlsmith, J.M., Bushwall, S.J., Ritter, P.L., Leiderman, P.H., Hastorf, A.H., & Gross, R.T. (1985). Single parents, extended households, and the control of adolescents. *Child Development, 56*, 326–341.

Dornbusch, S.M., Ritter, P.L., Leiderman, P.H., Roberts, D.F., & Fraleigh, M.J. (1987). The relation of parenting style to adolescent school performance. *Child Development, 58*, 1244–1257.

Eisenstadt, S.N. (1956). *From generation to generation*: Age groups and social structure. New York: Free Press.

Epstein, J.L. (1990). School and family connections. In D.G. Unger & M.B. Sussmayn (Eds.), *Families in community settings: Interdisciplinary perspectives* (pp. 99–126). New York: Haworth.

Farrington, D.P. (1986). Stepping stones to adult criminal careers. In D. Olweus, J. Block, & M. Radke-Yarrow (Eds.), *Development of antisocial and prosocial behavior* (pp. 359–384). New York: Academic Press.

Feldman, S.S., Rosenthal, D.A., Mont-Reynaud, R., Leung, K., & Lau, S. (1991). Ain't misbehavin': Adolescent values and family environments as correlates of misconduct in Australia, Hong Kong, and the United States. *Journal of Research on Adolescence, 1*, 109–134.

Hanna, J.L. (1988). *Disruptive school behavior: Class, race, and culture.* New York: Holmes & Meier.

Hansell, S. (1985). Adolescent friendship networks and distress in school. *Social Forces, 63*, 698–715.

Hirschi, T. & Hindelang, M.J. (1977). Intelligence and delinquency: A revisionist review. *American Sociological Review, 42*, 571–587.

Hollingshead, A.B. (1949). *Elmtown's youth.* New York: Free Press.

Kandel, D.B. (1986). Processes of peer influence in adolescence. In R.K. Silbereisen, K. Eyferth, & G. Rudinger (Eds.), *Development as action in context: Problem behavior and normal youth development* (pp. 203–227). New York: Springer.

Klingemann, H.-D. (1991). *Akzeptanz und Wirkung des Kabelfernsehens.* [Acceptance and effects of cabel TV]. Unpublished manuscript, Wissenschaftszentrum Berlin.

Kohn, M.L. (1987). Cross-national research as an analytic strategy. *American Sociological Review, 52*, 713–731.

McCord, J. (1990). Problem behaviors. In S.S. Feldman & G.R. Elliott (Eds.), *At the threshold: The developing adolescent* (pp. 414–430). Cambridge: Harvard University Press.

Miller, W.B. (1958). Lower class culture as a generating milieu of gang delinquency. *Journal of Social Issues, 24*, 5–19.

Olweus, D. (1983). Low school achievement and aggressive behavior in adolescent boys. In D. Magnusson & V.L. Allan (Eds.), *Human development: An interactional perspective* (pp. 353–365). New York: Academic Press.

Olweus, D. (1984a). Development of stable aggressive reaction patterns in males. In R. Blanchard & C. Blanchard (Eds.), *Advances in aggression research, Vol. 1* (pp. 103–137). New York: Academic Press.

Olweus, D. (1984b). *Bullying and harassment among school children in Scandinavia: Research and a nationwide campaign in Norway.* Unpublished manuscript, University of Bergen.

Oswald, H. (1992). Negotiations of norms and sanctions among children. In P. Adler & P.A. Adler (Eds.), *Sociological studies of child development* (pp. 99–113). Greenwich, CT: JAI Press.

Oswald, H., Baker, D.P., & Stevenson, D.L. (1988). School charter and parental management in West Germany. *Sociology of Education, 61*, 255–265.

Oswald, H. & Boll, W. (1992). Das Ende des Generationenkonflikts? [The end of the generation conflict]. *Zeitschrift für Sozialisationsforschung und Erziehungssoziologie, 12*(1), 30–51.

Parsons, T. (1942). Age and sex in the social structure of the United States. *American Sociological Review*, 7, 604–616.

Piaget, J. (1932). The moral judgement of the child. London: Kegan Paul.

Silbereisen, R.K., Boehnke, K., & Crockett, L. (1991). Zum Einfluss von Schul-milieu und elterlicher Erziehungshaltung auf Rauchen und Trinken im mittleren Jugendalter. [On the impact of school milieu and parental attitudes on smoking and drinking in mid-adolescence]. In R. Pekrun & H. Fend (Eds.), *Schule und Persönlichkeitsentwicklung: Ein Resümee der Längsschnittforschung* (pp. 272–293). Stuttgart: Enke.

Snyder, J., Dishion, T.J., & Patterson, G.R. (1986). Determinants and con-sequences of associating with deviant peers during preadolescence and adoles-cence. *Journal of Early Adolescence*, 6, 29–43.

Sroufe, L.A. & Fleeson, J. (1986). Attachment and the construction of relation-ships. In W.W. Hartup & L. Rubin (Eds.), *Relationships and development* (pp. 51–72). Hillsdale, NJ: Lawrence Erlbaum.

Steinberg, L. (1987). Single parents, stepparents, and the susceptibility of adoles-cents to antisocial peer pressure. *Child Development*, 58, 269–275.

Steinberg, L. (1990). Autonomy, conflict, and harmony in the family relationship. In S.S. Feldman & G.R. Elliott (Eds.), *At the threshold: The developing adolescent* (pp. 255–276). Cambridge: Harvard University Press.

Steinberg, L. & Brown, B.B. (1989). *Beyond the classroom: Parental and peer influence on high school achievement.* Invited paper presented to the Families as Educators Special Interest Groups at the annual meeting of the American Educational Research Association, San Francisco.

Steinberg, L., Mounts, N.S., Lamborn, S.D., & Dornbusch, S.M. (1991). Authoritative parenting and adolescent adjustment across varied ecological niches. *Journal of Research on Adolescence*, 1, 19–36.

Youniss, J. (1980). *Parents and peers in social development: A Sullivan-Piaget perspective.* Chicago: University of Chicago Press.

Youniss, J. & Smollar, J. (1985). *Adolescent relations with mothers, fathers, and friends.* Chicago: University of Chicago Press.

18
Interactions between Individual and Contextual Factors in the Development of Offending

DAVID P. FARRINGTON

The aim of this paper is to investigate interactions between individual and contextual (e.g., family, school, or work) factors in the development of offending. Factors A and B interact when the extent to which A predicts offending varies according to the value of B (and vice versa). For example, separation from parents might be associated with increased offending for children with unconvicted parents but with decreased offending for children with convicted parents, perhaps because separation shields children from criminogenic influences in the latter case.

Most prior research on the development of offending that uses multivariate techniques focuses on *independent main effects* rather than on interactions. For example, researchers might investigate whether individual factors predict offending independently of family factors. This focus partly reflects the major interest of many researchers in drawing conclusions about causes; it is often argued that, if a factor A does not predict offending independently of another factor B, then the factor A cannot be a cause of offending. However, it is often forgotten that such a factor A could be part of a causal chain leading to the factor B and later to offending. In other words, A could be a distal rather than a proximal cause.

The focus on discovering independent effects also partly reflects the difficulty, with currently available statistical techniques, of investigating interactions. In multiple regression, for example, it is common to study only multiplicative interaction effects, and all such effects have to be explicitly entered into the model. The number of possible interaction effects increases dramatically with the number of variables, making it necessary to have very large samples. Even with only 10 predictor variables, there are 45 possible two-way interaction effects, 120 possible three-way interaction effects, and so on.

Interaction effects can have important practical implications. For example, if a factor A predicts offending in the absence of B (or at low values of B) but not in the presence of B (or at high values of B), then B might be a protective factor for offending. In preventing the development of offending, it might be easier in some cases to provide or increase B than to eliminate or decrease A. Another possibility is that A might predict offending especially if it co-occurs with another factor C, which does not itself predict offending and essentially acts as a catalyst (e.g., Rutter & Giller, 1983, p. 241). Again, it might be easier in some cases to eliminate C rather than A. Hence, it is important to search for interaction effects.

Rutter (1985, p. 600) explicitly defined protective factors (nowadays sometimes termed "buffering" factors) in terms of their interactive effects:

Protective factors refer to influences that modify, ameliorate, or alter a person's response to some environmental hazard that predisposes to a maladaptive outcome . . . [They] may have no detectable effect in the absence of any subsequent stressor; their role is to modify the response to later adversity rather than to foster normal development in any direct sense.

He also pointed out that, if an adverse factor had a significant main effect, this did not necessarily mean that the adverse factor would have an effect in the absence of other adversities (i.e., when other factors were favorable rather than adverse). This is again a statement about interactive effects. Protective factors do not have to be defined in interactive terms (e.g., Farrington, Gallagher, Morley, St. Ledger, & West, 1988); for example, A might be defined as a protective factor if the risk of offending decreased as A increased. However, the focus of interest in this paper is on interactions.

Perhaps the most important research on interactive factors in offending has been carried out by Werner (e.g., Werner, 1983; Werner & Smith, 1982) and Kellam (e.g., Ensminger, Kellam, & Rubin, 1983; Kellam, Brown, Rubin, & Ensminger, 1983). Werner studied "vulnerable" children who were at high risk for delinquency, and compared those who were non-delinquent ("resilient") with those who were seriously delinquent. The resilient children were more likely to be firstborn, active and affectionate infants, and from smaller families characterized by low discord. They were unlikely to have absent fathers, or working mothers, were receiving a high degree of attention in infancy, and had high infant intelligence, high verbal skills, and high self-esteem in adolescence. Kellam found that while shy children generally had a low risk of delinquency, children who were both shy and aggressive had a particularly high risk. Similar results were reported by McCord (1987) and Farrington et al. (1988).

The Cambridge Study in Delinquent Development

The present research uses data collected in the Cambridge Study in Delinquent Development, which is a prospective longitudinal survey of 411 males. At the time they were first contacted in 1961–1962, they were all living in a working-class area of London, England. The vast majority of the sample were chosen by taking all the boys who were then aged 8, and on the registers of six state primary schools located within a one-mile radius of a research office that had been established. The boys were overwhelmingly white, working-class, and of British origin. The major results obtained in this survey have been reported in four books (West, 1969, 1982; West & Farrington, 1973, 1977) and in more than 60 papers listed by Farrington and West (1990).

The major aim in this survey was to measure as many factors as possible that were alleged to be causes or correlates of offending. The boys were interviewed and tested in their schools when they were aged about 8, 10, and 14, by male or female psychologists. They were interviewed in our research office at about 16, 18, and 21, and in their homes at about 25 and 32, by young male social science graduates. The tests in schools included measures of intelligence, attainment, personality, and psychomotor impulsivity, while information was collected in the interviews about such topics as living circumstances, employment histories, relationships with females, leisure activities, and offending behavior. On all occasions, except at ages 21 and 25, the aim was to interview the whole sample, and it was always possible to trace and interview a high proportion, For example, 389 of the 410 males still alive at 18 (94.9%) were interviewed, and 378 of the 403 still alive at age 32 (93.8%).

In addition to the interviews and tests with the boys, interviews with their parents were carried out by female social workers who visited their homes. These took place about once a year from when each boy was about 8 until when he was aged 14–15 and was in his last year of compulsory education. The primary informant was the mother, although many fathers were also seen. The parents provided details about such matters as family income, family size, their employment histories, their child-rearing practices (including attitudes, discipline, and parental agreement), their degree of supervision of the boy, and his temporary or permanent separations from them.

The boys' teachers completed questionnaires when the boys were aged about 8, 10, 12, and 14. These provided information about the boys' troublesome and aggressive school behavior, their attention deficit, their school attainments, and their truancy. Ratings were also obtained from the boys' peers when they were in their primary schools, about such topics as their daring, dishonesty, troublesomeness, and popularity.

Searches were carried out in the national Criminal Record Office in London to try and locate findings of guilt of the boys, of their parents, of their brothers and sisters, and (in recent years) of their wives and cohabitees. Convictions were counted only if they were for offenses normally recorded in this Office, thereby excluding minor crimes such as common (simple) assault, traffic offenses, and drunkenness. The most frequent offenses included were thefts and burglaries. However, we did not rely on official records for our information about offending, because we also obtained self-reports of offending from the boys themselves at every age from 14 onwards.

Summarizing, the Cambridge Study in Delinquent Development has a unique combination of features. Eight face-to-face interviews have been completed with the subjects over a period of 24 years, between ages 8 and 32. The attrition rate is unusually low for such a long-term survey. The main focus of interest is on crime and delinquency, but the survey also provides information about alcohol and drug abuse, educational problems, poverty and poor housing, unemployment, sexual behavior, aggression, and other social problems. The sample size of about 400 is large enough for many statistical analyses, but small enough to permit detailed case histories of the males and their families. Information has been obtained from multiple sources, including the subjects themselves, their parents, teachers, peers, and official records. Generally, the information came from parents, teachers or peers when the subjects were between ages 8 and 14, and from the males themselves between ages 16 and 32. Data has been collected about a wide variety of theoretical constructs at different ages, including biological (e.g., heart rate), psychological (e.g., intelligence), family (e.g., discipline), and social (e.g., socioeconomic status) factors.

Interactions have previously been studied in this project in two major ways. Farrington (1985), using 25 dichotomous predictor variables and four measures of offending, systematically searched for instances where a variable A had a (phi) correlation with offending greater than +.10 at one value of a variable B and less than −.10 at the other value. This happened in only 1.6% of cases (39 out of 2,400), in comparison with the chance expectation of about 1.3%. Farrington et al. (1988) searched for factors that might protect vulnerable boys with criminogenic backgrounds from becoming offenders. In agreement with previous research (West & Farrington, 1973, pp. 145–150) suggesting that being nervous or withdrawn was a protective factor, they found that vulnerable boys who had few or no friends at age 8 were particularly likely to remain unconvicted.

The main aim of this paper is to investigate interactions between factors that predict offending in three age ranges: adolescence (convictions between 10 and 14, self-reported offending up to 14), the teenage years (convictions and self-reported offending between 15 and 18), and adulthood (convictions between 21 and 32, self-reported offending between 27 and 32). Convictions and self-reports provide alternative windows on offending, subject to different biases. For example, convictions are affected by police behavior, while self-reports are affected by the willingness to admit offenses. Ideally, results obtained with one measure should be replicated with the other. These age ranges were chosen in light of the availability of data; because of inadequate funding, only about half of the males were interviewed at age 21 and only about a quarter at age 25. Hence, self-reported offending data for the whole sample is available primarily at ages 14, 18 and 32.

Methods of Analysis

A great deal of data reduction was carried out in this project to try to produce empirical variables that each measured only one theoretically distinct construct (Farrington, 1984). For example, clusters of variables were identified that were related empirically and theoretically, and then one variable might be chosen as the best representative of the cluster, or several cluster variables might be combined into a single composite variable. Similar variables obtained from different sources (e.g., peers and teachers) or at adjacent ages (e.g., 8 and 10) were often combined in the expectation that the combined variables would be more valid than the original variables.

In the interests of comparability, all variables were dichotomized, as far as possible, into the 'worst' quarter versus the remaining three-quarters of the sample. Because most variables were originally classified into a small number of categories, and because distinctions between categories often could not be made very accurately, this dichotomizing probably did not involve a great loss of information. It was completed prior to analyses of relationships between predictors and offending outcomes, and so was not influenced by any knowledge of results. The one-quarter/three-quarters split for predictors was chosen to match the prior expectation that about one quarter of the sample would be convicted.

Another reason for dichotomizing was that the relationships between predictor variables and offending measures were not usually linear (Farrington & Hawkins, 1991). In many cases, the risk of conviction increased only slowly in moving from "better" to "average" levels of a variable but then increased quite sharply for those in the "worst" quarter. Dichotomizing undoubtedly facilitates the presentation of easily under-standable and meaningful results, and encourages the analyses of "risk factors" for offending. It also facilitates the investigation and presentation of interaction effects.

Forward stepwise multiple linear regression (using ordinary least squares) was used to investigate how far the variables were independent predictors of offending. Strictly speaking, dichotomous data violate the underlying assumptions of multiple linear regression. However, with dichotomous variables, multiple regression is mathematically identical to discriminant analysis, and it produces very similar results to logistic regression in its identification of independent predictors (Cleary & Angel, 1984; Farrington, 1985, 1986). In fact, with dichotomous variables, discriminant analysis and logistic regression yield mathematically identical results under the assumption of multivariate normality of the predictors

(Schlesselman, 1982, p. 245). The use of the forward stepwise method avoids the problem with other methods in that the apparently most important predictors (i.e., those with the highest weightings) may be those that are represented least redundantly (Gordon, 1968).

Multiple regression was used because of the possibility of pairwise deletion of cases in calculating correlations, which minimizes the problem of missing data. Logistic regression involves listwise deletion of cases, so that if a subject is not known on any one variable he is completely deleted from the analysis. Even though the number of missing cases on any one variable in these analyses was never more than 10%, listwise deletion can have serious effects in reducing the effective sample size. This is especially important in research on offending, since the most uncooperative families tend to have particularly delinquent children (West & Farrington, 1973), and offending teenagers are differentially lost from samples interviewed (West & Farrington, 1977). Because the missing cases are disproportionally the worst offenders and hence the most interesting, listwise deletion can produce misleading and invalid results.

Predicting Adolescent Offending

Table 18.1 shows the most important independent predictors of adolescent offending, as identified by the stepwise multiple regressions. The aim was to predict the 54 males who were convicted between ages 10 and 14 and the 94 males who were the worst on self-reported offending at age 14 (each admitting 14 or more of the 38 acts inquired about; see Farrington, 1973). Fifteen predictor variables were studied: troublesomeness according to peers and teachers, daring according to peers and parents, peer-

TABLE 18.1. Independent predictors of adolescent official and self-reported offending.

	% Offending		Significance		Regression	
Predictor at age (N)	Worst	Re-mainder	Odds ratio	P	F change	P
Official offending 10–14 (54)						
High troublesomeness 8–10 (92)	29	8	4.5	.0001	26.2	.0001
Low nonverbal IQ 8–10 (103)	24	9	3.1	.0001	8.8	.0016
Low junior attainment 11 (90)	24	9	3.1	.0002	5.0	.013
Separated from parent 10 (90)	22	11	2.4	.003	3.7	.03
High daring 8–10 (121)	22	9	2.8	.0004	3.1	.04
Poor child-rearing 8 (96)	21	9	2.6	.002	2.5	.06
Self-reported offending 14 (94)						
High daring 8–10 (121)	36	18	2.5	.0001	15.4	.0001
Convicted parent 10 (104)	36	19	2.5	.0003	10.7	.0006
Low nonverbal IQ 8–10 (103)	32	20	1.8	.012	3.1	.04

rated unpopularity, parent-rated nervousness, psychomotor impulsivity, low nonverbal IQ (on the Progressive Matrices), low socioeconomic status family, low family income, large family size (5 or more children), convicted parent, separated from parent (for reasons other than death or hospitalization), poor child-rearing (harsh or erratic discipline and attitude), poor supervision (monitoring), low junior school leaving results, and going to a high-delinquency-rate secondary school. All were measured at age 8–10 except the last two variables, which were measured at age 11. (Only 6 boys were convicted at age 10.) Some variables were not included in this analysis (e.g., lacks concentration or restless at age 8–10, low verbal IQ at age 8–10) because of problems of multicollinearity. Even with only 15 predictors, listwise deletion would have reduced the sample size by one-quarter, to 313.

High troublesomeness was the best predictor of official offending. Of the 92 most troublesome boys, 29% were convicted, compared with 8% of the remaining 319, a significant difference (corrected $\chi^2 = 25.5$, 1 df, $p < .0001$, one-tailed in view of the clear directional predictions). The odds ratio for this comparison (a measure of predictive efficiency) was 4.5, in comparison with the chance expectation of 1. This is the ratio of the odds of becoming an offender for troublesome boys to the odds of becoming an offender for non-troublesome boys. Troublesomeness entered first in the multiple regression analysis, producing an F change of 26.2 ($p < .0001$, one-tailed).

The other independent predictors of official offending were low nonverbal IQ, low junior attainment, separation from parents, high daring and (almost significantly) poor parental child-rearing behavior. All independent predictors had positive weightings in all regressions. The most important independent predictors of self-reported offending were high daring, convicted parents, and low nonverbal IQ. Hence, high daring and a low IQ were independent predictors of both official and self-reported offending. Convicted parents were not characteristic of the boys convicted at the earliest ages (10–13) but were a feature of later-convicted boys (West & Farrington, 1973, p. 36). Although the boys were asked about offending up to age 14, their self-reports may have primarily reflected contemporaneous offending, which was associated with convicted parents at this age.

Convictions and self-reported offending have always been highly related in this research project (e.g., Farrington, 1989b). The agreement between those two measures was actually greater than suggested by Table 18.1. The strength of a relationship in a 2 × 2 table can be summarized by the phi correlation or by the logarithm of the odds ratio (OR). (These two measures are very highly correlated.) Comparing 15 predictor variables with official and self-reported offending, the 15 phi values for official offending correlated .50 ($p = .03$, one-tailed) with the 15 phi values for self-reported offending. Similarly, the 15 Log (OR) values for official offending correlated .52 (p = .023, one-tailed) with the 15 Log (OR) values for self-reported offending. Hence, the strength of relationships with official offending correlated quite highly with the strength of relationships with self-reported offending. This is not surprising, since 57% of the official offenders were also self-reported offenders, while 82% of the official non-offenders were also self-reported non-offenders. Hence, results with official offending tended to be replicated with self-reported offending.

In previous research on this study (e.g., Farrington, 1990), it was concluded that the most important independent childhood predictors of offending fell into six major conceptual categories: (a) socioeconomic deprivation (e.g., low family income, large family size); (b) poor parental child-rearing (e.g., harsh or erratic discipline, poor supervision, separation from parents); (c) family deviance (e.g., convicted parents); (d) school problems (e.g., low IQ, low attainment, high-delinquency-rate school); (e) hyperactivity-impulsivity–attention deficit (e.g., high daring, poor concentration or restlessness, high psychomotor impulsivity); and (f) antisocial child behavior (e.g., troublesomeness). Various theories have been proposed to explain the causes of childhood troublesomeness, why troublesomeness escalates into the onset of delinquency, why delinquency persists and escalates into adult crime, and why adult crime persists or desists after age 21 (e.g., Farrington, 1992). All these theories are essentially based on independent predictors of offending, with little attention to the possibility of interaction effects.

Investigating Interaction Effects

There are several possible types of interaction effects, and the simplest (two-way, in dichotomous data) will be investigated here. The focus of interest is on a variable B that modifies the significant relationship between a variable A and offending. B could be termed a "moderator" variable. In order to illustrate the possible interaction effects, I will assume that 50 males have A = 2 (are in the "worst" category) and are offenders, 50 are A = 1 and offenders, 50 are A = 2 and non-offenders, and 250 are A = 1 and non-offenders. These figures approximate the relationship between troublesomeness and juvenile (age 10–16) convictions, and show the link between the "worst" category and offending. I will also assume the same relationship between A and B; that is, A = 2, B = 2 ("worst"), 50 males; A = 2, B = 1, 50 males; A = 1, B = 2, 50 males; A = 1, B = 1, 250 males. Generally, "worst" categories, or adverse features, tend to be interrelated. The particular numbers chosen here help the exposition but are not critical to the argument.

Given these numbers, there are only two degrees of freedom in the 2 × 2 × 2 table (A × B × offending), and it is easy to investigate all possible

TABLE 18.2. Types of interaction effects.

	% Offending							Likelihood ratio		
	B = 2			B = 1						
	A = 2	A = 1		A = 2	A = 1					
Case	(50)	(50)	OR2	(50)	(250)	OR1	LOR	A	B	Int
1	50	16	5.3	50	17	5.0	0.06	36.5	0.0	0.0
2	62	30	3.8	38	14	3.8	0.01	24.4	12.6	0.0
3	84	20	21.0	16	16	1.0	3.04	20.2	26.9	24.3
4	98	2	2401	2	20	0.084	10.26	21.5	21.5	110.6
5	20	20	1.0	80	16	21.0	−3.04	55.5	16.4	22.6
6	2	20	0.082	98	16	257	−8.06	76.8	51.6	67.9
7	50	50	1.0	50	10	9.0	−2.20	21.5	21.5	16.9
8	60	2	73.5	40	20	2.7	3.29	38.9	0.5	16.7
9	38	20	2.5	62	16	8.6	−1.25	46.1	1.6	4.7

Note: LOR = Log(OR2) − Log(OR1); Int = Interaction; OR2 = Odds ratio, B = 2; OR1 = Odds ratio, B = 1.
The likelihood ratio test is from a logit analysis. Values are distributed as chi-squared with 1 df.

configurations. There are essentially nine possible types of interaction effects, exemplified in Table 18.2. Case 1 shows no interaction at all: The relationship between A and offending is essentially the same for B = 1 and B = 2. For B = 1, 17% (42) of the 250 with A = 1 are offenders, compared with 50% (25) of the 50 with A = 2 (referred to here as a positive relationship). For B = 2, 16% (8) of the 50 with A = 1 are offenders, compared with 50% (25) of the 50 with A = 2. The two odds ratios are very similar: 5.3 for the B = 2 table and 5.0 for the B = 1 table.

Using the GLIM statistical package, logit analysis (Fienberg, 1980) was carried out for the 2 × 2 × 2 table to investigate the independent effect of A on offending after controlling for B, the independent effect of B on offending after controlling for A, and the interaction effect of A and B on offending (after controlling for both main effects). The likelihood ratio chi-squared value of 36.5 shows that A had a significant effect on offending after controlling for B. (This statistic is distributed as chi-squared with 1 df, so 3.8 corresponds to $p = .05$ and 10.8 to $p = .001$, two-tailed; two-tailed tests must be used for interactions, but one-tailed tests are appropriate for main effects.) The two values of zero show that B had no effect on offending after controlling for A, and that there was no interaction effect.

Case 2 also shows no interaction effect. In this case, A and B both have additive and independent main effects. The percentage of offenders is greatest in the A = 2, B = 2 category, despite the absence of any interaction between A and B. Generally, if the percentage of offenders is greatest in the (A = 2, B = 2) category, this could reflect either an interaction effect or merely additive independent main effects. If the percentage of offenders is greatest when A = 2 and B = 1, this is evidence of an interaction effect.

Case 3 shows that A is related to offending when B = 2 but has no relationship when B = 1. This corresponds to significant independent effects of A and B on offending and a significant interaction. Case 4 shows a large positive relationship between A and offending at B = 2 and a small negative relationship at B = 1. Compared with Case 3, the interaction effect is now much bigger. Case 5 is basically the reverse of Case 3: A is related to offending when B = 1 but not when B = 2. Again, the independent effects of A and B and the interaction effect are all significant. Similarly, Case 6 is basically the reverse of Case 4, with a large positive relationship between A and offending at B = 1 and a small negative relationship at B = 2. Again, the interaction effect is much bigger in Case 6 than in Case 5.

Case 7 also shows an interaction effect that is somewhat the reverse of Case 3, but in a different way from Case 5. In Case 3, offending is disproportionally frequent when both A = 2 and B = 2, and infrequent in the other three categories. In Case 7, offending is disproportionally infrequent when both A = 1 and B = 1, and frequent in the other three categories. As with Case 5, A is related to offending when B = 1 and not when B = 2; but Case 5 shows that offending is disproportionally frequent when A = 2 and B = 1, and infrequent in the other three categories. The reverse of Case 7 (offending is disproportionally infrequent when A = 1 and B = 2, and frequent in the other three categories) does not occur in this example, because the maximum possible proportion of offenders when A = 1 and B = 1 is 20%.

Case 8 shows that A is related to offending at both B = 1 and B = 2, but the relationship is stronger for B = 2. In this case, A has a significant independent effect on offending but B does not, and the interaction is significant. Case 9 is essentially the reverse of Case 8: A is related to offending at both B = 1 and B = 2, but more strongly at B = 1. Again, A has a significant independent effect on offending, B does not, and the interaction is significant. Given the total positive relationship between A and offending, A must be positively related to offending at either or both values of B (excluding the trivial case where all those with B = 1 are non-offenders and all those with B = 2 are offenders). Hence, these are the only possible types of interaction effects in this 2 × 2 × 2 table.

All the significant interaction effects were readily detected by the size of the interaction term in the logit analysis. However, the size of this interaction term does not distinguish between different types of interaction effects. For example, Cases 3 and 5 show essentially opposite interaction effects, but the interaction terms are comparable. The following index of the nature of the interaction effect seems useful: LOR = Log(OR2) − Log(OR1) (where the ORs are odds ratios in the two sub-tables).

LOR is essentially the natural logarithm of the ratio of the two ORs. Case 3 has LOR = 3.04, and Case 5 has LOR = −3.04, indicating the equal and opposite interaction effects. Generally, LOR is positive when A is more strongly related to offending at B = 2 (when OR2 is greater than OR1) and negative when A is more strongly related to offending at B = 1 (when OR1 is greater than OR2). No interaction corresponds to LOR = 0. Both LOR and the interaction term are unaffected when A and B are reversed.

Interactions among Predictors of Adolescent Offending

All 105 possible 2 × 2 × 2 tables relating each of the 15 variables measured at age 8–11 to each other and to official offending were then constructed. Logit analyses were carried out to determine if the interaction term was significant in each case, and the 10 significant (or near-significant, in the case of the 3.7 value) interactions are shown in order of magnitude in Table 18.3. In general, individual variables are listed under A and contextual variables under B, to investigate how individual variables predict offending in different contexts.

TABLE 18.3. Interactions among predictors of adolescent official and self-reported offending.

| | | % Offending | | | | | | | |
| | | B = 2 | | | B = 1 | | | | LR |
A	B	A = 2	A = 1	OR2	A = 2	A = 1	OR1	LOR	Int
Official offending 10–14									
Separated	Low income	17	28	0.5	26	7	4.8	−2.23	11.8
Daring	Convicted parent	15	21	0.7	26	6	5.3	−2.05	10.2
Impulsive	Separated	21	23	0.9	25	6	5.2	−1.79	7.5
Low attainment	Poor supervision	16	20	0.8	26	6	5.4	−1.95	6.0
Troublesome	Convicted parent	23	15	1.7	34	7	7.2	−1.47	5.2
Delinquent school	Large family	22	25	0.8	24	8	3.7	−1.49	5.0
Convicted parent	Low class	32	8	5.2	12	12	1.0	1.62	4.9
Troublesome	Separated	29	19	1.8	30	6	6.4	−1.27	3.9
Daring	Low class	17	18	0.9	23	7	3.9	−1.41	3.9
Low attainment	Unpopular	18	14	1.3	28	7	4.8	−1.32	3.7
Self-reported offending 14									
Low IQ	Delinquent school	18	29	0.6	43	19	3.2	−1.75	7.6
Poor supervision	Low class	22	34	0.6	39	18	2.8	−1.64	6.5
Poor child-rearing	Low class	23	33	0.6	35	18	2.4	−1.39	5.1
Unpopular	Low class	44	16	4.2	23	22	1.1	1.39	4.9
Poor child-rearing	Poor supervision	50	20	4.1	21	20	1.0	1.38	4.8
Convicted parent	Low class	52	15	6.2	30	20	1.7	1.29	4.5
Daring	Troublesome	47	15	5.2	26	18	1.6	1.20	3.8
Daring	Unpopular	55	18	5.4	29	17	1.9	1.04	3.7

Note: OR = Odds ratio; LOR = Log(OR2) − Log(OR1); LR Int = likelihood ratio chi-squared for interaction.

For example, among 307 boys with non-convicted parents, 34% of the 53 troublesome boys were convicted, in comparison with 7% of the 254 non-troublesome ones, a significant difference (corrected $\chi^2 = 29.6$, $p <$ .0001, odds ratio = 7.2). However, among 104 boys with convicted parents, 23% of the 39 troublesome boys were convicted, in comparison with 15% of the 65 non-troublesome ones, a nonsignificant difference (corrected $\chi^2 = 0.52$, NS, odds ratio = 1.7). The logit analysis showed that troublesomeness had a significant independent effect on offending (likelihood ratio $\chi^2 = 20.9$, $p < .0001$), that convicted parents did not (L.R. $\chi^2 = 0.5$), and that there was a significant interaction (L.R. $\chi^2 =$ 5.2, $p = .023$, two-tailed). The negative value of LOR shows that troublesomeness predicted offending more strongly for those with unconvicted parents than for those with convicted parents.

The LORs for official offending in Table 3 show that, with one exception, all the significant interactions were of the same type: Variable A was more strongly related to offending at B = 1 than at B = 2. Most of these interactions resemble Case 7 in Table 18.2. They occurred because offending was disproportionally infrequent when A = 1 and B = 1, or, in other words, when neither adverse feature was present. However, because offending was always less frequent for A = 2, B = 2 than for A = 2, B = 1, the variables listed under B might be having counteracting or masking effects on the variables listed under A. In particular, the most significant interaction, between separation from a parent and low income, resembled Case 6 rather than Case 7, with a positive relationship between A and offending when B = 1 and a negative relationship when B = 2.

The one interaction that was different from the remainder was between convicted parents and low socioeconomic status families. This resembled Case 3 of Table 18.2. Offending was disproportionally frequent when convicted parents and low socioeconomic status families occurred together. Convicted parents were not related to offending in higher class families.

Summarizing the remainder of the interactions with official offending, boys from low income families were less likely to be convicted if they were separated from a parent (usually, the father), whereas boys from higher-income families were more likely to be convicted if they were separated. Daring predicted offending among those with unconvicted parents or from higher socioeconomic status families, but not among those with convicted parents or from low socioeconomic status families. Similarly, psychomotor impulsivity did not predict offending for those who were separated, low attainment did not predict offending for those receiving poor parental supervision or who were unpopular, troublesomeness did not predict offending for those with convicted parents or who were separated, and going to a high-delinquency-rate school did not predict offending for those from large-sized families.

The pattern of interactions seemed somewhat different for self-reported offending. The first three interactions (low nonverbal IQ with delinquent school, poor supervision and poor child-rearing with low social class) showed that A was positively related to offending for B = 1 and negatively related for B = 2, as in Case 6 of Table 18.2. In other words, poor child-rearing and poor supervision in lower-class families seemed to be better than good child-rearing and good supervision, perhaps because the good upbringing was more successful in inculcating undesirable norms. Similarly, being a low-IQ boy at a high-delinquency-rate school was better than being a low-IQ boy at a low-delinquency-rate school, perhaps because the low-IQ boys may have perceived themselves as less deviant at the more delinquent school.

The last five interactions showed that A was more strongly related to offending at B = 2 than at B = 1. The first two of these resemble Case 3 and the last three resemble Case 8. These factors had disproportionally additive effects when they occurred together. This was true for unpopularity or convicted parents in combination with low social class, poor child-rearing in combination with poor supervision, and daring in combination with troublesomeness or unpopularity. It is interesting that low socioeconomic status appeared so often in interactions, since it showed little sign of being related to either official or self-reported offending.

The interaction between convicted parents and lower-class families was the only one that was significant for both official and self-reported offending. However, interactions with official offending were generally similar to interactions with self-reported offending. Over all 105 interactions, the LOR values for official offending correlated .47 ($p < .0001$, one-tailed) with the LOR values for self-reported offending. Interactions had to be quite extreme to reach the $p = .05$ (two-tailed) significance level. For example, as Table 18.3 shows, the interaction between unpopularity and low social class in predicting self-reported offending was significant. The interaction between unpopularity and low social class in predicting official offending was very similar, with the highest prevalence of offending in the (A = 2, B = 2) category, and with an almost identical LOR of 1.38. However, this interaction was not quite statistically significant (likelihood ratio $\chi^2 = 3.0$, $p = .086$, two-tailed).

One problem in interpreting these results is that the percentage of significant interactions (8.6%, or 18 out of 210) was not much greater than the 5% expected by chance. However, the results are more convincing when the variables are partitioned into those with independent effects on offending (shown in Table 18.1) and the remainder. For comparisons involving variables shown in Table 18.1, 8 out of 69 for official offending and 4 out of 39 for self-reported offending yielded significant interactions: more than twice chance expectation. Twelve out of 108 is significantly more than chance expectation ($p = .001$, one-tailed). One of these interactions was significant at $p = .0006$ (with a probability of less than 1 in 1,600 of occurring by chance) and another at

.0014 (with a chance probability of less than 1 in 700). For comparisons involving other variables, only 2 out of 36 for official offending and 4 out of 66 for self-reported offending yielded significant interactions: close to chance expectation. From now on, the focus of interest will be on variables that are independent predictors of offending and on other variables that have significant interactions with them.

Three-way interactions were investigated for sets of three variables where all two-way interactions were significant. These were the interaction between daring, convicted parents, and low socioeconomic status in predicting official offending, and the interaction between poor supervision, poor child-rearing, and low socioeconomic status in predicting self-reported offending. However, these three-way interactions (and some others that were investigated) showed no sign of being statistically significant.

Predicting Teenage Offending

Table 18.4 shows the independent predictors of convictions and self-reported offending between ages 15 and 18. The self-reported offending measure was based on seven types of offenses, including burglary, vandalism, taking vehicles, and different types of theft (West & Farrington, 1977). The analysis included 29 predictor variables measured up to age 14. These were the 15 measured at age 8–11, the two previous

TABLE 18.4. Independent predictors of teenage official and self-reported offending.

	% Offending		Significance		Regression	
Predictor at age (N)	Worst	Re-mainder	Odds ratio	P	F change	P
Official offending 15–18 (94)						
Official offender 10–14 (54)	69	16	11.5	.0001	80.5	.0001
Convicted parent 10 (104)	44	16	4.3	.0001	33.0	.0001
High daring 8–10 (121)	44	14	4.7	.0001	26.4	.0001
Sexual intercourse 14 (47)	62	18	7.3	.0001	19.7	.0001
Frequent truancy 12–14 (73)	55	16	6.4	.0001	17.4	.0001
Frequent lying 12–14 (122)	45	13	5.3	.0001	9.4	.0012
Self-reported offender 14 (94)	48	15	3.0	.0001	4.2	.021
Large family size 14 (85)	40	18	3.0	.0001	4.0	.023
Poor child-rearing 8 (96)	39	18	2.9	.0001	3.6	.03
Attention deficit 12–14 (107)	44	15	4.3	.0001	2.3	.06
Self-reported offending 15–18 (97)						
Self-reported offender 14 (94)	51	17	4.9	.0001	45.4	.0001
Official offender 10–14 (54)	52	21	4.1	.0001	10.2	.0008
Sexual intercourse 14 (47)	51	22	3.8	.0001	6.0	.007
High troublesomeness 8–10 (92)	40	21	2.6	.0003	4.1	.021

measures of official and self-reported offending up to age 14, and the following 12 variables measured at age 12–14: attention deficit (lacks concentration or restless), frequent lying, frequent truancy (all rated by teachers), nervousness according to parents and teachers, nonverbal IQ (on the Progressive Matrices), verbal attainment (on the Mill Hill vocabulary test), hostility to the police, regular smoking, having sexual intercourse, low socioeconomic status family, large family size, and poor parenting (harshness and disharmony). Because of problems of multi-collinearity, some variables were excluded completely from the analyses (e.g., delinquent friends at age 14, which was highly related to self-reported offending at age 14, probably because most offenses were committed in groups). Other variables were excluded from the regression analyses but included in the analyses of interactions; for example, large family size at age 10 was excluded because it was highly related to large family size at age 14 and because large family size at age 14 was the better predictor of teenage offending.

Convictions between 15 and 18 were independently predicted by earlier convictions and self-reported offending, convicted parents up to the 10th birthday, high daring at age 8–10, having sexual intercourse by age 14, frequent truancy and lying at age 12–14, large family size at age 14, poor parental child-rearing behavior at age 8, and (almost significantly) attention deficit at age 12–14. High self-reported offending at age 15–18 was independently predicted only by earlier convictions and self-reported offending, having sexual intercourse by age 14 and high troublesomeness at 8–10.

Interactions among Predictors of Teenage Offending

Table 18.5 shows the results of the interaction analyses for teenage offending. Early sexual intercourse predicted official offending especially for those who were not suffering poor child-rearing and who were frequent truants. Psychomotor impulsivity and daring predicted offending especially for those who were suffering poor child-rearing. Offending was low among those who were not from large families and not hostile to the police, and also among those who were not nervous and not suffering poor child-rearing. Replicating the result seen in Table 18.3, convicted parents predicted offending especially for those from lower socioeconomic status families. Daring predicted offending especially for those suffering poor child-rearing and those who were not nervous. Those who were not suffering poor child-rearing either at 8 or at 14 were especially unlikely to become offenders. Frequent lying predicted official offending, especially for those who were separated from a parent, and those who were not adolescent official offenders and who did not have convicted parents were particularly unlikely to be teenage official offenders.

TABLE 18.5. Interactions among predictors of teenage official and self-reported offending.

| | | % Offending | | | | | | | |
| | | B = 2 | | | B = 1 | | | | LR |
A	B	A = 2	A = 1	OR2	A = 2	A = 1	OR1	LOR	Int
Official offending 15–18									
Intercourse 14	Poor child-rearing 8	50	37	1.7	68	13	14.7	−2.14	8.5
Impulsive 8–10	Poor child-rearing 8	63	29	4.2	17	18	0.9	1.52	6.7
Hostile to police 14	Large family 14	38	40	1.0	36	12	4.1	−1.46	6.6
Nervous 12–14	Poor child-rearing 8	34	42	0.7	29	14	2.6	−1.29	5.9
Convicted parent 10	Low class 8–10	65	13	12.7	36	16	2.9	1.49	5.8
Intercourse 14	Truancy 12–14	100	43	18.9*	44	13	5.1	1.32	5.6
Daring 8–10	Poor child-rearing 8	71	18	11.5	31	13	3.0	1.34	5.4
Poor child-rearing 14	Poor child-rearing 8	34	41	0.8	32	15	2.6	−1.24	4.9
Lying 12–14	Separated 10	64	13	12.6	35	14	3.4	1.31	4.8
Daring 8–10	Nervous 8–10	24	16	1.6	48	13	6.1	−1.35	4.3
Official offender 10–14	Convicted parent 10	74	38	4.6	66	9	18.9	−1.41	3.7
Self-reported offending 15–18									
Self-reported 14	Hostile to police 14	41	30	1.6	60	14	9.2	−1.73	10.0
Troublesome 8–10	Low class 14	22	27	0.8	50	19	4.2	−1.72	8.6
Official offender 10–14	Daring 8–10	48	34	1.8	56	16	6.6	−1.32	7.0
Intercourse 14	Unpopular 10	68	18	9.9	38	23	2.0	1.59	5.2
Intercourse 14	Daring 8–10	46	36	1.5	57	17	6.5	−1.45	5.0
Intercourse 14	Low IQ 8–10	35	27	1.5	60	20	6.0	−1.40	4.2
Intercourse 14	Official offender 10–14	53	51	1.1	50	18	4.5	−1.45	4.1
Intercourse 14	Convicted parent 10	44	35	1.5	55	18	5.8	−1.34	4.0

Note: OR = Odds ratio; LOR = Log(OR2) − Log(OR1); LR Int = Likelihood ratio chi-squared for interaction; * 1 case deducted from 100% in order to calculate odds ratio.

Turning to self-reported offending at age 15–18, most of the significant interactions had negative LORs and included early sexual intercourse. Earlier self-reported offending was a predictor especially for those who were not hostile to the police, and earlier official offending was a predictor especially for those who were not daring. Early intercourse predicted self-reported offending especially for those who were unpopular, who had higher IQs and who had unconvicted parents. Offending was especially infrequent for those who had not had early intercourse and had not been convicted earlier. In the only interaction to show effects in different directions, troublesome boys were particularly likely to become offenders if they did not come from low socio-economic status families, and rather unlikely if they came from low socio-economic status families.

Unfortunately, the number of significant interactions in these analyses (19 out of 341 tests) was hardly greater than chance expectation.

TABLE 18.6. Independent predictors of adult official and self-reported offending.

Predictor at age (N)	% Offending		Significance		Regression	
	Worst	Re-mainder	Odds ratio	P	F change	P
Official offending 21–32 (89)						
Official offender 10–20 (128)	52	8	11.9	.0001	114.6	.0001
Low junior attainment 11 (90)	40	16	3.6	.0001	10.7	.0006
Separated from parent 10 (90)	39	17	3.1	.0001	8.9	.0015
Heavy drinker 18 (98)	40	17	3.4	.0001	7.9	.003
Frequent lying 12–14 (122)	39	15	3.8	.0001	4.7	.015
Self-reported offender 18 (97)	43	16	4.1	.0001	4.5	.017
Hangs around 18 (61)	41	19	2.9	.0002	2.8	.05
Large family size 10 (99)	38	17	3.1	.0001	2.3	.07
Self-reported offending 27–32 (85)						
Official offender 10–20 (128)	39	15	3.5	.0001	26.4	.0001
Drug user 18 (122)	37	16	3.1	.0001	12.6	.0002
Attention deficit 12–14 (107)	37	17	2.9	.0001	7.9	.003
Regular smoking 14 (67)	38	19	2.6	.0007	5.8	.008
Heavy gambler 18 (87)	36	19	2.5	.0008	3.5	.03
Self-reported offender 18 (97)	39	17	3.2	.0001	3.3	.03
Unstable job record 18 (92)	37	18	2.6	.0003	2.6	.06

Predicting Adult Offending

Table 18.6 shows the independent predictors of adult convictions (between ages 21 and 32) and adult self-reported offending (between 27 and 32). The adult self-reported offending measure was similar to that at age 18, including burglary, vandalism, taking vehicles, and different types of theft (Farrington, 1989a). The analysis included 48 predictor variables measured up to age 18–20. These were the previous 27 variables measured up to age 14, convictions between 10 and 20, self-reported offending at 14 and 18, and the following 18 variables measured at age 18: heavy drinking, drunk driving, heavy smoking, prohibited drug use, taking no examinations, going out with male friends in the evenings, having a girlfriend, sexual promiscuity (having intercourse with three or more girls), poor relationship with parents, heavy gambling, high debts, unstable job record, unskilled manual job, member of antisocial group, hangs around the streets, self-reported violence, antiestablishment attitude, and high impulsivity. As before, steps were taken to reduce multicollinearity problems in the regression analyses.

Adult convictions were independently predicted by earlier convictions and self-reported offending, low junior leaving results at 11, separations up to the 10th birthday, heavy drinking at 18, frequent lying at 12–14, hanging around the streets at 18, and (almost significantly) large family size at 10. Adult self-reported offending was independently predicted by earlier convictions and self-reported offending, prohibited drug use at 18, attention deficit at 12–14, regular smoking at 14, heavy gambling at 18, and (almost significantly) an unstable job record at 18.

Interactions among Predictors of Adult Offending

Table 18.7 shows the results of the interaction analyses for adult offending. Official offending at 21–32 was disproportionally likely to occur when the following factors coincided: heavy drinking and an unskilled job; frequent lying and convicted parents; earlier self-reported offending and no examinations taken; unpopularity and separation from a parent; and heavy drinking and convicted parents. Offending was disproportionally unlikely to occur when the following factors were both absent: earlier self-reported offending and troublesomeness; earlier self-reported offend-

TABLE 18.7. Interactions among predictors of adult official and self-reported offending.

| A | B | % Offending B = 2 | | | B = 1 | | | LOR | LR Int |
		A = 2	A = 1	OR2	A = 2	A = 1	OR1		
Official offending 21–32									
Heavy drinker 18	Unskilled job 18	75	22	11.1	25	16	1.7	1.85	7.9
Hangs around 18	Impulsive 8–10	29	31	0.9	48	16	4.9	−1.69	7.0
Self-report 18	Troublesome 8–10	44	37	1.4	43	11	5.9	−1.47	6.8
Self-report 18	Daring 8–10	42	29	1.8	44	12	6.1	−1.23	5.9
Heavy drinker 18	Heavy gambler 18	39	33	1.3	41	13	4.5	−1.23	4.8
Lying 12–14	Convicted parent 10	64	19	7.5	26	13	2.3	1.19	4.7
Lying 12–14	Nervous 12–14	48	10	8.7	33	16	2.6	1.22	4.7
Self-report 18	No exams 18	58	20	5.4	17	12	1.6	1.22	4.2
Low attainment 11	Nervous 8–10	46	8	9.5	36	19	2.4	1.36	4.0
Unpopular 10	Separated 10	55	29	3.0	16	17	1.0	1.14	3.9
Heavy drinker 18	Convicted parent 10	69	25	6.6	26	14	2.1	1.13	3.8
Self-reported 18	Poor child-rearing 14	63	16	8.6	33	15	2.8	1.12	3.8
Self-reported offending 27–32									
Smoker 14	Poor child-rearing 14	15	26	0.5	47	16	4.6	−2.24	10.1
Attention deficit 12–14	Low attainment 11	27	30	0.9	47	14	5.2	−1.77	8.8
Attention deficit 12–14	Troublesome 8–10	40	3	23.3	35	19	2.3	2.33	7.0
Self-report 18	Daring 8–10	30	26	1.2	46	14	5.3	−1.45	6.8
Smoker 14	Unpopular 10	55	13	8.1	32	22	1.6	1.60	6.2
Smoker 14	Male companions 18	23	22	1.0	47	16	4.7	−1.52	5.6
Smoker 14	Hangs around 18	29	36	0.7	41	16	3.6	−1.60	4.9
Official offender 10–20	Low IQ 14	44	8	9.2	36	18	2.6	1.27	4.4
Drug user 18	Large family 14	24	22	1.1	41	14	4.1	−1.32	4.4
Self-report 18	Low class 8–10	50	10	9.4	36	19	2.5	1.33	3.8

Note: OR = Odds ratio; LOR = Log(OR2) − Log(OR1); LR Int = Likelihood ratio chi-squared for interaction.

ing and daring; and heavy drinking and heavy gambling. Hanging around the streets predicted offending only for those who were not impulsive; frequent lying and low attainment predicted offending especially for those who were nervous; and earlier self-reported offending predicted official offending especially for those who suffered poor child-rearing.

Turning to self-reported offending at 27–32, early regular smoking predicted offending for those who were not suffering poor child-rearing but was negatively related to offending for those who were suffering poor child-rearing. Attention deficit was a predictor especially for those who were troublesome children or who did not have low junior attainment. Earlier self-reported offending was a predictor especially for those who were not daring or who were from low socioeconomic status families. Early regular smoking was a predictor especially for those who were unpopular children and those who spent time hanging around the streets and mostly went out with other males at age 18. Earlier official offending was a predictor especially for those with low IQs, and drug use at age 18 was a predictor especially for those who did not come from large families.

The number of significant interactions in these analyses (22 out of 656 tests) was rather less than chance expectation.

Independently Important Interaction Effects

The final set of analyses investigated which interaction effects were important independently of the main effects in predicting the various measures of offending. The most obvious statistical technique to use was logistic regression, which (in the SPSS package) produced identical results to the GLIM logit analysis described above. However, logistic regression with 10 or more main effects and 10 or more interaction effects proved to be computationally very intensive, taking a prohibitive amount of computer time. Also, as explained above, the listwise deletion in logistic regression causes a serious loss of cases. Therefore, OLS multiple regression was again used.

The interaction effect was constructed by scoring 1 if both variables were present (e.g., separation and low income) or if both variables were absent (e.g., no separation and adequate income), and 0 for the other two combinations (separation and adequate income or no separation and low income). This is mathematically identical to the interaction effect in the logit analysis or logistic regression. All main effects that were independently important, or that were components of significant interaction effects, were entered first in the multiple regression, and then all the previously discovered interaction effects (shown in Tables 18.3, 18.5 or 18.7) were allowed to enter in a forward stepwise fashion.

TABLE 18.8. Independently important interaction effects.

A	B	F change	P
Official offending 10–14			
Separated 10	Low income 8	9.7	.002
Daring 8–10	Convicted parent 10	6.8	.010
Low attainment 11	Poor supervision 8	5.2	.023
Convicted parent 10	Low class 8–10	7.9	.005
Delinquent school 11	Large family 10	4.9	.028
Self-reported offending 14			
Low IQ 8–10	Delinquent school 11	7.6	.006
Daring 8–10	Unpopular 10	7.6	.006
Unpopular 10	Low class 8–10	7.4	.007
Poor child-rearing 8	Poor supervision 8	6.6	.010
Convicted parent 10	Low class 8–10	4.0	.045
Poor child-rearing 8	Low class 8–10	4.5	.034
Official offending 15–18			
Intercourse 14	Poor child-rearing 8	9.5	.002
Daring 8–10	Poor child-rearing 8	8.2	.005
Nervous 12–14	Poor child-rearing 8	5.0	.025
Self-reported offending 15–18			
Self-reported 14	Hostile to police 14	10.9	.001
Intercourse 14	Unpopular 10	6.4	.012
Intercourse 14	Official offender 10–14	6.7	.010
Troublesome 8–10	Low class 14	6.8	.010
Official offending 21–32			
Heavy drinker 18	Unskilled job 18	15.4	.0001
Self-report 18	Troublesome 8–10	8.6	.004
Self-report 18	No exams 18	12.0	.0006
Lying 12–14	Convicted parent 10	6.1	.014
Lying 12–14	Nervous 12–14	4.2	.040
Hangs around 18	Impulsive 8–10	4.4	.036
Heavy drinker 18	Heavy gambler 18	4.9	.028
Self-reported offending 27–32			
Smoker 14	Poor child-rearing 14	14.9	.0001
Attention deficit 12–14	Low attainment 11	12.9	.0004
Smoker 14	Unpopular 10	10.6	.001
Self-report 18	Low class 8–10	6.4	.012
Self-report 18	Daring 8–10	4.5	.034
Drug user 18	Large family 14	4.6	.032

Table 18.8 shows all the interaction effects that were important independently of main effects and of each other (with two-tailed p values). For example, the interaction between a convicted parent and low social class was independently important in predicting both official and self-reported adolescent offending. In both cases, the combination of a convicted parent and a low social class family caused a disproportionate

increase in the risk of offending. However, no other interaction effects were replicated.

Conclusions

Some important interaction effects were discovered in these analyses. However, the proportion of significant interaction effects clearly decreased with age. This is probably because people become less easy to change and their habits become more ingrained as they get older. For example, there was no sign of any variable interacting with and affecting the continuity between convictions at 10–20 and convictions at 21–32. Earlier convictions led to later convictions at all values of all other variables. In contrast, it was not true that troublesomeness at 8–10 predicted convictions at 10–14 irrespective of all other variables, and interaction effects occurred more often than chance at the earliest ages. Hence, the study of interaction effects in the prediction of offending is likely to be most valuable in childhood, rather than in adulthood.

Some of the interaction effects are plausible and may have theoretical importance. For example, the most significant effect showed that, from the viewpoint of later offending, early separation from a parent (usually the father) was harmful to boys from average or high-income families but beneficial to boys from low-income families. This may be because fathers in low-income families transmit values and norms that are conductive to offending, and separation protects the boys from the influence of these deviant values. Hence, single parent female-headed households may not always be harmful. Similarly, the most replicable significant interaction effect showed that a convicted parent predicted offending only in low socioeconomic status families. Hence, it may be that only convicted parents who also have unskilled manual jobs transmit deviant values to their children.

Some of the interaction effects may have implications for protective factors. For example, poor child-rearing predicted adolescent offending only when it was combined with poor supervision. Hence, good supervision might compensate for poor child-rearing, and good child-rearing might compensate for poor supervision. Similarly, it was the combination of heavy drinking and an unskilled job that predicted adult offending. This suggests that heavy drinking might not have deleterious effects on offending if it coincides with a high status job, and that an unskilled job does not have deleterious effects on offending unless it coincides with heavy drinking.

This analysis of interaction effects showed that some types occurred more often than others. Especially at the later ages, most interactions consisted of a significant positive effect on offending at one value of a variable B and no effect or a weaker positive effect at the other value. In contrast, at the earliest ages, many interactions consisted of a significant positive effect on offending at one value of a variable B and a negative effect at the other value. This again may reflect the greater plasticity of behavior at the earliest ages.

It was interesting that, as demonstrated for the prediction of adolescent offending, interaction effects for convictions were significantly correlated with interaction effects for self-reported offending. In other words, the pattern of interactions was similar for official and self-reported offending. To the best of my knowledge, this is the first paper that demonstrates this concordance. It is perhaps not surprising, since official and self-reported offending overlap significantly and since the pattern of predictors is similar for official and self-reported offending.

It might perhaps be argued that the small number of significant interaction effects discovered in this research is a function of the dichotomizing of data into the "worst" quarter versus the remainder. Perhaps more interaction effects would have been discovered if the "worst" quarter on one variable had been combined with the "best" quarter on another. However, the clustering of negative features means that this strategy would run into great problems of small numbers. For example, only 6 of those who were in the worst quarter on troublesomeness were in the best quarter on junior attainment, only 10 were in the best quarter on non-verbal IQ, only 15 were in the best "quarter" (actually 30%) on family income, and only 16 were in the best "quarter" (actually 30%) on child-rearing. It is not possible, of course, to identify a "best" quarter with some variables (e.g., convicted parents).

It might also be argued that it would have been better to have divided each variable into more than two categories. For example, many variables could have been divided into four categories. However, this would have caused problems of small cell numbers in the logit analyses, and problems of interpretation of the results would have been much greater. For example, a $4 \times 4 \times 4$ table involves 64 cells, with an average number of 6 in each cell for a sample of 400. Similarly, it might be argued that continuous variables should have been used where possible (which would, actually, have been in the minority of cases). However, because the interaction terms would then have been of the form $A \times B$, different types of interaction effects would have been confounded. For example, a low value of A combined with a high value of B, a high value of A combined with a low value of B, and medium values of both, could all produce the same value of $A \times B$. It could then be difficult to distinguish different types of interaction effects.

To the best of my knowledge, this analysis of interaction effects is the most systematic and extensive ever carried out in the prediction of offending. It was laborious to carry out, but has produced interesting results. Hence, researchers should not focus only on main effects, as they do almost invariably. However, there is a need for statistical packages that make it easier to investigate different types of interaction effects, while preserving as much of the data collected as possible.

References

Cleary, P.D. & Angel, R. (1984). The analysis of relationships involving dichotomous dependent variables. *Journal of Health and Social Behavior*, *25*, 334–348.

Ensminger, M.E., Kellam, S.G., & Rubin, B.R. (1983). School and family origins of delinquency: Comparisons by sex. In K.T. Van Dusen & S.A. Mednick (Eds.), *Prospective studies of crime and delinquency* (pp. 73–97). Boston: Kluwer-Nijhoff.

Farrington, D.P. (1973). Self-reports of deviant behavior: Predictive and stable? *Journal of Criminal Law and Criminology*, *64*, 99–110.

Farrington, D.P. (1984). Measuring the natural history of delinquency and crime. In R.A. Glow (Ed.), *Advances in the behavioral measurement of children* (vol. 1, pp. 217–263). Greenwich, CT: JAI press.

Farrington, D.P. (1985). Predicting self-reported and official delinquency. In D.P. Farrington & R. Tarling (Eds.), *Prediction in criminology* (pp. 150—173). Albany: SUNY Press.

Farrington, D.P. (1986). Stepping stones to adult criminal careers. In D. Olweus, J. Block, & M. Radke-Yarrow (Eds.), *Development of antisocial and prosocial Behavior* (pp. 359–384). New York: Academic Press.

Farrington, D.P. (1989a). Later adult life outcomes of offenders and non-offenders. In M. Brambring, F. Losel, & H. Skowronek (Eds.), *Children at risk* (pp. 220–244). Berlin: De Gruyter.

Farrington, D.P. (1989b). Self-reported and official offending from adolescence to adulthood. In M. Klein (Ed.), *Cross-national research in self-reported crime and delinquency* (pp. 399–423). Dordrecht, Netherlands: Kluwer.

Farrington, D.P. (1990). Implications of criminal career research for the prevention of offending. *Journal of Adolescence*, *13*, 93–113.

Farrington, D.P. (1992). Explaining the beginning, progress and ending of anti-social behavior from birth to adulthood. In J. McCord (Ed.), *Facts, frameworks, and forecasts: Advances in criminological theory, Vol. 3* (pp 253–286). New Brunswick, NJ: Transaction.

Farrington, D.P., Gallagher, B., Morley, L., St. Ledger, R.J., & West, D.J. (1988). Are there any successful men from criminogenic backgrounds? *Psychiatry*, *51*, 116–130.

Farrington, D.P. & Hawkins, J.D. (1991). Predicting participation, early onset and later persistence in officially recorded offending. *Criminal Behaviour and Mental Health*, *1*, 1–33.

Farrington, D.P. & West, D.J. (1990). The Cambridge study in delinquent development: A long-term follow-up of 411 London males. In H.J. Kerner & G. Kaiser (Eds.), *Criminality: Personality, behaviour and life history* (pp. 115–138). Berlin: Springer-Verlag.

Fienberg, S.E. (1980). *The analysis of cross-classified categorical data*. Cambridge: MIT Press.

Gordon, R.A. (1968) Issues in multiple regression. *American Journal of Sociology*, *73*, 592–616.

Kellam, S.G., Brown, C.H., Rubin, B.R., & Ensminger, M.E. (1983). Paths leading to teenage psychiatric symptoms and substance use: Developmental epidemiological studies in Woodlawn. In S.B. Guze, F.J. Earls, & J.E. Barrett (Eds.), *Childhood psychopathology and development* (pp. 17–47). New York: Raven Press.

McCord, J. (1987, April). *Aggression and shyness as predictors of problems.* Paper presented at the biennial meeting of the Society for Research in Child Development, Baltimore.

Rutter, M. (1985). Resilience in the face of adversity: Protective factors and resistance to psychiatric disorder. *British Journal of Psychiatry, 147,* 598–611.

Rutter, M. & Giller, H. (1983). *Juvenile delinquency.* Harmondsworth, Middlesex: Penguin.

Schlesselman, J.J. (1982). *Case-control studies.* New York: Oxford University Press.

Werner, E.E. (1983, November). *Vulnerability and resiliency among children at risk for delinquency.* Paper presented at the annual meeting of the American Society of Criminology, Denver.

Werner, E.E. & Smith, R.S. (1982). *Vulnerable but invincible.* New York: McGraw Hill.

West, D.J. (1969). *Present conduct and future delinquency.* London: Heinemann.

West, D.J. (1982). *Delinquency: Its roots, careers and prospects.* London: Heinemann.

West, D.J. & Farrington, D.P. (1973). *Who becomes delinquent?* London: Heinemann.

West, D.J. & Farrington, D.P. (1977). *The delinquent way of life.* London: Heinemann.

19
The Social Field of the Classroom: Context for the Developmental Epidemiological Study of Aggressive Behavior

Sheppard G. Kellam, George W. Rebok, Renate Wilson, and Lawrence S. Mayer

Social adaptation to the early elementary school classroom requires that young children meet the social task demands of both the teacher and classmates/peers. The adequacy of the children's performance in response to these demands will have long-lasting importance to their adolescent and adult developmental course (Ensminger, Kellam, & Rubin, 1983; Ensminger & Slusarick, 1992; Kellam, Brown, Rubin, & Ensminger, 1983; Robins, 1978; Tomas, Vlahov, & Anthony, 1990). While this volume is on contextual influences on adolescence, from a developmental perspective adolescent outcomes can best be understood by looking at earlier childhood adaptation to centrally important social fields. This paper is concerned with the antecedents found in the child's responses to social task demands in the context of the classroom leading to adolescent outcomes.

At this early stage of the life-course in industrial societies, the elementary school classroom is the social field where both peer group and teacher share the same ecological context, with the family as the third source of social task demands. While the three social fields overlap geographically, teachers set the tasks of the students and rate the adequacy of performance of the children from their perspective as teachers; the peers/classmates do so from their viewpoint; and the parents do so from the family's perspective. All of these contextual influences on behavior impact the developmental paths of the children (Kellam, Branch, Agrawal, & Ensminger, 1975).

The focus of this chapter is on the classroom and on the social task demands of teacher and classmates, particularly in regard to aggressive behavior and its long-term developmental sequellae. We will first examine epidemiological variation in the level of aggressive behavior in classroom environments in urban settings. We will then present analyses of the impact of classroom aggression on the children's achievement and their own aggressive behavior. Lastly, we will attempt to demonstrate the important developmental potential of the classroom social field in either promoting or inhibiting children's aggressive behavior. We will use a preventive intervention trial aimed at changing the classroom environment in regard to its reinforcement of aggressive behavior. The results are intended to illustrate the importance of classroom context on aggressive behavior through experimentally changing the classroom environment (Dolan et al., in press; Kellam & Rebok, 1992).

In a major review of the United States and European literature linking childhood maladaptive behavior to adolescent and adult disorder, Kohlberg, Ricks, and Snarey (1984) concluded that global indicators of childhood maladaptation (e.g., school failure, poor peer relations, antisocial behavior) predict later disorder. Aggressive behavior occurring as early as first grade in the form of breaking rules, truancy, and fighting has been found to predict antisocial behavior and criminality as well as heavy substance use, including intravenous drug use, through adolescence and well into adulthood, especially in males (Block, Block, & Keyes, 1988; Ensminger et al., 1983; Farrington, Gallagher, Morley, St. Ledger, & West, 1988; Kellam, et al., 1983; Robins, 1978; Shedler & Block, 1990; Tomas, et al., 1990; Tremblay, Masse, Perron, LeBlanc, Schwartzman, & Ledingham, 1992).

The work described here is based upon an integration of a life-course developmental perspective with that of community epidemiology to bring into focus both the variation in developmental paths in cohorts of individuals in defined communities or populations, and long-term continuities and discontinuities in behavior as children develop. We have termed this integration of orientations and methods *developmental epidemiology* (Kellam, 1990; Kellam et al., 1975; Kellam et al., 1983; Kellam & Ensminger, 1980; Kellam & Rebok, 1992; Kellam & Werthamer-Larsson, 1986; Kellam et al., 1991).

A Developmental Epidemiological Perspective: The Life-course Social Field Concept

Developmental epidemiology permits us to formulate questions concerning variation in developmental paths to be assessed; rates, distributions, and variation in functions of developmental models to be studied; questions about whom generalizations can be made; and tools and concepts for integrating disciplines into a broader, more ecological perspective. This perspective guides the study of developmental paths within representative samples from a defined community population over significant portions of the life-course. At each stage of life, an individual is involved in a few major social fields that constitute both present context and set the stage for future development. As children, individuals are first involved in their family, then in the school and their peer group. The social fields involved in later developmental stages shift to the workplace and its peer relations, the marital family with spouse and children, and still later, their children's families. Thus, there is an intimate relationship between life stages and key social fields.

Each of these social fields sets specific social task demands whose performance is judged by *natural raters*, as we call the parents, the teacher, and the significant peers in each context. These task demands may overlap considerably, but they are not necessarily identical and may even be in conflict. Parents require that children perform certain kinds of tasks or exhibit specific behaviors; the classroom teacher makes analogous demands but with a different emphasis. The demands and expectations of the peer group may be similar or quite different, depending on the cultural and developmental context.

As an example, aggressive behavior in the home environment may be defined differently and have different consequences from aggressive behavior in the classroom; aggressive behavior in these two fields may be different from that within the peer group. Aggressive behavior can be defined as an individual's behavioral responses within a specific social field involving breaking rules, and/or actively opposing physically or verbally the rules of acceptable behavior defined by the natural rater(s) in that social field. However, while aggressive behavior is socially maladaptive behavior that elicits poor ratings by parents or poor conduct grades from teachers, it may stimulate like or dislike, acceptance or rejection by peers, depending on the context. Thus, aggressive behavior, as the other social maladaptive behaviors, is specifically defined in each social field and by each natural rater. In fact, we often find disagreement between parents and teachers in their assessments of how well a child is performing the same task. Even more likely are discrepancies between parents and teachers in their assessments of children's performance of task demands that are confined primarily to the school (Kellam et al., 1975).

For researchers interested in the interplay between individual developmental stages and their specific context, it is important to look at the social task demands in each social field and at the behavioral responses of individuals in that social field. Both provide the necessary contextual information for assessing the relative importance of psychological, biological, or environmental processes that influence these interactions and determine individual success or failure in each field—what we call *Social Adaptational Status* (SAS). We use the parents', teachers', and peers' assessments of the child's performance in each specific field as measures of SAS.

In addition, we are concerned with *Psychological Well-Being* (PWB), that is, the individual's internal states such as depression, anxiety, self-esteem, and the status of an individual's thought processes. In regard to classroom performance, PWB variables might include the depression or anxiety a child feels upon receiving a failing grade. In regard to peer relations, PWB variables might include the perceptual biases that the child brings to peer interactions and the information-processing abilities used to process social cues. Although the SAS and PWB are often highly correlated (as in the example of failing grades and feeling depressed), they are conceptually distinct. We measure them independently of each other, so that we can study their long-term interrelationships and the outcomes of each. Unlike SAS, which can be measured by outside raters, PWB must be inferred from the child's self-reports of feelings; direct observations by peers, teachers, and parents; clinical observation; or by laboratory information-processing measures.

Developmental Epidemiology of the Classroom: Teacher Ratings of Aggressive Behavior

As developmental epidemiologists, we have been keenly interested in the distribution of aggressive behavior within and across schools and classrooms. The developmental epidemiological studies of mental health done in the poor, black ghetto community of Woodlawn, Chicago in the late 1960s clearly demonstrated that school-age children who are identified by teachers as aggressive, withdrawn, or both aggressive and withdrawn represent distinct populations who are at increased risk for later psychopathology (Kellam et al., 1983). First-grade aggressiveness without shyness in males (but not in females) was a strong predictor of increased teenage delinquency and of drug, alcohol, and cigarette use. Analyses of the Woodlawn data also revealed that aggressive behavior interacted with shy behavior to enhance the aggressive effect in later delinquency and drug use (Ensminger et al., 1983; Kellam, Ensminger, & Simon, 1980). These shy/aggressive children—a group to which we and several other groups have been calling attention—are children who are loners, who do not participate much with others, but who break rules and fight (Block et al., 1988; Ensminger et al., 1983; Farrington et al., 1988; Farrington & Gunn 1985; Hans, Marcus, Henson, Auerbach, & Mirsky, 1992; Kellam, Brown, & Fleming, 1982; Kellam et al., 1983; McCord, 1988; Schwartzman, Ledingham, & Serbin, 1985).

An unanswered question in these studies concerns the neighborhood epidemiology for these socially maladaptive behaviors. In our Woodlawn studies, we asked such questions as: Why do some children from the same neighborhood environment become aggressive adolescents and others not? Within this low-income community we found extraordinary variation in the developmental courses from early childhood through adolescence. We also found markedly varied rates of aggressive behavior among first-grade students attending the 12 elementary schools in that neighborhood (Kellam, 1990). As shown in Figure 19.1, we looked at 12 neighborhood elementary schools, which included both public and parochial schools, using the same cutoff point: teacher ratings at the moderate or severe

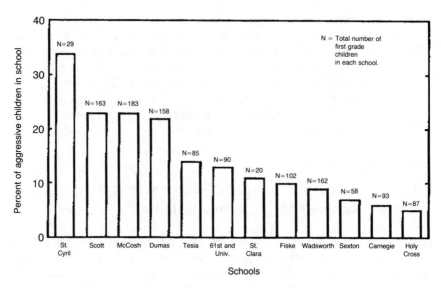

FIGURE 19.1. Prevalence of moderate or severe aggression among first grade children in Woodlawn public and private elementary schools: 1966–1967. (Reprinted with permission from Kellman, Tillman, & Albert, 1985.)

level of aggression. We found that, in one school, 35% of the children were rated as moderately to severely aggressive by their teachers. In another school, less than 10% of the children were rated as moderately to severely aggressive. Figure 19.1 shows the varied distribution of the prevalence of teacher-rated aggressive behavior across the 12 schools, each of which served a catchment area of families. This raises the question of the specific contribution of family-school-neighborhood constellations to variations in rates of aggression, as reflected in teacher ratings.

The micro-epidemiology of the classrooms within schools was equally revealing. Within each of these 12 elementary schools, first-grade classrooms differed markedly as to rates of aggressive behavior (see Figure 19.2). For example, in the second school, Scott, a public elementary school with eight classrooms, the overall prevalence of teacher-rated aggressive behavior was about 25%. But the variation within Scott was dramatic: In one classroom 7% or 8% of the children were rated as moderately to severely aggressive; in another classroom 63% of the children were so rated by their first-grade teachers. In one of these classrooms, it was deviant to be aggressive, while in another it was deviant not to be aggressive.

In fact, we know that this within-school distribution was not random: It reflects a frequent school district policy of "ability grouping," or "tracking," which often occurs very quickly after children enter the first grade in the United States. It is deliberate—that is, planned by principals

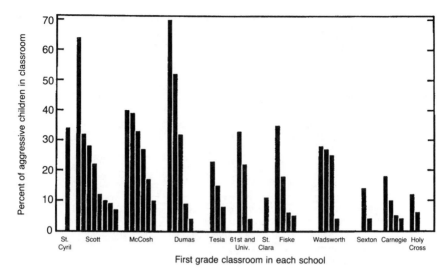

FIGURE 19.2. Prevalence of moderate or severe aggression in each Woodlawn first grade classroom: 1966–1967. (Reprinted with permission from Kellman, Tillman, & Albert, 1985.)

based on readiness test scores, on kindergarten teacher reports, and on principals' policies regarding assignment of children to classrooms. In this school, where the principal selectively assigned children to certain classes and teachers, an administrative policy decision induced important contextual variation among classrooms.

These findings suggest the types of data that we need to study when examining the contextual influences on child and adolescent development. One can ask: Is the prediction from early aggression the same across different kinds and levels of environments? What are the developmental consequences of these variations in contexts? We have cited evidence that the classroom environment influences the child's own aggressive behavior by enhancing or inhibiting the risk of long-term poor developmental outcomes.

We recently investigated the effect of the classroom context on the aggressive and shy behaviors of 609 children in 19 East Baltimore public schools in terms of dominant pattern of classroom achievement and behavior (Werthamer-Larsson, Kellam, & Wheeler, 1991). Structured teacher ratings on a teacher interview called the Teacher Observation of Classroom Adaptation-Revised (TOCA-R) assessed aggressive and shy behavior at the end of first grade. Children in low-achieving classrooms had significantly higher teacher ratings of both aggressive and shy behavior than children in higher-achieving classrooms, even after controlling for potentially confounding child characteristics and classroom behavior ef-

TABLE 19.1. Effect of classroom environment on child behavior, controlling for child characteristics.[a]

Class environment	Shy behavior		Aggressive behavior	
	M	F	M	F
Class achievement		3.45[b]		4.15[b]
Low-achieving	.31		.33	
Mixed-achieving	.25		.27	
High-achieving	.25		.31	
Class behavior		22.90[c]		0.01
Satisfactory	.25		.30	
Poorly-behaving	.35		.30	

[a] Gender, age, kindergarten grades, kindergarten work habit problems, first-grade repeater, preschool experience, and between-year change were entered into the model before the class environment variables in the model.
[b] $p < .05$.
[c] $P < .001$.
Source: Adapted from Werthamer-Larsson, Kellam, & Wheeler (1991).

fects. Analyses controlling for child characteristics and classroom achievement effects indicated that children in poor-behavior classrooms also had significantly higher teacher ratings of shy behavior alone than children in better-behaving classrooms. Results of a hierarchical analysis of variance for both the classroom achievement environment hierarchical model and the classroom environment hierarchical model are shown in Table 19.1. These findings indicate the importance of the differential influence of classroom environment, both in terms of group-level achievement and behavior.

Developmental Epidemiology of the Classroom: Peer Ratings of Aggressive Behavior

Much of the literature on the prediction from early aggressive behavior to adolescent and adult antisocial behavior, criminality, and heavy substance use, including that based on the Woodlawn studies, derives from teacher ratings of aggressive/disruptive maladaptive behavioral responses or school records of behavior. However, the growing literature on the effects of early peer rejection (Bierman, 1986; Bierman & McCauley, 1987; Coie & Dodge, 1983; Dodge, 1983; Dodge, Coie, Pettit, & Price, 1990; Patterson & Capaldi, 1990), possibly coupled with aggressive behavior, suggests that the peer group is an important part of children's vulnerability to later problems. There is evidence that teacher ratings of adjustment are not as sensitive as peer ratings for the prediction of subsequent psychopathology (Cowen, Pederson, Babigian, Izzo, & Trost, 1973). As Younger, Schwartzman, and Ledingham (1986) suggest, the sensitivity of peer ratings to childhood maladaptation may relate to their predictive power in that peer-raters may react negatively to children whom they label maladjusted. The relationship of variation in peer ratings over time to the developmental course of children is, therefore, central to the aims of our developmental epidemiological research.

Maladaptation to the peer group plays a developmentally important role in the emergence of maladaptive behavior patterns in elementary school-aged children and in the prediction of psychopathology, school drop out, and delinquency in adolescence and adulthood (Coie & Dodge, 1983; Cowen et al., 1973; Landau & Milich, 1985; Ledingham & Schwartzman, 1984; Parker & Asher, 1987; Robins, 1978). Further, several psychological disturbances in childhood (e.g., conduct disorder, shyness disorder, adjustment disorder with withdrawal) include peer relation difficulties as a diagnostic criterion of psychopathology (e.g., DSM III-R; Rubin, 1990). In the early school years, classmates typically serve as a child's most important peer group, defining the behaviors expected within the peer group and judging the adequacy of behavioral responses. We infer that children who meet the demands of the peer group are typically well-liked and popular; those who fail to meet those demands are typically disliked and either neglected or rejected.

In the Baltimore study, the Peer Assessment Inventory (PAI), a classroom-administered modified version of The Pupil Evaluation Inventory (PEI) (Pekarik, Prinz, Liebert, Weintraub, & Neale, 1976), has been used to obtain peer assessments of all children in each classroom of 19 East Baltimore public schools. Three items were selected to measure aggressive behavior. Children were asked to nominate classmates who *start fights, always get into trouble, and are mean to others.* Children were asked to indicate their choices by filling in a circle on an answer sheet next to the names of children who were really like those in the question. Children could nominate as many children for each item as they wished (including themselves), and they were free not to nominate any child if no one fit the question. The internal consistency of the aggressive behavior scale of the PAI, as assessed by standardized alpha coefficients, was .91.

Figures 19.3 and 19.4 show the percent of peer-nominated aggressive behavior for males and females across the 19 schools, using a cutoff of peer nominations for aggressive behavior by one third or more of classmates. For males, schools are ordered from the highest percent of male children receiving nominations for aggressive behavior to the lowest.

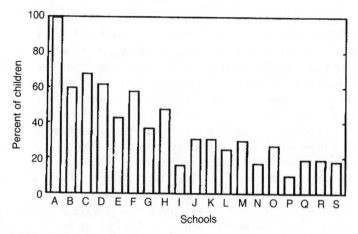

FIGURE 19.3. Prevalence of male aggressive behavior measured by classmates' nominations in 19 schools: one third or more of classmates.

For females, the schools correspond exactly to the ordering for male aggressive behavior. As in the Woodlawn data based on teacher ratings, we found tremendous variation in peer-nominated aggressive behavior across schools for both genders. As Figure 19.3 indicates, in School A 100% of the males were nominated by a third or more of their classmates as aggressive. In School P less than 10% of the males were nominated by a third or more of their classmates as aggressive. The overall level and variation of peer-nominated aggressive behavior for females was much less than that found for males. As seen in Figure 19.4, in School F about

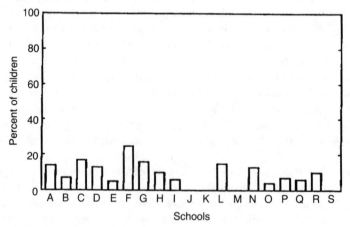

FIGURE 19.4. Prevalence of female aggressive behavior measured by classmates' nominations in 19 schools: one third or more of classmates.

25% of the females were nominated by a third or more of their classmates as aggressive, while in four schools (J, K, M, and S) 0% of the females were so nominated.

We are now analyzing findings indicating that within schools, there was even more variation across classrooms in peer nominations for aggression. For example, in one school the prevalence of peer-nominated aggressive behavior in males was about 60%, placing it among the top five schools in terms of prevalence of aggression. However, the variation across classrooms within the school in peer nominations for aggression was striking. In one classroom almost 85% of the males were nominated by their classmates as aggressive; in another classroom, only about 33% of the males received aggressive-behavior nominations. Understanding the relationship of this variation across different classroom environments over time, and its effect on the developmental course of individuals is central to developmental epidemiological studies of mental health and disorder.

We also examined the effects of classroom environment on children's behavior using peer nominations of aggressive behavior in first-grade children in the same East Baltimore public schools. Peer nominations were obtained in the fall and spring of the first-grade year. We first examined the stability regression of spring aggressive behavior on fall aggressive behavior. The regression of spring aggression on fall aggression was $R^2 = .57$ for males and .39 for females, showing that aggressive behavior is a fairly stable behavior as early as first grade. The stability among the children already aggressive in the fall was even greater.

Analyses were then performed to examine the relationship of classroom level of aggression and the aggressive behavior of each child. For both males and females, fall classroom average aggression was a weak but significant predictor of spring aggression. Classroom average aggression in the fall was fairly highly related to classroom average aggression in the spring for both genders. We then created two new variables by subtracting the classroom average aggression from aggression in the fall and spring, which we label *adjusted aggression*. As shown in Table 19.2, for males, adjusted aggression in the fall and adjusted aggression in the spring were as highly correlated as were fall aggression and spring aggression unadjusted for classroom aggression.

For females, adjusted fall aggression and adjusted spring aggression were uncorrelated. This latter result suggests that aggressive behavior in females was correlated from fall to spring because the level of aggression of the classroom environment remained stable. The classroom correlation accounted for the female correlation. For males, the stability of aggression was in their individual aggressive behavior.

Understanding the variation in these results is useful in planning universal interventions (interventions that are applied to an entire population) aimed at decreasing risk of adolescent and adult maladaptation.

TABLE 19.2. Regression analyses of fall to spring aggression in first-grade males and females, unadjusted and adjusted for classroom average aggression.

Independent variable	Spring aggression—males			
	B	SE	T-value	p
Fall aggress—unadj.	.902	.054	16.80	.001
Fall agress—adj.	.897	.055	16.24	.001

Independent variable	Spring aggression—females			
	B	SE	T-value	p
Fall aggress—unadj.	.739	.063	11.72	.001
Fall aggress—adj.	−.023	.059	−.37	ns

Note: $R^2 = 57.33\%$ and 55.66% for males' unadjusted and adjusted aggression; $r = .76$ and $.75$, respectively. $R^2 = 36.97\%$ and $.06\%$ for females' unadjusted and adjusted aggression; $r = .62$ and $−.03$, respectively.

Testing Classroom Contextual Influences through Preventive Intervention Trials

Experimental interventions represent an important strategy for examining contextual influences on children's behavior. In our work at the Johns Hopkins Prevention Research Center in Baltimore, Maryland, we have developed and implemented classroom-based experimental field trials directed at specific antecedents in developmental models to help determine whether the risk of specific problem outcomes in adolescence and adulthood can be reduced (Kellam & Rebok, 1992; Kellam et al., 1991). They provide data on the malleability of the early risk behaviors and their etiologic significance for later outcomes through shifting the social context of the classroom.

Two preventive trials in the Baltimore City Public Schools have been directed at children's early behavioral responses, demonstrated to be predictors for later antisocial behavior, criminality, heavy substance use, to teacher task demands in the classroom environment. A classroom team-based behavior-management strategy called the *Good Behavior Game* (GBG) (Barrish, Saunders, & Wolfe, 1969) targeted aggressive behavior in the classroom as measured by teacher and peer ratings (Dolan et al., in press). This preventive intervention promoted good behavior by rewarding teams that did not exceed maladaptive behavior standards. The goal was to determine whether improving behavior through shifts in the reinforcement characteristics of the classroom would reduce risk of later maladaptive behavior. A second preventive intervention, *Mastery*

Learning (ML), was aimed at improving reading achievement (Dolan et al., in press). The goal was to determine whether improved mastery of reading and other core skills would reduce risk of later psychiatric symptoms, particularly depressive symptoms and possibly depressive disorder.

This ongoing population-based prevention trial is based on a strong collaborative relationship with the Baltimore City Public Schools and with the wider community of parents whose children are involved in our classroom-based studies. Such close partnerships are essential for this type of population- and community-based research (Kellam, 1990; Kellam & Hunter, 1990; Rebok et al., 1991).

The Baltimore City Public Schools designated a widely varied set of elementary schools in the eastern half of Baltimore City, where five quite different urban areas were selected. Some of the areas exhibited many of the characteristics of community decay and poverty that are associated with high risk of problem behavior. Some were more middle-class areas and had many characteristics of community organization and access to resources associated with lower risk. Each urban area was served by at least three public elementary schools with two or more first-grade classrooms.

One or two of the set of schools in each urban area was randomly assigned as an external control school with no experimental interventions, another as a GBG school, and the third (or fourth) as a ML school. Within each intervention school, children were randomly assigned to an intervention classroom or an internal control classroom, with teachers also randomly chosen. The interventions were implemented over 2 years for each cohort after intensive baseline assessments. Classrooms of children were kept together over the 2 years.

The design for this preventive trial provided for some control over leakage or spillover effects that might happen if all or part of the intervention strategies were adopted in the comparison classrooms. These problems were addressed in the research design by having both internal comparison classrooms within the intervention schools and external comparison classrooms in schools not receiving any special intervention. This design also controlled for critical school-level effects.

The results reported here focus on impact at the end of the first-grade year. To be included in the analyses, all students had to remain in the same design condition for the entire year. Students who transferred into the school system or who left the system during the first-grade year were not included in these analyses. A total of 864 students met these criteria. The sample for the GBG condition was 182 students from 8 classrooms; the sample for the GBG internal control condition was 107 from 6 classrooms; and the sample for the external control condition was 212 from 11 classrooms. The sample for the ML condition was 207 students from 9 classrooms; the sample for the ML internal control condition was 156 from 7 classrooms.

Teacher-rated aggressive behavior, peer-nominated aggressive behavior, and standardized student achievement data from the California Achievement Test (CAT, Forms E and F) were assessed for the GBG, ML, internal control, and external control conditions. Assessments were conducted in the fall of first grade at first report card time, and in the following spring near the end of first grade.

As hypothesized, short-term proximal or direct effects of both the GBG and ML interventions on their target antecedents were found in our initial analyses of impact (Dolan et al., in press). For both males and females, the GBG had a significant impact on aggressive behavior as rated by teachers. Peer nominations of aggressive behavior among males by their classmates were also significantly reduced. By examining scatterplots of aggressive behavior ratings in the fall and the spring of first grade, along with the regression slopes, it appeared that the more severe end of aggressive behavior was affected by the GBG for both genders. We hypothesize that changes in aggressive behavior resulting from the GBG intervention were due to shifts in the precision of the teacher's task demands, and in the group pressure to behave within the specified acceptable range.

We are examining the longer-term impact of the two preventive interventions on developmental outcomes in early adolescence. Thus far, we have focused much of our effort on understanding the effect of the GBG on the course and evolving level of aggression from first through sixth grade.

In a recent paper (Kellam, Rebok, Ialongo, & Mayer, in press), we tested the hypotheses that the course of aggression is malleable and that the children in the GBG who were more aggressive in the fall of first grade would exhibit a greater reduction in the prevalence of aggressive behavior through the transition to middle school than children in the control or the ML classrooms. We also hypothesized that GBG participants who were not aggressive in the fall of first grade would exhibit a lower incidence of aggressive behavior over the course of the 6 years than initially nonaggressive children in either the control or ML classrooms. The ML classrooms were included here as an active control for attention.

There was a clear indication of the long-term impact of the GBG on aggressive behavior in males who were in the upper half of teacher-rated aggression in fall of first grade. Specifically, aggressive behavior dropped steadily for the initially aggressive males in the GBG from fourth through sixth grade after reaching a peak in third grade. Aggression among males in the control conditions and in ML continued at high levels into sixth grade. The drop in aggression for the GBG condition was not seen for females and for lower-aggression males.

It is important to note that the GBG supplied external structure in behavioral rules and reinforcement. The conclusion we draw from these preliminary results is that external structure with clear reinforcers is an important characteristic of preventive interventions for aggressive behavior. Also, results suggest that children manifesting aggressive behavior are likely to respond to fairly simple but nonlabeling, universal interventions (Kellam, Rebok, Wilson, & Edwards, 1993). These inferences—which have a common focus on contextual influences on adolescent behavior—need validation through continued analyses and replication.

Cautions should be noted in the GBG short-term reports. Although teacher ratings are considered an important measure of SAS, they are confounded by the fact that the teacher was the main intervention agent and was knowledgeable about specific outcome targets. Therefore, the internal validity of the teacher ratings is at issue. Further, because teachers in the intervention condition knew they were in a contrast condition, they may have wanted to improve the rating within their classroom. This concern is substantially reduced because this study included peer ratings to measure impact in addition to observations by independent observers.

The classroom peers within the GBG classrooms received the expectation of better behavior by their teacher, and hence may have inferred better behavior among their peers than existed in reality, thereby creating a self-fulfilling vision of a better-behaved class. Alternatively, they may have rated children more harshly because the cost of maladaptation increased with the GBG. There was some evidence of this in the results from the earlier Woodlawn prevention trials (Kellam et al., 1975). Furthermore, other investigators have questioned whether children at age 6 or 7 can draw valid inferences about each other (Younger, Schwartzman, & Ledingham, 1985, 1986). The results of our psychometric analyses support the inference that first-grade children can evaluate each other on constructs requiring attributions such as *is mean to others*, *fights a lot*, and *gets into trouble*. Peer nominations for these three aggressive-behavior items had sufficient alpha and met criteria for validity.

For the ML intervention, we found significant short-term impact on reading achievement at the end of the spring of first grade for both males and females, in covariance analyses controlling for baseline achievement. Importantly, the nature of the intervention impact differed by gender. Female high achievers benefited more from the ML intervention than female low achievers, whereas male low achievers benefited more than male high achievers. From fall to spring of first grade neither intervention had impact on the proximal target of the other, either as a main effect or as an interaction that involved effects on their own proximal target as a condition for altering the proximal target of the other. Each intervention thus appears to be specific to its own proximal target.

The choice of first grade as a context for experimental intervention aimed at adolescent and adult outcomes is consistent with empirical evidence as well as with our developmental epidemiological and life-course perspective. Clearly, the transition to first grade entails adaptation to a new social field and a new and potentially difficult set of social, behavioral, and cognitive developmental tasks. Moreover, because of the stabilization of these early patterns, success or failure in social adaptation to the early elementary school environment has significant consequences across the life span. The use of experimental interventions targeted at antecedent risk behaviors has provided us a powerful way of addressing questions about the effects of epidemiological context on variations in classroom behaviors.

The next series of preventive trials has been designed to show whether the target risk behaviors can be improved in various, carefully designed intervention configurations. First, we are combining the GBG intervention with an enhanced outcome-based curriculum similar to ML to test if their joint impact is redundant, additive, or synergistic. In addition, a family behavioral and learning environment intervention has been designed and will be tested alone and together with the combined classroom inter-vention. Looking at child behavior situated in the family as well as investigating the power of family-based interventions—with and without comparable classroom-based support—represents an important research agenda for understanding contextual influences on life-course develop-mental outcomes and their malleability.

Cross-cultural Implications

Our research concepts, measures, understanding of etiology, and pre-vention methods would benefit substantially by investigations in other cultures and societies. A major question on any cross-cultural research agenda is not so much whether, but in what ways antecedents and risk factors are similar or different in different settings. Given the develop-mental epidemiological perspective we have elaborated here and else-where, we propose cross-cultural studies of the antecedents and paths leading to mental health and disorder, and social adaptation and mal-adaptation. We further propose that this agenda include the continued elaboration and systematic evaluation of school-based preventive inter-vention trials directed at specific antecedents along the developmental paths leading to specific problem outcomes.

The field of prevention research has moved rapidly toward a model that emphasizes early antecedents as targets of preventive interventions. These early targets have been shown in some cases to be responsive to intervention. We need to determine if these targets and interventions are valid in other cultural contexts and under what conditions. A major focus must be the roles of the school and the community in influencing the effectiveness of the intervention, and the roles that the classroom, family, and the peer group assume in different cultures.

In most societies, the school is a fundamentally important social field that replaces exclusive reliance on the family during early childhood. Its importance grows over the course of middle childhood and early adolesence and offers a range of measurement points for assessing the course of development toward mental health or illness. The school context is, therefore, a strategic locale for developing and testing prevention programs and for evaluating the cross-cultural validity of the concepts underlying our research into risk behaviors, vulnerability, and resilience (Kellam, Anthony, Brown, Dolan, Werthamer-Larsson, & Wilson, 1989; Kellam, Wilson, & Rebok, in press).

In the context of our contribution to the present volume, this raises, as noted, the question of the specific impact of family-school-neighborhood constellations to variations in rates of aggression, as reflected in teacher and peer ratings. These constellations will differ by urban, rural, and urban/rural settings. They will be influenced by whether school systems and the peer groups which they create, are exclusively or predominantly public or private, secular or denominational, and coherent or diverse in terms of socioeconomic and demographic variables, including access to systems of pediatric and adolescent health care and referral for special services. The importance of this research agenda is all too obvious in view of the alarming rise in different social and political contexts of patterns of aggression by adolescents and young adults.

References

Barrish, H.H., Saunders, M., & Wolfe, M.D. (1969). Good Behavior Game. Effects of individual contingencies for group consequences and disruptive behavior in a classroom. *Journal of Applied Behavioral Analysis, 2,* 119–124.

Bierman, K.L. (1986). The relationship between social aggression and peer rejection in middle childhood. In R. Prinz (Ed.), *Advances in behavioral assessment of children and families* (Vol. 2, pp. 151–178). Greenwich, CT: JAI Press.

Bierman, K.L. & McCauley, E. (1987). Children's descriptions of their peer interactions: Useful information for clinical child assessment. *Journal of Clinical Child Psychology, 16,* 9–18.

Block, J., Block, J.H., & Keyes, S. (1988). Longitudinally foretelling drug usage in adolescence: Early childhood personality and environmental precursors. *Child Development, 59,* 336–355.

Coie, J.D. & Dodge, K.A. (1983). Continuities and changes in children's social status: a five-year longitudinal study. *Merrill-Palmer Quarterly, 29,* 261–281.

Cowen, E.L., Pederson, A., Babigian, H., Izzo, L.D., & Trost, M.A. (1973). Long-term follow-up of early detected vulnerable children. *Journal of Consulting and Clinical Psychology, 41,* 438–446.

Dodge, K.A. (1983). Behavioral antecedents of peer social status. *Child Development*, *54*, 1386–1399.

Dodge, K.A., Coie, J.D., Pettit, G.S., & Price, J.M. (1990). Peer status and aggression in boys' groups: Developmental and contextual analysis. *Child Development*, *61*, 1289–1309.

Dolan, L., Kellam, S.G., Brown, C.H., Werthamer-Larsson, L., Rebok, G., Mayer, L., Laudolff, J., Turkkan, J.S., Ford, C., & Wheeler, L. (in press). The short-term impact of two classroom-based preventive interventions on aggressive and shy behaviors and poor achievement. *Journal of Applied Developmental Psychology*.

Ensminger, M.E., Kellam, S.G., & Rubin B.R. (1983). School and family origins of delinquency: Comparisons by sex. In K.T. Van Dusen & S.A. Mednick (Eds.), *Prospective studies of crime and delinquency* (pp. 73–97). Boston: Kluwer-Nijhoff.

Ensminger, M.E. & Slusarick, A.L. (1992). Paths to high school graduation or dropout: A longitudinal study of a first grade cohort. *Sociology of Education*, *65*, 95–113.

Farrington, D.P., Gallagher, B., Morley, L., St. Ledger, R.J., & West, D.J. (1988). Are there successful men from criminogenic backgrounds? *Psychiatry*, *51*, 116–130.

Farrington, D.P. & Gunn, J. (Eds.). (1985). *Aggression and dangerousness*. New York: Wiley.

Hans, S.L., Marcus, J., Henson, L., Auerbach, J.G., & Mirsky, A.F. (1992). *Interpersonal behavior of children at risk for schizophrenia*. Manuscript submitted for publication.

Kellam, S.G. (1990). Developmental epidemiological framework for family research on depression and aggression. In G.R. Patterson (Ed.), *Depression and aggression in family interaction* (pp. 11–48). Hillsdale, NJ: Lawrence Erlbaum.

Kellam, S.G., Anthony, J.C., Brown, C.H., Dolan, L., Werthamer-Larsson, L., & Wilson, R. (1989). Prevention research on early risk behaviors in cross-cultural studies. In M.H. Schmidt & H. Remschmidt (Eds.), *Needs and prospects of child and adolescent psychiatry* (pp. 241–254). Stuttgart: Hogrefe & Huber.

Kellam, S.G., Branch, J.D., Agrawal, K.C., & Ensminger, M.E. (1975). *Mental health and going to school: The Woodlawn program of assessment, early intervention and evaluation*. Chicago: University of Chicago Press.

Kellam, S.G., Brown C.H., & Fleming J.P. (1982). Social adaptation to first grade and teenage drug, alcohol, and cigarette use. *The Journal of School Health*, *52*, 301–306.

Kellam, S.G., Brown, C.H., Rubin, B.R., & Ensminger M.E. (1983). Paths leading to teenage psychiatric symptoms and substance use: Developmental epidemiological studies in Woodlawn. In S.B. Guze, F.J. Earls, & J.E. Barrett (Eds.), *Childhood psychopathology and development* (pp. 17–51). New York: Raven Press.

Kellam, S.G. & Ensminger, M.E. (1980). Theory and method in child psychiatric epidemiology. In F. Earls (Ed.), *Studies of children* (pp. 145–180). New York: Prodist.

Kellam, S.G., Ensminger, M.E., & Simon, M.B. (1980). Mental health in first grade and teenage drug, alcohol, and cigarette use. *Drug and Alcohol Dependence*, *5*, 273–304.

Kellam, S.G. & Hunter, R.C. (1990). Prevention begins in first grade. *Principal*, *70*, 17–19.

Kellam, S.G. & Rebok, G.W. (1992). Building etiological theory through developmental epidemiologically-based preventive intervention trials. In J. McCord & R.E. Tremblay (Eds.), *Preventing antisocial behavior: Interventions from birth through adolescence* (pp. 162–195). New York: Guilford Press.

Kellam, S.G., Rebok, G.W., Ialongo, N., Mayer, L.S. (in press). The course and malleability of aggressive behavior from early first grade into middle school: Results of a developmental epidemiologically-based preventive trial. *Journal of Child Psychology and Psychiatry and Allied Disciplines*.

Kellam, S.G., Rebok, G.W., Wilson, R., & Edwards, E.J. (1993). *Two preventive interventions to improve behavior and learning in school: Developmental epidemiological studies in Baltimore*. Manuscript submitted for publication.

Kellam, S.G. & Werthamer-Larsson, L. (1986). Developmental epidemiology a basis for prevention. In M. Kessler & S.E. Goldston (Eds.), *A decade of progress in primary prevention* (pp. 154–180). Hanover, NH: University Press of New England.

Kellam, S.G., Werthamer-Larsson, L., Dolan, L., Brown, C.H., Mayer, L.S., Rebok, G.W., Anthony, J.C., Laudolff, J., & Edelsohn, G. (1991). Developmental epidemiologically-based preventive trials: Baseline modeling of early target behaviors and depressive symptoms. *American Journal of Community Psychology*, *19*, 563–584.

Kellam, S.G., Wilson, R., & Rebok, G.W. (in press). The next stage of child mental health research: Developmental epidemiology in cross-national perspective. In M. Kapur, S.G. Kellam, R. Tarter, & R. Wilson (Eds.), *Child mental health: A cross-cultural perspective*. Proceedings of a Symposium on Child Mental Health, Bangalore, India, March 6–10, 1989. NIMHANS, ADAMHA.

Kohlberg, L., Ricks, D., & Snarey, J. (1984). Childhood development as a predictor of adaptation in adulthood. *Genetic Psychology Monographs*, *110*, 91–172.

Landau, S. & Milich, R. (1985). Social status of aggressive and aggressive/withdrawn boys: A replication across age and method. *Journal of Consulting and Clinical Psychology*, *53*, 141.

Ledingham, J.E. & Schwartzman, A.E. (1984). A 3-year follow-up of aggressive and withdrawn behavior in childhood: Preliminary findings. *Journal of Abnormal Child Psychology*, *12*, 157–168.

McCord, J. (1988). Parental behavior in the cycle of aggression. *Psychiatry*, *51*, 14–23.

Parker, J.G. & Asher, S.R. (1987). Peer relations and later personal adjustment: Are low-accepted children at risk? *Psychological Bulletin*, *102*, 357–389.

Patterson, G.R. & Capaldi, D. (1990). A mediational model for boys' depressed mood. In J.E. Rolf, A. Masten, D. Cicchetti, K. Neuchterlein, & S. Weintraub (Eds.), *Risk and protective factors in the development of psychopathology* (pp. 141–163). Boston: Syndicate of the Press, Cambridge University.

Pekarik, E.G., Prinz, R.J., Liebert, D.E., Weintraub, S., & Neale, J.M. (1976). The Pupil Evaluation Inventory: A sociometric technique for assessing children's social behavior. *Journal of Abnormal Child Psychology*, *4*, 83–97.

Rebok, G.W., Kellam, S.G., Dolan, L.J., Werthamer-Larsson, L., Edwards, E.J., Mayer, L.S., Brown, C.H. (1991). Early risk behaviors: Process issues and problem areas in prevention research. *The Community Psychologist, 24,* 18–21.

Robins, L.N. (1978). Sturdy childhood predictors of adult antisocial behavior: Replications from longitudinal studies. *Psychological Medicine, 8,* 611–622.

Rubin, K.H. (1990). Peer relationships and social skills in childhood: An international perspective. *Human Development, 33,* 221–224.

Schwartzman, A.E., Ledingham, J.E., & Serbin, L.A. (1985). Identification of children at-risk for adult schizophrenia: A longitudinal study. *International Review of Applied Psychology, 34,* 363–380.

Shedler, J. & Block, J. (1990). Adolescent drug use and psychological health: A longitudinal inquiry. *American Psychologist, 45,* 612–630.

Tomas, J.M., Vlahov, D., & Anthony, J.C. (1990). Association between intravenous drug use and early misbehavior. *Drug and Alcohol Dependence, 25,* 79–89.

Tremblay, R.E., Masse, B., Perron, D., LeBlanc, M., Schwartzman, A.E., & Ledingham, J.E. (1992). Early disruptive behavior, poor school achievement, delinquent behavior, and delinquent personality: Longitudinal analyses. *Journal of Consulting and Clinical Psychology, 60,* 64–72.

Werthamer-Larsson, L., Kellam, S.G., & Wheeler, L. (1991). Effect of first-grade classroom environment on child shy behavior, aggressive behavior, and concentration problems. *American Journal of Community Psychology, 19,* 585–602.

Younger, A.J., Schwartzman, A.E., & Ledingham, J.E. (1985). Grade-related changes in children's perceptions of aggression and withdrawal in their peers. *Developmental Psychology, 21,* 70–75.

Younger, A.J., Schwartzman, A.E., & Ledingham, J.E. (1986). Age-related differences in children's perceptions of social deviance: Change in behavior or in perspective? *Developmental Psychology, 22,* 531–542.

Name Index

Subject Index